Understanding and Managing

TOURISM

John I Richardson & Martin Fluker

PEARSON
Hospitality
Press

Pearson Education Australia
Unit 4, Level 2
14 Aquatic Drive
Frenchs Forest NSW 2086

www.pearsoned.com.au

Acquisitions Editor: David Cunningham
Project Editor: Jane Roy/Rebecca Pomponio
Copy Editor: Janice Keynton
Proofreader: Sonnet Editorial
Cover and internal design by Natalie Bowra
Typeset by Midland Typesetters, Maryborough, Vic.

Printed in Malaysia

1 2 3 4 5 08 07 06 05 04

National Library of Australia
Cataloguing-in-Publication Data

Richardson, John I. (John Ivor), 1931-.
Understanding and managing tourism.

Bibliography.
Includes index.
ISBN 1 86250 463 6.

    1. Tourism. 2. Tourism – Australia. 3. Tourism – Economic
    Aspects – Australia. 4. Tourism – Australia – Management.
    I. Fluker, Martin, 1962-. II. Title.

338.479194

PEARSON
Hospitality
Press

An imprint of Pearson Education Australia
(a division of Pearson Australia Group Pty Ltd)

CONTENTS

CHAPTER 9 MANAGING TOURISM DEVELOPMENT   239

CHAPTER 10 MANAGING QUALITY   267

CHAPTER 11 MANAGING VISITORS

CHAPTER 12 MANAGING CHANGE

PREFACE

A person who studies law may become a lawyer. A person who studies medicine may become a doctor. A person who studies tourism may become a . . .? This is the problem many students face when they consider studying tourism: what do they become? A common experience for first-year university students enrolled in a tourism degree is to hear people say: 'So you're going to be a travel agent'. That *can* be one outcome, however it must be recognised that there is an extremely wide variety of other enjoyable and fulfilling careers associated with tourism. This book provides twelve profiles of people whose stories give insight into the diversity of the Australian travel and tourism industry. *Understanding and Managing Tourism* is directed primarily at young Australians who will pursue a career in one of the many kinds of businesses that make up that industry.

The book is organised in two parts. The first part presents the basic building blocks of tourism to the reader. This involves:

- exploring the nature of tourism
- examining the make-up of the industry that serves it
- considering tourism as a system, and thus the relationships between the tourist, the industry, markets, destinations and transit routes
- understanding what motivates people to become tourists and decide on a particular form of tourism
- discussing the complex interaction of tourism with the economic, social and physical environments in which it operates.

By understanding these phenomena, students are better able to deal with the management of tourism, which is the theme of the second part of the book. Management in the 21st century has an increasing number of dimensions, including not only demand and development, but also service quality, visitor behaviour at the destination, and change.

At one time Australian tourism interests were focused primarily on demand. The emphasis was on what motivated markets and the techniques for influencing them. The overriding objective was to increase tourism flows because growth brings money which swells economies and creates jobs. That objective is still important. Those in businesses are especially conscious of attracting more customers because they need them for profits to survive and grow their companies. But now there are other concerns and other objectives as well.

Much more attention has to be paid to supply than was the case in the past; there is an ever-increasing need to ensure the right facilities, including trained people, are provided to cater for the tourists who are not only coming in greater numbers but are also more discerning in what they want. Much more attention has to be paid to the impact of tourism, not only within the larger picture of worldwide concerns on what the human race is doing to the natural and social environments, but particularly on small communities where resources can be strained by even a modest increase in tourism. Some Australian communities are overwhelmed at times because they lack basic infrastructure, like adequate sewerage systems. There are those who dread the opening up of a new road which will bring more and more people to their town and what they see as its inability to cope with them comfortably. Other important matters require attention: for example, the conservation of tourism assets, the provision of quality service in a competitive, globalised world and the preparation for crises and disasters – some man-made like wars and terrorism and others beyond humankind's control, like cyclones and earthquakes. In all these matters the common thread is the requirement for competent and at times innovative management, and, given the nature of tourism, that implies a public–private sector partnership.

The theoretical framework of tourism is universal but issues, current practice and management requirements create the Australian context within which the book introduces the subject of tourism. The authors have had much assistance in preparing it. In particular, they thank Professor Neil Leiper of Southern Cross University, for offering sound advice on theoretical questions, Maureen Griffiths of Monash University's marketing department, who was generous with her time and expert knowledge, and Professor Larry Dwyer of the University of New South Wales, who read the chapter on economic impact and made valuable suggestions for improving it. Associate Professor David Foster, of RMIT University, was similarly helpful with the chapter on quality service. Nick Evers, chairman of the Australian Tourist Commission and of the TT-Line, and a former Minister in the Tasmanian Government, and Laurie Stroud, who was for many years the senior tourism bureaucrat in Canberra, read the chapter which includes the role of governments in tourism and it now bears the mark of their many years of practical experience.

Lois Peeler, chairperson of Aboriginal Tourism Australia, provided information and advice on indigenous tourism, David Crinion of the South Australian Tourism Commission was helpful on planning issues and Malcolm Wells of Tourism Tasmania, on development issues. The authors had the benefit of the expert views of Koos de Keijzer of dKO Architecture Pty Ltd, Melbourne, an authority on the development process and its practical application, of Athol Yates of the Institution of Engineers, Australia who advised on infrastructure, and Margot Homersham, a specialist in industry standards and accreditation. Jim Sloman, former deputy chief executive officer and chief operating officer of SOCOG, provided 'hands-on' information about visitor management at the Sydney Olympics. David Kanaley of Byron Bay Shire Council and June Smith of Tamworth City Council went out of their way to help with tourism matters affecting their areas.

When the first draft was written, Professor Brian King of Victoria University was an interested and discerning critic. The authors also appreciate the comments of Professor Chris Cooper of the University of Queensland and Professor Peter Murphy of LaTrobe University. They thank Janet Richardson for keeping extensive files before and during the writing of the book and for her enthusiastic help with research.

PART 1

UNDERSTANDING TOURISM

THE FIRST PART OF THE BOOK DEALS WITH THE THEORETICAL BASIS OF tourism and some of the practical consequences of its influence. This approach is illustrated in the first chapter which deals with the nature of tourism and the industry that serves it. Tourism is seen as a many-sided phenomenon which can be understood only by examining it from different viewpoints. However, statisticians successfully use a set of 'technical' definitions to count the number of tourists around the world and trace their travel patterns. The make-up of the travel and tourism industry is discussed, with special reference to the 'primary trades' in Australia.

In the second chapter, the tourism system is modelled as an aid to understanding the way tourism works and influences many facets of national, business and social life. The system has influenced the structure of the book; both parts are related to the five essential elements of the tourism system and the environments which influence it and which it influences. Discussion of the elements leads to an explanation of the theory of markets and destinations.

The central element of the system, the tourist, is the subject of the third chapter. The principal issue is what motivates tourists to travel and how that motivation is expressed in the type of tourism they choose to follow. A number of the forms of tourism are discussed, from indulgent tourism on huge luxury cruise ships to the 'new tourism' in which tourists get away from assembly-line packages, to experiences for the dedicated such as special interest tourism or ecotourism.

The last three chapters of this first part examine in detail the impact of tourism on three environments that embrace most of human existence – the economic, socio-cultural and natural environments.

FUNDAMENTALS 1

CHAPTER 1

LEARNING OBJECTIVES

Recognise the multi-dimensional nature of tourism and how this makes it difficult to produce a single definition satisfying every viewpoint.

Examine examples of conceptual definitions and note the inclusion or implication of leisure in those concerned with tourist behaviour.

Appreciate the requirement for technical definitions which the nations of the world can agree on for collecting statistics. Examine the definitions used worldwide and in Australia.

Understand that the travel and tourism industry, which is defined in terms of the circumstances in which goods and services are consumed, is unlike other industries which are defined in terms of their products.

Examine the distinction between businesses that are directly involved with tourists, those that are indirectly involved and those in the wider economy that benefit from tourism.

Review the categories of goods and services required by tourists.

Understand the scope of the 'primary tourism trades' in Australia: transport, travel services, hospitality, attractions and activities.

Appreciate the range of interests involved in a case study of attractions in Devonport.

**UNDERSTAND
THE MEANING OF:**

* *conceptual view
  of tourism*
* *day-tripper*
* *tourismology*
* *usual environment*
* *tourism's three
  essentials*
* *travel and tourism
  industry*
* *technical definitions*
* *tourism-related
  industries*
* *domestic tourism*
* *primary trades*
* *inbound tourism*
* *tour operator*
* *outbound tourism*
* *packaging*
* *traveller*
* *travel agent*
* *visitor*
* *consolidator*
* *tourist*
* *MICE sector*
* *international visitor*
* *meeting*
* *domestic visitor*
* *incentive travel*
* *trip*
* *attraction*
* *visit*

WHAT IS TOURISM?

Asking the question 'What is tourism?' may sound a little strange because the answer seems obvious: it is usually thought of by the person in the street as describing the activity of people travelling on holiday. However, tourism is more than people having holidays and travelling away from home. It is one of the modern world's most pervasive activities, with significant economic consequences for governments, localities and businesses. It is a vast employer. It also has important impacts on social, cultural and physical environments.

It is no less than 'an activity essential to the life of nations', according to a world meeting called to discuss it in 1980. This is 'because of its direct effects on the social, cultural, educational and economic sectors of national societies and on their international relations' (World Tourism Organisation 1995c, p. 1).

Australia is very much involved with tourism. Australians are enthusiastic travellers themselves within their own country and overseas. In the early years of the 21st century we were making about 75 million domestic trips a year (within Australia) and about 3.5 million trips overseas. In that period, some 5 million visitors from other countries – equal to about one-quarter of our population – were coming here annually.[1]

The evidence of this vast activity is very apparent. It can be witnessed in the coaches carrying tour groups around the country, and in the growing number of hotels, resorts, motels and 'bed and breakfasts' in cities and towns and along the highways. Menus in different languages can be found in cafés and restaurants and foreign credit card stickers on the doors of duty-free shops.

Although it is difficult to ignore tourism and most people can say what a certain aspect of it includes, presenting a clear definition is another matter. Definitions are important in that they set out the parameters of what is being discussed or studied. The problem with defining tourism is that it means different things to different people.

This complexity is indicated by the number of academic disciplines involved with its study. A World Tourism Organisation assessment listed psychology, anthropology, sociology, economics, business administration, geography, ecology, law and education as being related areas of study (1995a).

Jovicic (cited in Echtner & Jamal 1997) was so taken with the diversity of interests that he suggested that 'tourismology' should be established as a distinct science of tourism. The idea has not gained much support, but it is an illustration of how people have recognised the problem of coming to grips with tourism in all its dimensions.[2]

DEFINITIONS

Essential attributes

Despite the differing interests in tourism, it is commonly agreed that it has three essential attributes:

1. It involves travel – this literally means going from one place to another
2. It requires a temporary stay away from home
3. Its prime purpose is something other than earning money in the place or places visited.

There is no shortage of definitions and they can be broadly categorised as 'conceptual' or 'technical'. Conceptual definitions seek to throw light on the true nature of tourism or, less ambitiously, be appropriate to a particular area of research. Technical definitions have been devised so that tourists can be identified and counted; they use such measures as the distance people travel and how long they stay at a destination to say whether a traveller is or is not a tourist. They also define tourists by their reasons for travelling.

Conceptual definitions

Conceptual definitions have been formulated by scholars seeking to explain the phenomenon of tourism. However, as we have seen, tourism has many dimensions and it can be conceived in more than one way. It is generally accepted there will never be a single conceptual definition of tourism which satisfies everyone.

'Some have used the word "tourism" as being synonymous with the actions and impacts of tourists. Others use the term to refer to a course of study and body of research. Still others apply the term to a broad, conceptual system of people, places, businesses, and activities' (Smith 1988, p. 180).

In other words, tourism is defined in different ways because of different perceptions and interests. An academic researcher may define it comprehensively as 'the study of man away from his usual habitat, of the industry which responds to his needs, and of the impacts that both he and the industry have on the host's socio-cultural, economic, and physical environments' (Jafari 1977, p. 8). But a definition may be specific; for example, where the interest is regional and economic, tourism 'is a generic term for expenditure or activity in a region by non-residents' (Frost 1999, p. 7).

These differences should be borne in mind when reading other parts of this book. For example, a supply-side definition of tourism by Smith (1988) is quoted later in this chapter in a discussion about which businesses should be included in the travel and tourism industry. It states that tourism is the 'aggregate of all businesses that directly provide goods or services to facilitate business, pleasure, and leisure activities away from the home environment' (p. 123).

Tourism (conceptual)
The ideas and opinions people hold which shape their decisions about going on trips, about where to go (and where not to go) and what to do or not to do, about how to relate to other tourists, locals and service personnel. And it is all the behavioural manifestations of those ideas and opinions (Leiper 1995).

DEFINITIONS

Attitudes and behaviour

Chapter 3 deals with the motivations of tourists and the forms of tourism they prefer as a result. In this case it is more appropriate to define tourism in psychological terms. Leiper has offered these definitions, one of tourism and the other of tourists:

> *Tourism comprises the ideas and opinions people hold which shape their decisions about going on trips, about where to go (and where not to go) and what to do or not to do, about how to relate to other tourists, locals and service personnel. And it is all the behavioural manifestations of those ideas and opinions'* (Leiper 1995, p. 20).

Tourist

A visitor who spends at least one night away from home.

> *Tourists can be defined in behavioural terms as persons who travel away from their normal residential region for a temporary period of at least one night, to the extent that their behaviour involves a search for leisure experiences from interactions with features or characteristics of places they choose to visit* (Leiper 1995, p. 11).[3]

The second of Leiper's definitions and many other conceptual definitions add a fourth 'essential attribute' of tourism to the three identified earlier – leisure. In other words, they separate tourism entirely from work, thus excluding business travel as a form of tourism. Leisure experiences are those valued for their own sake, for personal pleasure and are pursued in a non-obligatory context, with a sense of freedom (Leiper 1990).

This is consistent with definitions of leisure which emphasise 'free time', in essence freedom from work (Moore, Cushman & Simmons 1995). The terms 'recreation' and 'leisure' are often used interchangeably or 'recreation' can be used to describe the activities undertaken during leisure time. In one sense tourism can be seen as a form of leisure, in another the leisure/recreation sector can be regarded as part of the travel and tourism industry (Hobson & Teaff 1994). Whatever the point of view, the two are closely related.

Tourism (technical)

The activities of persons travelling to and staying in places outside their usual environment for not more than one consecutive year for leisure, business and other purposes

Technical definitions

Technical definitions – those used by statisticians, governments, planners and businesses – do not restrict tourism to leisure pursuits. They include business travel in its various forms. This is because the primary interest of organisations using technical definitions is in visitor spending. From an economic perspective, all visitors staying overnight at a destination have a similarity, whatever their purpose for being there—that is, whether they are on holiday, conducting business or visiting friends and relatives. They all need transport, accommodation, food and drink and spend money on these needs, and so they are all included as tourists, although many scholars do not think some of them are (Leiper 1990).

Traveller

Any person on a trip between two or more localities.

On the other hand, the measures that technical definitions use to distinguish tourists from other **travellers** may result in some people who are tourists being excluded from the statistics. Examples of the measures are the requirement that tourists stay away from home no more than a year and, in Australia, travel at least 40 km from their place of residence in some circumstances.[4]

Despite these qualifications, technical definitions have proved generally effective in allowing those who use them to say who is a tourist and who is not. Experience has shown they can be relied upon for business planning, marketing and operations.

The World Tourism Organisation's (technical) definition is: 'Tourism comprises the activities of persons, travelling to and staying in places outside their usual environment for not more than one consecutive year for leisure, business and other purposes, (1995b, p. 12).

The WTO defines the usual environment of persons as a certain area around their place of residence plus all other places they frequently visit. It is an important concept, but imprecise because of different circumstances in different countries, and to some extent, each person's different habits and lifestyle. It is discussed in further detail in the Australian context later in the chapter.

GOVERNMENT AND BUSINESS NEEDS

Tourism activity around the world requires an enormous business effort to service it. As a result, tourism has become one of the world's biggest industries. Some authorities say it is the biggest.[5]

Tourism is very important to the economy of Australia. The amount of consumption of goods and services caused by tourism in 2000-01 was $71.2 billion, of which 24 per cent was attributable to inbound tourism. Additionally, tourism accounts for about 10 per cent of employment in Australia and is the fourth biggest export industry after mining, manufacturing and agriculture (Australian Bureau of Statistics 2000a and 2002).

Governments and business managers need to have accurate data on tourism to make sound policy and business decisions. They must be able to quantify markets, to trace travel patterns, discern trends, and distinguish between the different kinds of tourists.

Gathering the data requires a huge worldwide effort and, at the start, a level of agreement among the collectors in different countries about who should be called a tourist, and who should not, so that statistics from different countries and regions can be compared.

The technical definitions that statisticians use have been refined over a long period. Serious work began in 1937, when the Council of the League of Nations first recommended a definition of 'international tourist' for statistical purposes. Even now, it is not a perfect system. Not all statistics are strictly compatible; the collections of some countries, including Australia, do not adhere precisely to the standards laid down by the World Tourism Organisation and the United Nations Statistical Commission.[6] However overall the system works quite well for business and government planners. It enables them to follow travel patterns around the world and within Australia, the reaction of tourists to economic and political events, and trends from year to year.

DEFINITIONS

....

GATHERING STATISTICS

There are three basic types of tourism for which statistics are needed:

- domestic tourism, involving Australian residents travelling within Australia
- inbound tourism, involving non-residents travelling (as tourists) to Australia
- outbound tourism, involving Australian residents travelling (as tourists) outside Australia.

Statistics gathering starts with the collecting of data on the number of people arriving in and departing from Australia, with more detailed information about overseas and domestic tourism supplied by the International Visitor Survey, the National Visitor Survey, regional and specialist studies.

All of these employ definitions that use specific terms related to place of residence, length of journey, purpose of visits and length of stay.

These are the key international definitions.

- **Traveller** Any person on a trip between two or more localities.

Visitor

Any person travelling to a place other than their usual environment for less than 12 consecutive months and whose main purpose of travelling is other than the exercise of an activity remunerated from within the place visited.

- **Visitor** Any person travelling to a place other than his or her usual environment for less than 12 consecutive months and whose main purpose of travelling is other than the exercise of an activity remunerated from within the place visited.
- **Tourist** A visitor who spends at least one night away from home (World Tourism Organisation 1995b).

Apart from cruise ship passengers, almost all international visitors to Australia are tourists; it is hard to imagine anyone visiting Australia and failing to spend at least one night away from home.[7] Passengers on cruise ships usually spend the night on board ship and are classified internationally as same-day visitors, not tourists. In Australia, it is usual to keep count of same-day visitors (day-trippers and cruise passengers) and estimate their spending.

WHICH TRAVELLERS ARE TOURISTS?

Not all travellers are tourists. The WTO method of separating travellers who are included in international tourism statistics from those who are not is shown on page 9.

The Australian Bureau of Statistics (ABS) has excluded the following types of people from its definition of visitors in its Tourism Satellite Account (which is discussed in Chapter 4). Persons who are travelling:

- as an intrinsic part of their job, e.g. bus driver, air crew
- for the purpose of being admitted to or detained in a residential facility such as a hospital, prison or long-stay care
- as part of a move to a new permanent residence
- in association with military duties
- between two parts of their usual environment (Australian Bureau of Statistics 2000a).

Figure 1.1 Classification of international visitors

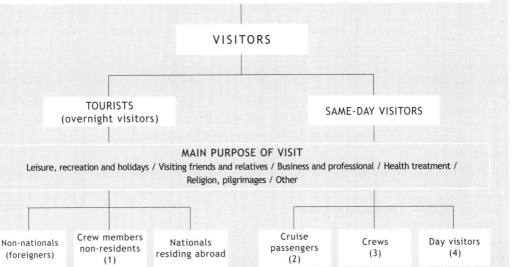

TRAVELLERS INCLUDED IN TOURISM STATISTICS

VISITORS

TOURISTS
(overnight visitors)

SAME-DAY VISITORS

MAIN PURPOSE OF VISIT
Leisure, recreation and holidays / Visiting friends and relatives / Business and professional / Health treatment /
Religion, pilgrimages / Other

| Non-nationals (foreigners) | Crew members non-residents (1) | Nationals residing abroad | Cruise passengers (2) | Crews (3) | Day visitors (4) |

TRAVELLERS NOT INCLUDED IN TOURISM STATISTICS

| Border workers | Temporary immigrants (5) | Permanent immigrants (5) | Nomads (5) | Transit passengers (6) |

| Refugees (7) | Members of the armed forces (8) | Representation of consulates (8) | Diplomats (8) |

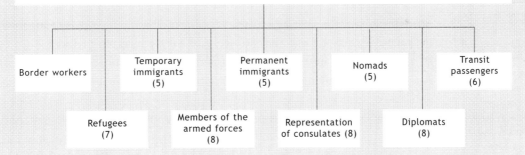

1   Foreign air or ship crews docked or in lay-over and who use the accommodation establishments of the country visited.
2   Persons who arrive in a country aboard cruise ships and who spend the night aboard ship even when disembarking for one or more day visits.
3   Crews who are not residents of the country visited and who stay in the country for the day.
4   Visitors who arrive and leave the same day for: leisure, recreation and holidays; visiting friends and relatives; business and professional; health treatment; religion/pilgrimages and other tourism purposes, including transit day visitors en route to or from their destination countries.

5   As defined by the United Nations in the Recommendations on Statistics of International Migration.
6   Who do not leave the transit area of the airport or the port, including transfer between airports and ports.
7   As defined by the United Nations High Commissioner for Refugees.
8   When they travel from their country of origin to the duty station and vice versa (including household servants and dependants accompanying or joining them).

(Source: Classification of International Visitors, adapted from *Recommendations on World Statistics* (1999), World Tourism Organisation.)

International and domestic visitors

The ABS Framework for the Collection and Publication of Tourism Statistics (Australian Bureau of Statistics 1997a) is a valuable reference work and conforms to WTO and the United Nations Statistical Office recommendations. It says that because the characteristics of different types of visitors differ significantly, it is necessary to have separate data according to whether the visitor is an international or domestic visitor and whether the visitor is staying overnight or is a same-day visitor.

According to its definition, an **international visitor** is:

> *A person who resides in another country and travels to Australia for a period not exceeding twelve months and whose main purpose of visit is other than the exercise of an activity remunerated from within Australia* (p. 13).

An overnight visitor is one who stays at least one night in Australia and a same-day visitor is an international visitor who does not spend a night in Australia.

A **domestic visitor** is:

> *A person residing in Australia who travels to a place within this country, outside his/her usual environment (i.e. more than 40 kms from place of residence and not on a regular trip between home and work/education) for a period not exceeding twelve months and whose main purpose of visit is other than the exercise of an activity remunerated from within the place visited* (p. 14).

An overnight visitor is a domestic visitor who stays at least one night in the place visited and a same-day visitor is one who does not spend a night in the place visited.

'Trip' and 'visit' have specific meanings in Australian statistics gathering and add detail to the above definitions. For example, a **trip** is a single journey covering the whole period away from home. The National Visitor Survey defines it as a single journey involving a stay of one or more nights but less than three months away from home involving a journey of at least 40 km from home. The trip can be undertaken for any reason except where the journey is related to taking up employment. An international trip to Australia is a journey by any person who resides overseas, enters Australia (i.e. clears Customs) and stays less than 12 months. The trip can be undertaken for any reason.

Day-trippers are those who travel for a round-trip distance of at least 50 km, are away from home for at least four hours, and who do not spend a night away from home as part of their travel. Same-day travel as part of overnight travel is excluded, as is routine travel such as commuting between work/school and home.

A **visit** can be a trip or part of a trip. Thus a visit is made to every place where a traveller makes an overnight stay during their trip. Therefore there may be more than one visit associated with a trip.[8]

▓ The concept of 'usual environment'

The term '**usual environment**' used in definitions is of great importance as a concept because it is the first criterion that distinguishes tourism from other travel. Everyday travel, for example going to work, school or university, even though it might involve considerable distance, is still staying within a person's usual environment and is therefore not tourism. Although the distinction seems clear from this example, 'usual environment' is one of the trickiest issues in tourism definitions and is explained by the following quotation:

> *The concept of usual environment, and therefore tourism, has two dimensions. The first is frequency. Places which are frequently (on a routine basis) visited by a person are part of the usual environment of that person, even though these places may be located at a considerable distance from the place of residence. The second dimension is distance. Places located close to the place of residence of a person are also part of the usual environment, even though the actual spots are rarely visited. Therefore, the usual environment consists of a certain area around the place of residence plus all places visited rather frequently* (World Tourism Organisation 1995b, p. 23).

The ABS added some specifics for the Tourism Satellite Account when it said that 'usual environment' was made up of one or more areas in which a person undertakes regular activities such as place of residence, place of work, place of study and other places frequently visited. 'Frequently visited' meant at least once a week. The standard Australian distance criteria were included: locations up to 40 km from home for overnight trips and up to 50 km from home (round trip) for day trips were regarded as a visitor's usual environment (Australian Bureau of Statistics 2000a).

No single definition of 'usual environment' has been found which can be applied all over the world. As we have seen, the Australian standard of 40 km from home on an overnight trip is the threshold beyond which a person must travel to be defined as a visitor but in the United States the distance threshold is 100 miles. However, such long distances may not be appropriate in a close-knit country like Holland and would certainly not be appropriate for a country where the majority of people travel on foot.

The WTO recommendation is that with the aid of mobility surveys, countries should look for a practical definition of 'usual environment' that excludes from tourism virtually all routine travel of their residents and travel to places very close to the place of usual residence.

THE TRAVEL AND TOURISM INDUSTRY

The idiosyncratic nature of tourism, which makes its defining a less than completely satisfying exercise, extends to the industry that serves it. Conventionally, the term 'industry' refers to groupings of businesses with similar economic activity; they are

---

DEFINITIONS

Trip
*(a) A single journey covering the whole period from home.
(b) A single journey involving a stay of one or more nights but less than three months away from home involving a journey of at least 40 km from home.*

Day-tripper
In Australia, one who travels for a round-trip distance of at least 50 kilometres, is away from home for at least four hours, and who does not spend a night away from home as part of the travel.

Visit
A trip or part of a trip. Thus a visit is made to every place where a traveller makes an overnight stay during their trip. Therefore there may be more than one visit associated with a trip.

Usual environment
One or more areas in which a person undertakes regular activities such as place of residence, place of work, place of study and other places frequently visited.

defined by the nature of the goods and services they produce, like wheat, coal, cars, accounting services or entertainment. But tourism is not a product. Tourists consume all sorts of goods and services provided by businesses with disparate economic activities: in theory, tourists can consume any product.

In Australia, industries are classified according to the Australian and New Zealand Standard Industrial Classification (ANZSIC), which is used in the preparation of the National Accounts. There is no industry identified as tourism in ANZSIC, nor is tourism defined as a category of demand in the international System of National Accounts. The Australian Tourism Satellite Account, which is derived from the National Accounts, refers to 'tourism-related industries', which it defines as industries that produce products that are strongly associated with tourism and which are consumed by both visitors and non-visitors (Australian Bureau of Statistics 2000a).[9]

The businesses that provide tourists with the goods and services they need belong to separate industries in their own right (e.g. the airline industry or accommodation industry or the retail industry). As Jefferson and Lickorish (1988) point out, these industries usually have their own distinct markets and some sell to both residents and visitors. Although independent of each other and often fiercely competitive, they are also interdependent, at least as far as tourism is concerned. What holds these industries together is tourism itself, the demand tourists have for their services. In other words, they have the same customers, who can be identified, segmented and marketed to. The various sectors cooperate in marketing, in industry associations and sometimes in the delivery of services.

As a result, despite some scholarly concern over the use of the word, there *is* a travel and tourism 'industry', sustained not by classic supply-side definition, but by common interests and practice. It is described not in terms of production, but in terms of the circumstances in which goods and services are both produced and consumed.

For those people in businesses that exist for travellers, such as airlines, coachlines, hotels, tour companies and travel agencies, there is no argument about the existence of an industry. They may call it variously the 'travel industry' or the 'tourism industry'. The term '**travel and tourism industry**' is widely used as a more appropriate description, especially in professional and academic circles (Leiper 1990).

The theory behind the 'double-barrelled' description is that there are two different industries involved: the travel industry gets the tourist to and from the destination and the tourism industry is the aggregate of the businesses supplying tourism services at the destination. The combination could be called travel and tourism 'industries', but the two groups of businesses are usually regarded as units of one industry, hence travel and tourism 'industry'.

Travel and tourism industry
The aggregate of all businesses that directly provide goods or services to facilitate business, pleasure and leisure activities away from the home environment (Smith, 1988).

▣ Businesses that benefit from tourism

Businesses that benefit from tourism either supply directly to tourists or indirectly. The staff of the first category have face-to-face contact with tourists and may include those

Table 1.1 Industry recipients of tourist expenditure, 1996–97

INDUSTRY/COMMODITY	TOURIST EXPENDITURE	INDUSTRY/COMMODITY	TOURIST EXPENDITURE
	$m		$m
Restaurants, hotels and clubs	13,570	Water transport	90
Air transport	10,380	Electronic equipment	750
Retail trade	(a)	Margarine, oils, fats	100
Road transport	1,780	Printing and stationery	110
Entertainment	2,890	Rubber products	160
Wholesale trade	(a)	Scientific equipment	160
Petroleum and coal products	6,040	Electricity	20
Services to transport	1,880	Banking	10
Education, libraries	1,580	Furniture and mattresses	20
Meat products	1,600	Public administration	10
Clothing	2,790	Soaps and detergents	20
Communication	850	Pharmaceuticals	50
Personal services (b)	660	Insurance	10
Rail transport	230	Leather products	250
Milk products	900	Joinery, wood products	20
Health	540	Gas	10
Food products	1,010	Electrical equipment	20
Beer and malt	1,610	Water, sewerage and drainage	(a)
Mechanical repairs	470	Glass and glass products	(a)
Business services	450	Clay products, refractories	(a)
Bread, cakes and biscuits	680	Flour mill and cereal products	250
Soft drinks and cordials	630		
Fruit and vegetable products	780	Total	59,410
Household appliances	950		
Publishing and printing	750		
Alcoholic beverages	1,090		
Confectionery	490		
Plastic-related products	370		
Cosmetics	510		
Tobacco products	740		
Footwear	530		
Welfare services	70		
Manufacturing	520		

(a) Less than $5m or less than 0.05 per cent of total expenditure.

(b) Personal services include hiring personal household goods (e.g. videos, bicycles), laundry and dry cleaning, photographic processing, chauffeur services, hairdressing and beauty salons, baby-sitting services.

(Source: Buchanan (1999), pp. 8–9 (much simplified).)

employed by a coach company or travel agent, or by a chemist's shop or a supermarket which sells goods to tourists.

Indirect suppliers produce goods or services which they provide to the direct suppliers who then provide them to tourists or use them in their businesses to enable them to provide goods or services to tourists.

As tourists consume many different goods and services the overall effect of tourism on the economy is very wide and a large number of industries benefit from it. This is of importance when considering the economic impact of tourism. Positive economic impacts create jobs, wealth and a vibrant community and methods have been developed for tracking the effects of tourism throughout the economy. The table on page 13, which traces the effects of tourism expenditure in Australia in a single year in the 1990s, demonstrates the extent of tourism's economic influence.

▓ Businesses directly involved in tourism

Two categories of businesses directly supply services to tourists – those existing specific-ally for the purpose (they would go out of business if travel stopped) and those that serve both tourists and residents. Examples of the first category include airlines, coach companies, travel agencies, hotels and duty free stores – all businesses clearly engaged in tourism.

In the second category, in which tourists and local residents are both customers, a business engages in tourism when it supplies a visitor, but not when it supplies a local resident. This category includes city department stores, most restaurants, local shops, postal services, taxis and suburban bus companies. Attractions fall into both categories, depending on what and where they are. For example, major theme parks would go out of business if sales to tourists stopped whereas some zoos and museums would continue to exist, albeit usually on a reduced level of activity.

Smith (1988) classifies six categories of goods and services required by tourists:
1. Transportation
2. Travel services
3. Accommodation
4. Food services
5. Activities and attractions (recreation/culture/entertainment)
6. Retail goods.

Listed on page 15 are the main types of enterprises supplying those services (the list is not exhaustive).

Table 1.2 Businesses directly involved in tourism

TRAVEL

Transportation	Travel services
Airlines	Travel agencies
Airports	Tour operators
Coachlines	Convention organisers
Railways	Incentive travel houses
Rent-a-car operators	Information agencies
Taxi operators	Tour guides
Cruise ship lines	Motoring organisations
Ferries	Financial services

HOSPITALITY

Accommodation	Food services
Hotels	Restaurants
Motels	Bars and cafés
Resorts	Catering companies
Caravan parks	Function centres
Hostels	Fast-food outlets

ATTRACTIONS AND ACTIVITIES

Natural attractions including national parks, zoos, animal parks	Festivals, gatherings
	Sporting
Museums/galleries	Political
Theme parks	Theatrical
Heritage sites	Cultural
	Religious

RETAIL GOODS

Duty free shops	Shopping centres
Souvenir shops	General retail
Photographic shops	Service stations

Businesses indirectly involved in tourism

These are the businesses which serve the direct suppliers with goods and services but have no direct contact with tourists. For example, motels are supplied with goods like orange juice and linen and services like laundry services.

The list of businesses 'indirectly involved' with tourism is so large that it is helpful to divide it into categories as shown below.

- The suppliers of goods and services to travel and tourism companies; for example, aircraft manufacturers, food and drink suppliers, contract laundries, oil companies, tyre manufacturers
- Providers of marketing services such as the trade media, market research companies and advertising agencies
- Organisations involved in tourism development – planners of various kinds, architects, developers, financiers, hotel and motel builders
- Education and training institutions
- Emergency services such as medical and dental.

Extent of tourism-related business

The number of businesses dependent on tourism demand in Australia – that is businesses directly and indirectly involved – is huge. A Bureau of Tourism Research study of tourism-related businesses in 1998 showed a total of 353,473 employing businesses were either directly or indirectly involved. Most were small businesses: 91 per cent employed fewer than 20 people. In addition, there were about 223,000 non-employing businesses in tourism-related categories.

By far the majority of tourism-related businesses were indirectly involved in tourism. The BTR classification was based on that developed by the Australian Bureau of Statistics for the Tourism Satellite Account. The classification closest to the 'directly involved' category is 'tourism characteristic', applied to businesses where at least 25 per cent of output is consumed by visitors. Of the 353,473 employing businesses, some 60,054 were 'tourism characteristic', and of these nearly 40,000 were connected with food services – cafés, restaurants and takeaways. Other prominent types of businesses were those in travel agencies and tour operator services, taxis, air and water transport, and motor vehicle hiring.

The other ABS–BTR classification of relevant businesses is 'tourism connected', where the products are consumed by visitors in 'significant amounts for the visitor and/or the producer'. There were more than 293,000 of these employing businesses and they were located predominantly in the following ABS industry categories: 'Retail', 'Transport equipment and other manufacturing', 'Other road transport', 'Education', and 'Other entertainment' services (Bolin & Greenwood 2003).

The study once more emphasises the importance of tourism to the Australian economy as a whole but is of limited help in determining the extent of the travel and tourism industry.

The 'primary trades'

People working in tourism think in much smaller numbers when considering the businesses making up the 'industry'. They usually limit its meaning to include only those businesses that provide goods and services directly to tourists and whose sole or main activity is serving tourists.

Smith (1988) accepts that there is a conceptual argument for including some portion of businesses 'indirectly involved' in a definition of the travel and tourism industry, but omits them on the basis that the conservative approach to the scope of tourism is more credible and acceptable. He offers a supply-side definition of tourism as 'the aggregate of all businesses that directly provide goods or services to facilitate business, pleasure, and leisure activities away from the home environment' (p. 123).

This view of the 'true' travel and tourism industry restricts it to what Jefferson and Lickorish (1988) have called the 'primary trades'. It is not only the common view of those people working in companies directly involved, but it is also the more likely view of those indirectly involved in tourism.

Buchanan (1999) has remarked that even when other types of businesses are included in the definition of the travel and tourism industry because their output is directed to tourists, those businesses would not see themselves as being part of the industry. He cites a business that makes only travel sickness pills. It might be classed as part of the travel and tourism industry because almost all its output is consumed by tourists, but the owner of the business and its employees would probably consider they were part of the pharmaceutical industry.

Status of government agencies

The wide-ranging roles of governments and their agencies involved in tourism raises the question of whether they should be included as members of the travel and tourism industry. However, despite the interwoven links, most industry people draw a distinction. When they speak of 'the industry' they do not include government agencies in its meaning. Similarly, people in government agencies in Australia are not thinking of themselves when they speak of 'the industry'; they use the term deliberately to make the distinction.

THE 'PRIMARY TRADES' IN AUSTRALIA

The 'primary tourism trades' in Australia, as classified in Table 1.2 (on page 15), are discussed in this section.

▓ Transport

This includes companies which offer transport by air, sea, and land, with a number of sub-categories in each classification, presenting a picture of diversity in size of company as well as type of operation.

Air transport

Air transport is a major factor in the growth of tourism, especially in Australia. All but a fraction of Australia's overseas visitors come by air and similarly almost all Australians travelling overseas go by plane. Additionally, because of the vast distances within Australia, airlines are a major force in the development of domestic tourism.

In Australia the main categories of air transport are:

(a) International scheduled airlines which fly into and within Australia. There were about 45 of them in early 2003. They do or can service all state capitals and Darwin, Cairns, Townsville and Coolangatta. The top five city pairs in 2001 were Auckland/Sydney, Singapore/Sydney, Los Angeles/Sydney, Hong Kong/Sydney and Singapore/Perth.

(b) International charter airlines which fly to Australia on an irregular basis. Examples have been charter series from Europe in the European off-season and charters from Asia to Tasmania, Broome and Hamilton Island.

(c) Domestic trunk carriers. They fly on the main domestic routes, mainly between capital cities. The top two city pairs (Melbourne/Sydney and Sydney/Brisbane) account for more than one-third of the total of domestic passengers. Qantas and Virgin Blue were the remaining trunk carriers following the cessation of Ansett Australia services at the beginning of 2002.[10]

(d) Regional airlines, which serve routes between regional centres and capital cities. They fly smaller aircraft than the trunk carriers – a regional airline has been defined for statistical purposes as one flying scheduled services with planes with fewer than 39 passenger seats or a payload of less than 4200 kg. About 30 regional airlines were flying in Australia in 2003.

(e) Aircraft tour companies. These are usually small companies using light aircraft (e.g. Beechcraft Kingairs and Piper Chieftains), though sometimes Fokker prop-jet sized planes or small jets are used, particularly for overseas touring.

(f) Executive and other charterers of small aircraft.

In the early 21st century, Qantas Airways was not only the dominant airline in Australia, it was also a powerful force in Australian travel and tourism. In size alone, with more than 30,000 employees, it was much bigger than any other company in the industry. It carried about 35 per cent of air travellers to and from Australia, had the bulk of the domestic trunk market (in 2003 about 70 per cent) and through subsidiaries was the major force in regional air transport.

Airport operators

All Australia's capital city airports are leased by the Commonwealth Government to private operators. The leases are for 50 years with an option to renew for another 49 years. The airports are subject to Commonwealth regulation in areas such as ownership, access, development and environmental control.

The airports in Australia are:

- 18 privatised Commonwealth civilian airports, including the capital city airports
- Three airports in the Sydney area (Bankstown, Campden and Hoxton Park) which remained under Commonwealth ownership in mid-2003. However the Government had announced they would be sold
- 16 military airports controlled by the Department of Defence
- About 260 licensed airports owned by local authorities or private organisations/ individuals.

Motoring organisations

For all the tourism power of other forms of transportation, the private motor car is the most popular vehicle in Australia. Air travel has taken away some of the car's dominance of domestic travel since deregulation of the aviation system within Australia, but the number of overnight trips taken by car is still six or seven times that taken by plane. As domestic tourism accounts for three-quarters of tourism within Australia a large portion of the basic structure of the travel and tourism industry is dependent upon the car.

Much car travel for tourism purposes makes minimal use of the travel and tourism industry. However, motoring organisations play a significant role in domestic tourism and an important one in inbound tourism. Australia has seven motoring organisations – one in every state and the Northern Territory – and their memberships total more than 6.4 million.[11]

The motoring organisations administer an accommodation rating system which requires the inspection of 17,000 properties each year. While individual associations are responsible for their territories, the work is coordinated by AAA Tourism in Melbourne, a company formed by the associations. It publishes Australia-wide accommodation guides derived from a national database and state guides, maps and brochures. The motoring organisations distribute more than 18 million pieces of this literature each year.

Coach companies

Coaches provide basic services within cities and link cities, towns and smaller places throughout Australia. These services are commonly shared by locals and tourists. Coaches are also used extensively in pure tourism roles: touring, sightseeing and transferring tourists from one facility within a destination to another, e.g. airports to hotels, hotels to convention centres. The coach is the transport workhorse of the destination system.

There are nearly 3,000 coach companies affiliated with the Australian Bus and Coach Association, ranging from giants like Murrays and McCafferty's, to suburban and country companies with just one coach. Most companies are small – the average number of employees in Australian coach companies in 1994 was seven (Richardson 1995).

The biggest express coach business in 2003 was McCafferty's, based in Toowomba. McCafferty's network spans the continent and provides the only form of transport to many outlying communities. Melbourne-based AAT–King's is a major coach touring company while Murrays Australia, the largest coach operator, is primarily a charter company though it does run some regular sightseeing and touring programs. It operates from depots in Sydney, Melbourne, Brisbane, Canberra, the Gold Coast and Cairns.

Rental cars

The rental car business in Australia provides easy access to cars and other vehicles throughout Australia. Each of the major companies operates from several hundred locations, including airports.

The business is dominated by four international companies – Hertz, Avis, Budget and Thrifty – and one Australian, which operates the Europcar franchise. They have the advantage of international connections – brand names, worldwide computer reservation systems and specialised marketing programs. The first three are owned by parent companies with the same name in the United States while Thrifty's shareholders are not only Thrifty Rent A Car–USA, but also Mitsubishi Motors Australia. There are many smaller rental companies.

Recreational vehicles

There is a growing demand for recreational vehicles such as motorhomes, campervans and 4-wheel drives, from within Australia and particular markets overseas (e.g. Germany). This demand is serviced by rental companies, the biggest of which in 2003 was Britz: Australia, followed by Maui Rentals. The two companies had the same owner – Tourism Holdings Ltd, a major New Zealand operator of tourism services and facilities. Hertz has a franchised recreational vehicle operation. A specialist operator, Aussie Outback Tours, organises escorted tours for recreational vehicle owners and renters.

Rail transport

Australia is one of the world's great tourist train destinations. It has a number of first class hotel trains crossing the continent, penetrating the interior and running up part of its east coast. These include trains like the Indian–Pacific and the Ghan. European-style fast trains operate out of Sydney, Brisbane and Perth.

The Queensland rail system includes the Queenslander, an all-first-class train which runs between Brisbane and Cairns, and the scenic railway which winds its way from

Cairns through rainforest to Kuranda. The 160 km/h Tilt Train operates between Brisbane and Rockhampton.

A private company, Great Southern Railway Ltd., runs the Indian–Pacific which makes the 4,352 km journey between Sydney and Perth, the Ghan which links Melbourne, Adelaide, Alice Springs and Darwin, and the Overland, the Melbourne/Adelaide express. West Coast Railway operates services between Melbourne/Geelong/Warrnambool.

Water transport

This includes cruise ships, ferries, reef, coastal, harbour and river cruising, and other water activities.

P&O Cruises has two Australian-based ships, the *Pacific Sky* and *Pacific Princess* (for half the year) and Sydney is the home port for South Pacific cruises. Ships sailing from Europe, North America and Asia on extended cruises call at Australian ports during the year. Other vessels come to Australian waters in the northern winter, running coastal cruises and shuttle voyages across the Tasman Sea. Cruise ship calls are eagerly sought at Australian ports. The usual ship stay is less than 24 hours but the amount of money they bring to a port can be significant; for example Tourism Victoria estimates that the average ship call at Melbourne is worth $1 million to the state economy.[12]

Ferries operate in a number of Australian waters. The TT Line, owned by the Tasmanian Government, runs a daily service both ways across Bass Strait, with two 29,000-ton vessels called *Spirit of Tasmania*. A large catamaran, *Sealion 2000*, provides a service between Cape Jervis, on the South Australian mainland, and Kangaroo Island. It is operated by K.I. Sealink, a private company.

The Great Barrier Reef is an area much frequented by cruise boats, most of them visiting islands or pontoons on the reef on day trips. Among cruise companies that operate for longer periods within the Great Barrier Reef are Captain Cook Cruises, which has the 3,000-ton *Reef Endeavour*, and Coral Princess Cruises, which has two cruising catamarans with cabins for about 50 each. Sydney Harbour is the most competitive of Australia's cruising waters. Captain Cook Cruises is a major company on the Harbour and also operates the 1,700-ton paddlesteamer *Murray Princess* on the Murray River. Its rivals on Sydney Harbour include Blue Line, owned by Accor Asia Pacific, and Matilda Cruises, owned by Amalgamated Holdings.

There are centres of water activity all around the coast. Queensland offers a number of examples such as in Cairns where tourists can find sightseeing craft, reef cruisers and big game-fishing boats. In the Whitsundays a number of different companies offer yachting cruises and cruising in sheltered waters is a major attraction on the Gold Coast. In other states, too, some kind of tourism experience is offered where there is access to water.

▓ Travel services

This category is for a variety of services which travellers need beyond the basics of transport, accommodation, food and drink. Among the companies represented are travel agents and the packagers of travel, the providers of financial services and the myriad suppliers of services for the ever-growing components of the MICE sector.

Tour operators

Most tour operators package services needed by tourists following a specified itinerary. Packaging involves stages which can take several months and sometimes years before sales are made. It requires knowing what the market wants, negotiating with the different suppliers (e.g. airlines, hotels, coach companies), designing the product, pricing it and then marketing it.

However, some tour operators are one-person operations, such as a specialist in a particular area (e.g. wilderness) or a particular activity (e.g. fishing). They need not offer anything but their own services. At the other end of the spectrum are tour operators which are very large international companies.

Wholesale tour operators, often just called wholesalers, sell their products widely through other distributors, usually travel agents. But some smaller operators, including some coach companies, do not wholesale; they do all the selling themselves.

Tour operators may be suppliers – such as airlines or coach companies – adding components from other suppliers with the prime objective of increasing the sale of their own products. Others are not suppliers of services such as accommodation or travel, they simply package other companies' products. Among these are government tourism organisations like Tourism Tasmania which packages and sells under the Tasmania's Temptations brand.[13]

Wholesalers are very important to the marketing of products and destinations. Even when travellers make their own arrangements, they may still look at a wholesaler's package to help plan a trip because wholesalers set standards in itinerary planning, acceptability of component products and price. They are often influential in establishing new destination areas.

Wholesalers usually specialise, distinguishing their markets by age groups, preferences for destinations, individual or group travel, mode of transport and type of experience (e.g. adventure or general sightseeing). Inbound tour operators package Australian travel products to promote and sell to overseas buyers such as wholesalers, travel agents, meeting planners and event managers in countries other than Australia. They may also be called 'ground operators' or 'destination marketing companies'.

The biggest wholesale tour operator in Australia in 2003 was Qantas Holidays. Other major domestic operators were Great Aussie Tours and Travelpoint. The coach company AAT–King's was another big operator. The latter's biggest rival in coach touring,

Australian Pacific Touring, outsources the running of its coaches to other companies. Examples of prominent international wholesalers are Creative Holidays, Insight International Tours, Contiki Holidays for 18 to 35s, Peregrine Adventures, Abercrombie and Kent, Adventure World, Cosmos and Trafalgar Tours. Among well-known Australian inbound operators are The Australian Outback Travel Company, General Travel Australia, ID Tours South Pacific, Bob Wood South Pacific Tours and Australian Tours Management.

Travel agents

Whether in a storefront building or online, travel agents are the industry's retailers. They sell travel and tourism products on a commission basis to consumers. They must be licensed and be members of the Travel Compensation Fund, which indemnifies consumers against an agency's insolvency.

There are about 4,700 licensed travel agency outlets in Australia, though the number of agency companies is probably about 1,000 fewer than that because some companies have multiple outlets and several hundred licences are held by organisations other than travel agents (e.g. coach operators, tourist information offices). Flight Centre, which is listed on the Australian Stock Exchange, is a large company owning (in 2002) more than 500 agencies in Australia (it also has operations overseas). However, the typical agency is a small company, employing a few people. The majority of agencies belong to a group of some kind, a buying/marketing group, a cooperative or franchise, and carry a well-promoted brand. They are in a better bargaining position with suppliers if they are part of a group.

Jetset Travelworld, owned by a public company, includes the Travelworld and Jetset brands as well as unbranded groups; in early 2003, it had about 750 agencies affiliated. Besides Flight Centre, other groups with several hundred agencies included Travelscene (formerly UTAG) and Harvey World Travel. Examples of online agencies are www.travel.com.au and www.webjet.com.au.

Consolidators

Consolidators are travel companies that write airline tickets for agents who are not qualified under the rules of the International Air Transport Association (IATA) or do not want to issue tickets themselves. Therefore the customers of consolidators are travel agents, not tourists.

Concorde International Travel is the biggest consolidator in Australia. It also owns Metro Travel. Consolidated Travel is another big consolidator.

The MICE sector

MICE is an acronym for Meetings, Incentives, Conventions and Exhibitions and refers to those sectors of the travel and tourism industry which cater for such activities. The term

Consolidators
Travel companies which write airline tickets for agents who are not qualified under the rules of the International Air Transport Association (IATA) or do not want to issue tickets themselves.

MICE sector
Businesses, government agencies and other organisations involved in bidding for, staging, facilitating and/or promoting meetings, incentives, conventions and/or exhibitions.

'meetings' can have different connotations. It can be given a specialised meaning for those gatherings primarily organised by companies. This distinguishes them from 'conventions' and 'conferences' which are usually run by associations. 'Meetings' can be used also in a broader sense for all off-site gatherings, including those organised by corporations, but also conventions, congresses, conferences, seminars, workshops, symposiums; indeed, any event which brings people together for the purpose of sharing information.

Incentive travel is a motivational tool to encourage employees or distributors (e.g. car dealers) to improve their work performance or results. The Society for Incentive Travel Executives (SITE) defines it as a 'global management tool that uses an exceptional travel experience to motivate and/or recognise participants for increased levels of performance in support of organisational goals (Australian Tourist Commission 1997, p. 4)'.

Exhibitions bring together suppliers of products, equipment and services in an environment where they can demonstrate their products and services. An exhibition can target either trade, industry or the consumer and can be either an integral part of a meeting or an independent event.

One category of exhibitions, trade shows (or fairs), is an important part of the selling mechanism of travel and tourism itself. The Australian Tourism Exchange is a familiar trade show in the Australian promotional calendar, but there are many more well known to the travel and tourism industry (e.g. ITB – International Tourismus Börse – Berlin; Asia/Pacific Incentives and Meetings Expo, Melbourne). A trade show is organised exclusively for a particular trade or industry and provides a forum for the exchange of information between companies and potential clients. Attendance is usually by invitation.

There are, however, many different kinds of exhibitions, some of them open to the public. Research by the Exhibition Industry Association of Australia suggests that arts, recreation, hobbies and sports are the largest categories of exhibition types, followed by home and lifestyle, computers, electronics and telecommunications.

The MICE sector includes diverse activities, but they are related because of the nature of the travel involved. The main stakeholders are associations (potential hosts), professional conference organisers, purpose-built convention centres, hotels (meeting facilities and rooms), other venues (e.g. Parliament Houses, High Court), convention bureaus, transport operators (e.g. air, coaches, shuttle buses, trains, trams and taxis), catering services, technical services (e.g. furniture and equipment hirers, printers, photographers), incentive travel planners, travel-related service companies (packaging transport and accommodation), event managers, government organisations (e.g. Australian Tourist Commission).

Financial services

Financial services are designed to give travellers access to spendable cash (currency that is accepted at the destination) or to credit. This is achieved through money exchange facilities, credit cards, traveller's cheques and disposable cash cards. Insurance for travellers is another important service.

The nationwide network of automatic teller machines makes accessing bank accounts easy for domestic travellers. They therefore have no problem in obtaining cash, and, of course, most of them have credit cards. Providing for the financial needs of international travellers requires more attention.

Some banks and hotels provide money exchange services. Specialised exchange bureaus are located at airports and in city locations.

Travelex Australia, a subsidiary of the British Travelex Group, is the biggest operator of foreign exchange bureaus. It also offers an online service for travellers who wish to purchase foreign currency (www.travelex.com.au). American Express issues the world's best-known traveller's cheques, including those in Australian dollars. It also has a family of credit cards for individuals and corporate clients which form the basis of the American Express travel system. The Diners Club credit card can be used with a personal identification number (PIN) to get cash from 2,800 bank automatic teller machines in Australia and a total of 232,000 in nearly 50 other countries. The international bank credit card systems, Visa and MasterCard, operate in most parts of the world tourists are likely to travel. Visa-branded cards are said to be accepted at more than 22 million locations around the world and MasterCard says its cards are accepted at 'more locations than any other card' (www.visa-asia.com and www.mastercard.com.au).

Most travel insurance is sold through the travel agency network and there is fierce competition among insurance providers to gain preferred product status with agency groups. About a dozen companies provide travel insurance, either insurance companies or brokers underwritten by insurance companies. Products are similar, providing coverage against illness while travelling, lost baggage, theft, expenses because of transport delays and so on. Special policies are available for frequent flyers and for domestic travellers who wish to insure against being forced to cancel discount air tickets (which cannot be changed or cashed in with the airline).

The hospitality sector

The Australian Oxford Concise Dictionary (1987, p. 515) defines hospitality as the 'friendly and generous reception of guests or strangers'. It is one of the basic constituents of the travel and tourism industry, the purpose of which has not changed over the ages. In industry terms it embraces the supply of accommodation, food and drink.

Accommodation

The volume of tourism to a particular destination is directly influenced by the size of the accommodation sector, by the way it reacts to demand and by the quality of the accommodation it offers. According to the World Tourism Organisation (1999b) Australia is one of more than 40 countries in the world with more than 100,000 hotel beds. Australia easily qualifies, as it has almost double that number of beds. But, of course, hotels are only one form of tourist accommodation. The accommodation directories produced by the motoring organisations classify and rate hotels, motels, self-catering accommodation, caravan parks and bed and breakfast accommodation.[14] The Australian Bureau of Statistics collects information on hotels, motels, guest houses and serviced apartments.

Most of the big hotels bear familiar brand names – Hyatt, Hilton, Sheraton, Novotel, Holiday Inn and so on. They are operated by hotel management companies, which either have the same name or manage hotels of different star ratings under different brands, e.g. Accor Asia Pacific Corporation works with the Sofitel, Novotel, Mercure, Ibis and Formule 1 names. According to Jones, Lang LaSalle Hotels, an international hotel investment group, the six top operators, in terms of number of rooms, at November 2001 were Accor Asia Pacific, Six Continents Hotels and Resorts, Rydges Hotels and Resorts, Starwood Hotels, Tourast Hotels and Hilton Hotels of Australia.

In 2001 Australian hotel investors and owner/operators owned 55 per cent of the accommodation covered in a Jones, Lang LaSalle Hotels survey (137 major owners, 395 establishments and more than 69,200 rooms). Three Australian listed companies led the owners' list: Tourism Asset Holdings, the Grand Hotel Group and Thakral Holdings Ltd. Next were British-based Six Continents Hotels & Resorts, Stamford Land Corporation and General Property Trust.

Most motels are owned individually but many of them are organised in groups for marketing purposes. Major groups are Best Western and the Budget Motel Chain. Best Western, descended from the oldest Australian motel referral chain, is part of the international Best Western Group. The Budget Motel Chain is a low cost, basic referral group, based on the Budget Motel 6 concept in the United States.

Flag Choice Hotels, majority owned by US-based Choice Hotels, is said to be the largest accommodation group in the Southern Hemisphere. It is a franchise group with properties in Australia, New Zealand, the South Pacific and Asia. It includes hotels and motels and is headquartered in Melbourne.

There are more than 350,000 caravans in Australia and some 2,700 short-term caravan parks, with annual revenues in the late 1990s of about $1.5 billion, employing 15,000 people (Office of National Tourism, 1998a). Recreational vehicles with sleeping accommodation are also popular. Camping is another form of low-cost accommodation. The Australian Camping Association fosters the use of bunk house and cabin accommodation, mainly by school groups who account for about 90 per cent of the customers. Another section of the youth market is catered for by the Youth Hostels Association, which represents some 140 hostels in Australia. Backpackers patronise hostels as well as specialised accommodation.

Tourists can also stay in Australian homes. There are about 5,000 bed and breakfast establishments in Australia, not all of them homes – accommodation can be in cottages or self-contained apartments. In any case, visitors can expect the 'home touch': it is a requirement of the Australian Bed and Breakfast Council that the host/hostess should be present to offer personal service and that breakfast should be available (Peterkin 1998). There is some overlap with host farms. These have representative organisations in each state and a national body, Australian Farm and Country Tourism.

Food services

Food and drink are necessities, but they are also part of a destination's stock-in-trade in ensuring tourists have a satisfying, memorable, stay. The demand for good quality meals, unusual or distinctive cuisine, can be an important secondary attraction for any destination.

Tourists eat in a variety of situations – in planes and trains and on ships, in airports, seaports, railway stations, coach terminals and, of course, in restaurants, cafés and other kinds of specific eating establishments. Many domestic tourists cook for themselves some of the time and eat out on special occasions during a holiday. Sometimes self-catering foodpacks are provided where they are staying.

The bigger hotels provide more than one restaurant and keep up with international trends in food and its preparation. Some international travellers prefer this because they know what they are getting. Standardisation can be a problem for others, who wish to sample what the locals eat and drink.

The experimentation with Australian ingredients in recent years to produce the distinctive style of cuisine for which Australia is becoming known has taken place in the independent restaurants. They and the cafés, bars, pubs and clubs represent an important part of the nation's culture and provide visitors with an opportunity to mix with the locals in a convivial atmosphere.

▓ Attractions and activities

Attractions and activities provide the reason for travelling to particular destinations and they are the first essential ingredient in developing leisure tourism. They are those events, places, people or features that draw visitors from near and far. An attraction must be interesting and pleasurable enough to sufficiently motivate people to travel for the purpose of experiencing it (Timothy & Butler 1995).

The term 'attraction' can be interpreted very broadly so that a destination's major attraction can be a whole city, with the opportunity to share the lifestyle of its residents. The Western Australian Tourism Commission regards Fremantle as a specific attraction, but the concept can be applied to much bigger cities, destination areas or even countries. The term can also be applied more specifically: the major attraction of a resort area may be the weather. A safe, hospitable environment is an attraction. 'Friendly people' has often been said by visitors to be one of Australia's attractions.

Attractions
(a) Those events, places, people or features that draw visitors to a destination. (b) Natural wonders or built establishments designed to educate or entertain visitors, which are managed and promoted.

The place is the Gold Coast and the theme is Hollywood. Warner Bros. Movieworld exemplifies the popular theme park in the Disneyland tradition. The picture shows the Wild West Falls Adventure Ride, which takes six minutes and ends in a 20-metre, 60 km per hour drop to the final splashdown.

(Source: Warner Bros. Movieworld.)

'Attraction' also has a narrow meaning – for a natural wonder or built establishment which is managed and promoted. It is this version of attraction which is of interest in determining who is part of the travel and tourism industry. A building may be an attraction but designed for a specific function which in itself had little to do with tourism. An example is Parliament House in Canberra. It is managed by the Joint House Department which not only looks after the needs of the Commonwealth legislature, but also the marketing and guidance needs of an Australian 'super-attraction' with yearly patronage of more than one million.[15]

Public/private sector mix

There is a mix of ownership and management of Australian attractions; some are run by the private sector but many of them are owned by the public and managed by a variety of agencies, boards and management committees, and so governments are ultimately responsible for them.

The travel and tourism industry is often reluctant to regard the managers of government-owned attractions as 'of the industry'. And on the whole managers of such attractions as national parks and heritage sites are reluctant to take the usual industry marketing-led approach to management, with its emphasis on fulfilling the needs and wants of the consumer.

Table 1.3 shows how a range of Australian attractions are owned and managed.

Table 1.3 Selected Australian attractions

Natural attractions	Most of Australia's great natural attractions are managed within a multi-government national park and reserves system. The Commonwealth administers some 18 sites under the National Park and Wildlife Conservation Act, among them the Uluru-Kata Tjuta National Park (Ayers Rock and the Olgas) and Kakadu National Park in the Northern Territory. The Great Barrier Reef Marine Park has been set up under its own Act of Parliament. Most of the other parks and reserves are administered by state/territory government departments or authorities although in some cases local government authorities have set up committees of management.
Heritage sites	National heritage sites are managed under a cooperative arrangement between the Commonwealth Government, state and territory governments and private owners. Management plans are mandatory for places owned or controlled by the government and named on the Commonwealth Heritage List. The Commonwealth is required to use best endeavours to ensure there are plans prepared in cooperation with states and territories for places on the National Heritage List. Additionally, the Register of the National Estate has the names of 13,000 significant sites. Tourists are encouraged to visit most of them.[16] See Chapter 5.
Indigenous tourism	Some Aboriginal communities, companies and individuals conduct cultural tours and there are a number of successful cultural centres and dance theatres. Aboriginal art is popular with tourists. See Chapter 3.
Museums, galleries and other cultural facilities	Australia has many different museums with themes such as maritime history, science, technology, toys, natural history, art and Antarctic exploration. The term 'museum' includes art galleries and an international definition excludes those run for profit. At the end of June 2000 there were 2,049 'museum establishments' in Australia, the total being made up of 249 art museums/galleries, 411 historic properties and 1,389 other museums (e.g. social history, natural history and science museums) (Australian Bureau of Statistics, 2001). Governments at all levels operate museums, including the most prominent, but a number are run privately, including important art galleries, and some do not figure in the above statistics because they are intended to make a profit.
Theme parks	There are two major categories of theme parks – those in the Disneyland tradition with popular themes designed to attract the largest possible market and those that have been built to tell part of Australia's history in an entertaining way. Most of the major Disneyland-type parks are concentrated in the Brisbane-Gold Coast corridor and on the Gold Coast itself, three of them managed centrally as the Warner Bros. Village Theme Park Group: Warner Bros. Movieworld, Sea World and Wet 'n' Wild Water World. A fourth major Gold

continued . . .

Table 1.3 continued

	Coast theme park, Dreamworld, is owned by the Leisurewide Property Trust. The biggest theme park – in area at least – is Wonderland Sydney which occupies 213 hectares west of the city near Penrith. A prominent historical theme park, Ballarat's Sovereign Hill, a recreated gold mining township of the 1850s, qualifies as a museum because it is operated by a not-for-profit organisation.
Zoos, animal parks, aquariums	Zoos, bird and animal parks and aquariums are managed under three different systems – government, trusts and private enterprise. Governments typically set up organisations with their own legislation to manage major zoos under their control. Examples are the Zoological Board of New South Wales, which manages the Taronga Park Zoo in Sydney and the Western Plains Zoo in Dubbo, the Royal Zoological Society of South Australia which runs the Adelaide Zoo and the Monato Zoo, and the Zoological Parks and Gardens Board which manages three Victorian zoos and parks – Melbourne Zoo, Healesville Sanctuary and the Victorian Open Range Zoo at Werribee. The Currumbin Sanctuary on the Gold Coast was given to the National Trust of Queensland by its founder, Alex Griffiths. Some specialised parks are owned in the private sector – the Crocodile Farm out of Darwin is an example. Aquariums tend to be owned privately.
Events	All the states and territories have organisations to attract events, develop them and sometimes to manage them. Western Australia set the trend when it established Eventscorp in the mid-1980s to develop, attract and manage events of economic importance to the state. The Queensland Events Corporation, the Melbourne Major Events Company and the Northern Territory Major Events Company have been created to attract events. The Canberra Tourism Commission incorporated events into a new name in the late 1990s, becoming the Canberra Tourism and Events Corporation. The Queensland Events Corporation is a proprietary limited company owned by the Queensland Government. South Australia's Australian Major Events and Special Events New South Wales are part of their governments' tourism commissions. The Hobart City Council manages Tasmania's most significant event, the Festival of Tasmania, which is held each year in January around the time of the Sydney-Hobart Yacht Race.
Performing arts	A Sydney company, Showbiz International, specialises in selling tickets for major theatrical and sporting events to the travel and tourism industry in Australia and overseas. It also packages tickets with accommodation for major hotel groups and other clients and provides priority tickets for loyalty programs. The Sydney Opera House is Australia's best-known cultural icon. It is operated by a trust, set up under an Act of the New South Wales Parliament, which is charged with its care, maintenance and control.[17]

Table 1.3 continued	
	Similar arrangements are in place in some other states – the State Theatre complex in Melbourne, for example – but, of course, much of the theatre business is in the hands of private entrepreneurs. Casino complexes usually include theatres which attract local and visitor audiences.
Handicrafts	Handicrafts venues range from sophisticated permanent exhibitions in tourism precincts, to periodic markets in city or suburban locations or at country fairs. Markets are usually administered by local authorities. Thus the Hobart City Council manages one of its city's best known attractions, the Salamanca Place Market.

▥ Retail goods

Researchers rate shopping as an attraction and International Visitor Surveys show it at the top of the list, e.g. in Sydney more overseas tourists shop than visit the Opera House, Darling Harbour, the Rocks or go on a harbour cruise.

Shopping can be rated thus:

1. exclusively for travellers (e.g. duty free shops)
2. almost exclusively for travellers/visitors[18] (e.g. shops at airports, service stations[19] on highways, shops in hotel lobbies, shops at theme parks and other attractions
3. mainly for visitors (e.g shops in tourism precincts like the Rocks and Darling Harbour in Sydney, the Pacific Fair Shopping Centre on the Gold Coast)
4. for visitors and residents alike (e.g. shopping centres like Adelaide's Myer Centre and Melbourne Central)
5. mainly for locals (e.g. major department stores in big cities)
6. almost exclusively for locals (e.g. the general run of shopping in places only occasionally visited by non-locals).

CASE STUDY

The management diversity of Devonport's attractions

Devonport is an attractive city of about 25,000 on Tasmania's fertile north-west coast. It was created in the 1890s by merging two towns, Formby on the west bank of the Derwent River and Torquay on the east bank. It is known as the 'Gateway to Tasmania' because it is the site of the terminal for the TT-Line's *Spirit of Tasmania* ferries which cross Bass Strait daily between Devonport and Melbourne.

It is an ideal place to start a tour of Tasmania, but it also has an array of attractions of its own to interest the visitor. These provide an example not only of the range of attractions in a small city, but also of the diversity of management in a destination's attractions. The official 'Guide to Devonport' lists the following:

- Tiagarra, a Tasmanian Aboriginal cultural and arts centre
- Home Hill, a National Trust house which was the home of Tasmania's only Prime Minister, Joseph Lyons, and Dame Enid Lyons
- the Tasmanian Arboretum, a tree park of native and exotic species
- Devonport Gallery and Arts Centre, in a converted old church
- the Don River Railway, a railway museum and vintage railway with steam train
- the Maritime Museum, a collection of models from the days of sail to the current passenger ferries
- Australian Weaving Mills, manufacturers of several brands of towels.

The mills are run by private enterprise, Tiagarra by the Mersey–Leven Aboriginal Corporation, the gallery and arts centre by the Devonport City Council, Home Hill by the National Trust (Tasmania) and the Don River Railway, Arboretum and the Maritime Museum by incorporated associations. Volunteers help staff Home Hill, the Arboretum, the gallery and arts centre, the Don River Railway and the Maritime Museum (Moore 1999).[20]

INDUSTRY PROFILE

JULIE SINCLAIR PUBLIC RELATIONS CONSULTANT, QUEENSLAND RAIL

I'm responsible for promoting QR's passenger trains – namely its long distance Traveltrain services and urban Citytrain services – as a travel option. Primarily this involves building relationships with the media to ensure positive editorial coverage. This is usually achieved by providing media with information about our services, either in person or via media release, and offering them opportunities to experience them first-hand.

I look to supplement the editorial coverage we receive with consumer promotions with radio, newspaper and television partners. I'm also the resident copywriter, providing the words for editorial features, advertisements, brochures, newsletters and the like.

How did I get here?

I've been in public relations for more than eight years. Most of this time has been spent in the tourism and leisure sectors, with stints at Tourism Queensland, Warner Bros. Movieworld, 2001 Goodwill Games Brisbane and Brisbane Festival.

Travel and tourism is a very attractive industry, so getting in – especially in PR – can be difficult. I got my role at Tourism Queensland after extensive unpaid work experience there. But it's also a very close-knit industry and once you're in you're always hearing about new opportunities. Word of mouth and industry contacts have played an important role in securing some of my other positions.

What do I like about my job?

Travel and tourism is a very exciting industry to be involved in and presents a great variety of opportunities for a public relations practitioner. It's a dynamic industry that is constantly evolving, with an ever-growing suite of products and developments. And, while it's often seen as young and glamorous, it's also economically important and, as such, faces social, economic and legislative issues in the same way as other big industries. From a PR perspective, this means the opportunity to work on positive, fun projects such as product promotions and launches, as well as issues and crisis management. Few industries afford this level of diversity.

SUMMARY

Tourism is so pervasive just about everybody is conscious of it. It is important because of its value as a leisure pursuit, its economic effect on businesses, destinations and nations, and its sociocultural and physical environmental impacts. But it is difficult to say exactly what it is because it means different things to different people, depending on their interests. It is usually agreed, however, that tourism has three attributes:

- it involves travel
- it requires a temporary stay away from home
- its prime purpose is something other than earning money in the place or places visited.

Definitions can be placed in two broad categories: conceptual and technical. Conceptual definitions may reflect a particular interest – e.g. study or economics – or try to encapsulate the true nature of tourism, usually through the attitudes or behaviour of tourists. Technical definitions have been framed so that tourists can be distinguished from other travellers and be counted. They employ such measures as the distance travelled and length of stay. They include business travellers while most conceptual definitions do not; the latter see tourism as being the result of leisure, essentially the freedom from work.

In Australia statistics on international tourism are gathered when people arrive in or leave the country. More detailed information about overseas and domestic tourism is supplied by the International Visitor Survey, the National Visitor Survey, regional and specialist studies. All of these employ definitions which use specific terms related to place of residence, length of journey, the purpose of visits and length of stay.

Tourism is not a product; this means that the 'industry' that serves it cannot be defined by conventional means. Usually the term refers to groupings of businesses with similar economic activity; they are defined by the nature of the goods and services they produce. But tourists consume all sorts of goods and services provided by businesses with different economic activities.

Those businesses belong to separate industries in their own right. They are linked because of the demand tourists have for their services; they have the same customers. While there is scholarly argument about the use of the word 'industry', in common usage there is a travel and tourism industry.

Many different types of businesses are involved in supplying tourists with their needs. They fit into two major categories: those that supply services directly to tourists and those that supply them indirectly. Those that supply tourists indirectly provide goods and services to the businesses which have face-to-face contact with tourists.

People working in tourism usually limit the meaning of the 'industry' to include only those businesses which provide goods and services directly to tourists, and more particularly those whose sole or main activity is serving tourists. These have been called the 'primary trades' and have been classified under six headings: transportation, travel services, accommodation, food services, activities and attractions, retail goods.

QUESTIONS

1. Tourism is more than people having holidays and travelling away from home. What do you think that statement means?
2. What are the main differences between conceptual and technical definitions?
3. Tourism has three essential attributes. What are they and what is a fourth that is usually added in conceptual definitions?
4. Why do governments and business managers want business travellers included in tourism statistics?
5. What is the difference between a 'trip' and a 'visit'? Do you think the language devised for technical definitions is logical and easy to understand?
6. How do you explain the concept of 'usual environment'?
7. Why does tourism not fit into standard classifications of industries?
8. What is the rationale for the description 'travel and tourism industry'?
9. What is the difference between businesses directly involved in tourism and those indirectly involved?
10. How would you describe travel and tourism's 'primary trades'?

THE TOURISM SYSTEM AND THE THEORY OF MARKETS AND DESTINATIONS

Understand what models and systems are and how they are used in tourism analysis.

Understand the elements of the tourism system and their relationships.

Examine the system from the perspective of four of the elements: the tourist destination region, the traveller generating region, the transit route region and the travel and tourism industry (the fifth element – the tourist – is discussed in Chapter 3).

Identify the types of linkages that are important in the tourism system – communications, transportation and infrastructure – and the part each plays in developing tourism flows.

Examine what is meant by 'market', 'demand' and 'segmentation', the different types of segmentation research and how the family lifecycle model can be used to help understand a market and its tourism potential.

Understand the use of the term 'destination', how 'product' is related to it and how destination lifestyle models are of value for analysis.

Review a case study of the Japanese market: how it was once seen as Australia's dominant inbound market for years to come, how it faltered and eventually was downgraded in importance in comparison with others.

| UNDERSTAND
THE MEANING OF:

- *model*
- *system*
- *elements of a system*
- *Tourist destination region (TDR)*
- *Traveller generating region (TGR)*
- *Transit route region (TRR)*
- *destination marketing organisation*
- *Passenger Vehicle Equalisation Scheme*
- *node and spokes*
- *market*
- *demand*
- *needs and wants*
- *product*
- *competitor*
- *marketing information system*
- *market research*
- *market segmentation*
- *demographic research*
- *psychographic research*
- *family lifecycle*
- *destination*
- *destination area*
- *tourist region*
- *service*
- *overall destination product*
- *destination lifecycle*
- *allocentric, midcentric, psychocentric*

A SYSTEMS APPROACH TO STUDYING TOURISM

Now that a general understanding of the nature of tourism has been set out in Chapter 1, this chapter begins by describing a way of conceptualising, or imagining, the way in which tourism occurs. The method uses a model of the tourism system. A model may be defined as a theoretical system of relationships which tries to capture the essential elements in a real-world situation (Bannock, Baxter & Rees 1977).

Models are used to demonstrate a conceptual framework, the way in which ideas concerning a particular phenomenon are related to each other. They can also have an active role, as in forecasting future situations. Thus different kinds of models are described in this book. Some of them are complex like the computable general equilibrium (CGE) models, the most sophisticated of a number of models referred to in Chapter 4, or the Tourism Futures Simulator, which is the subject of a case study in Chapter 9.

CGE models represent the whole economy as a system of flows of goods and services between sectors, including industry, the household, government and foreign sectors. They provide the most detailed and informative modelling technique available for estimating the economic impact of tourism. The Tourism Futures Simulator uses inter-connected mathematical equations to help predict future occurrences for entire tourism regions.

Other models are less complex and indeed their purpose is to make situations easier to understand. They display connected elements so that it is possible to appreciate relationships and what is likely to happen if a change occurs to one or more elements. A model of the tourism system is an example.

The Macquarie Dictionary (1997, p. 1775) defines a **system** as 'an assemblage or combination of things or parts forming a complex or unitary whole'. Systems are found in many different situations. The human body contains a number, among them the digestive system, the **elements** of which include the oesophagus, stomach, liver, pancreas and colon. They all form a 'unitary whole', but if one part suddenly does not work properly, it will affect the rest of the system in some way. Another system which is necessary for existence on earth is the ecosystem, the attributes of which are discussed in Chapter 6.

The tourism system is fundamental to the study of tourism. Like the digestive system, it is made up of elements. Elements are essential, but need not be dissected to understand the system and how it functions (Leiper

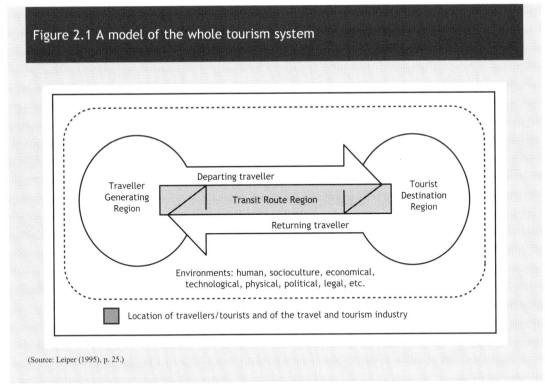

Figure 2.1 A model of the whole tourism system

(Source: Leiper (1995), p. 25.)

1990). The model in Figure 2.1 is of the whole tourism system, in contrast to sub-systems, such as tourist attractions or the travel and tourism industry.

The model shows that three of the five essential elements of the tourism system are geographic:

1. The **traveller generating region** (TGR) – where the tourist comes from.
2. The **transit route region** (TRR) – through which the tourist must pass to reach the intended destination and return home.
3. The **tourist destination region** (TDR) to which the tourist intends to travel.

The other two elements are human and they are to be found in all three regions. One is the tourist, the central feature of the system; there has to be at least one of them, otherwise tourism cannot exist. The fifth element is the travel and tourism industry. It is required to enable the transition of tourists from the TGR to and from the TDR via the TRR and to provide them with goods and services at the TDR.

The model includes a number of environments – human, sociocultural, technological, economic, physical, political, legal – within which tourism occurs. Changes in these environments may cause changes in the way that tourism is provided and consumed.

Should a change occur in the technological environment, such as the development of a jet engine that is cheaper to operate, the cost of tourism involving air travel can be expected

DEFINITIONS

Model
A theoretical system of relationships which tries to capture the essential elements in a real-world situation.

System
An assemblage or combination of things or parts forming a complex or unitary whole.

Elements
(of a system) are the basic building blocks. They are essential, but need not be dissected for an understanding of the system and how it functions.

to decrease, resulting in an increase of tourists from particular TGRs. This shows how all the elements in the model are related to each other. A change in one area can create a ripple effect throughout the rest of the system. Types of change which affect tourism are discussed in Chapter 12.

The interaction of tourism with environments is two-way. While a change in any environment can change the pattern of tourism, so too can changes in tourism impact on environments, e.g. a large increase in numbers of tourists visiting a destination will have a powerful impact on a range of environments. Such impacts are the subjects of Chapters 4, 5 and 6. In fact, the subject matter of all chapters can be related to the tourism system.

USING THE MODEL

The system model can be used for general analysis and discussion. It is also suitable for interdisciplinary studies of tourism. It is so constructed that each discipline (such as geography, psychology, economics, management) can play its part in research or educational programs. Further, it shows how their contributions can be organised to form a cohesive understanding of the subject (Leiper 1990).

It can also be a valuable business tool. The model may be used from the perspective of any element, four of which are discussed in this chapter and the fifth, the tourist perspective, is the subject of the next chapter.

Figures 2.2 and 2.3 show Australia in different roles, as a tourist destination region and also as a traveller generating region. In fact, a place can function in all three geographic roles in the system. In addition to it being a tourist destination region and a traveller generating region Australia may also be on a transit route region for some tourists, for example, when a European or American visitor passes through on the way to the South Pacific (e.g. on a cruise) without choosing to stay for any length of time.

Tourist destination region (TDR)

A place visited by tourists.

THE TDR PERSPECTIVE

Figure 2.2 shows how Leiper's system can be extended to display a number of traveller generating regions (TGRs) from the perspective of the tourist destination region (TDR). This is a common use of the model. In this case the TDR is Australia and the TGRs are its five major suppliers of overseas tourists in the eight-month period ending August 2002.

This type of display is of interest to marketers in the TDR because most of their marketing effort will take place in the TGRs. It is in them that tourists make the initial decisions about itineraries, destinations to be visited and products that will be purchased, including transport and accommodation. Many will buy a package combining a number of the elements of a tour.[1] National tourism organisations will do most of the research and much of the promotional work in overseas TGRs, often in association with travel and tourism businesses. The latter also promote independently and forge relationships with relevant members of the home industry.

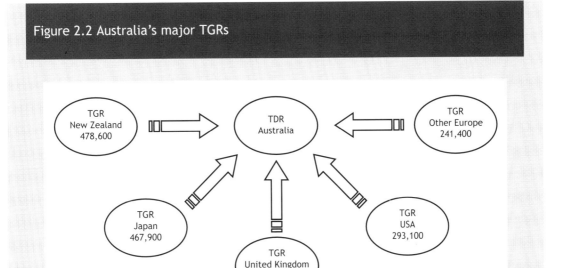

Figure 2.2 Australia's major TGRs

Arrival figures are for the eight month period ending August 2002. (Source: *Impact Fact Sheet* (September 2002), Department of Industry, Tourism and Resources.)

THE TGR PERSPECTIVE

The basic model may also be adapted in the reverse of the Figure 2.2 display, with the focus being on Australia as a TGR. This is shown in Figure 2.3 with the top five TDRs for short-term Australian citizen departures, for the seven-month period ending July 2002 being modelled.

There are three dimensions to the way places generate travellers for tourism: (a) geographically, because travel is generated by the physical act of setting out on a trip; (b) economically, because the economic resources which tourists use, consume or spend during a trip are usually generated in the economy of the TGR; and (c) psychologically, because a place generates travel when its environments shape the needs and motivations of its residents, impelling a proportion of them to travel (these so-called 'push' factors are discussed in the next chapter) (Leiper 1995).

THE TRR PERSPECTIVE

Being in the middle, it is no surprise that the perspective of the transit route region is influenced by both the TGR and TDR. The TGR is where the tourists come from and they will have their own ideas about which route to take to the destination (if there is a choice),

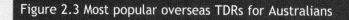

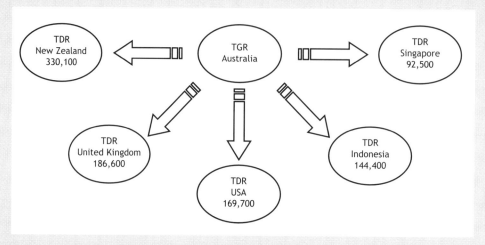

Figure 2.3 Most popular overseas TDRs for Australians

Australian short-term departure figures show the five most popular tourist destination regions for the seven month period ending July 2002. (Source: *Overseas Arrivals and Departures Fact Sheet* (26 September 2002), Australian Bureau of Statistics.)

what transport they will use and whether or not they will stop over on the way. They may also decide to take a different route home.

The TDR's influence derives from its transport and related links with the TGR and intermediate destinations: e.g. airline services or road systems, terminals, signage etc. These considerations also largely define the influence of the TRR. If it is efficient, allowing easy and attractive access to the TDR, then the latter's tourism will benefit. If it is inefficient, then the TDR's tourism will suffer. There are many factors, including distance, the frequency and capacity of transport services, the adequacy of road systems (if applicable), travel time, cost, stopover places and attractions along the way.

THE TRAVEL AND TOURISM INDUSTRY PERSPECTIVE

For the system to work, business activity must take place in at least the TGR and the TDR. When tourism products are bought and sold in the traveller generating region, it becomes a market. Tourists spend money there and at the destination. They may not spend directly in the transit route region but they will at least consume resources there. This is easy to understand in organised tourism involving the travel and tourism industry, particularly when an international journey is involved. In a typical case, tourists buy a package from travel agents in the TGR (the market), stop over at an intermediate destination in the TRR and of course spend most of their time and money in the TDR (the destination), sampling its attractions and using services like accommodation, destination transport, shopping and other attractions. The 'travel' parts of the travel and tourism industry are in generating regions and the 'tourism' parts are in destinations, all working cooperatively, to some extent, to form an industrial chain along the itinerary (Leiper 1995).

But even when tourists have little or no contact with the travel and tourism industry, they still will spend money in the three areas, except in instances where the TRR is short. For example, a family going on holiday to its holiday home will buy at least petrol or transport tickets in the TGR and will buy at least food and drink at the destination as well as paying for the running of the holiday home. When the distance between homes is very short they may not actually spend money in the TRR, but they will have consumed resources in passing through it.

Because some tourists are not dependent on services from the travel and tourism industry, or are dependent to a limited extent only, Leiper uses the term 'partial-industrialisation' in respect to the tourism system. There are degrees of industrialisation, ranging from 100 per cent (all money spent with the travel and tourism industry) to zero (tourists present and spending money but no travel and tourism industry).

PROMOTION

Tourism planners and businesspeople think of the TGR as the marketplace where tourists and potential tourists reside. It may be overseas, interstate or intrastate. Part of the travel and tourism industry functions in the generating region: the ticketing services, travel agents, tour operators, plus the marketing arms of the competing destinations.

Tourists and potential tourists present certain demographic and psychographic characteristics which are important to marketers' assessments of their needs and motivations. They have preferences of what they want to see and do and which transportation, accommodation and other services they wish to use. They are influenced by a variety of communications including personal correspondence, weather information, news stories and so on (Blank 1989).

TDR promoters also try to influence tourists' preferences. Promotion of the destination is in two parts: (1) attempts to directly influence consumers favourably, and (2) the building of relationships with key members of the travel and tourism industry within the TGR. These are mainly the distribution companies – the tour operators and travel agents – but usually also airlines, particularly the national carrier of the TGR if it flies to the destination.

Destination promotion is carried out by (1) destination marketing organisations representing collective destination interests and (2) the travel and tourism businesses which operate in their own sub-markets (e.g. airline market, hotel market, tour market). In some cases, tour operators from the industry in the TGR will take the initiative in creating or servicing linkages between the destination and markets.

Australia has a large number of destination marketing organisations. The national body is the Australian Tourist Commission, a statutory authority of the Commonwealth Government, which operates in overseas markets only. Each of the eight states and territories has a tourism commission which promotes its destination in Australia and overseas. City visitor and convention bureaus promote to specialised markets – meetings, incentive travel and exhibitions.

Tourism organisations representing regions or local destinations also are active in domestic and overseas markets. A national domestic promotion organisation, See Australia, encourages Australians to travel within Australia.

TRANSPORT LINKAGES

Australian government organisations take a keen interest in transport from Australia's TGRs. These include the Commonwealth Government departments responsible for transport and tourism. Most of the state/territory tourism commissions have units responsible for enhancing air services from tourism markets.

As for sea links, the most prominent example of state concern is Bass Strait, where car ferries, run by a Tasmanian Government-owned company, provide service between Melbourne and Devonport. As most Australians take a holiday by driving their own vehicle in their own country, Tasmania has long seen itself as being at a disadvantage by being an island. Since September 1966, when the Bass Strait Passenger Vehicle Equalisation

The Transit Route Region between Tasmania and the mainland is traversed by sea or air. The sea route is serviced by two ferries called the Spirit of Tasmania I *and* II *(shown right) which make nightly crossings of Bass Strait in both directions, linking Melbourne and Devonport. Each ferry can carry 650 cars as well as 1,400 passengers. The cost of taking a car is subsidised by the Commonwealth Government through the Bass Strait Passenger Vehicle Equalisation Scheme (BSPVES). This is done to remove a disadvantage to Tasmania by reducing the cost of taking a vehicle across Bass Strait to the cost of driving the same vehicle the same distance on a mainland highway. As a promotional inducement, the TT Line, which is wholly owned by the Tasmanian Government, carries cars free of charge in off-peak periods.*

(Source: TT Line Company Pty Ltd.)

Scheme (BSPVES) was introduced, the cost of taking a car between the mainland and Tasmania has been subsidised by the Commonwealth Government.

The principle behind the Passenger Vehicle Equalisation Scheme is to reduce the cost of taking a vehicle across Bass Strait to the cost of driving the same vehicle the same distance on a mainland highway. The subsidy relates to the vehicle, not the passenger. The Department of Transport and Regional Services calculates recurrent adjustments to the level of the subsidy based on its own analysis along with cost data provided by motoring bodies.

INFRASTRUCTURE

Infrastructure plays an important role in the linkage of a TDR with its TGRs. Tourists arrive at a gateway – an airport, seaport, border point or turn-off on a highway. All of these require infrastructure of one kind or another, ranging from an international airport costing hundreds of millions of dollars to a directional sign costing a tiny fraction of that expenditure.

The designation of particular TDRs for development and linking them with appropriate transport has become attractive to state and regional planners. Tourism New South Wales (1996) recommends a 'node and spoke' system as a means of rationalising the development of TDRs. A node is a destination area with high attraction value and concentrated infra-structure and spokes are smaller attractions in the local area. What links them are roads. Nodes themselves should be linked to encourage overnight stays. Therefore designated tourism transportation links need to be established.

Tourism Tasmania uses the term 'clusters' rather than 'nodes' and applies different criteria to them. But otherwise the basic principles are similar. Clusters involve major attrac-tions, activities and associated visitor services. The clusters are linked by road systems.

THE THEORY OF MARKETS AND DESTINATIONS

The TGRs which supply tourists and the TDRs which receive them are, of course, the major fields of activity for the travel and tourism industry. These require study in some detail from a business point of view and a change to the more familiar industry terminology of markets and destinations.

▨ Markets — where tourism is generated

Markets are where tourism demand is, or put in the terms of tourism businesses, where their customers are, at least potentially. A straightforward way to think of a **tourism market** is that it consists of all the potential customers sharing a particular need or want who might be willing and able to satisfy it by buying a tourism product.

Demand is the desire of would-be purchasers for products and, to be realistic for businesses, the desire must also be accompanied by the ability to make the purchase.

Tourism market
All the potential customers sharing a particular need or want who might be willing and able to satisfy it by buying a tourism product.

Demand
The desire of would-be purchasers for products, who have the ability to make the purchase.

DEFINITIONS

....

Need

A state of felt deprivation of some basic satisfaction, like food and clothing, shelter and safety, belonging and esteem.

Indeed, economists define demand not in terms of needs and wants but as the willingness and ability of a consumer to purchase a product at a particular price. No matter how great the **need**, the lack of money to back it will mean that it does not constitute demand or exert any pressure in the market (Hughes 1986).

Demand can be created in customers who do have the money; they can be made aware that they have unsatisfied needs. That is a marketing role, creating a good fit between the customers' needs and wants, and the service providers' offerings. Demand can be latent or 'pent-up'; that is, the desire is there but the ability to purchase is not, even though the constraint is not lack of money (e.g. it could be government regulations). Demand can be analysed and it can be measured.

A human need is a state of felt deprivation of some basic satisfaction. Food and clothing, shelter and safety, belonging and esteem are needs; they are not created by society or marketers but are fundamental to the condition of a human being.

Want

The expression of a need, the desire for something specific to satisfy it.

Wants are the expressions of those needs, the desires for something specific to satisfy them. Needs are few, but wants are many and shaped and reshaped by society and its institutions such as schools, churches and business corporations (Kotler 1991).

The term 'product', which will be discussed again later, includes any kind of travel and tourism service.

'Market' itself has more than one meaning. In economics terminology, it is where buyers and sellers of a single product are in touch with each other; and so there is an hotel market, an airline market, a tour market and so on. There may be hundreds of these markets, some of them having little in common with others, but they are usually thought of as a single market as a matter of convenience and for promotional purposes.

Identifying markets

Markets can be identifed geographically (e.g. the Melbourne market, the German market), by purpose (e.g. business or leisure), by demographics (e.g. age, income), by psychographics (e.g. lifestyle, attitudes), by the things the people in them tend to buy (e.g. group tours, ecotourism packages) or by combining any number of these criteria.

Defining a market allows marketers to identify competition and break down the market into segments. These steps are essential to the development of a satisfactory marketing strategy. O'Shaughnessy (1984) sums up the conditions for successful strategy this way: sufficient demand must exist at the prices envisaged; the organisation must have the products to meet demand; and, last but not least, the organisation must have an edge over its competition.

Competitor

Someone or some company, organisation or destination satisfying the same customer need or serving the same customer group.

Competitors are those who satisfy the same customer need or serve the same customer group (Kotler 1991). Coach companies offering express service on the same route are an example. Destinations that offer beach holidays with shopping and night-time entertainment are another.

▓ Information about markets

Marketers need a constant flow of information about markets, those they are operating in and others which might have potential for their products. They need data from which they can make judgments about the size of the markets, the products that are selling and can be sold there, present tourism flows, and likely influences in the future. They need an understanding of the travel and tourism industry operating in the markets, particularly those businesses involved in product distribution.

A **marketing information system (MkIS)** is an organised way of continually gathering and analysing data to provide marketing managers with information they need to make decisions. Much of the information required is already available, collected by the organisation itself or someone else. This is called **secondary data**. Other information has to be gathered for a specific purpose, usually by commissioning research; this is called **primary data**.

The supply of secondary data starts with the organisation's own records. Cash flows, sales records, distribution data, reports from branch managers and salespeople provide invaluable information about the company's markets and the acceptability of its products. Consultants such as advertising agencies can also usually provide information.

Australian travel and tourism businesses have access to a steady flow of outside data on aspects of the markets and their behaviour from:

- International organisations such as the World Tourism Organisation, the World Travel and Tourism Council, the Pacific Asia Travel Association, the International Air Transport Association
- Commonwealth departments, particularly those responsible for tourism and transport
- specialist agencies such as the Australian Tourist Commission, the Australian Bureau of Statistics, Bureau of Tourism Research and the Tourism Forecasting Council
- state and territory tourism organisations
- visitor and convention bureaus
- regional tourism organisations
- trade associations
- the general and trade press.

However, information from these sources is unlikely to be enough. Information specific to the business (e.g. its competitors and distributors) is vital. Some of this information can be gathered at industry functions or by participating in trade missions and organised business exchanges. An effective method is to build personal relationships with well-informed associates in the markets.

One way to start is simply to visit likely candidates. This means identifying potential sellers of the business's product (e.g. tour operators and leading travel agents) and visiting them for discussions. While it can be a tiring exercise, particularly in a strange city, in terms

DEFINITIONS

Marketing information system (MkIS)
An organised way of continually gathering and analysing data to provide marketing managers with information they need to make decisions.

Secondary data
Information that already exists, having been collected for another purpose.

Primary data
Information gathered for a specific purpose, usually by commissioning research.

of gaining information about the market and how it works, it is not formidable. The language of travel is the same in Chicago and Mumbai, Jakarta and Sydney, or anywhere else; only the accents are different.

Market research

Research is needed to systematically gather and analyse data on markets and is routinely carried out in such studies as the International Visitor Survey and the National Visitor Survey. Additionally, a considerable number of one-off studies are undertaken by both government organisations and businesses to provide information for a particular project or to help decision making at some point.

Market research

The systematic gathering and analysis of data on a market. It provides an overall picture, at a given point of time, of the market, its segments, or some aspect of buyer behaviour.

Market research provides an overall picture, at a given point of time, of the market, its segments, or some aspect of buyer behaviour. It can be quantitative, based on numbers; or qualitative, based on opinions, attitudes, needs and motivations of people. Quantitative research is used as a measuring tool; qualitative research helps marketers understand why people act as they do.

Segmenting the market

Markets can be divided into groups whose members are more similar in their market needs and wants than the market at large. This is called segmentation.

A market segment is a group of potential travellers with similar characteristics who share similar needs and wants. Segmentation allows marketers to select target markets. They distinguish between the market segments, target one or more of them and develop products and marketing programs tailored to reach each target market.

The first step in segmenting a market is to try to understand who potential customers are and what they want in terms of tourism destinations and products.

This requires:

- studying who those in the market are – that is determining their demographic characteristics by research
- studying what those in the market do – that is determining characteristics of their lifestyle by research
- determining their travel and tourism preferences by research.

Researchers segment markets by demographic factors (age, sex, occupation, education) or psychographic factors (lifestyle, attitudes, opinions).

Demographic research

Dividing the market into groups based on variables such as age, income, family lifecycle, income, occupation, education, religion and race.

Demographic research and family lifecycle

Demographic research divides the market into groups based on variables such as age, income, family lifecycle, occupation, education, religion and race. They are easier to measure than most other types of variables and it is usually relatively easy to select media to reach them with a promotional message because demographic research divides total populations into a limited number of groups.

Demographic information can be used to group people in terms of their **family lifecycle**. There are said to be distinct stages in the life of an ordinary family and each stage has different characteristics in terms of commercial behaviour and these affect the probability of travelling. By determining from census information or other research the approximate numbers in the various stages, the marketer can take the important first step in identifying target markets.

For example, it can usually be assumed that older people whose children have grown up and left home (see Empty nest 1 in Table 2.1) are good travel prospects. That was usually a key assumption when many of Australia's early promotional campaigns in overseas markets were designed. Later, promotion was extended to other groups such as affluent young marrieds without children, while in Japan young unmarried working women and honeymooners have always been regarded as important groups. Some businesses cater especially for people at a particular stage in the family lifecycle, e.g. in Australia, many accommodation establishments especially cater for family groups with children (Full nest 2 and 3).

The table on page 48 shows consumer behaviour in various stages of the lifecycle.

Classifications can vary. Some marketing writers put in alternative stages for people who are not in the conventional family of mother, father and children, e.g. a young or middle-aged person with dependent children, the single parent, a divorced person without dependent children, middle-aged married couples without children.

Psychographic research

Psychographic research provides data on lifestyles, personalities, activities, values, interests and opinions and enables segmentation into groups with similar characteristics. Much of the media is directed at specific pyschographic audiences, which makes those audiences easy to reach with advertising.

Lifestyle factors are important when it comes to choosing a destination, and are important to tourism operators of all kinds. Are potential travellers likely to be adventurous? Will they want to roam in the outback or stick to the cities? Will they want to travel independently or seek the 'safety' of groups? In the last 20 years, this kind of research has become an indispensable part of tourism marketing.

Researchers group a market's population into segments in which there are people with similar psychographic characteristics. Sometimes demographic and psychographic research is combined in sophisticated segmentation studies, such as the Roy Morgan Research Centre's system of Value Segmentation which has been used in successive Tourism Victoria Strategic Business Plans. In these studies a detailed analysis of both quantitative and qualitative data was undertaken to identify potential high yield markets and their holiday needs.

DEFINITIONS

Family lifecycle
Stages in the life of an ordinary family which have different characteristics of commercial behaviour affecting the probability of travelling.

Psychographic research
Provides data on lifestyles, personalities, activities, values, interests and opinions and enables the segmentation of a population into groups with similar characteristics.

Table 2.1 Consumption characteristics over family lifecycle

STAGE	CHARACTERISTICS	CONSUMER BEHAVIOUR
Bachelor	Young, single people not living at home	Few financial burdens; recreation orientated; buy basic equipment, cars, vacations
Newly married	Young, no children	Financially better off than will be later; buy cars, durables, vacations
Full nest 1	Youngest child under 6	Low liquid assets; buying conditioned by young children
Full nest 2	Youngest child 6 or over	Financial situation better; buy bicycles, educational items
Full nest 3	Older married with dependent children	Financial situation still improving; buy durables, leisure items
Empty nest 1	Older married, no children at home, still working	Optimum financial position; buy luxuries vacations
Empty nest 2	Older married, no children at home, retired	Income falls; health/medical products important
Solitary survivor in labour force		Income good; similar to empty nest 1 but often gives up home commitments
Solitary survivor retired		As for other retired but special needs for affection and security

(Source: Reprinted with permission from the *Journal of Marketing Research*, published by the American Marketing Association, Wells and Guba (November 1966).)

DEFINITIONS

Destination

A significant place visited on a trip, with some form of actual or perceived boundary. The basic geographic unit for the production of tourism statistics.

Destination area

Part of a destination. A homogeneous tourism region or a group of local government administrative regions.

▉ Destinations — the places tourists visit

A **destination** is a significant place visited on a trip. Kotler (1999) says it is a place with some form of actual or perceived boundary. To the statisticians it is the basic geographic unit for the production of tourism statistics. It can be split into '**destination areas**', which represent homogeneous tourism regions or which may be groups of local government administrative regions (World Tourism Organisation 1995c).

In discussing destinations we must also must consider the meaning of the word '**region**'. It may refer to a grouping of countries, usually in a common geographic area. This kind of grouping was discussed in Chapter 1, in relation to the way the World Tourism Organisation divides the world for statistical purposes. Australia is in the East Asia and Pacific Region.

A region may also be an area within a country, usually a tourism destination area. In Australia the word has a specific tourism meaning because the states and the Northern

Table 2.2 Tourism regions by state/territory[2]	
New South Wales	15
Northern Territory	4
Queensland	14
South Australia	12
Tasmania	3
Victoria	13
Western Australia	11
Total	72

Territory have all developed systems of designated tourism regions administered by regional tourism organisations, with links to the state/territory tourism commissions. Table 2.2 shows there are more than 70 such regions throughout the country.

A service industry

While at the destination, tourists will require services, such as accommodation, transport around the region, food, shops, and things to do and see. Thus they will consume products, and the term '**product**' related to tourism can include just about anything – 'any good or service purchased by, or consumed by, a person defined as a visitor' (World Tourism Organisation 1995c, p. 102).

Tourists buy manufactured products, of course, including some, like souvenirs, made just for them. But most travel and tourism businesses provide **services**, like advice and ticketing, transportation, a place to sleep, the preparation of food, sightseeing services and so on.

Unlike manufactured or other physical products, you cannot see or touch a service. It is defined as any activity or benefit one party can offer to another that is essentially intangible and does not result in the ownership of anything. Its production may or may not be tied to a physical product (Kotler 1991).

A service has four characteristics:

1. **Intangibility**. You cannot smell, hear, see, feel or taste it. Although you cannot sample it, you can be shown the concept – and almost always are when contemplating buying a tourism service. After experiencing it, you might take a souvenir away, and plenty of photographs and memories, but once the experience itself is over that is the end of the service.

2. **Inseparability**. A service cannot be separated from its providers – if the provider is not there the service cannot be performed. However, a service can be *sold* by someone representing the provider, such as a travel agent or tour operator.

DEFINITIONS

Region
(1) A grouping of countries, usually in a common geographic area. (2) An area within a country, usually a tourism destination area.

Product (tourism)
Any good or service purchased by, or consumed by, a person defined as a visitor.

Service
Any activity or benefit one party can offer to another that is essentially intangible and does not result in the ownership of anything. Its production may or may not be tied to a physical product.

DEFINITIONS

3. **Variability**. A service industry or individual provider of services cannot standardise output. No matter how hard it may try, an airline or coach company cannot give exactly the same quality of service on each trip, nor does a hotel or a restaurant produce exactly the same service each time a guest visits it.

4. **Perishability**. Services are perishable, they cannot be stored. A bed not slept in on a particular night or a seat not used on a particular journey means revenue lost for ever.

▒ The overall destination product

Total tourism product

The combination of all the service elements which a tourist consumes from leaving home, to returning.

The 'total tourism product' describes the aggregate of productive activities and services which satisfy the needs of tourists. It is the combination of all the service elements which a tourist consumes from leaving home, to returning. At the point of sale, before the journey begins, this product is an idea or an expectation in the customer's mind. The major portion of the tourism product is, however, consumed at the destination, making up what Middleton (1989, p. 573) has called a 'bundle of tangible and intangible components, based on activity at a destination. The package is perceived by the tourist as an experience, available at a price'. This is called the **overall destination product**.

Overall destination product

A bundle of tangible and intangible components, based on activity at a destination. The package is perceived by the tourist as an experience, available at a price.

In Middleton's view it has five main components:

1. **Destination attractions** are the elements within the destination's environment which, individually and combined, serve as the primary motivation for tourist visits. They are natural attractions, such as landscape, seascape, beaches and climate; built attractions, such as historic towns, theme parks and resorts; cultural attractions such as theatrical attractions, festivals, museums and galleries; and social attractions defined as opportunities to mix with the residents of destinations and experience their way of life, to some extent (sometimes called 'lifeseeing'). For non-leisure tourists, such as those travelling for business or to see friends and relatives, the primary motivation is provided by their connections or associations within the destination, although the leisure attractions may still be an influence and used by such visitors.

2. **Destination facilities** are the elements within the destination, or linked to it, which make it possible for tourists to stay at destinations and to enjoy and participate in the attractions. They include accommodation of all types, restaurants, cafés and bars, transport at the destination including car rental and taxis, and other services including shops, hairdressing and visitor information.

3. **Accessibility**, or the relative ease or difficulty with which tourists can reach the destination of their choice. Access is a matter of transport infrastructure, such as airports, harbours, highways and rail networks. It is also a matter of transport technology which alters the costs of travel and the time it takes to reach a destination.

4. **Images**, or the ideas and beliefs that people hold about all forms of products they buy or contemplate buying. Destination images are not necessarilly based on experience or fact, but they are very powerful motivating forces in leisure travel.

DEFINITIONS

5. **Price**, or the sum of what it costs for travel, accommodation, and participation in a range of selected services at the destination. The price varies by choice of accommodation, the class of travel, the season, the types of activity chosen and the distance travelled to a destination.

(Source: Witt and Moutinho, *Tourism Marketing and Management Handbook* © 1989, Prentice Hall International (UK) Limited, reprinted by permission of Pearson Education Limited.)

Destination lifecycle models

Destinations (and destination areas and resort areas) go through a cycle of evolution which includes introduction, growth, maturity and decline and/or rejuvenation. Models characterising each stage have been produced as planning and marketing tools. They have implications for the provision of products appropriate to each stage and for the management of a destination's tourism.

The main use of the **destination lifecycle model** is as an aid to understanding the evolution of tourism products and destinations (Cooper 1989). To get the best from a lifecycle model, tourism businesses and destinations should adopt a long-term planning horizon and use the model as an organising framework for marketing and development decisions.

Modelling of tourism development goes back to the early 1960s. Some writers, drawing on product lifecycle models, have suggested four stages: (1) inception – discovery; (2) growth – local response and initiative; (3) maturity – institutionalisation; and (4) decline – saturation and alienation (Gee, Makens & Choy 1989).

Another view is that the rise and fall of a destination is due to the psychology of tourists. In this model, Plog (1973) identified three types of tourists: the allocentric (adventurous, ever seeking new destinations), the midcentric (the bulk of the market representing characteristics of both the others) and psychocentric (seeking familiar destinations and the security of the travel and tourism industry). The continuum of personality types can actually be divided into five segments: allocentric, near-allocentric, midcentric, near-psychocentric and psychocentric.

Allocentrics tend to be self-confident, not suffering from unfocused anxiety. They like to travel, with a higher preference for air travel, and are the first to visit or discover a new destination. As more and more allocentrics visit a destination, near-allocentrics also start going there. Tourism facilities begin to expand and as they do midcentrics are also attracted. These are the majority of tourists who like destinations to be accessible, predictable and comfortable. Development occurs to offer a full array of facilities, services and attractions; the destination matures, it has reached its maximum potential and attracted the broadest possible range of participants.

The increased popularity eventually convinces the near-psychocentrics and, finally, even the least venturesome psychocentrics, to visit. These are people who travel less, stay a shorter time and spend less money, typically preferring destinations to be as familiar as

Destination lifecycle model
A model that characterises each stage in the lifecycle of a destination (and destination areas and resort areas) including introduction, growth, maturity and decline and/or rejuvenation.

possible. They tend to travel by a personal car or camper where the familiar is always close at hand. Psychocentrics have a stronger than normal feeling of anxiety. As the destination becomes more accessible and more commercialised, it becomes less and less of what attracted tourists in the first place. The original visitors stop coming and go searching for new discoveries. As this process completes itself, the psychocentrics eventually become the majority tourists and the resort is in decline.[3]

Models evolving

The destination lifecycle model is still evolving and the uses to which it can be put are being tested by researchers in different situations. Butler's model, the best known, is shown in Table 2.3 below:

Table 2.3 Destination lifecycle	
Exploration	Limited and sporadic visitation by a few adventuresome people. There is a high degree of contact with locals and use of their facilities but with very little social and economic impact.
Involvement	Increasing visitation induces some locals to offer facilities primarily or exclusively for visitors. Contact with locals is still high and many adjust their social patterns to accommodate the changing economic conditions. A tourism destination and season emerges and advertising is initiated.
Development	Outside investment is attracted to the destination as a well-defined tourism market emerges. Accessibility is enhanced, advertising becomes more intensive and extensive, and local facilities are displaced by more elaborate and up-to-date ones. This results in a decline in local participation and control. Artificial attractions supplant original ones. Imported labour and auxiliary facilities and services become necessary to support the rapidly growing tourism industry.
Consolidation	The major portion of the local economy is tied to tourism and dominated by major chains and franchises. Visitation levels continue to increase but at declining rates. Marketing efforts are further widened to extend the tourism season and attract more distant visitors. Older facilities are now second-rate and mostly undesirable.
Stagnation	Capacity levels for many relevant factors are reached or exceeded, resulting in economic, social and/or environmental problems. A peak number of possible visitations is achieved forcing facility managers to rely on repeat visitations and conventions for business. Artificial attractions supersede the natural or cultural ones and the destination is no longer considered fashionable.

Table 2.3 continued

Post-stagnation stage

Part 1: decline	Tourists are drawn away by newer destinations; those remaining are mostly weekend or day visitors. Tourism facilities become replaced by non-tourism establishments as the area disengages from the industry. This results in even less attraction for visitors and remaining facilities become less viable. Local involvement probably increases again as the price of facilities drops along with the market decline. The destination either becomes a tourism slum or finds itself devoid of tourism activity altogether.
Part 2: rejuvenation	A dramatic change in the resource base is established. Either a new set of artificial attractions is created or a previously unexploited natural resource is used.

(Source: Reprinted from *The Canadian Geographer*, Vol. 24, No. 1 (1980), article by Butler, R.)

Obviously the model as it is laid out in the table doesn't suit every situation. The popularity of one of the world's greatest holiday destinations, Walt Disney World in Florida, did not start with the exploration by a few adventuresome people. The Disney organisation searched for a place to put a version of the Disneyland theme park and surround it with additional attractions and resort facilities. They found it near Orlando but the raw site was not attractive to even the most venturesome – much of it was swamp and there were plenty of snakes around.

Australian entrepreneur Keith Williams followed the same pattern in developing Hamilton Island in the Whitsundays. He had a big idea for a rarely visited island, developed it as a major resort and promoted it heavily to tourists.

Figure 2.4 illustrates both Butler's and Plog's models and shows where the starting point for Hamilton Island Resort is placed.

Modifications to Butler's model are accepted. It is widely agreed that the first stage or two may be avoided, depending on circumstances and Figure 2.4 shows how this can be done. Usually it is thought the final stages should be left intact, but Agarwal (1994) has advocated adding to them, which has important implications for destination areas which are showing signs of decline.

In assessing the validity of the model in relation to certain English seaside resorts, he concluded there was a problem in accepting decline of a destination area because of the economic and political consequences for the community. While the model properly directed attention to the fact that the popularity of an area goes through a series of

Figure 2.4 Stages in destination development

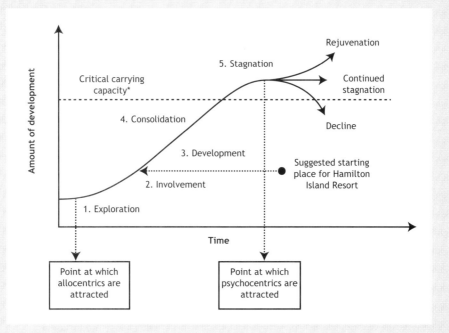

* Carrying capacity refers to the level of human activity an area can accommodate without it deteriorating, the resident community being adversely affected or the quality of visitor experience declining. It is discussed in detail in Chapter 11.

acceleration and decay stages, it was necessary to ensure the successful continuation of destination areas before the decline stage.

In the model itself, he said, more emphasis should be placed on rejuvenation as opposed to decline in the post-stagnation phase and an intermediary stage should be added between the stagnation and post-stagnation phases of Butler's model.

Agarwal called this the 're-orientation stage'. It would represent continual efforts at restructuring, and would be characterised by market targeting, specialisation and segmentation on the one hand and substantial investment in tourist accommodation and attractions on the other. The image of the destination area would be radically transformed. The prospect of inevitable decline would not be accepted; the prospect of total decline would be regarded as inconceivable.

The re-orientation phase could be repeated as many times as necessary in the short term until circumstances changed and the post-stagnation period was finally entered. From this point onwards, the events described by Butler for the post-stagnation phase would proceed: the destination would be rejuvenated indefinitely or enter a period of long, slow decline.

Limitations

Researchers have identified other limitations of the lifecycle model, including:

- the difficulty of identifying when one stage finishes and another begins
- the model is not seen as an independent guide for decision making which is determined by the strategic decisions of management and heavily dependent on external factors such as competition, development of substitute products, changes in consumer taste and government legislation
- the model is not seen as a reliable forecasting tool.

These are but examples. Prosser (1997) has found enough criticisms to classify them into five categories: (1) scepticism about the feasibility of a single model of tourism development; (2) conceptual limitations of carrying capacity and the product lifecycle; (3) conceptual limitations of the lifecycle model as it has been applied to tourist destination areas; (4) lack of empirical support for the destination lifecycle concept; and (5) the limited practical utility of the lifecycle concept in tourism planning.

Also it may be misleading to think in terms of a single lifecycle for a destination. In the case of the Gold Coast, for instance, there are distinct lifecycles for the domestic and international sectors of the market and the introduction of new attractions such as theme parks and the Indy Grand Prix may also have introduced new lifecycles.

Strengths

Despite the doubts about the original model developed by Butler and the criticism it has received, Prosser points to its 'enduring attraction'. After two decades it survives largely intact. He sees three main factors contributing to its acceptance: (1) it offers an easily comprehended conceptual framework where relatively few such frameworks are available; (2) it has sufficient descriptive power to provide intuitive appeal for researchers; and (3) research completed in a range of different tourist areas has provided (qualified) empirical support for the model.

Prosser regards some of the criticism as having been based on unrealistic expectations of the model's explanatory and predictive capability. Cooper (1989) discourages its use for day-to-day marketing decisions. He believes it is best used to understand the evolution of tourism products and destinations. Tourism businesses and destinations should adopt a long-term planning horizon, then use the model as an organising framework for marketing and development decisions. But the model is far less successful in providing detailed prescriptions for marketing actions.

CASE STUDY

The rise and fall of the Japanese market

K otler (1991) has postulated that a market evolves through four stages: emergence, growth, maturity and decline. The Japanese market for Australia between 1964 and 2001 can be examined in these terms.

Emergence (1964–79)

Overseas travel from Japan was restricted until April 1964 and most of the 3,307 Japanese who visited Australia that year were businesspeople. However, in 1965 the American consultants who compiled a report on the Australian travel and tourism industry for the Australian National Travel Association (ANTA) concluded that a substantial tourism market for Australia could be developed. It recommended that ANTA establish an office in Tokyo.

The report resulted in the formation of the Australian Tourist Commission in 1967 and one of its first acts was to appoint a manager in Japan.[4]

Progress was slow in building a market for Australia, although the number of Japanese travelling overseas was increasing rapidly, from 353,500 in 1968 to 4,038,300 in 1979.[5] At that time Japanese wholesalers, the major influence on the market, did not consider a destination of much consequence until it reached a figure of 40,000 visitors from Japan. Australia crossed that threshold in 1979 and the event was celebrated with some fanfare (Richardson 1995).

Growth (1980–93)

Travel from Japan to Australia grew slowly in the early 1980s. By 1983 there were 72,000 arrivals from Japan. And then the boom started. Only two years later in 1985 there were 198,000. In 1989 – 10 years after the wholesalers accepted Australia as a destination – the number had grown to nearly 350,000. The Japanese were changing Australia's tourism outlook.

Price was a major force in this change of fortune. One factor was the introduction of tour-basing fares for tour operators after a delay brought about by the fuel crisis of the 1970s. This reduced the cost of getting to Australia and changes in the exchange rate made the cost of accommodation, food, sightseeing and travel within Australia cheaper. The next table shows how many yen it cost to buy one dollar's worth of goods and services in different years during this period.

It should also be noted that Australia was benefiting from a general rise in Japanese overseas travel. In this period of 13 years, it tripled, from about 4 million in 1980 to

Table 2.4 Exchange rate – Yen to A$						
JUNE						
1981	**1983**	**1985**	**1987**	**1989**	**1991**	**1993**
260	209	166	106	109	106	72

(Source: © Reserve Bank of Australia.)

12 million in 1993.[6] Growth in Japanese travel to Australia averaged 22 per cent annually in the first three years of the 1990s, with the number of arrivals reaching 670,000 in 1993.

Maturity (1994–97)

By 1994 Japan was well established as Australia's biggest source market. In that year this is how it compared with other sources of overseas visitors.

Table 2.5 International arrivals in Australia, 1994		
1	Japan	721,100
2	South-East Asia	487,800
3	New Zealand	480,400
4	North-East Asia	395,300
5	Other Europe	370,700
6	United Kingdom/Ireland	350,500
7	United States	289,700
8	Rest of world	266,200
	Total	3,361,700

(Source: Australian Bureau of Statistics.)

The Tourism Forecasting Council issued its first estimates of future inbound travel in 1995 and saw Japan as the dominant inbound market for as far ahead as it forecast – to 2003, a year in which it expected 1,456,000 Japanese to visit Australia (Tourism Forecasting Council 1995).

The market ran ahead of the forecasts for two years, but fell behind in 1997, when growth was a mere 0.1 per cent. Arrivals totalled 813,900 against a forecast 856,000.

Overseas travel from Japan was continuing to expand although by this time the country was experiencing the severe economic problems which were to continue into the next decade. Australia was having to fight for its share of the market against strong competition. Although it looked upon Japan as its leading overseas market, Australia rated but tenth in

Table 2.6 Top 10 overseas destinations for Japanese travellers, 1997

	DESTINATION	ARRIVALS
1	United States*	5,367,700
2	Hong Kong	1,968,900
3	Korea	1,676,400
4	China	1,581,700
5	Singapore	1,094,000
6	Thailand	965,500
7	France	960,000
8	Taiwan	905,500
9	German	819,300
10	Australia	813,900

* Includes Hawaii 2,092,500, Guam 1,118,000.

(Source: Japanese National Tourist Organisation. Note these are arrival figures (not departures) compiled from data supplied by national tourism organisations, WTO, PATA and OECD.)

Japanese preferred destinations in 1997, when numbers coming to Australia reached their peak. See Table 2.6.

There were rumblings, too, signs that all was not going as well as in the periods of rapid growth. It was said Australia was widely perceived in Japan as a 'once only' destination, without the depth of tourism product necessary to encourage visitors to return (Dowling 1993). And in 1994 a leading Japanese wholesaler spoke of product problems to a joint meeting of the Australia–Japan Business Cooperation Committees in Brisbane. Mr Kazuo Riko, director of the Japan Travel Bureau, told of accommodation difficulties, resort areas without top-class facilities and the need for a more balanced promotion of destination areas throughout Australia. 'I venture to say that greater coordination is needed in destination development policies, airline business policies and investment policies,' he said (Collins 1994).

Although arrival figures for 1996 and 1997 were the highest so far recorded, Qantas saw its market fall during part of that period, putting it down to the Australian dollar's appreciation against the yen and cheaper tour prices in Hawaii and other destinations.[7] It responded by reducing capacity on the route.

Decline (1998–2001)

The Japanese market for Australia went into decline in 1998 when arrival numbers dropped by a notable 7.7 per cent from the previous year. Figures for the years 1998 to 2001 are shown in the next table.

These figures represented a considerable loss of market share because Japanese travel overseas continued to increase – there were more than 16 million departures in 2000 and

Table 2.7 Japanese arrival figures 1998–2001

1998	1999	2000	2001
751,100	707,500	720,300	681,400

(Source: Australian Bureau of Statistics.)

2001. However, Australia was not alone in suffering a decrease. Five out of seven of Japan's leading medium- and long-haul destinations lost ground during the period. The exceptions were Thailand and France. The next table shows what happened.

Table 2.8 Japanese medium- and long-haul destinations

DESTINATION	ARRIVALS 1997–2000			
	1997	1998	1999	2000
United States	5,367,578	4,885,369	4,826,369	5,061,337
Italy	1,264,987	1,110,356	877,275	NA
Singapore	1,094,036	843,713	860,561	929,687
France	990,000	1,030,000	987,000	1,035,000
Thailand	934,111	986,264	1,059,872	1,202,164
Germany	819,254	814,889	818,482	NA
Australia	813,900	751,100	707,500	720,400
Indonesia	706,942	469,409	606,042	662,045

(Source: Japanese National Tourist Organisation.)

On the other hand, travel to all destinations close to Japan increased, particularly Korea and China.

The trend was clearly towards short-haul destinations at the expense of those further away. The Australian Tourist Commission noted the trend towards 'an-kin-tan' (cheap, close and short) travel in a Japan market report in early 2002. It regarded this as a result of unwillingness by Japanese consumers to spend during uncertain economic times (www.atc.australia.com). See Table 2.9.

However, a new trend appeared in the recovery period following the 11 September terrorist attacks in the US. By late 2002 it was clear that Japanese traffic to Australia was increasing at a growth rate unknown since the mid-1990s (an annual rate of 6–7 per cent in the later months). The Tourism Forecasting Council suggested that this was partly driven by Qantas' new lower-cost subsidiary Australian Airlines and the Australian Tourist

Table 2.9 Japanese short-haul destinations

ARRIVALS 1997–2000

DESTINATION	1997	1998	1999	2000
Korea	1,676,543	1,954,416	2,184,121	2,472,054
China	1,581,743	1,572,054	1,855,197	2,201,513
Hong Kong	1,368,988	954,334	1,174,071	1,382,417
Taiwan	905,527	826,632	826,222	916,301

(Source: Japanese National Tourist Organisation.)

Commission's promotional efforts. It predicted an average annual growth rate of 3.2 per cent leading to 953,000 visitor arrivals in 2012 (Tourism Forecasting Council 2002). Encouraging as this appeared, there was no expectation of a bounceback to the rosy picture of earlier days. In 1995 the TFC had forecast 1.456 million Japanese arrivals in 2003; in 2002 it forecast half that number (726,000).

INDUSTRY PROFILE

HILARY WATT PRODUCT MANAGER, GREAT AUSSIE HOLIDAYS

I am responsible for a variety of functions. From August to March each year our brochure production team is in full swing preparing our range of full colour domestic wholesale brochures. Of the six brochures we produce annually, the largest is well over 100 pages and the others average about 60 pages, so it keeps our small team very busy.

All the graphic work is done in-house. My role is to negotiate rates, source new product, oversee the day-to-day production of the brochures, write copy and proofread final copies.

In between, we have to ensure that there are plenty of special flyers out in the market promoting Great Aussie Holidays packages. These vary from a basic return air and two nights accommodation package to any of the Australian capital cities, to self-drive packages, to specific tactical campaigns involving tourism commissions. This often means embarking on a separate round of rate negotiation to obtain short-term reduced rates and bonus offers from operators.

How did I get here?

Before emigrating to Perth in January 1999 and joining Great Aussie Holidays, I had had 16 years in the UK travel industry, the last eight of them with a major UK wholesaler where I became Operations Manager.

I started with Great Aussie Holidays as a casual reservations consultant. Within a couple of months I had been made a permanent member of staff and within six months was offered the role of Reservations Supervisor. After a couple of years in that role I transferred over to the product area and worked my way up to my present position.

What do I like about my job?

Very few days are ever the same (particularly since September 11 and the Ansett collapse) so there is never a chance of getting bored with doing the same thing. As a small company we pride ourselves on being able to respond to new activities such as 'fare dumps' within hours and to get new product out immediately, so I enjoy the challenge of having to respond to that sort of pressure and to working in a small team to achieve it.

I love being part of such a fascinating and vibrant industry and thrive on the contact with operators Australia-wide – from the hobby people running B&B establishments in the country to sales managers of big hotel chains like Accor.

It is also great to be able to wander around shopping centres, see your brochures sitting on travel agents' shelves and know that you helped create them.

SUMMARY

In conceptualising, or imagining, the way in which tourism occurs, models are useful tools. There are different kinds, including some very complex ones, such as those used for estimating the economic impact of tourism or to predict future occurrences in entire tourism regions. But other models are simpler and are used to illustrate a conceptual framework so that relationships of the various elements can be studied. Thus the tourism system itself can be modelled, its geographic elements displayed and its environments noted. The geographic elements are the traveller generating region (TGR), the transit route region (TRR) and the tourist destination region (TDR). The other two elements are human – tourists and the travel and tourism industry. They operate in the geographic elements of the system.

The model shows that tourism occurs within a number of environments – e.g. technological, sociocultural, economic, physical, political – and changes within any of them can impact on tourism. Tourism can also impact on them.

The model can be examined from the point of view of any of the five elements. For example, derivative models show how a TDR's principal TGRs (markets) can be displayed and then, in the reverse, a TGR's main TDRs (destinations) can be shown. The viewpoints of the TRR, the travel and tourism industry and the central figure in the system – the tourist – are all important. Among other things, examining them leads to investigations of communication and transportation linkages between TDRs and TGRs and a detailed discussion on the theory of markets and destinations.

Sellers and buyers of tourism products gather in 'markets' to make their exchange. Markets can be identified in different ways: geographically, demographically, psychographically, by the things people buy, or by combining any of these criteria.

Markets can be segmented, that is divided into groups whose members are more similar in their needs and wants than the market at large. This allows target marketing: the designing, offering and promoting of products suitable to particular segments. Two types of research are used to determine segments and their characteristics: (1) demographic research, which divides the market into groups based on variables such as age, income, family lifestyle, occupation, education, religion and race, and (2) psychographic research, which provides data on lifestyles, personalities, activities, values, interests and opinions, thus enabling segmentation into groups of similar characteristics.

Demographic information can be used to group people in terms of their family lifecycle. There are said to be distinct stages in the life of an ordinary family and each stage has different characteristics in terms of commercial behaviour which affect the probability of travelling.

The word 'product' may relate to any goods or services purchased or consumed by a tourist. Most products supplied by the travel and tourism industry are services; that is, they are intangible, inseparable from their providers, variable and perishable.

There are collective products. For example, the term 'total tourism product' describes the combination of all the services a tourist consumes from leaving home until the moment of return. The 'overall destination product' refers to the 'bundle of tangible and intangible components' of a destination the tourist uses or encounters, such as attractions, facilities, accessibility, images and price.

Destinations go through stages in a lifecycle and the process has been modelled in various ways. Plog (1973) has suggested the rise and fall of a destination is due to the psychology of the tourists who visit it. Other models have been derived from product lifecycle models. The best known is Butler's, which suggests the destination goes through six stages: exploration, involvement, development, consolidation, stagnation and post-stagnation.

QUESTIONS

1. The model of the tourism system is an important aid in understanding tourism. What is a model? And what is a system?
2. What are the three geographic elements of the tourism system and the relationship between them? What is necessary for them to function?
3. How do environments and the tourism system interact?
4. How do you think the tourism system can be used to help make business decisions?

QUESTIONS continued

5. What part does the transit route region play in a destination's tourism? Can you give examples at a national, state and regional level?

6. Leiper uses the term 'partial-industrialisation' in respect to the tourism system. Why does he do this? How important is the concept in the Australian context?

7. How would you identify most tourism markets? How would you gather sufficient information about them to decide which would be given marketing priority?

8. What is the process for defining target markets? What are the commonly used methods of research and why would you decide to use one rather than the other?

9. How would a destination marketing organisation use the 'overall destination product' concept?

10. Do you think Butler's destination lifecycle model can be adapted to be relevant to most destinations?

MOTIVATION AND FORMS OF TOURISM

Understand how destination choices are made and the importance of motivation. This includes understanding motivation theory, push and pull factors and the destination choice process.

Recognise how motivational research can guide tourism planners and businesses in providing preferred forms of tourism.

Examine the following forms of tourism:

- Australian holidays by the sea
- Indulgent tourism
- The new tourism
- Special interest tourism
- Nature tourism
- Ecotourism
- Cultural tourism
- Industrial tourism
- Indigenous tourism.

Appreciate the issue of authenticity and its importance to certain forms of tourism.

Review a case study of Wundargoodie Aboriginal Safaris.

**I UNDERSTAND
THE MEANING OF:**

* *motivation*
* *push and pull factors*
* *indulgent tourism*
* *new tourism*
* *special interest
  tourism*
* *nature tourism*
* *ecotourism*
* *cultural tourism*
* *industrial tourism*
* *indigenous tourism*
* *Aboriginal tourism
  product*
* *authenticity*

DEFINITIONS

....

Motivation

*A process of
internal
psychological
factors (needs,
wants and goals)
generating an
uncomfortable level
of tension within the
minds and bodies of
individuals. This
leads to actions to
try to release
tension and satisfy
needs.*

MOTIVATION AND DESTINATION CHOICE

In the last chapter, four of the five essential elements of the tourism system were discussed. The fifth element is the tourist, without whom there is no tourism. Not everyone becomes a tourist of course; certain preconditions are necessary. Firstly, a person must have the time and money to travel and as Leiper (1990) points out touristic leisure is usually more expensive than other leisure. The poorer sections of society, even in a relatively rich country like Australia, cannot afford substantial travel. Price is an influential attribute of a destination, affecting its choice or rejection by potential tourists.

It follows that income is one of the characteristics of individual tourists which affect their propensity to travel for pleasure, their ability to travel and their choice of destinations. But it is only one characteristic: others include, age, psychological make-up and **motivation** (Morley 1990). This chapter is concerned with the motivation of tourists and the consequences it has for the type of tourism they wish to pursue. The second part of the chapter discusses a selection of the more popular forms of tourism, such as Australian holidays by the sea, indulgent tourism, ecotourism and cultural tourism.

What moves people to decide to travel and become tourists is of great interest to marketers. If they can unlock that secret they can frame appealing messages about their destination or tourism products in such a way that they make a good fit with the needs and wants of targeted tourism consumers. Understanding travel motivation is also important to destination planners and tourism businesses as a guide to products that are likely to appeal in the marketplace. The different forms of tourism are important in this context. They are varied as tourist preferences change, an example being the increased interest since the 1980s in various forms of nature tourism. There is a strong link therefore between motivation as it directly affects tourism demand and preferred forms of tourism as part of tourism supply at the destination.

Basic motivational theory describes a process of internal psychological factors (needs, wants and goals) generating an uncomfortable level of tension within the minds and bodies of individuals. This leads to actions to try to release tension and satisfy needs. From a marketing perspective tourism products can be designed and marketed as solutions to consumers' needs (Fodness 1994).

Motivation is one of a number of psychological variables in destination choice; others include perception, learning, beliefs and attitudes. However, motivation is the critical variable because it is the driving force behind all behaviour. Mansfield (1992) sees the destination choice process as a number of steps starting with motivation:

1. Travel motivation
2. Collection of travel information – phase 1
3. Establishment of alternatives
4. Collection of travel information – phase 2
5. Assessment of destination alternatives
6. Choosing the best alternative
7. Undertaking travel.

Push and pull factors

The external and internal factors which motivate tourists have been put into two categories: 'push' and 'pull'.

Push factors are all the economic, social, demographic, technological and political forces that stimulate a demand for tourism activity by 'pushing' consumers away from their usual place of residence. These are the dominant factors when people decide they want to 'get away from it all', but are vague about where they want to go.

Pull factors are those which 'pull' consumers towards a particular destination (e.g. a positive image, safety, attractions, climate). Forms of tourism are among pull factors – the destination's offerings to tourists.

Push motivations can be socio-psychological. Ryan (1991) reviewed academic research to come up with this list:

1. **Escape**. A wish to get away from a perceived mundane environment.
2. **Relaxation**. A wish for recuperation; it is partly related to the escape motivation.
3. **Play**. A wish to indulge in activities associated with childhood. Play on holiday is culturally sanctioned and adults indulge in games not otherwise permitted. There is a regression into the carefree state of childhood.
4. **Strengthening family bonds**. A holiday represents a time when partners who are working full time can renew their relationship. Sometimes the reverse happens: enforced sharing of each other's company on a holiday has been known to provide too much strain on a marriage and both parties have realised they have grown apart. However, on the positive side of relationships, holidays can provide a time when working parents can spend time with their young children, and so strengthen family bonding.
5. **Prestige**. The choice of a holiday destination is a statement about lifestyle and can be seen in terms of status and social enhancement. Martin Brackenbury, President of the International Federation of Tour Operators, has described how Northern Europeans reacted to a Mediterranean holiday when it first became the thing to do in the 1960s: 'The holiday abroad had a cachet of sophistication and a tingle of adventure. It was

DEFINITIONS

Push factors

The economic, social, demographic, technological and political forces that stimulate a demand for tourism activity by 'pushing' consumers away from their usual place of residence.

Pull factors

The positive image of a destination, availability of particular forms of smart and fashionable. The suntan became a statement of both material and physical well-being' (Brackenbury 1993, p. 15).

6. **Social interaction**. The holiday can be an important social forum for individuals. Sometimes, a group of like-minded people with common interests are brought together – special interest groups of those interested in painting or sailing or gemstone-collecting. Other holidays are designed for single people so they can become part of a group and not feel isolated.

7. **Romance**. The opportunity of meeting people for the purpose of romantic encounters which are free from the restraints of home is often a desired form of social interaction and a powerful influence in choosing a destination. 'Sun, sand and sex' is a description often applied to destinations such as the Gold Coast. The 'sex' may refer to romantic as well as physical relationships.

8. **Educational opportunity**. This goes to the heart of tourism: it is a chance to see new sights, to learn about other places and peoples, to understand something of other cultures and viewpoints.

9. **Self-fulfilment**. People sometimes return from a holiday with a changed life or a changed perspective. The journey has been as much a self-discovery as a discovery of new places and people.

10. **Wish-fulfilment**. The holiday is the answer to a dream, a dream which may have sustained a long period of saving. Ryan uses the example of a naturalist feeling the thrill of visiting the Galapagos Islands after reading about Charles Darwin's visit aboard the *Beagle*. But the dream may not be sourced as specifically as that: few of us don't have a dream about faraway places.

FORMS OF TOURISM

Some of the motivational factors described above can be related specifically to forms of tourism.

▓ Australian holidays by the sea

'Strengthening family bonds' is perhaps best expressed in Australia by the annual summer holiday by the sea. Families flood from the cities to stay for varying lengths of time in hotels, motels, guest houses, holiday homes and apartments by the sea, with friends or relatives or to camp on the foreshore.

This is a form of tourism that the travel and tourism industry has limited power to influence. While commercial accommodation at popular seaside resorts may be packed, many holidaymakers will stay privately. In even more cases, the trip will have been made in private vehicles and will have been organised without the help of travel agents or tour operators. According to Leiper (1999), surveys indicate that more than 80 per cent of domestic tourist trips are privately organised and use private vehicles while more than

60 per cent use private accommodation. The annual family holiday, more often than not, fits into this category.

Indulgent tourism

The industry does cater for those who want to get away from it all, escape, relax, play and/or flirt with romance. It provides glamour resorts, casinos, theme parks and themed hotels. Australia has them all. Worldwide there has been a growing trend towards a 'new mass tourism', or **indulgent tourism**, which is characterised by a search for luxury, glamour and name brands.

Wheeler noted as early as 1992, 'We have moved from travel to tourism to mass tourism. Pundits of the green movement advocate a kind of *back to travel* except that globally we are moving towards mega tourism . . . it seems highly probable that the next generation will, globally, consist of a large number – the critical mass – of tourists not behaving *correctly*' (p. 142).

Chamberlain (1997), a former chief executive of the Pacific Asia Travel Association, uses the term 'indulgent tourists' and has said, 'To a great extent their holiday is removed from the community and the natural environment in which they are staying . . . the "indulgent tourists" are, and for the foreseeable future will continue to be, the basis of our industry even if it does go against the grain for some of us to admit it. Sun, sea, sand, sex, shows and shops sell much more than trees and wildflowers and the developers know it' (pp. 7–8).

Perhaps nothing symbolises the 'new mass tourism' more than the huge cruise ships built in the late 1990s. The biggest launched at the turn of the century was the 142,000-ton[1] *Voyager of the Seas*, of the Royal Caribbean Line. It is as long as four Boeing 747 aircraft lined up nose to tail. The idea in building a ship so large was to have enough room for more attractions than were available on older ships. Ships like the *Voyager of the Seas* are destinations in themselves.

The vessel's attractions include a shopping and strolling mall called the Royal Promenade which connects two immense attria that soar 11 decks; the La Scala theatre which seats 1,350 people and reaches up five decks; another theatre which converts to an ice-skating rink; a rock-climbing wall up the side of the funnel; an in-line skating track, a miniature golf course, a casino, and a profusion of restaurants and cafés (Lofting 2000). That is not all: there are so many attractions the issue is whether a seven-day cruise to the Western Caribbean is long enough to discover them all.

Every Royal Caribbean International ship has a common feature, The Viking Crown Lounge, which symbolises the attraction of indulgence.

> *Ever since its appearance in Royal Caribbean's very first ship, the Viking Crown Lounge has been drawing the attention of passengers and architects alike. A giant multi-purpose entertainment area perched high above the sea produces not only a*

DEFINITIONS

. . . .

Indulgent tourism
Tourism characterised by a search for luxury, glamour and name brands rather than authenticity. It is often disconnected from local communities and the natural environment.

superior 360-degree view of the horizon, but a distinguished look that is solely Royal Caribbean. Inspired by Seattle's landmark 'Space Needle' of the 1962 World's Fair, the Viking Crown Lounge is the perfect gathering place for a cocktail, moonlight glance, or a ballroom dance lesson (www.royalcarribean.com).

The 'new tourism'

Escape and relaxation may be allied to other motives besides those that lead to indulgence – educational opportunity and self-fulfilment for instance. There has been a strong trend throughout the world towards product innovation to cater for what has been called the **'new tourism'**. Much of that innovation has been to meet the requirements of people who are interested in self-discovery, or travel to see new things and learn about them – places, people and cultures.

New tourism

Tourism in which flexibility is the hallmark; itineraries are individualised as distinct from tightly controlled 'assembly-line' packages.

Some tourism, particularly out of Asia, is still rigidly packaged, but in mature markets like those of Europe and the United States, the trend since the mid-1970s has been towards individualised itineraries, more flexibility and a changing social environment. This departure from 'assembly-line' tourism was called the 'new tourism'. Poon (1994) saw it being driven by a number of significant changes.

> *This new best practice is created by a number of factors, including the diffusion of a system of new information technologies in the tourist industry; deregulation of the airline industry and financial services; the negative impact of mass tourism on host countries; the movement from sun-lust to sun-plus tourists; environmental pressures; technology competitions; and changing consumer tastes, leisure time, work patterns and income distribution* (p. 92).

In some cases, product innovation has meant making more of what was already being done. Sightseeing is an example. It can be a routine experience crammed in between meals and entertainment or it can be, as Horne (1992) suggests, 'one of the most important conveyors of meaning in our times' (p. 377).

Special interest tourism

Tourism for which the main motivation is to follow a special interest (e.g. birdwatching or scuba diving). It is different from other travel because people choose a destination so they can follow their particular interest there.

Nature tourism, in all its manifestations, has become one of the major trends of the 'new tourism' era. It has been encouraged by the environmental movement which Heath (1991) has called 'the major movement of the age' (p. 600).

Special interest tourism

One of the causes of segmentation and specialisation within the travel and tourism industry, hallmarks of the 'new tourism', has been the growth of **special interest tourism** both in number of participants and areas of interest. It is different from other travel because people choose a destination so they can follow their particular interest there.

'It is the *hub* around which the *total* experience is planned and developed' and is travel 'with only four additives. That travel would be *rewarding*; it would be *enriching*; it would

Table 3.1 Examples of special interest tours

ACTIVE ADVENTURE	NATURE AND WILDLIFE	HISTORY/CULTURE	SPIRITUAL
Caving	Birdwatching	Agriculture	Biblical tours
Parachute jumping	Ecotourism	Art/architecture	Church tours
Trekking	Geology	Arts festivals	Pilgrimage/mythology
Off-road adventure	National parks	Film/film history	Religion/spirituality
Mountain climbing	Rainforest	Winery tours	Yoga and spiritual tours

AFFINITY	ROMANCE	HOBBY	SPORTS
Artists' workshops	Honeymoon	Antiques	Basketball
Gay tours	Island vacation	Brewer/beer festivals	Car racing
Lesbian tours	Nightlife	Craft tours	Olympic Games
Seniors tours	Singles tours	Gambling	Soccer
Tours for the handicapped	Spa/hot springs	Videography tours	Senior tours

FAMILY	SOFT ADVENTURE		
Amusement parks	Backpacking		
Camping	Bicycle touring		
Shopping trips	Canoing/kayaking		
Whalewatching	Scuba diving/snorkelling		
Gourmet/gastronomy	Walking tours		

be *adventuresome*; it would be a *learning* experience' (Read, cited in Zeppel & Hall 1991, p. 30).

Special interest touring is now well established on a large scale. For example, an American company, InfoHub Inc, provides for more than 150 interests in its Specialty Travel Guide on the Internet (www.biztravel.com).

It puts them into 10 categories which are listed in Table 3.1 with examples of interests.

The symmetry of the table is a convenient way of presenting examples but it does not reflect the numerical relationship of categories. There were more interests in the soft adventure category (36) than any other. Next was history/culture with 28.[2]

▓ Nature tourism

Nature tourism is the broad term used to describe tourism having contact with the natural environment. It can refer to both the flora and fauna of an area and can be associated with environments modified by man. Nature tourists may be doing something specific like

DEFINITIONS

Nature tourism
Tourism having contact with the natural environment. It can refer to both the flora and fauna of an area and can be associated with environments modified by man. It does not necessarily have any explicit conservation motive.

bird-watching or experiencing the wonders of a coral reef while scuba diving. But they may also be doing something simple like walking through a forest or enjoying watching a waterfall.

There is little that is new about it. People had been travelling away from their homes to see natural wonders long before modern tourism began. It has been recorded that centuries ago in China and Japan people travelled hundreds of kilometres to stand before a waterfall or a cherry tree (Richardson 1999). And love of nature is not restricted to a few cultures; it can be found everywhere.

Nature tourism has been called alternative tourism. Among others, it incorporates adventure tourism and ecotourism as special forms. 'Ecotourism' is a relatively new word. It was invented in the 1980s[3] to describe a specialised form of nature tourism and quickly took hold in a period of changing values and habits; so much so that by 1998 the United Nations General Assembly was prepared to nominate 2002 as the Year of Ecotourism.

Both with nature tourism generally and ecotourism particularly, consumer interest and the increased recognition of the dangers to the environment have brought about expansion in many parts of the world, including Australia. Nature tourism is not difficult to define. It is 'primarily concerned with the direct enjoyment of some relatively undisturbed phenomenon of nature' (Valentine cited by Hvenegaard 1994, p. 25). It does not necessarily have any explicit conservation motive.

An example of the kind of activities researchers think constitute nature tourism is given in a survey published by Tourism Queensland (2000a). Nature tourism was sub-divided into four categories of attraction:

1. Reef activities including reef tours and cruises
2. Adventure activities (horse riding, climbing, abseiling, canoeing, diving, white-water rafting)
3. Bushwalking and national parks
4. Built nature-based attractions such as theme parks, zoos and sanctuaries.

Ecotourism

Ecotourism

Nature-based tourism that involves education and interpretation of the natural environment and is managed to be ecologically sustainable (Commonwealth Department of Tourism 1994, p. 3).

Ecotourism has an active conservation role: it must enhance or maintain natural systems (Hvenegaard 1994). A relatively small proportion of tourists experience it, although the number is said to be growing rapidly (Beeton 1998). Understanding what the word means in operational terms has been a problem for some mainstream tour operators. This is how an executive of one of the big Australian coach tour operators responded when asked what 'ecotourism' meant to him:

> *What is it? No-one has really been able to understand it. Some say avoid breaking a blade of grass and that's ecotourism. Some say look over crystal waters and that's ecotourism. It's almost indefinable. We look upon it as being controlled tourism in small groups, off the beaten track. It suits our four-wheel-drive*

operation. But we don't use the term for marketing purposes. Some people have; they have called anything with a touch of nature in it ecotouring (Hill, 1998).

Tourists themselves can be puzzled, as the following example shows. Fogg Dam in the Northern Territory's Top End is not a natural area but one modified in the 1950s for rice growing. The permanent body of water created by the making of an earthwork dam and the rice grown as a result attracted such large flocks of waterbirds that agriculture was abandoned and the area declared a bird protection district. Ninety-four per cent of those surveyed during a visit to Fogg Dam in the mid-1990s regarded their visit as ecotourism, but only 48 per cent listed attributes suggesting they knew why (Chirgwin & Hughes 1997).

Tourism Queensland's (2000b) research of international visitors showed a similar confusion. About half indicated they understood 'ecotourism' was about 'not doing damage to the environment' while 31 per cent were simply unsure about the term and its meaning.

The differing perceptions of ecotourism are reflected in the lack of a standard definition, although in Australia, the following definition from the National Ecotourism Strategy, produced by the Commonwealth Department of Tourism (1994), has found wide acceptance:

> *Ecotourism is nature-based tourism that involves education and interpretation of the natural environment and is managed to be ecologically sustainable* (p. 3).

Nevertheless, it is still only one of many definitions. For example, the Ecotourism Association of Australia:

> *Ecotourism is ecologically sustainable tourism with a primary focus on experiencing natural areas that fosters environmental and cultural understanding, appreciation and conservation* (www.ecotourism.org.au).

A survey of government tourism agencies in the Americas showed that no single definition dominated. Indeed, most definitions reported in the study were 'homegrown' – that is they were developed by agencies to meet their own needs or understanding of ecotourism as opposed to being a definition taken from the tourism research literature or a professional tourism organisation (Edwards, McLaughlin & Ham 1998).

Rather than worry about definitions, the World Tourism Organisation (www.world-tourism.org) believes ecotourism is best understood from its generally accepted characteristics. They are:

1. Ecotourism includes all nature-based forms of tourism in which the main motivation of the tourists is the observation and appreciation of nature as well as the traditional cultures prevailing in natural areas.

2. It contains educational and interpretation features.

3. It is generally, but not exclusively, organised for small groups by specialised and small,

locally-owned businesses. Foreign operators of varying sizes also organise, operate and/or market ecotourism tours, generally for small groups.

4. It minimises negative impacts upon the natural and socio-cultural environment.

5. It supports the protection of natural areas by:

   – generating economic benefits for host communities, organisations and authorities managing natural areas with conservation purposes

   – providing alternative employment and income opportunities for local communities

   – increasing awareness of the conservation of natural and cultural assets, among both locals and tourists.

Tourism Queensland carried out a series of research programs into both nature tourism and ecotourism in the late 1990s. The differences should be recalled. Nature tourism is a non-specific term which describes all tourism activity relating to the natural environment. Ecotourism is a subset of nature tourism which goes beyond just appreciation of nature: learning and conservation are also necessary attributes. Specialist operators provide pro- grams for ecotourists. One of the Tourism Queensland programs surveyed 258 operators – 155 nature tour operators, 103 ecotourism operators. The businesses represented tours, attractions and accommodation operations.

The research showed ecotourists did much the same sort of thing as other nature tourists, but nevertheless there were marked differences which set them apart. Many ecotourists like to be closer to the natural resource, favouring resorts like Daintree Wilderness Lodge (Queensland) and Crystal Creek (New South Wales). Ecotourism operators were more likely to access protected areas often serviced by specialised accommodation – 78 per cent as against 58 per cent of nature-based operators. This was consistent with the heavy reliance by ecotourism operators on significant natural areas as the core feature of their product base. Protected areas included national parks, state forests, marine parks and world heritage areas.

The activities undertaken by ecotourists are similar to other nature tourists. The Tourism Queensland researchers listed these activities for nature tourists: bushwalking, birdwatching, viewing animals in the wild, diving or snorkelling, camping, adventure activities, farm/bush activities and fossils and minerals. But the difference the research shows is in dedication; in particular it is the addition of conservation and education criteria that differentiated ecotourism.

About half the businesses surveyed received 5,000 or more visitors annually. Size favoured nature-based businesses – twice as many nature-based businesses as ecotourism businesses attracted more than 50,000 visitors a year.[4]

The surveys also demonstrated the power of consumer influence. Almost all the operators – 95 per cent – believed consumers were becoming more knowledgeable about environmental issues and 80 per cent indicated this was influencing their business. A significant number of operators were prepared to nominate ways in which they were changing their business operations to meet consumer demand as a result of increased environmental awareness. For example, 34 per cent said they were supplying more information on wildlife and the environment, 15 per cent were offering more information-based tour products and 12 per cent saw the need for better staff training (Tourism Queensland 1999a, 1999b, 2000a, 2000b, 2000c).

DEFINITIONS

▓ Cultural tourism

Culture is very important to tourism. One of the most compelling motivations for people to travel is to see how other people live and to learn something of their cultural heritage. The industry recognises the role of culture as a 'pull' factor by promoting the cultural features of destinations. Promotion may also emphasise educational benefits because many tourists are eager to explore and learn about the social and historical significance of sites (Zeppel & Hall 1991). Hughes (1996) sees most tourism as 'cultural' in that visits will usually involve some exposure to aspects of other cultures. It may be the main activity of a trip and the prime motivation, or a secondary activity and an incidental motivation.

The popular use of the word 'culture', according to The Macquarie Dictionary (1997, p. 529) refers to literature and the fine arts. But the dictionary also defines it as meaning the total ways of living built up by a group of human beings, which is transmitted from one generation to another, the 'wider form of lifestyle and folk heritage' (Hollinshead 1990, p. 292). **Cultural tourism** embraces both meanings. It is experiential tourism involved in and stimulated by a great variety of things – the performing arts, visual arts, festivals, cuisines, history, experiencing nostalgia and other ways of life.

Cultural tourism
Experiential tourism involved in and stimulated by the performing arts, visual arts, festivals, cuisines, history, experiencing nostalgia and other ways of life.

Cultural tourism can begin early in life. These young visitors to the Australian War Memorial in Canberra dress the part to learn something of their nation's past in the Discovery Room.

(Source: The Australian War Memorial.)

However, Hughes says 'it is clear' it does not include popular culture, including variety shows, music hall, pantomime, pop concerts, rock, reggae, jazz, folk music, dancing, circus, comedy, and magic. He cites Williams for a definition of the arts as the 'works and practices of intellectual, spiritual and aesthetic development' using it to distinguish them from 'popular culture'. However, the role of popular entertainment in attracting tourists can be highly significant. Further, it may be an element of popular culture which plays a particularly important role in people's lives in offering escape and a sense of contentment and fulfilment. Hughes regards it as significant that the holiday resort is one of the places where live entertainment has endured. So there is no doubting its value in attracting tourists; the issue is whether it should be classified as cultural tourism.

The popular entertainment argument aside, cultural tourism can be viewed essentially as an opportunity for tourists to experience, understand and appreciate the character of a place, its richness and diversity. It offers personal contact with local people and those who have special knowledge of interesting features. It aims to convey meaning rather than simply to describe or give lists of facts.

It can include:

- visiting historic buildings, sites, monuments and streetscapes, museums, art galleries, Aboriginal art sites and established gardens and trails
- seeing contemporary art and sculptures, architecture, textiles, arts and crafts shops, design centres, artists' workshops, the work of the media, the film and publishing industries and other forms of expression
- experiencing the performing arts including folk singing, storytelling and street theatre, special events such as festivals, and the reenactment of historically significant moments
- appreciating religion(s) followed by residents, including its visible manifestations
- sampling the local way of life, including leisure activities, educational systems, the kinds of work engaged in by residents and the technology that is used
- travelling on historic and unusual forms of transportation (e.g. paddlewheelers on the Murray, heritage steam trains)
- trying the cuisine of the destination. Local foods and beverages, and the way they are prepared, are a significant attraction. Especially when tried in the company of residents, they can tell a visitor much about the local culture (Mathieson & Wall 1982; Commonwealth Department of Industry, Science and Resources 1999).

For the purposes of collecting data, many Australian researchers narrow the definition. International cultural tourists are considered as those who attend at least one of the following cultural attractions or events during their visit to Australia:

- Historic sites or heritage buildings, sites or monuments
- Aboriginal sites and culture
- Art and craft workshops or studios

- Festivals, fairs or markets
- Performing arts or concerts
- Museums or art galleries.

Studies in the mid-1990s by the Bureau of Tourism Research showed that the majority of international visitors to Australia were cultural tourists according to this definition (62 per cent in 1995). Six features distinguished them:

1. More of them were females than males (females were 52 per cent of the total in 1993, 56 per cent in 1995).
2. They tended to be holidaymakers rather than business visitors.
3. They stayed longer than other visitors (in 1995 28 nights as against 23 nights for all visitors). The longer a visitor stayed in Australia the more likely they were to participate in cultural activities.
4. They usually spent more on their trip to Australia than other visitors because of their longer duration of stay, but less on a per night basis.
5. A higher proportion of them than other visitors bought inclusive air fares. This was probably due to the aggressive marketing of packages including special cultural events or visits to a cultural attractions (Lee Mei Foo 1998).

Domestic cultural tourism is harder to pinpoint. While there are some figures to go on they cover only some cultural activities and it is not known how many of those who visited a museum or attended an opera were domestic overnight tourists and how many were locals. However, the interest in cultural activities is very high and Australia has a range of cultural experiences to offer visitors.

ABS figures show attendance in 1999–2000 at the 2,049 'museum establishments' in Australia[5] was 27.5 million, of whom just on 11 million paid and the remaining 16.5 million did not (Australian Bureau of Statistics 2001). By contrast attendance for the year 2000 at all Australian Football League matches (the best-attended football code in Australia) was 5.7 million. Attendance figures for some other venues and activities which are relevant to cultural tourism are shown in Table 3.2 on the next page.

Festivals are an important part of Australian cultural tourism. About 300 festivals devoted solely or partly to cultural activities are held each year in Australia. Among the biggest are Adelaide's biennial festival and the annual festivals in Sydney, Melbourne and Perth – each lasts several weeks and attracts many visitors.

Industrial tourism

Visits to factories, farms, vineyards and other places of work are known collectively as **industrial tourism**. It is usually considered as part of cultural tourism, although not everyone will find it easy to equate 'work' with 'culture'. It is perhaps not difficult to see that some work, like making wine, can fit a cultural label, but it is harder to include other work, like making cars. However, in accordance with the broad definition of culture as

DEFINITIONS

Industrial tourism
Organised visits by tourists to operational industrial sites where some facilities have been provided specifically for their use. The industrial enterprise must be operating.

Table 3.2 Attendance at selected cultural venues, year ending April 1999

VENUE/ACTIVITY	PERSONS '000
Popular music	3,781.8
Classical music	1,310.3
Theatre	2,464.9
Dance	1,345.0
Opera or musical	2,430.4
Other performing arts	2,648.0

(Source: Australian Bureau of Statistics (1999b), p. 3.)

reflecting the life of the community, it could be argued that car manufacture is an important factor in the life of a particular community and helps make it what it is.

Industrial tourism involves organised visits by tourists to operational industrial sites where some facilities have been provided specifically for their use. The industrial enterprise must be operating. If it is not then the site has become an example of industrial heritage.

Some workplaces have a tourist flavour to them. For example the Commonwealth Department of Industry, Science and Resources (n.d.) fact sheet on Cultural Tourism, says, 'Visitors can learn about industries such as wool, forestry, mining and beef through farmstays, interpretation centres, site tours or "hands on" activities like cattle musters'.

Industrial tourism covers a range of industries and can include farming, mining, manufacturing, public utilities, theatre production and financial services. In other words, industrial tourism can take in the production of either goods or services, and can be involved with industries concerned with the processing of raw materials or semi-processed inputs. Public or private sector ownership is not a consideration (Frew & Shaw 1996).

▓ Indigenous tourism

The culture of Aboriginal peoples is important in establishing an Australian national identity and in making the Australian tourism product distinctive. It is said to be 'integral to our "Australian-ness"' (Commonwealth Department of Industry, Science and Resources 1999). Aboriginal cultural forms – art, boomerangs, didgeridoos – have long been used in travel promotions. It is common for overseas visitors to buy Aboriginal art and artefacts as souvenirs – some genuine, some mass-produced.

While other Australians have 'borrowed' representations of Aboriginal culture for tourism purposes for decades, it is only in recent years that there has been a concerted effort to increase direct Aboriginal and Torres Strait Islander participation in tourism enterprises.

Australia's indigenous people are the various Aboriginal communities across Australia and the Torres Strait Islanders, who take their name from the islands of the strait that separates the Australian mainland at Cape York Peninsula from the south coast of Papua New Guinea.

The Torres Strait Islanders have cultural similarities with people of New Guinea and the western Pacific rather than Aboriginal communities of mainland Australia, with whom they differ culturally, historically and politically. There are not many Torres Strait Islanders – about 6,000 living in the Torres Strait Region and another 21,000 outside the region, mainly in the coastal towns of north Queensland, particularly Townsville and Cairns.

So Aboriginal people – at least 400,000 of them at the turn of the century – form by far the largest group of indigenous people in Australia. They are increasing at a faster rate than the rest of the population, one of the reasons being that more people are identifying themselves as Aboriginal.

Indigenous tourism includes all forms of participation by indigenous people in tourism:

- as employers
- as employees
- as investors
- as joint-venture partners
- providing indigenous cultural tourism products
- providing mainstream tourism products (Aboriginal and Torres Strait Islander Commission & Office of National Tourism 1997).

An **Aboriginal tourism produc**t has been defined as a tourism experience or service which is majority-owned by Aboriginal people and/or in partnership with non-Aboriginal people.[6]

Activity is widespread but it is usually small-scale. Overall it accounts for only a small part of the Australian tourism product.

At the heart of Aboriginal tourism is a powerful culture based on distinctive sets of beliefs and values. Aboriginal people believe their rights to land derive from the activities of ancestral heroes and creator figures. Representations based on these sources give effect to their traditions of ritual, dance, music, art and stories. Particular groups have authority over the ownership of such knowledge and strict protocols determine who may narrate or paint particular stories or use associated designs.

Aboriginal Tourism Australia, the peak body representing Aboriginal tourism operators, emphasises that the use of Aboriginal culture for tourism purposes should take place only with the agreement of the relevant communities, and on the terms established

DEFINITIONS

Indigenous tourism
All forms of participation by indigenous people in tourism as employers, employees, investors, or joint-venture partners, providing indigenous cultural tourism products and/or mainstream tourism products.

Aboriginal tourism product
A tourism experience or service which is majority owned by Aboriginal people and/or in partnership with non-Aboriginal people.

by those communities. It also believes that the communities should receive the benefits from tourism (www.ataust.org.au).

Surveys have consistently indicated a high proportion of visitors, especially those from overseas, want to experience Aboriginal art and culture. Nicholson (2000) quoted a survey of 700 overseas tourists which showed that 80 per cent wanted to visit an Aboriginal attraction. However, she also said more than a third left without any experience of indigenous culture and many others saw no more than a museum or art and craft shop.

Indigenous tourism is inextricably bound up with the Aboriginal arts industry, which though small scale, has a long history and has brought international recognition to the Aboriginal people and Australia. Aboriginal art takes many forms including rock art which goes back tens of thousands of years, as well as paintings and artefacts produced today.

Dreaming stories

Aboriginal Tourism Australia describes the themes of Aboriginal art as being involved with the Dreaming stories and the rituals and ceremonies that maintain the link between people and spirits and land. There are many different styles and subjects because Aboriginal people live in many different environments and have different stories.

While some of the best-known examples of rock art are in the Northern Territory's Uluru–Kata Tjuta National Park and Kakadu National Park, other areas of significance can be found in other parts of Australia, e.g. Mutawintji and Mungo National Park in New South Wales and the Grampians National Park in Victoria. Rock paintings known collectively as the Bradshaws are located in remote and largely inaccessible parts of the Kimberley region of Western Australia. They are considered to show remarkable artistic skill and their content has caused debate about their origins.

Permits are required to enter some Aboriginal lands, mostly in northern and central Australia and some parts of South Australia and Western Australia. They are issued through Land Councils acting on behalf of traditional owners. The system is designed to help protect the privacy of Aboriginal communities, preserve Aboriginal culture, safeguard the natural environment and promote visitor safety. Intending visitors should submit applications for permits to the relevant Land Council well in advance (www.ataust.org.au).

Cultural centres

Aboriginal cultural centres of various kinds are major attractions. One of the best known is the Tjapukai Cultural Park near Cairns, home of the Tjapukai Dance Theatre, which has won many tourism awards and also a place in the Guinness Book of Records for staging the longest-running play in Australia. In Adelaide, Tandanya, the National Aboriginal Cultural Institute, won a South Australian Tourism Award in 2000 for its program of traditional art, craft, music and dance.

The Brambuk Living Cultural Centre in Halls Gap, Victoria, offers exhibits, activities and the Gugijela Restaurant mixing Aboriginal and European cuisine. Dreamtime Cultural Centre in Rockhampton displays and explains Aboriginal and Torres Strait Islander culture and lifestyle to mainly domestic tourists. It is operated by a company which includes white as well as Aboriginal people on its board of directors. All its staff (about 30) are indigenous.

A variety of Aboriginal tour and learning experiences are available to the tourist. Examples are:

- Harry Nanya Outback Cultural Tours, headquartered in Wentworth, New South Wales, an accredited Aboriginal-owned and operated tour company which has won a New South Wales Tourism Award. It employs indigenous guides for its tours in a number of states and also operates the Harry Mitchell Art and Craft Gallery in Wentworth. This features the work of local Aboriginal artists and is incorporated with Harry Nanya Outback Cultural Tours.

- In the Bungle Bungles in the Kimberley, Bonnie Edwards and her sister Tamba lead bush walks twice a week for major tour companies, which bring thousands of visitors a year into the region. They tell visitors about bush tucker, medicines and the landscape, and also about life on the stations and their concerns about alcohol, unemployment and lost skills.

- At Fitzroy Crossing in the Kimberley, the Bunuba people take about 1,000 people a year on boat cruises through the Geikie Gorge. Further east along the Ord River, the Bell Springs Community offer story-telling over billy tea and damper.

- The Manyallaluk people invite tourists to sample bush tucker and try their hands at bark painting, basket-weaving and making fire on the former Eva Valley cattle station south east of Katherine, which is now Aboriginal land. Cultural tours of one to four days are conducted for both domestic and international tourists. Manyallaluk Tours has been inducted into the Australian Tourism Awards Hall of Fame – the first indigenous tourism operation to receive that honour.

▓ The issue of authenticity

As has been seen, some people satisfy the needs that motivate them by placing themselves in an entirely fabricated atmosphere. What could be more artificial than a vast cruise ship packed with manufactured attractions including a rock-climbing wall up the side of the funnel?

At the other end of the scale, are the people who set out to learn something they didn't know before, to enrich themselves by seeking out and experiencing some place that is new to them, interacting with people and environments that that will change their view of the world. In a time when 'virtual reality' has become part of our language, it is essential for some people that their experiences be real, **authentic**.

Authenticity is about being genuine, reliable and unspoiled and is a central issue in assessing the quality of a cultural experience.

DEFINITIONS

Authentic
A tourism experience which is genuine, reliable and unspoiled; the 'real thing'.

But what is authentic and what is not? What is the real thing? How does the tourist know? Aboriginal artisans use electric tools to make boomerangs and other artefacts these days. They use industrial paints instead of naturally-found ochres. Does this make their products less authentic? Some people think so, others think Aboriginal culture is simply adapting to the modern world (Clark & Larrieu 1998).

What is considered authentic depends on the person's own knowledge and beliefs and also how cultural objects and attractions are interpreted by professionals. People tend to accept the view of professionals about whether something is authentic or not. Museums have had a key function in presenting an authoritative interpretation of a place through time (McIntosh & Prentice 1999).

Authenticity is regarded as an important part of the experience by visitors to historic theme parks, even though such parks may be regarded as examples of 'staged authenticity' (Zeppel & Hall 1991). An authenticity test can also be used on contemporary culture. King (1994) says authenticity is neither static nor rooted in the past. It recognises evolving types of representation; it can be contemporary or even futuristic. Nevertheless, applying measures of authenticity to the contemporary Australian tourism experience requires an appreciation of the key stages of history.

Though interpretations of history are necessarily subjective, they can help us understand the multiplicity of influences which have created Australia and therefore improve our judgments about the relative authenticity of current events.

Four eras of Australian history can form settings for the Australian tourism experience:
1. the prehistoric era prior to the arrival of Aboriginals on the continent
2. the era of sole habitation by the Aboriginals. This period probably lasted for about 50,000 years
3. the European (and Anglo–Celtic dominated) era. This period lasted for approximately a century and a half after 1788
4. the post-World War II era of liberalised immigration and the advent of multi-culturalism (King 1994).

Authenticity as identity

Authenticity can be interpreted in terms of national identity, as an expression of what makes Australia and Australians what they are. On this basis, development of a tourism product should start with what is right for Australians and not be manufactured just for an external market.

King says most tourism products and facilities need to gain acceptance in the local market before they are likely to attract and satisfy international tourists. He cites Melbourne's Southgate development where food and beverage and retail outlets successfully sought local acceptance and then emerged as a magnet for international tourists.

However, he notes there are opponents of tourism who are sceptical of any claims to authenticity when the process is driven by a form of imagery contrived to package the destination for commercial tourist consumption. He points to the use of Uluru (Ayers Rock) as both a tourist symbol and as an embodiment of the national essence. Even if it is agreed that the symbol is authentic and an appropriate choice, there remains the dilemma over whether the reproduction of that object preserves the original authenticity. Images of Uluru itself may be reproduced in a variety of forms which may or may not preserve the original authenticity and meaning, particularly its spiritual significance to Aboriginal people. What is or is not authentic is a matter of judgment.

Areas of authenticity

Many different elements make up the overall tourism product. King sees how attention to authenticity in different areas can enhance the Australian product.

Souvenirs. Some loss of the meaning of an artefact may be inevitable in an age of mass production but Australian souvenirs and tourist merchandise should not be debased. To ensure authenticity requires (a) a sensitive use of local materials in souvenirs and crafts and (b) a proper understanding of and explanation of the original purpose of the artefact/souvenir.

Buildings and facilities. The style and relation to the immediate environment are important. The use of locally quarried stone or locally sourced timber can help to convey a sense of 'place' and authenticity to tourists. Authenticity should also be extended to the interior of such properties. Themed settings need to be approached with sensitivity and care, especially when they attempt to depict a unified décor, menu and possibly even theatrical or musical performance.

Atmosphere. This includes bush sensations such as the smell of eucalyptus oil, the sound of native birds, or the sun setting on the expansive outback horizon. The sights and sounds of tourists and local people mixing in such settings as Darling Harbour in Sydney, Salamanca Place in Hobart or Lygon Street in Melbourne provide tourists with an insight into the 'real' Australia.

Service. Quality service that is 'distinctly Australian' should incorporate high levels of craft skills, plus a knowledge and understanding of both Australia and overseas. In this sense 'authentic Australian' preserves some traditional values (e.g. laconic sense of humour and egalitarianism), but recognises the increasing openness of the country to the rest of the world

Authentic cuisine

The food offered to tourists and the ambience in which it is available are a reflection of our culture – 'a powerful vehicle of transmitting and experiencing' that culture, according to Handszuh (1999). Reynolds (1994) sees food as probably one of the last areas of authenticity that is affordable on a regular basis by the tourist.

However, there are barriers to tourists sampling foods which reflect local cultures. Firstly, there is the internationalisation of food and service. The most obvious examples are in fast food, but even before McDonalds and others spread their tentacles, internationally hotel chains were standardising their menus and their contents. This suits travellers who don't want to take risks with food; not only because they might try something they don't like, but they fear they might get sick – according to Reynolds, more people are ill on holiday from food-related incidents than any other source.

Also the travellers' own culture plays a large part in their choice of food. In some cultures, Indian for example, this plays a major role in where they are prepared to travel and to stay.

This is a synopsis of what Indian tour operators said about their clients' food habits at a symposium in Melbourne in 1997: Indians have rigid food habits. There are big areas of their country – the whole state of Gujarat, for example – which are predominantly vegetarian. Most Indians who are not vegetarian prefer meats curried and, if that is not available, would rather stay vegetarian than eat 'bland meats' or cold meats. Most North Indians would be happy to try Australian food, but they would still want Indian food at least once a day. South Indians must have curds, 'not flavoured sweet yoghurt, but plain and simple curds' (Symposium record, unpublished).

Despite the difficulties, Reynolds believes there is an increasing tourist interest in authentic local food experiences. The obvious evidence of Australians' own interest in food and drink, as seen in the bustling café and restaurant life in our cities, does not fail to attract tourists. Besides, Australia is one of the safest nations on earth in which to eat and it offers a great variety of cuisines.

King thinks the diversity of fresh food and beverages in Australia is 'worthy of highlight' (1994, p. 4). The styles of preparation are 'blatantly eclectic', which means Australian chefs can cater for a great variety of tastes and food habits and still offer food, service and ambience which is culturally Australian. After all, Australian culture in general is blatantly eclectic. The blend of Australian foods and beverages with cooking styles chosen from many nations is what makes Australian cuisine authentic.

CASE STUDY

Wundargoodie Aboriginal Safaris

Wundargoodie Aboriginal Safaris operates three- to nine-day bush tours out of Broome and Wyndham. Its customers include schoolchildren, university groups, specialists like geologists and those with a serious intention of learning about the bush and the ways of Aborigines.

The company was set up in 1994 by Colin and Maria Morgan in Wyndham. In 1998 it moved to Broome as an expansionary move and in 2003 went back to Wyndham as its second operating base.

The approval of the elders of Colin's father's language group was sought and given before Wundargoodie was established. 'They thought we had the guts to get up and do something different,' Colin said. He also asked the elders to extend his knowledge of Aboriginal culture so that he could pass it on to tourists.

The company networks with other Aboriginal people throughout the region. People from different tribal groups act as guides in some of the activities, allowing visitors to participate and appreciate the diversity of Aboriginal culture in the Kimberley region. The activities include crabbing, fish poisoning, viewing exclusive corroborees and having the songs and dances interpreted to them. Tourists also learn about the influences of the missionaries.

The tourists that Wundargoodie attracts include those with a serious intention of learning about the bush and the ways of Aborigines. Among them are large groups of American university students organised by a lecturer at Notre Dame University, local school groups, specialists like geologists, and Australian families who want to learn more about their country and its indigenous people.

The American group organiser sometimes sends 80 students at a time. Colin splits them into two groups of 40. He takes each into the bush for four full days, showing them how Aboriginal people lived and survived in the beautiful but harsh country, and teaches them aspects of Aboriginal culture and history. He shows the students how to find their way in the bush. They go out at night looking for animal tracks and for lessons on how to navigate by the stars, the Aboriginal way. They return to town on Day 5 and Colin takes the next group out bush.

He also teaches bush navigation to local schoolchildren from Broome during a week-long safari. He disorients the children by getting them to go round in the circles and then invites them to find a north or south reference. Of course, when they fail he shows them how. He teaches the children to fish, using a drug from a bush plant to stun the fish as they swim in rock pools off the Dampier Peninsula. The crushed roots of the plant are mixed with sand and water and put in a sack to take to the pools. Within two minutes of it being introduced to the pools the fish are rendered unconscious and float to the surface for easy retrieval. Fish poisoning allows the children – and other visitors – to experience first-hand ancient methods of conservation and preservation of food sources that Aboriginal people practised.

Colin sometimes guides specialists who value his knowledge of the country and its geological treasures. An example of this was his guiding of a group of 20 geologists from different parts of the world to the 60 million-year-old Devonian Reef in the Fitzroy Valley (Morgan 2002).

INDUSTRY PROFILE

COLIN AND MARIA MORGAN TOUR OPERATORS,
WUNDARGOODIE ABORIGINAL SAFARIS

Colin: We run tours out of Broome and Wyndham, and our customers learn about the Australian bush and Aboriginal culture. I am the guide and driver and Maria is also a guide and looks after the equipment. Maria is the driving force behind the business.

Maria: We have five children of whom four work in the family business. They have been groomed for it all their lives in the cultural sense and nine years in the industry sense. Each has expertise in different aspects of the business. The family all join in campfire sessions allowing visitors to get a perspective of Aboriginal family life.

How did we get here?

Colin: When I was an Aboriginal liaison officer at the hospital in Wyndham, some of the staff came with the family for outings and asked me about the bush. Maria worked at the hospital and also in the local tourist bureau. We thought we should try tourism as a business so I set out on a learning exercise. I got my first tour together by going to Kununnara and asking about 10 tourists to come come with me as a freebie. One was an American, the rest Australian and I listened to them; they gave me lots of tips. I then got a job with East Kimberley Tours as a driver–guide and I learned how they set up base camp, what sort of food they provided and anything else that was useful. We began Wundargoodie Aboriginal Safaris in 1994 with one-day bush tours. We started with practically nothing and often things were shaky; it was seven years before anyone believed in us enough to give us a loan and we could get our own vehicle.

Maria: I first worked in tourism as an information officer at the tourist bureau in Wyndham in 1984 for a season, then again in 1988 until the end of the season when our eldest son Ron, who was five, had kidney failure. We spent five months in Perth until he received one of my kidneys. He has kept well ever since. We have certainly gone through some hard times but we have always focused on our children and our future. Besides working on tours, I have a full time job. This allows bills to be paid and places food on the table because the tourism industry runs for only 6–7 months of the year due to the weather.

What do we like about our job?

Colin: Everything. I like talking to people. I especially like talking to a large group about Aboriginal culture. It makes me glow. And when the hard work is done and the group is gone we sit around as a family and relax and laugh.

Maria: It's really self-rewarding, bridging the gap between black and white people by taking tourists out and showing them who we are and how we live. It's very different to how our lives are portrayed in the media.

Characteristics of individual tourists affect their ability and propensity to travel and their choice of destinations. These characteristics include their age and income, the amount of free time they have and psychological factors, among them motivation, the driving force behind all behaviour.

Knowing what motivates tourists is important to destination planners and tourism businesses because they can then provide and market products that will appeal.

The factors that motivate tourists have been put into two categories: push and pull. Push factors (e.g. economic, social, demographic, technological and political) are the things which 'push' people away from their place of residence. They want to get away from those factors, at least for a while. On the other hand, pull factors draw them towards a particular destination. They include such things as a positive image, safety, attractions, climate and the opportunity to do the things they really like. Forms of tourism are among the pull factors.

Push motivations can also be socio-psychological. A review of academic research produced this list:

- **Escape** A wish to get away from a perceived mundane environment.
- **Relaxation** A wish for recuperation.
- **Play** A wish to indulge in activities associated with childhood.
- **Strengthening family bonds**.
- **Prestige** The choice of a holiday seen in terms of status and social enhancement.
- **Social interaction** The holiday can be an important social forum for individuals.
- **Romance** The opportunity of meeting people for romantic encounters.
- **Educational opportunity** A chance to learn about other places and peoples.
- **Self-fulfilment** Returning with a changed life or a changed perspective.
- **Wish-fulfilment** The holiday is the answer to a dream.

These motivations can be related to forms of tourism. Those of particular interest in the Australian context are described below.

- **Australian holiday by the sea** The annual family summer holiday (strengthening family bonds) is in total a huge domestic tourism movement. More often than not it is made with minimal or no assistance from the travel and tourism industry.
- **Indulgent tourism** The industry is certainly involved in this kind of tourism, which is characterised by a search for luxury and glamour and name brands and is not concerned with authenticity.
- **The 'new tourism'** This is characterised by flexibility and individualised tours and has important destination product consequences.
- **Special interest tourism** People choose a destination so they can follow their particular interest there.
- **Nature tourism** Nature tourism describes tourism having contact with the natural environment which does not necessarily have any explicit conservation motive.

SUMMARY

- **Ecotourism** This is a form of nature tourism with an active conservation and education role.
- **Cultural tourism** Cultural tourism is concerned with the performing and visual arts but also culture in the wider sense, e.g. lifestyles and heritage including festivals, cuisines, history, and the way people live.
- **Industrial tourism** This describes touristic visits to operating factories, farms, vineyards and other places of work.
- **Indigenous tourism** This is bound up with the Aboriginal arts industry, sustains cultural centres, and is the basis for many tours.

Authenticity (being genuine, reliable and unspoiled) is a central issue in assessing the quality of a cultural experience. What is considered authentic depends on the person's own knowledge and beliefs and also how cultural objects and attractions are interpreted by professionals. Attention to authenticity can enhance the Australian tourism product. Areas where it is applicable include souvenirs, buildings and facilities, atmosphere, service and a distinctive Australian cuisine.

QUESTIONS

1. What does 'travel motivation' mean? Why is it so important to marketers and product developers?
2. What are push and pull factors? Which do you think are the most forceful?
3. How do socio-psychological push factors affect the forms of tourism people choose?
4. What are the characteristics of indulgent tourism? Do you think it will become more or less prevalent?
5. Where did 'new tourism' start and what were those embracing it seeking?
6. Why do you think ecotourism is hard to define? Does defining it matter? If not, how can it better be described?
7. What sort of things do people do in pursuing cultural tourism? Can you name five of them?
8. Do you think industrial tourism should be developed as a separate form? If so, why?
9. What is the driving force behind Aboriginal culture? How is this expressed in tourism ventures?
10. Does authenticity matter to cultural tourists? If so, how can it best be guaranteed?

MEASURING TOURISM AND ITS ECONOMIC IMPACT

LEARNING OBJECTIVES

Understand that tourism is measured in people and money. Appreciate the importance of yield, which is dependent on the type of tourist attracted.

Examine how tourists are tracked around the world and identify the region which is of most importance to Australia.

Examine how tourists are tracked in Australia, and identify the major Australian tracking studies and the information they produce.

Understand how the Tourism Forecasting Council attempts to measure the future.

Examine how tourism expenditure is measured and appreciate its impact on the economy. Understand measures and concepts such as leakage, multipliers, tourism consumption, Gross Domestic Product, Gross Value Added, Balance of Payments, the Travel Account.

Investigate the Tourism Satellite Account, how it works and how it has given Australia a more reliable measure of the impact of tourism on the economy.

Examine other methods of assessing impact: input–output models, computable general equilibrium models, benefit–cost analysis.

Understand the impact of tourism on state and regional economies and how difficulties of assessment increase as the size of the destination area decreases.

**UNDERSTAND
THE MEANING OF:**

- *yield*
- *East Asia & Pacific Region*
- *arrival & departure cards*
- *International Visitor Survey*
- *National Visitor Survey*
- *Tourism Forecasting Council*
- *tourism expenditure*
- *direct, indirect & induced effects*
- *leakage*
- *tourism multipliers*
- *tourism consumption*
- *Gross Domestic Product*
- *Gross Value Added*
- *Balance of Payments*
- *travel account*
- *National Accounts*
- *Tourism Satellite Account*
- *input–output analysis*
- *computable general equilibrium model*
- *BTR's 1990s methodology*
- *benefit–cost analysis*

Understand how the impact of events and particular types of tourism on an economy is measured.

Appreciate how tourism employment is measured and recognise problems in understanding what is being measured and what are real tourism jobs.

Recognise the impact of taxation on tourism economics.

Examine a case study on the measurement of the economic impact of cruise shipping.

PEOPLE, MONEY AND THE IMPORTANCE OF YIELD

The subjects of the next three chapters are the environments in which the tourism system operates and which receive the most attention from researchers, governments and businesses. They are the economic, socio-cultural and physical environments. Usually at issue is the impact tourism makes on these environments but it should not be forgotten that the process can be two-way and changes in the environments can affect tourism.

The subject of this chapter is tourism's impact on the economic environment. It is also largely concerned with methods: how people moving around the world and in Australia are tracked, how their expenditure in Australia is calculated and its effect on the national and smaller economies assessed. Tourism is thus measured in people and money. Depending on circumstances, people can be thought of as arrivals, departures, tourists, visitors or day-trippers and the money from tourism can be reckoned as receipts or expenditure. As will be seen there are other economic measures derived from expenditure.

It is important to track and keep a count of the numbers of people moving around the world and within Australia. It can be demonstrated how countries and regions share tourism and, by looking at comparable figures from year to year, we can discern trends. Forecasters use these figures on which to base their estimates for the future. But in economic terms all tourists are not equal. Some stay longer than others, some spend more per day than others.

Developing countries are sometimes tempted to measure the success of their tourist activities in terms of the numbers of visitors rather than by the earnings from those visitors. This approach ignores differences in the daily expenditures of visitors, which can be increased by promotional and planning policies (Wheatcroft 1994, p. 41).

DEFINITIONS

The issue is **yield**, the return businesses and the economy of a destination receive from visitors. Australia had a yield problem in the early 1990s when the number of visitors from overseas increased but the amount of money they spent in the country decreased. The years were 1990 to 1993 and they were reported in the press as a period of 'record growth' because the number of arrivals grew impressively year by year.

In fact, tourism expenditure in each of the years 1991, 1992 and 1993 was less than in 1990 (Richardson 1995). The consequence was that businesses generally received less per tourist and the period is remembered by those elements of the industry which suffered (particularly the accommodation sector) as one of 'profitless volume'.

Yield is usually thought of as net return – what is left from revenue after costs have been deducted. But it is calculated in different ways by different industry sectors.

- In the accommodation sector, yield is the revenue on rooms on one night related to the maximum possible. Thus 100 per cent yield would require every room to be occupied at the full price or published rack rate.
- To airlines, yield means earnings per revenue passenger kilometre (RPK). Passenger revenue is obtained by multiplying yield by volume.
- To a travel agent, yield is retained commission.

Yield
(1) The net return – what is left from revenue after costs have been deducted. It is calculated in different ways by industry sectors.
(2) For a country or other destination, yield is the net benefit measured in social and physical terms as well as economic. However, it is difficult to measure. As an indicator, it is usually considered sufficient to take the gross expenditure.

To economists, tourism yield is the net benefit accruing to a country or destination area from visitors, i.e. the benefits minus the costs of tourism activity. But there is a problem. Benefits and costs to a destination are not only economic, but social and physical as well, and the latter two are difficult to measure.

Following the problems of the early 1990s, the Commonwealth Department of Tourism commissioned a study on yield from inbound tourism by consultant economists Professor Peter Forsyth and Associate Professor Larry Dwyer. But Forsyth and Dwyer found that 'there is insufficient information on many of the factors that have an impact on tourism yield and approaches to the measurement of different variables have yet to be properly developed' (Department of Tourism 1995b, p. 3).

They concluded that the best available indicator of the yield from inbound tourism was net domestic tourism expenditure (total expenditure less leakages on imports). As an indicator, it would normally be sufficient to take the gross expenditure. In reports and discussions about destination, gross expenditure is in fact the measure most used. But it should be remembered that it is an indicator rather than a measure embracing all relevant factors.

TRACKING TOURISTS AROUND THE WORLD

The World Tourism Organisation divides the world into six regions and gathers information on tourist arrivals and expenditure each year. Thus it is able to track travel patterns round the world and keep a check on trends (the changes from year to year) as they affect each region. The WTO measures tourism in terms of arrivals (i.e. people) and the money they spend.

The six regions are Africa, The Americas, East Asia/Pacific, Europe, Middle East and South Asia.

The World Tourism Organisation collects information from government authorities around the world and then processes it to show the world picture.[1] It distributes this information, in the form of tables and analysis, through a number of publications (www.world-tourism.org). The statistics enable the determination of trends, that is, whether there has been positive or negative growth in world tourism, as measured by international arrivals and receipts; and changing travel patterns in regions and individual destinations.

In addition to WTO sources, information is also directly available from the markets. Australian organisations can usually access this through national tourism organisations.

The East Asia and Pacific region

Australia is part of the East Asia and Pacific region, along with 36 other destinations which include strong tourism countries like Japan, Singapore, Hong Kong and mainland China. It also includes tiny destinations like Nieue and Yap State.

The region can be thought of as a sliver of the world enclosed in an ellipse which has China in its north-western corner and stretches south and east to enclose the islands of French Polynesia. The Hawaiian islands have to be removed from the ellipse because they are statistically part of the Americas, but otherwise the region takes in North Asia and South East Asia, Australia and New Zealand, Melanesia, Micronesia, Polynesia, a little of the Indian Ocean and a lot of the Pacific Ocean.

Although Europe is by far the most important tourism region, when measured by arrivals or receipts, the East Asia and Pacific Region is the fastest growing, increasing its share of arrivals from 12 per cent in 1990 to 16 per cent in 2000 (World Tourism Organisation 2001).

Australia's place in tourism when measured by arrivals was around the low- to mid-30s among the nations of the world during the 1990s.[2] But when measured by receipts it rose steadily in the top 20 – 15th in 1990, 13th in 1995 and 11th in 2000 (World Tourism Organisation 1999b).

Tracking tourists in Australia

Within Australia, the Bureau of Tourism Research conducts surveys to track both international visitors and Australians travelling in the country, and it gathers much more detail than the WTO collections discussed above. Thus it is possible tell things about domestic and international travellers in Australia like:

- where they came from
- why they travelled
- where they went in Australia
- what transport they used to travel within the country
- what kind of accommodation they stayed in
- what they spent.[3]

The major collections of statistics regarding tourists are:

(1) **International arrival and departure figures**, which are compiled by the Australian Bureau of Statistics from the arrival and departure cards filled in when people enter or leave Australia. Those indicating an intended duration of stay of less than one year are sampled.

The cards show the following:

- Category of movement
- Country of residence/main destination
- Country of birth
- Country of citizenship (nationality)
- Country of embarkation/disembarkation
- State of clearance/major port of clearance
- State of residence/stay
- Purpose of journey
- Duration of stay
- Sex and age.

(2) The **International Visitor Survey (IVS)**, conducted in airport departure lounges after visitors from overseas have completed their stay in Australia.

(3) The **National Visitor Survey (NVS)**, in which 80,000 Australian residents are surveyed each year by mail-out/mail-back questionnaires, telephone interviews and face-to-face personal interviews.

The surveys collect data on a number of items, including:

- Number of overnight, day and outbound visitors
- Number of visitor nights
- Expenditure by overnight, day and outbound visitors
- Places visited and purpose of visit
- Accommodation and transport used
- Leisure activities participated in
- Travel party type and size
- Travel package expenditure and itemised expenditure
- Port of departure and airline used (outbound only)

- Age, sex and lifecycle information
- Country of birth and years in Australia
- Employment status and annual household income
- Impact of long-term health conditions/impairments on ability to travel (Poole 1993).

The IVS and NVS are conducted by the Bureau of Tourism Research. Results are distributed in printed form and also on compact disk. In addition to the national surveys, there are a number of state and regional collections of statistics which show the characteristics and movements of tourists in various parts of Australia.

FORECASTING TOURISM FLOWS

The surveys discussed so far measure tourism movements of the past. It is also necessary to attempt to measure the future, providing forecasts as a tool for planning, marketing, budgeting and policy making for tourism businesses and all levels of government (Jackson 2000).

Even without some major disturbance there is obviously some uncertainty surrounding the forecasts because of the extent to which they are based on assumptions. Nevertheless, they represent 'the most likely outcome' at a given point of time and are a necessary part of tourism development.

The Tourism Forecasting Council was set up by the Commonwealth Government in 1993 to 'provide tourism-related businesses and the government sector with realistic and relevant forecasts so that tourism can develop based on sound investment decisions' (Tourism Forecasting Council 1994, p. 2).

The TFC uses econometric models to identify and explore past relationships between movements in visitor arrivals and economic conditions in major source markets and apply the results to the future. Models are developed for each market, relying to a large extent on economic factors. The decision to travel is related to people's ability to pay for the travel service and the price of the travel compared with other goods and services, including travel to other destinations.

MEASURING TOURISM'S ECONOMIC IMPACT

The money tourists spend increases the wealth of the areas in which they travel and creates employment. For nations, it increases their foreign exchange. As we saw in Chapter 1 (Table 1.1) it impacts on many industries throughout the economy.

It is essential to measure the impact of such expenditure accurately as a guide to policy development, planning, investment and marketing. A number of methods have been developed to do this with economies of various sizes and in different circumstances (e.g. annually or a one-off study of a particular event).

The economic impact of tourism varies widely within Australia. For example, the percentage of the work force engaged in a region with a high level of tourism activity, such as Cairns or Uluru, exceeds the national average, whereas tourism contributes much less in a region with little tourism activity (Allcock 1999). National estimates of the economic impact may not be of much use in establishing the impact in a state or region. Therefore, they must be measured separately.

Measuring tourism expenditure

The first step in determining impact is to measure what tourists spend.

Inbound tourism expenditure consists of:

- what overseas visitors spend on goods and services in Australia
- fares paid to Qantas Airways by overseas visitors
- expenditure in Australia by foreign airlines attributable to the carriage of foreign visitors.

The sources of information are the International Visitor Survey, the Commonwealth survey of international student expenditure and the Australian Bureau of Statistics balance of payments on international air receipts.

Domestic tourism expenditure consists of what Australians spend on

- overnight trips
- day trips
- the domestic component of overseas trips.

The main source of this information is the BTR's annual National Visitor Survey. The 1998 NVS showed the greatest proportion of domestic expenditure was on overnight trips – 74 per cent (Buchanan 1999).

A Qantas Airways 747-400 soars into the sky to start another international flight. Fares paid to Qantas by overseas visitors are included in calculations of inbound tourism expenditure. They are also an important item in the balance of payments.

(Source: Qantas Airways Ltd.)

DEFINITIONS

▓ Measures and concepts

To understand how tourism expenditure impacts on an economy it is necessary to appreciate some economic concepts. For a start, the total impact involves more than the receipt of money directly from tourists by those who deal with them. It is the sum of direct, indirect and induced effects on an economy.

Direct effects are those produced by initial spending by tourists at hotels, service stations, attractions, and other businesses. Those businesses use the money to pay for wages and salaries, taxes, services, supplies and distributed profits.

Indirect effects refer to the second round, the production changes resulting from various rounds of re-spending. Payments to suppliers as tourism establishments replenish their stocks are indirect effects of the initial, direct tourist expenditure. For instance, an increase in the demand for accommodation will cause hotels and motels to increase their demand for (among other things) electricity, food and laundry services. This brings about changes in those industries, reflected in sales, income and jobs, and businesses supplying goods and services to *those* businesses benefit in turn. The accommodation sector is linked to many other sectors.

Leakage

The money which 'escapes' from the destination, for example it may be paid for imports of food, fuel, equipment or other goods necessary for servicing tourists or as dividends or profits to outside investors.

Induced effects are the changes in economic activity resulting from household spending of income earned directly or indirectly as a result of tourism spending. As wages and salaries within an economy rise, consumption also increases and this provides an additional impetus for economic activity.

Leakage

Leakage is the term used for the money which 'escapes' from the destination, reducing the income received by the community from the tourism expenditure. It may be paid for imports of food, fuel, equipment or other goods necessary for servicing tourists. It may be paid to international hotel management companies operating within the destination area. It may be paid as dividends or profits to outside investors.

Multipliers

Mathematical tools which attempt to encapsulate the total effect of tourism on the economy of a destination area. Tourism mulitipliers can refer to the level of tourism expenditure on the level of output, income and employment of the national or regional economy.

Savings are a form of leakage because they withdraw money from the economy. Taxation – e.g. income tax, company tax, GST – is extracted by governments and also contributes to leakage.

Usually leakage is reduced as the size of the area being measured increases because of the greater ability of the larger area to supply the needs of the industry from within its boundaries.

Multipliers

Tourism **multipliers** attempt to encapsulate the total effect of tourism on the economy of a destination area. They take into account the secondary effects of visitor spending as well as the direct effects.

Multipliers vary according to the economic variables to which they apply (i.e. income, output, employment, value added) and the way they are calculated. There are thus many different multipliers. The so-called 'simple multiplier' is the sum of the direct **effects of tourism expenditure** and the indirect effects. Otherwise, multipliers are usually expressed in terms of a ratio. There are two standard types of 'ratio' multipliers:

$$\text{Type 1 multiplier} = \frac{\text{direct effects} + \text{indirect effects}}{\text{direct effects}}$$

$$\text{Type 2 multiplier} = \frac{\text{direct effects} + \text{indirect effects} + \text{induced effects}}{\text{direct effects}^4}$$

Multipliers are commonly used to assess the impact of tourism expenditure on the economic development of a community in these forms:

1. The sales or output multiplier, which reflects the change in total output of an economy as the result of tourism expenditure.
2. The income multiplier, which measures the change in income generated per dollar of new income earned.
3. The employment multiplier, which reflects a change in the total number of people employed as the result of tourism expenditure.

Output multipliers tend to be quite large. A US example shows a range of output multipliers of 1.5 to 3.0 as against income multipliers of 0.2 to 0.8. They are attractive to those seeking to justify development spending, but they can give false impressions of the true impact of tourism spending because sectors showing the greatest increases in tourism sales (output) are not necessarily those where the highest income and employment effects are generated (Stynes n.d.). In Australia, researchers argue against their use.

Multipliers of the same kind vary considerably from one destination area to another because they are particular to each area, expressing the degree of interdependency between sectors in the economy of each one. They cannot be safely transferred from one destination area to another. Therefore it is not practical to apply national multipliers to states or regions.

Tourism consumption

Consumption is sometimes spoken of as the ultimate end aim of all economic activity (Heilbroner & Thurow 1975). It has two meanings to economists. One is the act of consuming, e.g., a tourist consumes the services of an airline by booking a seat on a flight and travelling on it, and consumes a souvenir boomerang by taking it home and putting it on a mantelpiece. Once consumed in this way the aeroplane seat on a particular flight and the souvenir are no longer objects in the marketplace.

The second meaning of consumption refers to the total expenditure in an economy on

DEFINITIONS

Effects of tourism expenditure
(1) Direct effects are produced by initial spending by tourists. (2) Indirect effects are the production changes resulting from various rounds of re-spending of the direct expenditure, e.g. payments to suppliers as tourism establishments replenish their stocks. (3) Induced effects are the changes in economic activity resulting from household spending of income earned directly or indirectly as a result of tourism spending.

Tourism consumption
(1) The act of consuming a tourism product (e.g. booking a ticket on an airline flight and taking the flight). (2) The total expenditure by tourists in an economy on goods and services which are used up within a specified time.

DEFINITIONS
....

Gross domestic product (GDP)

The total value of all goods and services produced in the Australian economy for the year, after deducting the cost of goods and services used up in the process of production, but before deducting allowances for the consumption of fixed capital.

Gross value added

The gross output of goods and services produced, less the value of intermediate inputs required to produce them. Unlike the GDP, it is measured before net taxes on products are added to the value of industry gross output.

Balance of payments

The result of economic transactions during a period of time (usually a year) between Australia and the rest of the world, showing whether there was a surplus or a deficit on international trading at the end of the period.

goods and services which are used up within a specified time, usually a year. It includes not only consumer goods and services but also the raw materials used in the production system.

Gross domestic product

Gross domestic product, or GDP, is the summary measure of the nation's economic position provided in the National Accounts.[5] It represents the total value of all goods and services produced in the Australian economy for the year, after deducting the cost of goods and services used up in the process of production, but before deducting allowances for the consumption of fixed capital. It consists of three elements:

1. Goods and services produced for consumption
2. Goods produced for investment, or fixed capital formation to produce further goods and services
3. The value of exports.

Tourism figures in all three:

1. Most expenditure by tourists in Australia is consumption spending.
2. Businesses and governments invest in buildings, plant and equipment, roads, airports, sewerage systems to produce more goods and services for tourists.
3. Tourism is an export industry because residents of other countries visit Australia and spend money here (Bull 1995).

Tourism GDP is the total market value of Australian-produced goods and services consumed by tourists after deducting the cost of goods and services used up in the process of production.

Gross value added

Gross value added is the preferred National Accounts measure for the production of industries. One reason is that it enables comparisons between industries free of the effects of product taxes and subsidies on the price of industry outputs.

Gross value added is calculated as the gross output of goods and services produced, less the value of intermediate inputs required to produce them. Unlike GDP, it is measured before net taxes on products are added to the value of industry gross output (Australian Bureau of Statistics 2000a).

Balance of payments

The **balance of payments** records the result of economic transactions during a period of time (usually a year) between Australia and the rest of the world, showing whether there was a surplus or a deficit on international trading at the end of the period.

International transactions are divided into two broad groups:

1. The current account, which is made up of 'visible' transactions (i.e. merchandise

exports, reimports and imports) and 'invisible' transactions (i.e. tourism, banking, insurance and shipping, together with profits earned overseas and interest payments).

2. The capital account, which includes Australia's transactions with the rest of the world in financial assets and liabilities. These include foreign borrowing and lending by Australian residents, equity investments and Australia's foreign reserves.

Travel and tourism is part of international trade and appears on both credit and debit sides of the current account. Investment from overseas in Australian tourism developments are accounted for in the capital account.

The travel account

The **travel account** is an indicator of the degree to which a country attracts overseas visitors compared with its ability to persuade residents not to travel abroad. The balance on the travel account is the difference between the expenditures of residents travelling abroad and the expenditures of overseas visitors.

Money spent by overseas tourists on Australian transport or tourism services is a contribution to our export income, but when Australians travel overseas and make expenditures outside Australia they are, in effect, paying for imports. So there is a net effect which may appear to devalue international tourism's overall worth to the economy.

While tourism promoters sometimes take this view, from an economist's standpoint there is not much to be said for worrying about the travel account. Countries export those goods and services which they produce relatively efficiently and import those products they cannot produce at all or only relatively inefficiently. Overall the balance of payments should be in long-term equilibrium, but otherwise it is to be expected that different sections of the overall account will record deficits or surpluses.

Also, inbound tourism brings in money not previously in the country and creates a platform for employment and investment. On the other hand, money spent on outbound travel has been earned in Australia and tax paid on it. Considerable amounts of travel expenditure are paid before the traveller leaves the country (Bureau of Industry Economics 1979).

Travel account

The difference between the expenditures of residents travelling abroad and the expenditures of overseas visitors.

▓ The Tourism Satellite Account

The most authoritative method for measuring economic impact is the **Tourism Satellite Account** (TSA), which assesses Australian travel and tourism within the national accounting framework, allowing it to be compared with other industries. The emphasis is on the measurement of consumption and the size of the travel and tourism industry, including its contribution to GDP and employment (Australian Bureau of Statistics 2002).

The TSA can:

•   describe and interrelate current production, consumption and investment activities in the economy resulting from tourism demand

Tourism Satellite Account

An economic assessment of Australian travel and tourism within the national accounting framework, allowing it to be compared with other industries.

- measure the domestic supply of tourism products and how they are used – for example as inputs towards final demand or as the final end product.
- track the source and destination of tourism capital
- measure employment by tourism suppliers.

The TSA is a 'satellite' account because it provides the means by which the economic aspects of tourism can be drawn out and analysed separately within the structure of the National Accounts. The latter in themselves do not provide a mechanism for measuring tourism as they do other industries like mining, manufacturing or agriculture. The reason for this was discussed in Chapter 1 – tourism is not defined as are other industries by its products, but by the type of consumer it supplies with goods and services. As a result it is not included in conventional classification of industries and is not identified as a separate industry in the National Accounts.

Those accounts do however include tourism's economic activity and when it is sorted out in the TSA, tourism's contribution to major national accounting aggregates can be determined and compared with other industries.

The National Accounts, which are produced by the Australian Bureau of Statistics, can be thought of in the same terms as the accounts kept by a business to chart its progress and determine its worth. They show the income and expenditure transactions estimated for the nation as a whole over a given period. They also include a balance sheet which measures the net worth of the nation at a point in time, just as a balance sheet does for a company.

Of course, the National Accounts are much more complex: they provide a framework to combine data from many sources (e.g. the number of houses being built, the number of cars produced, the number of tourists arriving from overseas) and present it to describe the overall economic position of the nation.

Australia's National Accounts are produced according to the guidelines of the System of National Accounts endorsed by the United Nations Statistical Commission. Australia's Tourism Satellite Account derives from a satellite accounting system worked out by the World Tourism Organisation.

Producing the Tourism Satellite Account is an expensive and lengthy process. Some of the data on which it relies is available only every three years. For these reasons it is not practicable to produce a full-scale TSA every year. However, it is possible to produce estimates for other years using economic modelling.

The first TSA was produced for the 1997–98 year and released in 2000. The first update produced by economic modelling was for the 2000–01 year and released in 2002. Key results are shown in Table 4.1.

Table 4.1 Tourism's direct effects on the economy

TOURISM SATELLITE ACCOUNTS

1997-98 AND 2000–01

	1997–98	2000–01
Tourism consumption	$58.2 billion	$71.2 billion
Consumption by overseas visitors (exports)	22%	24%
Tourism gross value added	$22.4 billion	$26.3 billion
Tourism GDP	$25.2 billion	$31.8 billion
Tourism's share of GDP	4.5%	4.7%
Employment	513,000	551,000

(Source: Australian Bureau of Statistics (2000a and 2002).)

Notes on the 2000–01 results

International visitors consumed $17.1 billion worth of goods and services produced by the Australian economy. This represented 11.2 per cent of total exports of goods and services.

There are marked differences in consumption patterns by type of visitor. Long distance passenger transportation has been the dominant product consumed by domestic business/ government and international visitors. Shopping, including gifts and souvenirs, and take-aways and restaurant meals were the dominant products bought by domestic household visitors.

The sectors which accounted for the largest share of tourism gross value added were air and water transport (15%), accommodation (11%) and cafés, restaurants and takeaway foods (9%). Tourism gross value added ranked 12th out of the 18 industry divisions. Among those it exceeded were government administration and defence, agriculture, forestry and fishing, communication services and electricity, gas and water supply.

The introduction of the GST was a significant contributor to the high growth rate of Tourism GDP in 2000–01. This is because tourism GDP is measured in market prices, which include all taxes.

The indirect effects of tourism spending were regarded as outside the scope of the Tourism Satellite Account. However, following the release of the TSA figures for 1997–98, the Bureau of Tourism Research (BTR) used them as the basis for an input–output study to calculate the indirect effects of tourism in that year. This showed that they contributed almost as much as the direct effects – $24 billion as against $25 billion for direct Tourism GDP.

This means the total value of the tourism industry to the Australian economy in 1997–98 was estimated at $49 billion, or 9 per cent of GDP.

Tourism indirectly created an additional 341,000 jobs which took the total to 854,000, or 10 per cent of national employment. Of the jobs indirectly created by tourism, 78 per cent were full time. Property and business services accounted for the largest share of indirect employment (91,000 jobs), followed by the manufacturing sector (51,000 jobs). These are broad industrial classifications. 'Property and business services' covers many different types of business, including property owner and developers, equipment hirers, marketing, contract staff suppliers and interior decorators.

The BTR said that the fuller picture showed that behind travel and tourism businesses, there were significant suppliers of goods and services such as food and beverage, cleaning, building maintenance and souvenirs, many of which did not see themselves as being involved in the travel and tourism industry (BTR 2001 and Salma 2002).

Other methods of economic impact analysis

Besides the Tourism Satellite Account, several other methods of economic impact analysis have been employed in Australia.[6] They are:

- input–output models
- computable general equilibrium (CGE) models
- BTR's 1990s methodology
- benefit–cost analysis.

Each of these models is described below.

Input–output models

Input–outputs is a tabular technique that statistically analyses how an economy's industries interact to provide measures of the economic activity generated by tourist spending in terms of four key variables: value added, output, employment and household incomes.

Equations describe the relationships which link the output of one industry with all the other industries in an economy. Therefore, input–output analysis can determine the impact on supplier industries of production changes in any single industry. It can be used to measure the impact of changes in tourism expenditure throughout the economy in a particular year.

It can also be used to measure the changes in an economy brought about by something new, such as the development of a hotel or an attraction or the staging of a festival or major sporting event.

The Australian Bureau of Statistics produces input–output tables from surveys of industries on a national level and makes them available to researchers. The tables are arranged according to the standard ABS industry classification. Other organisations produce tables for states and territories. Victoria, New South Wales, Queensland and Tasmania have produced them for regions. They can be constructed for local government areas.

Computable general equilibrium (CGE) models

These models provide the most detailed and informative modelling technique available for estimating the economic impact of tourism. They are relatively expensive to set up and use, and require significant expertise to evaluate the results (Johnson, R 1999).[7]

They represent the economy as a system of flows of goods and services between sectors, including industry sectors, the household sector, government and the foreign sector. They can measure the same variables as input–output models and also the effects of tourism on prices and availability. The economic impact of tourism is only one of a wide range of issues to which **CGE** models can be applied; others include trade policy, taxation design, economic development and environmental issues.

They treat an economy as a whole, allowing for feedback effects of one sector on another. They can make explicit assumptions about government policy settings, and can incorporate a more realistic set of economy-wide constraints on the supply side of the economy than other models.

They are also capable of picking up the various 'crowding out' phenomena needed to evaluate the net benefits – and intersectoral effects – of growth in tourism demand for Australia (Adams & Parmenter 1991). 'Crowding out' occurs when the expansion of one industry has an adverse impact on others.

The models best known in Australian tourism are called ORANI and MONASH.[8]

The ORANI model dates back to the 1970s and is a comparative static model, referring to the economy in a particular year. The MONASH model, created at the Centre for Policy Studies at Monash University as ORANI's successor, is a more ambitious dynamic model, which can trace out paths of the future for the economy.

The forecasting version of ORANI, called ORANI-F was used for two important studies of the effects of an increase in overseas tourism to Australia conducted for the Bureau of Tourism Research in the early 1990s by Adams and Parmenter – *The Medium-Term Significance of International Tourism for the Australian Economy* (1991) and *The Medium-Term Significance of International Tourism for the State Economies* (1993).

The MONASH model has also been used for economic impact forecasts, for example estimating the impact of the GST for Tourism Council Australia.

BTR's 1990s methodology

The **Bureau of Tourism Research's 1990s methodology** was used for the principal economic impact studies of the Australian economy before the introduction of the Tourism Satellite Account. It linked tourism expenditure to overall expenditure so that tourism's contribution to the Australian economy, in terms of value added, employment, wages,

DEFINITIONS

Computable general equilibrium (CGE) model
A representation of the economy as a system of flows of goods and services between sectors, including industry sectors, the household sector, government and the foreign sector. They can measure the same variables as input–output models and also other effects on tourism, including prices.

BTR's 1990s methodology
A method for calculating the impact of tourism expenditure on the Australian economy before the introduction of the Tourism Satellite Account. It linked tourism expenditure to overall expenditure so that tourism's contribution to the Australian economy could be calculated in terms of its contribution to value added, employment, wages, gross operating surplus and taxation.

gross operating surplus and taxation could be calculated. It was first applied to the 1993–94 year and its methodology and data sources were refined in studies of tourism's effects on the Australian economy for 1995–96 and 1996–97.

The methodology had its limitations compared with the Tourism Satellite Account, which offers a much more detailed examination of tourism's economic contribution than is possible by looking solely at tourism expenditure. In particular, supply-side effects, measured through a series of surveys, are incorporated into the TSA.

Nevertheless the BTR work is still worth studying not only for its results for particular years but because of the detailed examination of the relationship of tourism expenditure to the rest of the economy. Table 1.1 in Chapter 1 is derived from the 1996–97 study. The methodology also demonstrates the use of CGE models, input–output analysis and multipliers.

Benefit–cost analysis

This technique is designed to calculate the social and environmental implications of expenditure as well as the economic factors. Thus it is concerned with valuing the tourism resource from society's point of view, and with the opportunity cost of funding tourism.[9]

It is being used more and more in Australian tourism development, for public sector projects such as airports and private sector developments like resorts and hotels. It may also be used to measure the impact of major events on a community or to consider the economic efficiency or desirability of tourism policies, programs and regulations. It is said to be the second most common model (after input–output analysis) used to analyse tourism developments (Johnson, R 1999).

In economic terms, **benefit–cost analysis** is closely related to the concepts of (a) opportunity and (b) willingness to pay. These state respectively (a) that the real cost of an economic activity is the alternative use of these resources and (b) benefits and costs from the activity are valued at the margin. For example, the real cost of government sponsorship of a special event may be the foregone use of the same amount of money in health or education (Hunn & Mangan 1999).

Benefits are defined in terms of willingness to pay and may include value of outputs, avoided costs, productivity savings, health, social or environmental benefits. Costs are defined in terms of marginal opportunity costs and may include capital and operating expenditures, labour costs and environmental and social impacts (Resource Assessment Commission cited by Gillespie 1999).

For example, in calculating the benefits of constructing a new airport not only the costs of the land, construction of the buildings and runways and subsequent operations should be calculated, but also the losses in welfare resulting from such things as aircraft noise and the despoiling of areas of scenic beauty.

Of course there are problems of measurement. Savings in travelling time can be measured in minutes and hours, and noise nuisance in decibels, but it is difficult to measure such things as the 'amount of pleasure' lost if a particular piece of scenery is removed.

It is helpful to reduce all magnitudes to some common 'unit of account', usually money. Economists have developed ways to do this, including:

- the Willingness to Pay (WTP) method in which survey techniques are used to find out how much households are willing to pay for an environmental asset;
- the Hedonic Pricing Method (HPM) in which environmental resources are valued by considering their effects on the goods and services that have readily observable market prices (e.g. house prices)
- the Travel Cost Method (TCM) which assumes that there is a relationship between the travel costs that a visitor has incurred to visit a tourism site and their valuation of that site (Tribe 1999).[10]

The Travel Cost Method has been used in Australia to estimate the economic value associated with tourism and recreation on public lands, including state forests, national parks and beaches.

IMPACTS ON STATE AND REGIONAL ECONOMIES

The magnitude of the impact of tourism expenditure on a state's or region's economy depends on the combined effect of three factors:

1. the relative size of tourism in the state/region's economy (its percentage contribution to GDP)
2. the growth rate of the tourism sector itself
3. the degree to which the tourism sector buys inputs from other industries in the state/region.

The third factor, which involves leakage, produces a difference between the impact of expenditure on the size of the state/regional economy and the income received by residents because part of the income is transferred outside the region to pay for imports. Some of these imports may come from overseas but most will be from other regions of the country (Harris 1997). As a general rule, leakage becomes more critical as the size and status of the destination area decreases.

The problems caused by leakage are not confined to tourism. The ABS produces estimates of Gross State Products (GSPs) for the states and territories, but calls them 'experimental' and advises users to 'exercise caution' when using them for economic analysis (Australian Bureau of Statistics 1999a). A major reason is leakage, for example allocating shares of expenditure with respect to some industries which operate nationally, including transport and storage, communication services and finance and insurance.

An air ticket provides a tourism example. It may be bought in one state or region for travel to another and a problem arises in allocating the expenditures to where the costs are incurred. The same problem occurs with other long distance transport fares, such as those for coaches, trains and ferries.

The treatment of long distance transport fares also has implications for package expenditure because transport is usually the most costly component of packages. The BTR allocates long distance fare expenditure equally between the two endpoints of a flight or other journey, believing this provides a close approximation to where the impact of the expenditure is primarily felt (Johnson, L 2000). Direct benefits of airfare expenditure include increased regional employment in the air transport industry, while indirect benefits can be found in increased demand for catering services, taxis and so on.

The ABS state and territory estimates for Gross State Products are essentially a dissection of the national estimates. There is no such dissection of the Tourism Satellite Account – not yet anyway – but some state tourism bodies are using the TSA results as a benchmark, reviewing the results from other methodologies against it.

Others have compiled their own 'supply and use' tables and by using these and the general methods adopted for the TSA account can construct their own tourism satellite accounts. Such work is not always the province of tourism organisations. Often treasuries and departments of state development are the main parties. Increasingly work is being commissioned through universities.

IMPACT OF EVENTS AND PARTICULAR TYPES OF TOURISM

As well as measuring the effect of tourism expenditure on the economy of a nation or smaller destination area, economic impact analysis can also be used to measure the effects on an economy of:

- a special event, such as an arts festival or an international motor race
- a particular type of tourism or niche market, such as alpine tourism or the hosting of cruise ship passengers.

Events come in many different forms – festivals, carnivals, sporting events, agricultural shows and so on. Some are part of the folklore of the location in which they are staged, some are of recent invention and some are international, attracted to an Australian location deliberately to increase exposure of a destination area and to lure visitors.

The number of visitors they attract and how much the visitors spend determines their economic impact; the size of the impact depends on the ratio of visitors to the normal population.

Events in major cities are usually associated with a low ratio of additional visitors to population and hence make a relatively small economic impact. This is not so in smaller locations. Harris (1997) instances the Country Music Festival at Tamworth which can double the normal population and has a large economic impact in the period of the festival.

States and regions pay a great deal of attention to measuring the economic impact of events. Partly this is to justify them. Events are highly visible and often controversial with a section of the community, and governments or other public authorities sometimes help meet the costs of staging them and there may be political overtones as a consequence. In both cases, it pays to show the events make a significant contribution to economies in terms of increased output, household income and employment.

But the reason for wanting to know the economic impact of events goes further than justification in the face of possible criticism. Governments at state and local levels now make events part of their economic strategy. For example, in the late 1990s the Victorian Government set out to acquire a minimum of 10 major events which, on a recurring basis every year, would have a continuing impact on the state's economy (Harris 1997). It is essential in those circumstances that financial authorities have an accurate estimate of the economic effect of such a policy.

On a different level it is important that organisers of even small events understand their economic impact. They need to know the return on their investment; it justifies their effort and helps them raise money and plan for the future.

Methods employed

The methods employed to measure economic impact vary but the most common are input–output and benefit–cost analyses.

For smaller events, Arts Victoria has produced a do-it-yourself economic impact assessment kit. It was developed for local festival organisers to determine the impact of their events on the economies of their regions, and may be applied to other events in other places (Morton 2000). Organisers are required to conduct a survey to estimate visitor expenditure as the result of the festival. They must also determine expenditure on the event itself as well as a picture of the regional economy.

An Excel-based program is used for the calculations. Multipliers are applied to the inputs to produce an estimate of the economic impact from the festival in terms of additional regional income and employment, the latter expressed as equivalent full time jobs. Only two multipliers are used – one for Metro Melbourne, which includes Geelong, and one for regional Victoria. This is considered acceptable for Victoria where the regional economic differences are not considered significant enough to make use of a single multiplier impractical. But in some states, Queensland for example, the regional differences are more striking and the Victorian methodology would have to be modified.

Impacts of particular types of tourism

Governments encourage particular forms of tourism – e.g. backpackers, cruise ship, indigenous tourism – but for such policies to succeed it is necessary to have estimates of their economic impact. For example, in developing strategies for the cruise ship sector it matters that the average expenditure per passenger per cruise injected into the Australian economy is twice as great for the coastal compared to the international cruise market (Dwyer & Forsyth 1996). This is because of leakages due to foreign ownership and the foreign sourcing of inputs.

On a state level it matters to policy-makers that manufacturing workers in Melbourne might be as reliant on the alpine industry for their jobs as a storekeeper in Bright (Buckby, Burgan & Molloy 1993). Examining the economic impact of particular types of tourism raises some issues which are similar to those found in event estimates, e.g. visitors may switch from some other kind of tourism and thus limit the net gain.

MEASURING TOURISM EMPLOYMENT

Tourism is an important generator of employment in Australia. It is more labour-intensive on average than other forms of economic activity, largely because of the requirement for personal service. Bull (1995) points to front office situations in travel, accommodation, restaurants and souvenir-selling as examples. Even where automation is available, the personal touch is often the most important factor.

In assessing figures on tourism employment, it is important to know what they mean – what is being included and what is not. This is a return to the discussion in Chapter 1 – defining what is the travel and tourism 'industry' as against determining the range of industries that benefit from tourism.

Three types of employment are generated as a result of the 'total effects' of tourism spending.

1. Direct employment results from the direct effects of visitor expenditure, e.g. for airline tickets, hotel rooms, taxis, souvenirs, food, travel agency services.
2. Indirect employment results from the building of hotels and the expansion of sewerage and water supply facilities, from the supply of food and beverages to hotels and restaurants (e.g. the increased demand for food creates jobs in agriculture), and from the making of skis and tyres and sightseeing boats and many other things that tourists need.
3. Induced employment is the additional employment as the result of local residents re-spending the additional money earned as the result of tourism expenditure.

If the objective is to calculate the impact of tourism expenditure on employment in the economy as a whole then all three categories must be included. The BTR 1990s method-ology did this, the method being to apply the tourism share of expenditure on domestic output to ABS labour force estimates.

The results are shown in Table 4.2.

These figures gave rise to reports at the time of tourism being 'a million-job industry' (Leiper 1999).[11] This is a misinterpretation of what they mean: they are not travel and tourism industry figures but employment throughout the economy as the result of tourists' expenditure.

Table 4.2 Employment from the total effects of tourism

	1995–96	1996–97
Direct employment	694,000	670,800
Indirect employment	334,000	291,100
Total	1,028,000	961,900

(Sources: O'Dea (1997a), p. 19 and Buchanan (1999), p. 29.)

DEFINITIONS

Tourism-characteristic industries
Industries that would either cease to exist in their present form, producing their present product(s), or be significantly affected if tourism were to cease.

The ABS comes closer to the 'industry view' of what constitutes the travel and tourism industry by describing employment in 'tourism-related' industries. Their products are strongly associated with tourism and they are classified into:

- **Tourism-characteristic industries** They would either cease to exist in their present form, producing their present product(s), or would be significantly affected if tourism were to cease.
- **Tourism-connected industries** They are industries other than tourism-characteristic ones, for which a tourism-related product is directly identifiable, and where the products are consumed by, visitors in volumes which are significant for the visitor and/or the producer.

Tourism-connected industries
Industries other than tourism-characteristic ones, for which a tourism-related product is directly identifiable to, and where the products are consumed by, visitors in significant volumes.

Table 4.3 shows tourism employment in these two categories in 1997–98. Not all people in the industries included are employed in tourism-related work, so the table shows first the total number of people employed in each industry, the ratio employed in tourism-related work, and then the total employed in tourism-related work, both as the number of actual people involved and the number it would be if they were all employed full time.

The total employed in tourism-related work – 513,000 (shown in column 4) – is still more than the number employed by the 'true' travel and tourism industry. It includes manufacturing and education which would not be seen as 'primary tourism trades'. Manufacturing is included because of the requirements of an international accounting standard.

Real jobs supported by tourism
Identifiable positions where individuals' knowledge and skills normally are related to attributes of tourism (Leiper 1999).

'Real jobs' in tourism

Leiper (1999) has used the term '**real jobs supported by tourism**' as the defining point for the 'true' industry. These are 'identifiable positions where individuals' knowledge and skills normally are related, in a conscious way, to attributes of tourism' (p. 607).

On this basis he estimated the number of 'real jobs supported by tourism' – full-time and real-time – at about 200,000.[12] This estimate was made before the Tourism Satellite

Account figures, arrived at by a new methodogy, were available. An assessment of Table 4.3 would suggest that his estimate is too low, but his work is a valuable examination of the difficulty in identifying 'tourism employment' as against 'employment generated by tourism'.

Table 4.3 Employment in tourism-related industries, 1997-98					
	TOTAL EMPLOYED PERSONS	FULL-TIME EQUIVALENT EMPLOYED PERSONS	TOURISM INDUSTRY RATIO (a)	TOURISM EMPLOYED PERSONS (b)	TOURISM FULL-TIME EQUIVALENT EMPLOYED PERSONS (c)
	'000	'000	%	'000	'000
Travel agency/tour operator services	25.7	23.2	96.6	24.9	22.4
Road transport & motor vehicle hiring	205.9	184.2	10.8	22.2	19.9
Air & water transport	47.7	43.0	64.2	30.6	27.6
Accommodation	103.2	76.5	89.0	91.8	68.0
Cafés & restaurants	149.0	77.7	29.5	43.9	22.9
Clubs, pubs, taverns & bars	149.0	83.7	18.4	27.4	15.4
Rail transport	39.6	39.4	9.6	3.8	3.8
Manufacturing	1,111.6	1,038.6	3.4	38.2	35.7
Retail trade	1,258.7	876.0	10.8	135.8	94.5
Casinos & other gambling services	33.5	26.4	7.2	2.4	1.9
Libraries, museums and arts	51.2	38.6	16.1	8.2	6.2
Other entertainment services	119.6	85.9	12.0	14.3	10.3
Education	588.2	478.7	3.0	17.8	14.5
Total tourism-related industries	3,882.9	3,071.9	11.9	461.4	343.1
All other industries	4,691.7	4,135.4	1.1	51.5	45.4
Total	8,574.6	7,207.3	6.0	512.9	388.5

(a) The tourism industry ratio is the proportion of the total value added of an industry which is related to tourism.

(b) Tourism employed persons is derived by multiplying the total number of employed persons in an industry by the relevant tourism industry ratio.

(c) Tourism full-time equivalent persons is derived by multiplying the total number of full-time equivalent persons in an industry by the relevant industry ratio.

(Source: Australian Bureau of Statistics (2000a), p. 37.)

Full-time equivalent employment

The concept of full-time equivalent employment (see Table 4.3) involves adjusting the number of employed persons by a measure of full-time employment, to give a result showing what the position would be if there were no part-time employees – if everyone working in each tourism-related business worked full-time.

In the Tourism Satellite Account the result is arrived at by employing a simple formula: the number of part-time employees is multiplied by the average hours they work as a proportion of the average hours worked by full-time workers. The resulting number of full-time equivalent employees is added to the number of full-time employees to give the final figure.

In Table 4.3 the results are particularly noticeable in hospitality businesses, such as accommodation, cafés and restaurants, clubs, pubs and taverns, and in retail trade. All of these employ a substantial proportion of their work force on a part-time basis.

The earlier BTR methodology arrived at a full-time equivalent figure by multiplying the persons directly employed in each industry by average weekly hours worked in that industry and dividing by a standard working week, taken as average hours worked by all persons in all industries.

Leiper challenged the BTR methodology on the basis that it measured full-time equivalent jobs across macroeconomics, but did not relate to real jobs in functioning industries. His contention was that sometimes full time equivalent jobs are not identifiable jobs at all but an economist's measure made up of shares of activity – a person may spend a small portion of their time attending to a tourist's needs and the rest concerned with local residents. Putting together a number of these 'small portions' from different persons adds up to the equivalent of a job.

Everyone involved with supplying goods and services to consumers has at least a fraction of their employment directly supported by tourism, in Leiper's view. But only a minor proportion were employed in 'real jobs' in tourism.

Volunteer employment

While it is difficult to reconcile them in terms of economic impact, the role of volunteers in Australian tourism should be noted in a discussion on tourism employment. For example, an ABS study in the early 1990s shows that 13,200 people were paid to organise fêtes and festivals in Australia at that time, but 411,400 were engaged in the activity without pay. Other categories such as museums, art galleries, art/craft shows, heritage organisations and information centres also have a proportion of volunteers. Even a premier attraction such as Victoria's 'Puffing Billy' train is overwhelmingly staffed by unpaid volunteers – 700 of them to 30 paid staff (Ham 2000).

TAXATION AND TOURISM

Taxation, the compulsory transfer of money from individuals, institutions or groups to governments, is an important part of the fabric of tourism. In the pre-GST days of 1997–98, governments in Australia gained some $3,625 million in taxes from tourism, according to the Tourism Satellite Account. They were in two broad categories: taxes on the products themselves, like sales tax, customs duties, motor vehicle registration, property tax, gaming tax, departure tax, landing charges; and taxes on the productive process and on businesses, like payroll tax.

The direct taxes made up most of what governments charged – $2,785 million. This was a net figure after subsidies for various transportation categories had been deducted. In some cases – long distance and local area passenger transportation and taxis – this led to a negative amount; governments paid out in subsidies more than they collected in taxes. By far the biggest single contributor to government taxation from tourism was fuel (petrol and diesel) which accounted for $1,685 million (Australian Bureau of Statistics 2000a).

It would seem fair that tourism contributes substantially to taxation because governments are expected to pay for infrastructure (everything from roads and bridges to sewerage systems), to market destinations and to provide the economic conditions and the regulatory framework for tourism to flourish. They need money to do all these things.

But there is often plenty of room for argument during the process of devising a tax and making it law. The industry has fought hard at times and won on such issues as Commonwealth government plans to extend the fringe benefits tax to corporate travellers (1993) and a 5 per cent bed tax on hotel accommodation (1995).[13]

In the early 1990s, travel and tourism industry associations and other groups made such a case for the industry being unfairly taxed that the House of Representatives Standing Committee on Banking, Finance and Public Administration spent a year examining the issue. It reported in April 1995 that while there was considerable doubt about whether the impact of taxation was equitable, it was difficult to argue that tourism had been targeted unfairly through the taxation regime or that it should be eligible for special tax breaks and concessions.

The world view

International organisations like the World Tourism Organisation and the World Travel and Tourism Council keep a close watch on taxation affecting the travel and tourism industry around the world. A year-long study of 50 destinations by the WTO Business Council in the 1990s showed that the application of discriminatory or inequitable taxes on tourism could distort the competitive position of the sector, both against other industries and against rival tourism destinations, and might also depress demand for a particular country.

This, in turn, could lead to business failures and job losses, both in the travel and tourism industry and other industries dependent upon it. The study included several examples of governments ending up with less revenue after increasing taxation related to tourism.

The key conclusions reached were:

- entry and exit taxes, including visa fees, should end
- taxes should be on consumption and be transparent to the consumer
- tax changes should be announced well in advance to the travel and tourism industry and the public
- part of tourism taxes should be dedicated to developing the industry
- tax increases decrease demand and can cause a net loss in revenues (World Tourism Organisation 1998).

Taxes in Australia

Australia meets some of the recommendations embodied in the conclusions reached in the WTO study and not others. Tax changes are usually announced well in advance and industry groups are usually given adequate opportunity to state their case. A consumption tax, the Goods and Services Tax (GST), was introduced in July 2000 as part of a New Tax System.

On the negative side, visa fees are applied to some visitors and everybody pays an exit tax.[14] The latter is sugar-coated by calling it an 'international movement charge' and having the airlines and port authorities collect it rather than public servants. In fact it is intended to cover the cost of customs, immigration and quarantine services despite arguments by tourism interests within the bureaucracy that the prime aim of those services is to protect the Australian community as a whole and not to provide a service to travellers (Stroud 2001).

Senior officials in the tourism area of the public service, have tried to persuade the Department of Treasury to the view that tourism more than paid its way for the service it received; in fact it was a profit centre for the government. But to no avail.

'My attempts to get Treasury to accept that funding tourism programs was an investment that yielded tax revenue far in excess of the cost were never accepted' (Stroud).

Taxes are imposed by the three levels of government. Most of the taxes paid directly by tourists (e.g. excise, GST) are federal. At the other two levels the taxes tend to be hidden, i.e. they are paid by the service provider and not shown on the tourist's bill, they are paid for such things as payroll tax and rates for water, sewerage and land.

Some taxes are dedicated to developing the industry. Examples are the charges on passengers at airports. Many of these are run by local authorities or by companies. The charges are used to help pay for the airports and their operations.

Some charges may be temporary, like the levy imposed in late 2001 by the Commonwealth Government to cover employee entitlements following the collapse of Ansett Australia. Such charges are usually opposed by the travel and tourism industry, which sees them as a disincentive to travel.[15]

'User-pays' charges and fees, like the airport examples, make up their own category and include:

- air navigation charges
- airport landing fees
- park entry fees
- vehicle registration fees
- fees for maritime moorings and ramps
- electricity costs which disadvantage island resorts compared with mainland facilities
- special water, sewerage or other selective rates
- entry to national parks
- access to 'white water'
- access to publicly-controlled waterways.

CASE STUDY

The economics of cruise tourism in Australia

A study by Dwyer and Forsyth (1996) raised the possibility that a proportion of increased demand for cruise tourism to Australia from overseas could be at the expense of growth in existing tourism markets and thus reduce the net foreign exchange earnings from cruise ship spending.

On the face of it there is every reason for trying to expand the markets overseas for cruise tourism in Australia. Cruise tourists spend on average much more per day in Australia than other categories of overseas tourists.[16]

However, what passengers spend is only part of the total expenditure. Table 4.4 shows the main categories of cruise ship tourism expenditure with a note on whether the effect is mainly on the national or regional economy.

Only expenditure on goods and services sourced in Australia is relevant to assessing the economic significance of cruise tourism to this country. More than 70 per cent of the cost of a cruise is for fixed operating costs, including crew and capital costs. Foreign companies operate most of the larger cruiseships which use Australian ports,[17] and almost none of these costs is for goods and services supplied by the Australian economy.

Even for a cruise that did not travel outside Australian waters, less than 30 per cent of

Table 4.4 Cruise expenditure and national and regional effect

TYPE OF EXPENDITURE	ITEM PURCHASES	IMPACT
Passenger		
Airfares to and from Australia	Road, rail, air	National
Internal travel	Accommodation, meals	National, significant regional
Add-on expenditure (before and after cruise)	Tours & attractions	National, significant regional
Port expenditure	Meals, tours, attractions, shopping	Mainly port region
Operator		
Port expenditure	State government	Regional and state
	Port charges	Regional
	Towage	Regional
	Stevedoring	Regional
Provedoring	Bunkering	National, small regional
	Stores	Regional and national
	Services (waste disposal, water)	Regional
Crewing	Australian crew	National, significant regional
	Port spending, foreign crew	Regional
Ship maintenance		Regional
Marketing in Australia		National and regional
Taxes in Australia	GST, income tax, customs duty and departure tax	National

(Source: Adapted from L Dwyer and P Forsyth, *National Cruise Shipping Strategy*, Commonwealth Department of Tourism (1995), p. 13.)

the total costs would represent expenditure in Australia. For international cruises, the Australian component would probably be between 10 to 20 per cent. For this reason the authors emphasised the importance of knowing more about the extent to which cruises were a substitute for shore-based holidays. There was a risk of shifts from shore to cruise holidays outweighing in expenditure terms the gains from additional foreign cruise passengers attracted by promotion overseas.

The importance of the operators' costs was demonstrated by the estimates of the economic impact on the Australian economy for two types of cruises, assumed by Dwyer and Forsyth, for the sake of the exercise, to have been taken by the same number of passengers who were all foreigners.

The first cruise was entirely in Australian waters, with a Sydney–Brisbane–Townsville–Cairns itinerary, and it was estimated to have injected $756,000 of foreign exchange into the economy (ship operating costs $517,000; passenger and crew injection $239,000).

The second cruise included South Pacific ports. Only expenditure in the home port of Sydney was relevant to assessing its economic impact on Australia. This was estimated at $367,000 (ship operating costs $195,000; passenger and crew injection $172,000).

INDUSTRY PROFILE

DAVID CRINION GROUP MANAGER OF POLICY AND PLANNING, SOUTH AUSTRALIAN TOURISM COMMISSION (SATC)

My career in tourism has spanned the exciting and demanding period of the past 25 years of Australia's tourism industry growth. During this time I worked principally in the strategic areas of research, policy and planning. In broad terms, this involves high-level strategic planning for the industry (joint government/industry tourism plans) and SATC corporate and business plans. It also involves tourism advocacy to ensure a favourable policy environment so sustainable tourism can flourish.

More specifically, it includes tourism forecasting and economic analysis, competitive analysis, consumer and community attitudes research, product research, marketing evaluation, industry performance measurement, tracking of global, national and local trends, regional strategic planning, policy formulation and advice, sector planning (e.g. cultural tourism, ecotourism, indigenous tourism, wine tourism), development advice and destination management.

How did I get here?

I started my working life as a draftsman with a civil engineering firm while studying town planning part-time at what is now known as the University of South Australia. My early planning experience was in private consulting and in local government. However, after joining the SATC in 1978, I enjoyed the opportunities and challenges of tourism so much that, with the exception of three separate periods each of 12 months (i.e. Executive Development Program, travelling around Australia and a secondment to the Department of Premier and Cabinet working on SA Vision 2020), I have worked in tourism ever since.

What do I like about my job?

Even after 25 years, I still find tourism a fascinating industry. The strategic nature of my work is extremely diverse and connects with and value-adds to so many other aspects of government, private sector and community life. Focusing on the big picture offers opportunities to envision, identify new challenges and opportunities as well as challenging conventional wisdom, while at the project level I enjoy contributing to sound decision-making and continuous improvement through learning from experience. I find particular satisfaction in collaborative initiatives that focus on achieving sustainable and triple bottom line outcomes.

It is important to track people moving around the world, estimate their numbers and expenditure and calculate the effect of that expenditure on economies. It is possible then to see how countries and regions share tourism and, by looking at comparable figures from year to year, determine trends. Forecasters use these figures as a base for their estimates for the future.

In economic terms all tourists are not equal. Some stay longer than others, some spend more per day than others. The issue is yield, the return that businesses and the economy of a destination receive from visitors.

The Australian Bureau of Statistics compiles arrival and departure figures showing the number of visitors who come to the country as well as the number of Australians travelling overseas. Within Australia, the Bureau of Tourism Research conducts surveys to track both international visitors and Australians travelling in the country. A number of state and regional collections of statistics show the characteristics and movements of tourists in various parts of Australia in more detail. The Tourism Forecasting Council produces forecasts intended to provide tourism-related businesses and the government sector with information on which to base investment decisions.

Expenditure is also calculated during tourism studies. The money tourists spend increases the wealth of the areas in which they travel and creates employment. A number of methods can be used to measure the impact of tourists' expenditure as a guide to policy development, planning, investment and marketing. The most authoritative method is the Tourism Satellite Account (TSA), which assesses Australian travel and tourism within the national accounting framework, allowing it to be compared with other industries. Other methods used in Australia are input–output modelling, computable general equilibrium (CGE) modelling, BTR's 1990s methodology and benefit–cost analysis.

Some of these methods are also used to measure the impact of tourism expenditure on state, regional and smaller economies. They can provide estimates of the the effects on an economy of a special event such as an arts festival, and a particular form of tourism or niche market such as alpine tourism.

Tourism is an important generator of employment in Australia. It is important to differentiate between those employed by the travel and tourism industry and those whose employers benefit from tourism spending although their businesses are seen as part of the wider economy.

Leiper (1999) thinks that the number of 'real jobs supported by tourism' is far fewer than the numbers produced by economic impact analysis. He defines 'real jobs' as those which are 'identifiable positions where individuals' knowledge and skills normally are related, in a conscious way, to attributes of tourism'.

The role of volunteers in Australian tourism should be not overlooked, although it is difficult to reconcile them in terms of economic impact. Studies have shown that in one

SUMMARY

category alone, fêtes and festivals, the number of volunteers was in the hundreds of thousands.

Finally, taxation plays an important part in the economics of tourism. A year-long study by the World Tourism Organisation Business Council in the 1990s showed that the application of discriminatory or inequitable taxes on tourism could distort the competitive position of the sector, both against other industries and against rival tourism destinations, and might also depress demand for a particular country. Australia meets some of the recommendations embodied in the conclusions reached in the WTO study and not others.

Taxes are imposed by the three levels of government. Most of those paid directly by tourists (e.g. excise, GST) are federal. At the other two levels the taxes tend to be hidden, that is they are paid by the service provider and not shown on the tourist's bill (e.g. such things as payroll tax and rates for water, sewerage and land).

QUESTIONS

1. How is world tourism tracked and measured?
2. Why is destination yield important? What problems did Australia experience in the early 1990s? What can be done to ensure satisfactory yield?
3. In assessing tourist expenditure how would you describe direct, indirect and induced effects? Is it necessary to attempt to measure all three?
4. Do you think the travel account has any value in determining a country's tourism performance?
5. Why is the Tourism Satellite Account superior to other methods of measuring the economic impact of tourism?
6. Think of two ways in which environmental resources can be valued by relating them to something else which has a 'dollar and cents' value. Can you think of examples of when and where these two methods have been used in Australia?
7. Is the reliability of economic impact analysis much the same for a region as for a state?
8. Why is it important that the economic impact of events and niche markets should be measured?
9. Do you think published figures for travel and tourism employment are accurate? What are 'real jobs' in tourism?
10. Has the Commonwealth Department of Treasury generally been sympathetic to tourism in respect to taxation? If not, what are some of the effects of its attitude?

THE SOCIOCULTURAL INFLUENCES OF TOURISM

LEARNING OBJECTIVES

Understand key concepts in relation to tourism impacts: environment, heritage, conservation, sustainable tourism.

Examine the impacts that tourism can make on host communities.

Investigate tourist–host relationships, including the marketing factor.

Appreciate the international viewpoint on tourism's sociocultural influences–WTO's Code of Ethics and the International Charter on Cultural Tourism.

Understand that tourism does have positive sociocultural effects and that adequate tourism management is essential to achieving the best results.

Examine Doxey's sociocultural impact model and some reservations about it as the result of more recent research.

Review community reaction to the Indy car event on the Gold Coast as a case study.

UNDERSTAND
THE MEANING OF:

- *heritage*
- *World Heritage Area*
- *National Estate*
- *conservation*
- *sustainable tourism*
- *ecologically sustainable tourism*
- *sustainable development*
- *demonstration effect (acculturation)*
- *marginal person*
- *cultural commodification*
- *ICOMOS*
- *Irridex*

TOURISM HAS COSTS AS WELL AS BENEFITS

In the last chapter it was shown that tourism brings economic benefits to a nation or a smaller community. It creates wealth and jobs. Tourism continues to grow and we live in a society where growth is the measure of success. The individual businesses serving tourists – the airlines, coach companies, hotels, restaurants, convention organisers, attractions and shops – need profits to exist and expand. Therefore, they constantly look for ways to attract more customers.

Governments approve of this; they are anxious to see tourism increased because it can bring with it income, foreign exchange, employment and a means of spreading prosperity to otherwise poor or economically declining regions.

But there are costs to having more tourism and these have to be weighed against the benefits. Much attention was given in the last decades of the 20th century to the dangers from tourism to the natural environment, of visitors sometimes polluting or destroying the very things that attract them – the shorelines, the rainforests and the mountains.

Tourism also changes host communities because it alters attitudes, expectations and personal habits. These changes may bring unexpected tensions. And while tourism can help preserve the diversity of cultures, it can, if badly handled, diminish them or 'McDonaldise' them – that is, destroy what makes them different so that they seem the same as everywhere else. Sustainability has become a word of great importance: it means preserving cultural treasures as well as natural so they may be passed on to future generations.

▓ Limits to growth

Growth has built-in limits and these will become increasingly pressing in the future. In Australia tourism's growth is already causing problems for some smaller communities. The case study on Byron Bay in Chapter 7 is an example. But when measured against the size of the continent, tourism in Australia is relatively small compared with other parts of the world and overall its effects much less noticeable. The problems are more widespread and acute elsewhere. In opening the 1994 ITB tourism trade fair in Berlin, the then Secretary-General of the World Tourism Organisation, Antonio Enríquez Savignac, spoke of the problems – and the responsiblity for managing them:

In recent years there are an increasing number of warning signs: the oversaturation and deterioration of some destinations, heritage sites and facilities; the overwhelming of some cultures and local populations; more bottlenecks in transportation facilities; and a growing resentment by residents in some of our host destinations.

We need to realise that there are limits: limits to the number of visitors in the same place at the same time; limits to the patience and welcome of our hosts; and limits to the number of persons who can visit our national resources (World Tourism Organisation 1994).

The meaning of environment

A number of concepts relevant to this chapter overlap with the subject of the next chapter which deals with the impact of tourism on the natural environment. One of them is the word '**environment**' itself. It means the aggregate of surrounding things, conditions or influences (Macquarie Dictionary 1997, p. 711). It is often used to mean only natural resources – land, air, water, flora and fauna – but its wider meaning includes people, their creations, and the social, economic and cultural conditions that affect their lives.

The environment can be considered to have three components:

1. **The natural environment**. This includes the air, land, sea, lakes, rivers, clear light, climate, flora and fauna.
2. **The built environment**. The urban fabric – buildings, infrastructure such as roads and bridges, open space and elements of townscape.
3. **The sociocultural environment**. This includes the values, beliefs, behaviours, morals, arts, law and history of communities (Lerner, cited in Mathieson & Wall 1982; Green & Hunter 1991).

The subject of this chapter is the sociocultural environment and the way tourism influences it. '**Sociocultural**' is a hybrid term which, as Gartner (1996) observes, encompasses change to both the social organisation and the culture of a group of people. Social change comes first but it is not easy to pick the point where it results in cultural change. Most studies do not try; they review impacts from a 'sociocultural' point of view.

In the early part of the chapter, there are references to other parts of the environment because some concepts cover more than one part. Three such concepts are heritage, conservation and sustainable tourism.

Heritage

Heritage is about a nation's or community's collective inheritance: what was here when we came on this part of the earth, what nature has bequeathed us and what has been left by those who have gone before us; not only dwellings and public buildings and monuments, but also language, paintings and music, beliefs and symbols, and ways of doing things.

DEFINITIONS

Environment
The aggregate of surrounding things, conditions or influences with three components (a) natural environment (air, land sea, climate, flora, fauna; (b) built environment (buildings, infrastructure, elements of townscape); and (c) the sociocultural environment (values, beliefs, arts, laws, history).

Sociocultural
A term used to indicate impacts bringing about change to the social organisation of a group of people as well as more fundamental reorganisation of a society's culture.

Heritage
What may be inherited. A nation's collective inheritance includes what nature bequeathed it and what has been left by earlier generations.

Heritage also refers to the things we want to keep because some form of value has been ascribed to them. It encompasses landscapes, historic places, sites and built environments, as well as biodiversity, collections, past and continuing cultural practices, knowledge and living experiences.

It follows that heritage tourism is 'tourism centred on what we have inherited, which can mean anything from historic buildings, to art works, to beautiful scenery' (Yale, cited in Garrod & Fyall 2000).

Common forms of heritage are places, artefacts, people and practices:

- a place, such as a national park or historic building
- an artefact, such as an Aboriginal painting or convict uniform
- people, who might be an indigenous tribe or regulars at a country bar
- practice, such as a seasonal whale migration or an annual camel race (McArthur 2000).

McArthur has pointed out changing needs and expectations have altered the Australian perception of heritage in some respects. Post-war migration from Europe and, more recently, Asia has led to a reduction in the significance of British heritage ideals and values. In addition, the resurgence in presenting Aboriginal culture has led to a far greater appreciation of indigenous cultural values.

Heritage has thus become a means by which a wide range of groups and communities within Australian society are able to assert their identities within broader national cultures. Societies, in turn, have grasped various symbols, icons and mythologies in order to try and fashion a collective national identity.

While heritage can be thought of as either cultural or natural in character, some sites (e.g. Kakadu National Park in the Northern Territory) may be significant in terms of both.

World Heritage List

Heritage must be protected. On a world scale this is done by entering natural and cultural properties of 'outstanding universal value', and which meet the strict criteria of the World Heritage Convention, on a list compiled by the World Heritage Committee. This convention was adopted by the General Assembly of the United Nations Educational, Scientific and Cultural Organisation (UNESCO) in Paris in 1972 and Australia was one of the first countries to ratify it in 1974. Signatories to the convention are required to identify, protect, conserve, present and transmit to future generations the properties entered on the list.

As of June 2001, there were 690 properties on the World Heritage List, most of them cultural assets. They included the Taj Mahal, the Great Wall of China, the pyramids in Egypt and the Acropolis in Greece. Most of Australia's 14 properties are natural wonders, though some also have cultural values. The Australian World Heritage Areas are shown below, with the year of their inscription on the list.

1981 Great Barrier Reef

1981 Kakadu National Park

1981 Willandra Lakes Region

1982 Tasmanian Wilderness

1982 Lord Howe Island Group

1987 Uluru–Kata Tjuta National Park

1987 Central Eastern Rainforest Reserves

1988 Wet Tropics of Queensland

1991 Shark Bay, Western Australia

1992 Fraser Island

1994 Australian Fossil Mammal Sites (Riversleigh/Naracoorte)

1997 Heard and McDonald Islands

1997 Macquarie Island

2000 The Greater Blue Mountains Area

(Source: www.unesco.org)

The National Estate and the National Heritage List

The Commonwealth Government administers three major lists of places it wants to preserve for future generations – the National Estate, the National Heritage List and the Commonwealth Heritage List. The National Estate goes back to 1976 following the setting up of the Australian Heritage Commission while the National Heritage List and Commonwealth Heritage List were provided for in legislation passed in 2003. This also abolished the Australian Heritage Commission. At that time the Register of the National Estate contained the names of more than 13,000 places in three categories – natural environment, historical and indigenous. Responsibility for the register was transferred to a new body, the Australian Heritage Council.

The 2003 legislation was designed to improve the way the Commonwealth Government protects Australia's heritage. It amended the Environment Protection and Biodiversity Act of 1999 to identify, conserve and protect places of national heritage significance. The National Heritage List was established to name places or groups of places considered of outstanding significance to the nation chosen through a public nomination process. The Commonwealth Heritage List was established to protect and manage in a systematic way heritage places under Commonwealth control.

The National Estate and the National Heritage List are significantly different, though it is possible for sites to be on both lists. Places can be thought of as of world, national, state/territory or local significance and the National Estate consists of places at all those levels. The National Heritage List is to consist of places of national significance only but it could include places of significance to Australians who are not in Australia. Anzac Cove at Gallipoli has been cited as a possible candidate for inclusion on that basis.

Overseas heritage places will only be listed with the agreement of the country in which they are located.

The Australian Heritage Council is an independent body of heritage experts established to assess places nominated for the National Heritage List and the Commonwealth Heritage List and to advise the Minister for the Environment and Heritage on conserving and protecting listed places.

State and territory governments have much of the responsibility for the day-to-day management of heritage and environmental issues. Each has an agency which looks after its national parks, wildlife and other types of conservation reserves.[1] Most have separate agencies for heritage matters. In addition there are community-based National Trusts in each state and territory, which have lists largely made up of buildings, although they also include some natural and Aboriginal places (Australian Heritage Commission 1994 and 1998, Simmons 1996, www.environment.gov.au).

Natural, indigenous and historic heritage assets provide the basis for a big proportion of Australia's tourism products. In particular, they provide the opportunity for the development of regional products. There is concern that rural and regional heritage is being depleted where rural economies are declining.

Conservation

The planned management of specific sites and places and natural and cultural resources in general. It implies that some use and controlled change can take place if the basic integrity of the site, place or resource is maintained.

▓ Conservation

Conservation refers to the planned management of specific sites and places and natural and cultural resources in general. It does not necessarily mean categorical preservation, which dictates no change of the site, place, or resources. Conservation sometimes includes restoration to an original condition. It implies that some use and controlled change can take place if the basic integrity of the site, place or resource is maintained (Inskeep 1991).

People interested in conservation may not necessarily be environmentalists, although they are usually sympathetic to their aims. Conservationists are not concerned with humans, though they may be with things built by humans, such as historic buildings or monuments. They care about non-humans (wildlife) and their habitat. Environmentalists are concerned about humans and human habitat (Allaby 1986).

Sustainable tourism

All forms of tourism development, management and operations that maintain the environmental, social and economic integrity and well-being of natural, built and cultural resources.

▓ Sustainable tourism

According to the World Tourism Organisation (2000), **sustainable tourism** 'includes all forms of tourism development, management and operations that maintain the environmental, social and economic integrity and well-being of . . . natural, built and cultural resources'.

Sustainability itself is closely related to survival; it means living within the boundaries of the biophysical environment. It requires that environmental resources be preserved so that they may be passed on intact to future generations.

The term ecologically sustainable tourism (EST) is also used. Moscardo, Morrison and Pearce (1996) relate its principles to two major forces in modern tourism: the first calling for greater responsibility towards people and places that act as hosts for tourism and the second for greater responsibility towards individual tourists. They believe it is best defined through an understanding of its goals and a description of its characteristics.

The Australian Government Ecologically Sustainable Development Working Group described those characteristics in 1991 as:

- Tourism which is concerned with the quality of experiences.
- Tourism which has social equity and community involvement.
- Tourism which operates within the limits of the resource – this includes minimisation of impacts and use of energy and the use of effective waste management and recycling techniques.
- Tourism which maintains the full range of recreational, educational and cultural opportunities within and across generations.
- Tourism which is based upon activities or designs that reflect the character of a region.
- Tourism which allows the guest to gain an understanding of the region visited and which encourages guests to be concerned about and protective of the host community and environment.
- Tourism which does not compromise the capacity of other industries or activities to be sustainable.
- Tourism which is integrated into local, regional and national plans (Moscardo, Morrison & Pearce 1996).

Sustainable development

Development can be defined as the modification of the environment and the application of human, financial, living and non-living resources to satisfy human needs and improve the quality of human life. **Sustainable development** means achieving growth in a manner that does not deplete the natural and built environment and preserves the culture of the local community (Organisation of American States 1997).

IMPACTS ON HOST COMMUNITIES

Sociocultural impacts result whenever different cultures come in contact. They can be thought of as occurring when people of markedly different races, backgrounds and/or experiences meet through tourism – such as when somebody from a Western society visits a developing country. But it can also happen in Australia when somebody from one state (or smaller community) visits another. For example, during a football final 'out-of-towners' may be identified by the way they behave as well as the club colours they are wearing.

Whatever its origin, when tourism reaches a certain level it changes the destination for the people who live there. As Ringer (1996) says, developing and marketing communities as tourism destinations rarely comes without human costs, including a transfiguration of the inhabitants' social history and the dynamics of their place.

Sustainable development
Achieving growth in a manner that does not deplete the natural and built environment and preserves the culture of the local community.

The range of possible impacts on a host community is considerable, involving changes in value systems, individual behaviour, family relationships, collective lifestyles, safety levels, moral conduct, creative expressions, traditional ceremonies and community organisations.

Tourism may bring pollution and overcrowding to the streets, problems with parking, and noise. It may increase crime and prostitution. It may cause changes to a community's social structures, its culture and its traditional ways of doing things.

Changes can be good or bad, however. If tourism brings prosperity to a community – better incomes, education, employment opportunities, and local infrastructure – and provides opportunities for enhancing the local culture, all without unwelcome dislocation of people's lives, then it is of obvious benefit.

On the broad scale, the expansion of international tourism has increased the contact among different societies and cultures in a way it would have been difficult to comprehend before World War II. The consequences have been profound and so have the reactions.

> *To some, this interaction threatens to destroy traditional cultures and societies and to others it represents an opportunity for peace, understanding and greater knowledge among societies and nations* (Brunt & Courtney, 1999).

WTO's code addresses issues

The World Tourism Organisation and other international tourism organisations have recognised social and cultural impacts as critical issues which affect tourism's future. In 1997, the WTO called a meeting in Manila to discuss how to maximise the positive social impacts of tourism while reducing its negative effects around the world.

In broad terms there is not much argument about what should happen, though making it happen is another matter. The WTO returned to the subject in its 1999 'Global Code of Ethics for Tourism' which makes these points.

- Tourism activities should be conducted in harmony with the attributes and traditions of the host regions and countries and in respect for their laws, practices and customs.
- The host communities on the one hand, and local professionals on the other, should acquaint themselves with and respect the tourists who visit them and find out about their lifestyles, tastes and expectations; the education and training imparted to professionals contribute to a hospitable welcome.
- Tourists and visitors have the responsibility to acquaint themselves, even before their departures, with the characteristics of the countries they are preparing to visit; they must be aware of the health and security risks inherent in any travel outside their normal environment and behave in such a way as to minimise those risks.

- Travel for purposes of religion, health, education and cultural or linguistic exchanges are particularly beneficial forms of tourism, and deserve encouragement.

- Tourism policies and activities should be conducted with respect for artistic, archeological and cultural heritage, which they should protect and pass on to future generations; particular care should be devoted to preserving and upgrading monuments, shrines and museums as well as archeological and historic sites which should be widely open to tourist visits; encouragement should be given to public access to privately-owned cultural property and monuments, with respect for the rights of their owners, as well as to religious buildings, without prejudice to normal needs of worship.

- Financial resources derived from visits to cultural sites and monuments should, at least in part, be used for the upkeep, safeguarding, development and embellishment of this heritage.

- Tourism activity should be planned in such a way as to allow traditional cultural products, crafts and folklore to survive and flourish, rather than causing them to degenerate and become standardised.

- Tourism policies should be applied in such a way as to help to raise the standard of living of the populations of the regions visited and meet their needs; the planning and architectural approach to and operation of tourism resorts and accommodation should aim to integrate them, to the extent possible, in the local economic and social fabric; where skills are equal, priority should be given to local manpower.

- Tourism professionals, particularly investors, should . . . deliver, with the greatest transparency and objectivity, information on their future programs and their foreseeable repercussions and foster dialogue on their contents with the populations concerned (World Tourism Organisation 1999c).[2]

Tourist–host relationships

It will be noted that the code places obligations on host communities as well as the tourists and tourist professionals. Sometimes host communities try to exploit tourists or they may react forcefully to what they don't like about visitors. As Chamberlain (1996a) observes, by nature, people are strong believers in the 'not in my backyard' philosophy. They don't like crowds of visitors invading their territory, pushing them aside, inflating prices, congesting the place, imposing their values and, generally, changing things. However, the more a local economy becomes dependent on tourism, the greater the degree of local involvement in the travel and tourism industry becomes. After all, the host community is expected to provide services for tourists and that level of service will become increasingly intensive as tourism increases. The chapter case study indicates considerable differences within a community in attitudes towards tourism depending on whether or not a person is involved with the travel or tourism industry or derives a direct benefit from tourism.

As Gartner points out, tourism may be only one of a number of factors bringing about sociocultural change. There are global forces which are redefining and shaping just about everyone's lives. There may be other forces of change than tourism more particular to the area, such as population changes or specific economic problems. Nevertheless, there is a special quality about the impact of tourism because it brings two cultures into contact and when their norms and standards differ change can result.

Often there is not much residents can do about it. If tourists are not comfortable with the experience of visiting a particular area they can leave. On the other hand members of a host community usually have to stay where they are for financial or sentimental reasons; they have to put up with change whether they like it or not.

Tourists exist in a 'non-ordinary world' at the destination. Tourist cultures are formed by observing the behaviour of other tourists who preceded them. If the tourist culture is based on play, pleasure and the free spending of money which makes it all possible, then there is a high degree of difference between the tourists' non-ordinary world and the ordinary world of their hosts. The tourist culture may be regarded as the dominant culture. The inability of host societies to become part of the tourist culture – 'to free themselves from ordinary life' – can cause negative reactions throughout the host society (Gartner 1996).

The marketing factor

Marketing may be a factor in relationships between host communities and tourists. It is the marketers who project images of destination areas and arouse the expectations of tourists with their selling message. The marketers may be the destination marketing organisation of the area itself or local companies which have gone out into the marketplace to sell their services. Opportunities exist for the host community to influence their messages and there is little excuse for them if they overstate the attractions of the destination area or promote traffic flows beyond its capacity.

But often the communication linkage is provided by marketers who are not responsible directly to the destination area and they have their own reasons for wanting to promote increased tourism. They may project tourism images host communities do not want used or which lead to unjustified expectations. They may ignore difficulties the host community has in coping with tourism. This happened to Byron Bay. The Shire Council perceived its problems were sufficient to ask Tourism New South Wales to stop promoting it. The request was refused (Chapter 7).

The style of promotion can encourage a particular tourist culture and it is often in the interests of the host community to influence it. Marketers provide 'the cues of behaviour' which form the tourist culture even before the tourist arrives at the destination (Gartner 1996). When the marketers are outside the destination the host community may have little or no opportunity to put their points of view.

Types of changes within the community

The impact of tourism on host communities is examined under these headings.

- Impact on population structure
- Transformation of occupation structure
- Transformation of values
- Influence on daily life.[3]

Impact on population structure

Increased tourism will require new people to work in tourism establishments and to run the extra services needed. Some of them will be locals who change from other jobs or decide to stay in the area instead of leaving because of the lack of employment opportunity, but others will come from elsewhere.

The result is not only an increase in the population but a change in its composition. Tourism employment can be age and sex selective. An example can be seen in a study in Queenstown, New Zealand, a major resort area: it showed that compared with the national average the population had more residents aged from 20 to 30, fewer under-15-year-olds and a larger proportion of females (Pearce 1989).

Transformation of occupation structure

Job opportunities in tourism will attract people from other occupations. In regional communities, those occupations often have been directly concerned with agriculture or in a servicing role connected with agriculture. Certain types of jobs – e.g. housekeeping in motels – often attract housewives who previously did not work.

Seasonality affects employment and this may be socially disruptive to a community as a significant proportion of the workforce comes and goes according to tourism demand.

Transformation of values

An increased population, with new people with different attitudes attracted to a destination area, can alter the mix of values in a destination area. As tourism – and the population – rapidly increased in Far North Queensland in the 1980s, the Cairns City Council said:

> *We do have concerns with social consequences . . . the major issue that tourism has brought to this area has been a divergence of the community. There are locals who describe themselves as the people who have lived here for yonks, and do not want to see things change. There are the newer locals who have come into town and who now are permanent residents but who are going at 100 miles an*

hour to provide services to tourism (Industries Assistance Commission 1989, pp 184–185).

Influence on the values held by a community from tourists – rather than those working in tourism – can take a number of forms. Gartner lists the demonstration effect, marginal person and cultural commodification.

Demonstration effect

Acculturation

A theory which assumes that when two cultures interact the dominant one overpowers the weaker one, bringing about changes within the weaker culture.

This is another name for the process of **acculturation**, a theory that assumes that when two cultures interact the dominant one overpowers the weaker one, bringing about changes within the weaker culture.

> *Certain aspects of one culture are adopted by another, resulting in the emergence of a new culture based more on the patterns of behaviour of the strong or dominant culture. It is the reactions to acculturation which result in sociocultural impacts* (Gartner 1996, p. 161).

It is most noticeable when there is a significant difference between the economic status of hosts and tourists: members of the host community are attracted by the tourist culture because of the emphasis on pleasure and the money to indulge it. As a result, residents may adopt new dress styles and begin eating food and drinking beverages favoured by tourists. However, as Pearce (1989) points out, this may not be a one-way process: on their return home tourists may retain a taste for food and drink they had while they were away and seek out ethnic restaurants or food stores.

Marginal person

One who has rejected his or her ordinary life as the result of trying to fully assimilate into the tourist culture.

Marginal person

The **marginal person** is one who has rejected his or her ordinary life as the result of trying to fully assimilate into the tourist culture, but full assimilation is unlikely because it is 'often based on excessive play behaviour made possible by large amounts of money' (Gartner 1996, p. 169).

The marginal person does not adopt a set of norms and standards acceptable to either culture and his or her behaviour is considered deviant by both groups, further separating him/her from either culture.

Cultural commodification

Packaging cultural events for sale, fitting them into a tourist's time frame, or staging them in an area to suit tourists rather than the event itself. Commodification also occurs when handicrafts are produced to sell to tourists, though traditional manu-facturing methods are not used.

Cultural commodification

This means packaging cultural events for sale, fitting them into a tourist's time frame, or staging them in an area to suit tourists rather than the event itself. **Commodification** also occurs when handicrafts are produced to sell to tourists, though traditional manufacturing methods are not used.

Influence on daily life

Besides the influence of tourism on values and the way people think, tourism can produce very tangible problems for host communities which affect the way people go about their daily lives.

People congestion

A small community can be overwhelmed by a sudden arrival of comparatively large numbers of tourists. Chamberlain gives the example of a cruise ship unloading hundreds of passengers at a small island off the coast of Sumatra, visited because of its ancient culture and beautiful scenery.

> These passengers live mainly in cities and are not exactly nature lovers or culture buffs. They are there for possibly eight or ten hours and then they are gone. This is a scenario for negative social and environmental impacts unless the whole situation is very carefully and sensitively managed (Chamberlain 1997, p. 2).

People congestion also affects Australian communities, most noticeably relatively small seaside towns during the summer or on special occasions such as New Year's Eve. The problem can be ameliorated by visitor management techniques (Chapter 11).

Traffic congestion

Traffic congestion is a more general problem. It usually takes one or more of three forms: the conflict between pedestrians and cars, traffic overload at key points and the lack of sufficient parking space. As with people congestion, it can occur during a whole season at places like resort areas or at certain times for events, such as New Year's Eve or a festival. To an extent, at least, it can also be managed.

Overloading of infrastructure

Inadequacy of sewerage systems is one of the most common – and regrettably most obvious – infrastructure problems faced by authorities attempting to cater for increased tourism. However, water and energy may also be restricted and the solutions required to provide for extra demand may also be beyond the capacity of local communities. The result is supply failures, pollution and health hazards.

Change in land prices

Tourism can force land prices up because it needs land for accommodation and other facilities. One result may be that land is taken out of primary production. Another can be the displacement of people from low-cost accommodation. The Industries Assistance Commission, during its 1989 hearings on travel and tourism, considered reports of evictions of pensioners in Sydney because of tourism, of low-income earners displaced in Brisbane because of World Expo 88, and cases of homelessness in Cairns as the result of increased tourism.

Land use loss

The use of land for tourism purposes may be at the expense of another kind of amenity enjoyed by at least part of the local population. For example, a decision to build a tourism complex on parkland or along an otherwise deserted stretch of coastline could cause loss of amenity for local residents who used the land for recreation before the complex was built.

Tourism growth in the Great Barrier Reef World Heritage Area is said to have resulted in loss of access to traditional Aboriginal hunting grounds and damage to significant cultural sites and values (Tourism Review Steering Committee 1997).

Losses to other businesses

The development of tourism may cause other kinds of business activity to suffer losses. For example, the Queensland Commercial Fishermen's Organisation told the 1989 Industries Assistance Commission inquiry that the use of wetlands and mangrove swamps for tourism developments imposed direct costs on the fishing industry, because those areas included fish habitats which were an integral part of the marine lifecycle.

Architectural pollution

Architectural pollution

Inappropriate designs for hotels, terminals, theme parks and other attractions and facilities which disturb the social and cultural integrity of the landscape.

Inappropriate designs for hotels, terminals, theme parks and other attractions and facilities can disturb the social and cultural integrity of the landscape by creating **architectural pollution**. This is not rare. Buildings for tourism purposes are often built to attract attention and/or to make the most money out of a particular land area. There has often been a failure to integrate resort infrastructure with aesthetically pleasing characteristics of the natural environment. Large, dominating hotel buildings are often out of scale and clash with their surroundings.

Mathieson and Wall (1982) note that the failure to incorporate adequate environmental considerations into the architectural designs of hotels and other tourism buildings can affect their financial performance – design and ambience have economic value because the attractiveness of physical structures is important to their success.

Peter Goulding, a tourism businessman and experienced international marketer, became concerned about architectural trends in Cairns in the 1990s. Among other things, he protested about hotels and motels built with little or no cognisance of the unique environment and the pressure for more high-rise hotels and marinas.

'We don't want pink buildings and garish road signs,' he said in a letter to the Far North Queensland Promotion Board in 1995. 'We do want small friendly accommodation establishments where interchange amongst guests and with hosts supports and strengthens "natural" touristic experiences.' (Goulding 1995).

Changes in urban fabric

Tourism buildings may cast shadows or take away views. Access to beaches may be blocked, the ecology of an area may be altered. Ribbon development and sprawl may result from overall design failure, resulting in new roads and pavements, bridges and round-abouts. This applies particularly to coastal resort development where it is desired to take advantage of the beach as a primary resource.

Crimes against tourists

Successful destinations make money out of tourism and crime follows money. A study by Kelly (1993) showed significantly higher crime rates in Cairns and the Gold Coast than in other parts of Queensland. Cairns ranked high in offences against both persons and property, while offences against property were much more frequent on the Gold Coast.

He cited a report by Clark (1988) that crime increased in Cairns between 1976 and 1987 by 217 per cent while the population increased by 64 per cent. Later statistics had confirmed that the trend continued in the 1990s.

Crotts (1996) has pointed out some of the reasons why tourists are suitable targets for criminals: they are perceived to have items of wealth such as cameras, cash and credit cards; they are relatively easy to observe due to differences in dress and types of places they visit; they are often in environments easy for an offender to get to them as well as escaping once the crime has occurred (e.g. motel rooms that open to dimly lit parking areas, parking areas themselves, highways).

Kelly noted the failure of tourists to take normal precautions with their persons and property, which he considered may be attributed, in part, to the marketing of tourist destinations, which are often described as virtual paradises, friendly and hospitable, and offering opportunities for romantic experiences.

He also thought some of the malicious damage offences committed on the Gold Coast and at Cairns could reflect community resentment over the impacts of tourism on the local community. At the time of his study, there had been reports of concern and dissatisfaction in the Cairns and Gold Coast communities over the perceived dominance of the local tourism industry by Japanese interests, and practices (e.g. importation of Japanese tour guides, and inducements to tour guides to take visitors to Japanese gift shops).[4]

Offences by tourists

Offences frequently attributed to tourists include vandalism, drug abuse and disorderly behaviour, which is often alcohol-induced. This kind of behaviour often accompanies annual hallmark events such as music festivals and motorcycle rallies.

People on holiday are likely to drop some of their inhibitions, a process which Kelly has noted may be stimulated by more than normal consumption of alcohol and drugs. He found that Cairns demonstrated by far the highest concentration of drug-related offences of any Queensland police district between 1986 and 1990, followed by Mount Isa and the Gold Coast.

A high level of drug offences at a tourist destination may or may not be primarily attributable to visitors. It can also be caused by people attracted to live in areas with attractive settings as part of their search for an alternative lifestyle.

THE POSITIVE SOCIOCULTURAL EFFECTS OF TOURISM

Some of the positive sociocultural results of tourism were referred to early in the chapter but the long list of possible negative consequences discussed since then may make it appear that the scales are inevitably weighted against tourism.

This is not so. Detailing negative impacts is as much a warning against bad tourism management as anything else. The second part of this book deals with management and it should be read with the solutions to possible problems in mind.

There are a number of issues involved. One is the mitigation of visitor impacts and the measures to achieve it. Some measures involve direct visitor controls, others are directed at the way development is planned or tourism marketed.

Managing cultural resources is an allied issue. There are a host of public and private organisations involved with managing Australia's cultural heritage. In general, they take a positive view of tourism. Few communities reject tourism. Most embrace it, primarily because it brings wealth and jobs. The management tests are to ensure that locals benefit from both: that they get their share of jobs including the better paid ones, that as much of the money spent by tourists stays within the community (i.e. it is not 'leaked' to outsiders) and that it is shared by as many as possible.

Tourism can help nurture cultural activity. The pros and cons were detailed in an International Cultural Tourism Charter, produced in 1999 by ICOMOS, the International Council on Monuments and Sites. The charter acknowledges that excessive or poorly-managed tourism can threaten cultural heritage and living cultures. But it also notes that tourism is increasingly appreciated as a positive force for natural and cultural conservation. It can capture the economic characteristics of heritage and harness them for conservation by generating funding, educating the community and influencing policy (www.unesco.org/culture/development/highlights/decades/tourism).

Zeppel and Hall (1991) regard the involvement of tourism with the arts in general as a two-way benefit of great potency. Citing Johnson (1983), they say:

To the world of tourism, the arts bring style, culture, beauty and a sense of continuity of living. They interpret cultural change, convert sound to music, turn colour and language into painting and theatre. In commercial terms, the arts revitalise the tourism product, sharpen its market appeal, give new meaning to national character, and permit much tighter sales and promotional efforts. Simply stated, the arts, as an element of tourism, improve the product and strengthen its appeal, making tourism saleable.

For the arts, tourism can bring the vitality needed to draw upon new audiences, improve attendances and open up the marketplace. Moving into the mainstream of tourism can attract an array of new partners who can provide promotional funds, fresh promotional skills, and a whole new distribution system. New sources of funding, new revenue opportunities, and programmed attendance revenue must be found to sustain a growing and vital arts community, and tourism can provide this important source of planned revenue. The benefits to both are obvious (p. 29).

Finally, there is the issue of relationships between tourists and the host communities. On the whole, Australians are unlikely to be overwhelmed by the cultures of their visitors. It may be difficult to measure, but it would seem there can be only benefit in this country from cross-national contacts. In general, there is, according to Gartner (1996) 'compelling evidence' supporting tourism as a means of promoting understanding and exchange (social and economic). And . . .

Although no substantial evidence exists to support the statement that tourism is a force for peace, it is clear that peace is not attainable without tourism. People-to-people interaction is necessary for understanding and discovery of common ground, and tourism provides the stage for social exchange to occur (p. 177).

DOXEY'S SOCIOCULTURAL IMPACT MODEL

The intensity and types of sociocultural impacts depend on the speed and extent of tourism development. These factors also influence the way residents react. One of the most influential works in the field has been the 'Irritation index' or 'Irridex', a model produced by Doxey and cited by Gartner (1996), which can be used as a guide to the likely reaction of residents as tourism increases.

Doxey identified four time-related stages linked to an increasing number of tourists. He argued that as numbers increase, resident populations react with increasing hostility towards tourists, passing through stages from euphoria to antagonism. The stages are described below.

Stage 1: euphoria

Residents support tourism development and are ready to share their community with visitors. Among the benefits forecast are new jobs, increased incomes and higher property values. There are few opponents. This stage is most likely to occur when local economies have been stagnant and tourism can be seen to offer new opportunities for growth. Or it may be that there is unemployment because an existing industry is shut down or is in decline. Tourism is then seen as a replacement. Support is based on economic projections that ignore or downplay social factors.

Stage 2: apathy

Eventually, the growth that fuelled rapid tourism development begins to slow. The rate of increase of rising land values and business expansion has eased. Tourism is accepted as part of the community's economic base; it is no longer a novelty. The social structure of the area most likely changes with new migrants arriving in search of jobs, and family roles change as different members (e.g. youths) find employment within the industry. The promise of economic 'good times' which pervaded the euphoria stage is now viewed as accruing to only a limited number of residents, with the rest not realising or believing the potential.

Stage 3: irritation

If the level of tourism continues to expand, a stage of irritation may occur. Most likely, tourism development has been unplanned and has spread into environmentally sensitive areas. Locals must now share with outsiders what used to be their own recreation areas. Prices of staple goods (such as food) rise at a much faster rate than local incomes. Income growth realised in earlier stages vanishes as inflation takes back earlier gains. If the environment or the attractiveness of the local area is drastically modified through development, visitor numbers may decrease, resulting in an over-abundance of facilities and eventually economic decline. During the irritation stage, the social and environmental impacts of unplanned tourism development begin to receive attention. Local residents perceive a loss of 'place' and blame tourism for it.

Stage 4: antagonism

As a sense of loss of 'place' becomes more profound, residents blame tourists for the changes rather than the unplanned and uncontrolled developments. Most likely, the type of tourist who arrived when the area was in the euphoria stage has been replaced with an entirely new type of visitor who is less interested in local customs and traditions and more drawn to specific physical attractions.

Residents show their antagonism by, for example, writing angry letters to the local newspaper complaining about different types of tourist behavior. They may devise names for tourists which have a derogatory connotation understood only by locals. This kind of passive-aggressive behaviour may shift to overtly aggressive actions, as when cars with out-of-state number plates are chosen as objects for criminal activity.

Antagonistic activity can occur in any area, but it is more apparent where a wide gap between the lifestyle of the tourists and locals exists. In developing countries it may occur after local residents realise that the tourism industry does not offer the type of jobs desired.

If development is of an enclave, 'environmental bubble' nature, very little social exchange between locals and tourists occurs, in contrast to the first tourists who arrived when the area was relatively undeveloped and mixing between the groups was necessary and desired. The stage of antagonism can occur whenever either group, and most likely both, is perceived as a commodity to be exploited rather than a guest or a host (Gartner 1996).

One of the criticisms of Doxey's model is that it assumes a degree of homogeneity in community attitudes and reactions to tourism which has not been sustained by other research. Indeed, more recent research suggests that communities hold diverse opinions about developments in their destination areas. This was borne out by the study of Fredline and Faulkner (2000) involving the measurement of resident perceptions, attitudes and behavioural adjustments to the IndyCar event it is the subject of this chapter's case study.

CASE STUDY

The Indy car race and the Gold Coast community

The Gold Coast Indy has been a major event in Australia since 1991. The four-day affair is held at Surfers Paradise, the heart of the Gold Coast, and the main focus is on the IndyCar race held on the final afternoon. A number of support events from Australian motor racing codes are also included, and there are many social activities in the days leading up to and including the IndyCar race.

Fredline and Faulkner set out to explore clusters evident among resident reactions to the event and investigate the similarities that could be observed between them and those identified in two previous studies.

The first of these – Davis et al (1988) – involved the segmentation of Florida residents in terms of their attitudes and opinions regarding tourism development in that state. The second – Madrigal (1995) – was more ambitious. It adopted a cluster analysis approach to examine community reactions to the impact of tourism and local government's involvement with tourism development in two different types of cities in the United States and the United Kingdom. The US city was Sedona, Arizona, a rural community of 7,720 people with extensive tourism development based on natural attractions and an active artisan community. The British city, York, has a population of 100,000 and a long history of urban-based tourism. Madrigal found that residents in the two cities showed similar clustering tendencies despite their differences in size, level of tourism development, and national context.

The method adopted for the Gold Coast survey was to engage in face-to-face interviews with residents. This resulted in 337 valid cases (16 responses were rejected due to missing data).

The survey instrument had three parts:

1. A 'battery' of 36 statements referred to positive and negative economic, social and environmental impacts of the Indy, in relation to which respondents were asked to indicate the degree of their agreement or disagreement on a five point scale.
2. The second part included questions concerned with demographic background and the involvement of respondents in the event and/or tourism.
3. This part consisted of a question about activities undertaken by residents during the period of the event. Residents were asked which of the following best described the activities engaged in during the weekend of the Indy in 1996: attended Indy, watched it on television, worked, usual weekend activities, went away for the weekend, and 'other'.

In choosing the respondents it was considered necessary to have those living closest to the Indy zone over-represented because the disruptive effects were concentrated in a small area around the track. Those living close to it were affected by street closures, noise levels and crowding by spectators. For the purposes of the survey, the non-Indy zone, which was very large compared with the Indy zone, was divided into ten zones to ensure representation of all sectors of the relevant population.

Resident responses were summarised into six factors:

1. Community benefits (such as increased pride, community spirit, business and trade opportunities, improved levels of service)
2. Short-term negative impacts (e.g. noise, encouragement of 'hoons', overcrowding, traffic congestion and disruption to lifestyle)
3. International profile and economic benefits (e.g. tourism promotion and a range of statements similar to factor 1)[5]
4. Negative economic impacts (such as demand-driven price increases)
5. Negative physical impacts (such as litter, noise levels, parking congestion)
6. Facility development benefits (such as maintenance and development of facilities, improved appearance of the area).

The respondents were clustered in relation to their responses to the factors in this way:

Cluster One: Ambivalent supporter (cautious romantics) This group contained 99 residents, whose response patterns were described as 'fairly ambivalent', as they tended toward moderate responses. The vast majority were in favour of continuation of the Indy (97 per cent) and many were in favour of the current location (60 per cent). They were more likely to live in the non-Indy zone (62 per cent).

Cluster Two: Haters This cluster contained 50 residents and the group could be 'quite clearly' labelled as haters of the event. They showed a high level of disagreement with the community benefit items and agreed strongly with the negative impacts. Sixty-five per cent were not in favour of continuation of the Indy and only two of the residents were in favour of the event remaining in its current location. The preferred options were 'not on the Gold Coast', or Dreamworld, an alternative site on the northern outskirts of the city. They were mostly older residents, 66 per cent of them over 50 years and 44 over 60 years. Very few attended the Indy (2 per cent) or watched it on TV (4 per cent). Forty per cent went away for the weekend. A relatively large proportion had lived on the Gold Coast for more than 20 years (36 per cent).

Cluster Three: Realists The label was not intended to indicate the 80 residents in the group were more correct in their opinions than others, rather that they acknowledged that there were both positive and negative impacts, which was regarded as intuitively realistic. Of the residents in the cluster who were employed, 51 per cent worked in tourism, with an additional 32 per cent working in industries whose volume of business was affected by tourism. A relatively large percentage were low-income earners.

Cluster Four: Lovers Made up of 77 residents, this group agreed with the community benefits (factor 1), the international profile and economic benefits (factor 3), and the amenity and facility benefits (factor 6). They were the only group to disagree with the short-term negative impacts in factor 2 and also disagreed with all of the negative economic and physical impacts except for saying that during the Indy it was difficult to find a parking space. They were more likely to fit the demographic profile of spectators (predominantly male and under the age of 40), but less likely to be involved in tourism. Some 38 per cent attended the Indy and a further 35 per cent watched it on TV.

Cluster Five: Concerned for a reason The final group contained 31 residents who appeared to be deeply concerned about specific impacts of the Indy, but did not have completely negative perceptions of the event. They disagreed with most of the community benefits in factor 1, but did agree that the Indy made nightlife more exciting. They very strongly agreed with the short-term negative impacts, except that they disagreed that the Indy had led to increased crime.

These responses were similar to those in Cluster Two. But the two clusters differed in their perceptions of the remaining impacts. Cluster Five agreed with most of the international profile and economic benefits in factor 3, and were largely ambivalent to the negative economic and physical impacts of factors 4 and 5. They disagreed slightly with the amenity and facility benefits of factor 6.

The residents in this cluster were largely supportive of the continuation of the Indy (92 per cent), despite their concern about some impacts, but many of them favoured it being relocated, with 39 per cent favouring the Broadwater option and 26 per cent favouring the Dreamworld option. The majority did not fit the demographic profile of spectators and most lived in the Indy zone (90 per cent). They tended to be higher income earners.

The authors expressed concern about the precision of the process, commenting that while it was obviously relatively easy to identify corresponding groups among those who have the most extreme views (lovers and haters) the complexity of views among the remainder created difficulties.

They also said that differences in methodology made impossible a direct comparison with studies conducted by Madrigal and Davis *et al*. However, all three studies produced in common clearly identifiable clusters of residents who either loved or hated tourism/the Indy. Among the remainder of the population there was a diversity of views ranging from conditional support/concern to ambivalence. Parallels between the clusters in the three studies are shown in Table 5.1.

Table 5.1 Parallels between Indy clusters and those in other studies

FLORIDA STUDY	SEDONA/YORK STUDY	INDY STUDY
Haters (16%)	Haters (31%)	Haters (15%)
Lovers (20%)	Lovers (13%)	Lovers (23%)
Cautious romantics (21%)		Ambivalent supporters (29%)
In-betweeners (18%)	Realists (56%)	Realists (24%)
Love 'em for a reason (26%)		Concerned for a reason (9%)

(Source: Reprinted from *Annals of Tourism Research*, Fredline and Faulkner Vol 27 (3)(2000), p. 76, with permission from Elsevier.)

Fredline and Faulkner commented that the identification of similar response patterns across different communities may bring researchers closer to developing more general theory concerning the interface between communities and tourism/events. Real progress, however, depended upon a better understanding of the factors underlying these patterns.

INDUSTRY PROFILE

CHRISTINE BEDDOE MANAGER, CHILD WISE TOURISM

I am the founder and manager of Child Wise Tourism, a program that provides training and policy advice to the tourism sector on the prevention of child sex tourism. I have been working for almost 10 years with Child Wise (formally known as ECPAT), an Australian organisation dedicated to ending the sexual exploitation of children. Child Wise Tourism has worked with government tourism authorities and private sector tourism businesses across the world, including partnerships with the World Tourism Organisation and the Pacific Asia Travel Association. In 2001 Child Wise Tourism was selected by a United Nations panel as a model of best practice for the protection of children. Recently I worked with Accor Asia Pacific to develop training and a child protection policy for their hotels across Asia.

How did I get here?

I came into this work having completed a Bachelor of Business in Tourism Management, and a Master of Arts in Sociology and Anthropology of Tourism. I had also worked for several years with retail and wholesale tourism operators. I left the private sector because I was frustrated by the lack of attention paid to the sociocultural effects of tourism by tourism decision makers. But that was 10 years ago and now we are starting to see positive change.

What do I like about my job?

I love the work I do because it makes a difference – to the quality of tourism, to enhancing people's knowledge about sustainable and ethical tourism – and ultimately because it helps to protect children, the most valuable resource for the future of tourism.

SUMMARY

The chapter is concerned with the sociocultural environment and the way tourism influences it. While governments and tourism businesses are constantly trying to increase tourism, chiefly because of its economic benefits, it is necessary to count the costs and weigh them against the benefits. Much attention has been given to the threat from tourism to the natural environment but tourism also changes host communities and may bring unexpected tensions.

Sociocultural impacts result whenever people of different races, backgrounds and/or experiences meet through tourism. Scale is important: when tourism reaches a certain level it changes the destination for the people who live there, including changes in value systems, individual behaviour, family relationships, collective lifestyles, safety levels, moral conduct, creative expressions, traditional ceremonies and community organisations.

Often a host community is in two minds about tourism. People don't like crowds of visitors invading their territory, pushing them aside, inflating prices, congesting the place, imposing their values and, generally, changing things. But the more a local economy becomes dependent on tourism, the greater the degree of local involvement in the travel and tourism industry becomes.

Marketing may be a factor in relationships between host communities and tourists. It is the marketers who project images of destination areas and arouse the expectations of tourists with their selling message. The host community usually can influence the messages of the destination marketing organisation of the area itself or local companies, but not outside marketers who have their own reasons for wanting to promote increased tourism to the destination.

The types of changes within the community which tourism can bring include (a) a change in population; (b) transformation of forms and types of occupation; (c) transformation of values (e.g. copying tourists' ways of dressing and eating, trying to fully assimilate with a tourist culture, organising cultural events or producing artefacts to suit tourists rather than for traditional purposes).

Tourism can also produce very tangible problems for host communities, such as people and traffic congestion, overloading of infrastructure, changes in land prices, the loss of land use for other purposes, losses of other businesses, architectural pollution, undesirable changes in the urban fabric, and an increase in crime. However, negative impacts are a warning against bad tourism management. There are measures available to mitigate against visitor impacts discussed in Chapter 11. Managing cultural resources is an allied issue. Generally the many organisations that manage Australia's cultural heritage take a positive view of tourism.

Communities as a whole favour tourism, primarily because it brings wealth and jobs. It can also nurture cultural activity and is seen internationally (by the International Council on Monuments and Sites) as being a positive force for natural and cultural conservation.

A guide to the likely reaction of residents to tourism was produced by Doxey in 1975 and continues to be studied. His model, called the 'Irritation index' or 'Irridex', is based on the proposition that the intensity and types of sociocultural impacts depend on the speed and extent of tourism development and these factors also influence the way residents react to tourism. Doxey identified four time-related stages linked to an increasing number of tourists. He argued that as numbers increase, resident populations react with increasing hostility towards tourists, passing through stages from euphoria to antagonism.

One of the criticisms of Doxey's model is that it assumes a degree of homogeneity in community attitudes and reactions to tourism which has not been sustained by other research. Indeed, more recent research suggests that communities hold diverse opinions about developments in their destination areas. This is borne out by the chapter's case study, based on research by Fredline and Faulkner (2000), which involved the measurement of resident perceptions, attitudes and behavioural adjustments to the IndyCar event.

QUESTIONS

1. The statement has been made that tourism growth has built-in limits. If that is so, how is it a problem for Australia?

2. What does the word 'environment' mean in its tourism context and why is the hybrid word 'sociocultural' used in this chapter?

QUESTIONS continued

3. What is heritage and what part does the Australian Heritage Council play in preserving it?

4. Sustainability has become a much-used word in recent years. Why? And what does it mean when applied to tourism?

5. What are some of the principal sociocultural impacts of tourism? How can they be managed to produce the best possible result for a community?

6. In what ways can a powerful tourism culture change the values of some people in a host community and therefore change the way they behave?

7. What are the characteristics of the relationship between tourists and host communities? How can marketing influence them?

8. How can tourism help preserve and expand the appreciation of a destination's cultural heritage?

9. Doxey's model links community irritation and disillusionment with tourism to a growing number of tourists. Can you think of examples where this has happened and where it has not?

10. In the case study, Fredline and Faulkner put residents into categories according to their attitudes towards the IndyCar motor race. Two of these categories were labelled 'lovers' and 'haters'. How did the characteristics of the groups differ?

TOURISM AND THE NATURAL ENVIRONMENT

Understand the relationship between population and tourism growth and appreciate that both exert pressure on the natural environment.

Appreciate the nature and causes of the global problems with which tourism is principally concerned: global warming, pollution and deforestation.

Examine the causes of tourism impact: transport, development and operations.

Understand what is being done to manage problems and protect the future, specifically: an increase in research, the quest for sustainable transport, the protection of special areas, commitment programs to improve companies' environmental performance, company-initiated 'best practice' programs and codes of conduct.

Review the lessons from a case study of what Australian companies have done, and are doing: adopting pro-environment practices, constructing environment-friendly accommodation and finding innovative ways of fulfilling tourism purposes and at the same time being compatible with natural surroundings.

UNDERSTAND THE MEANING OF:

* *ecology*
* *biodiversity*
* *ecosystem*
* *climate change*
* *cleaner production*
* *global warming*
* *IPCC*
* *UNFCC*
* *greenhouse gas*
* *Kyoto Protocol*
* *sustainable transport*
* *Cooperative Research Centre*
* *CSIRO*
* *Tourism Futures Simulator*
* *National System of Reserves*
* *Green Globe*
* *Greenhouse Challenge*
* *environment policy statement*

ENVIRONMENTAL DANGERS

The importance of the natural environment to tourism cannot be overstated. It goes to the heart of why people travel from one part of the earth to another; even when it is not the main attraction it usually has a significant influence on why tourists chose one destination over another. The other side of the coin is the impact tourism has on the natural environment, and this is a matter of great concern. But tourism is only one human activity that affects the environment. The state of the planet and the way the human race was using and despoiling its resources in general became a matter of increasing public concern in the last two decades of the 20th century.

Recognition of the need to protect the natural environment goes back at least to the 19th century; the first international environment regulation was passed in 1886. In more modern times there has been development of regulation since the late 1930s, mainly as a reaction to pollution and environmental change, and resulting from our better understanding of the effects of environmental degradation on human life. Regulation concentrated on specific issues that could not be resolved at a national level, e.g. pollution of the seas. Such regulation has had a very limited impact on the practices of travel and tourism organisations (Middleton & Hawkins 1998).

However, since the mid-1980s there has been a more powerful force– public awareness and concern about such issues as the hole in the ozone layer, global warming, destruction of the landscape, air pollution, dying forests, excessive noise levels, energy crises, depletion of basic resources, and waste-disposal problems. Concern has been directed at tourism because it contributes substantially to at least some of these problems. As a result, travel and tourism companies have become increasingly environmentally conscious, displaying growing awareness that good environmental practice makes sound business sense.

Tourism's relationship with the natural environment is complex and should be viewed in the context of how human beings relate to the environment generally.

Population and tourism growth

The number of people on earth, the world's population, is central to this issue. Obviously, the demands human beings place on the environment increase as the population continues to grow. So far advances in science have allowed this growth. Without science, population growth would have been controlled (unpleasantly) by lack of food and resources (Shearman &

The environment is the attraction that has caused a huge increase in Outback touring. Here a convoy of caravans in the Victorian Mallee region is led by a specially equipped vehicle of the tour organiser, Aussie Outback Tours. Not only is there a growing use of four-wheel-drive vehicles in remote areas, but caravans are now made for touring on non-bitumised roads. The increase in the number of vehicles and people in the Outback can be a danger to a fragile environment. Touring in groups with expert guidance helps manage the risk.

(Source: Aussie Outback Tours.)

Sauer-Thompson 1997). Scientific knowledge will need to be applied to an even greater extent to sustain the kind of numbers foreseen by the middle of the 21st century.

The number of people in the world is expected to grow, though at a declining rate. As a result, it has been forecast that by 2050 the population will have increased by more than three and a half times in 100 years. In 1950 the world's population was 2.5 billion, in 2000 it was just over 6 billion, and the US Bureau of the Census forecasts it will be more than 9 billion in 2050. It is anticipated the average annual growth rate, 1.47 per cent in 1950, will have slowed to at most 0.43 per cent in 2050 (US Bureau of the Census 2000).

The movement of tourists around the world is expected to increase at a much greater pace. In the first 20 years of the 21st century the number of international arrivals is forecast to show an annual average growth rate of about 4 per cent. There were 25 million arrivals in 1950 and 668 million in 2000. The billion is expected in 2010 and more than 1.5 billion by 2020 (World Tourism Organisation 1999b).

International tourism is only part of tourism, the smaller part. Producing accurate worldwide figures and predicting growth for domestic tourism is not possible because of the lack of comparable data from all countries. But its scale is much greater than international tourism, accounting for about 75 per cent of the total of tourism in Australia and the United States (measured by expenditure) and more than that in some other countries. There is expectation of continuing growth as populations and standards of living increase, at least in the short term.[1]

Travel requires large quantities of energy and adding numbers of tourists at destinations brings pressure on local resources, sometimes at the expense of host communities.

CONCEPTS RELATED TO THE ENVIRONMENT

In the last chapter concepts were discussed which helped an understanding of the socio-cultural impacts of tourism. Some of those concepts also relate to the natural environment: heritage, conservation, sustainable tourism. They should be referred to again for this chapter. Specific concepts related to the natural environment are now discussed:

- ecology
- biodiversity
- ecosystem
- climate change
- cleaner production.

Ecology

Ecology

The study of organisms and their environment, a branch of biology concerned with relationships among species and between species and the physical and chemical environments they inhabit.

Ecology is the study of organisms and their environment, a branch of biology concerned with relationships among species and between species and the physical and chemical environments they inhabit. The most obvious relationships are between organisms in which one eats the other. But there are many other kinds of relationship: between males and females, adults and their young, dominant and subordinate individuals, or between resident animals and 'visitors' from outside.

Darwin's theory of evolution by natural selection is an ecological theory. It states that minor differences among individual members of a particular population of a particular species equip some better than others to thrive and reproduce in the environmental circumstances in which they live. The inherited differences provide the basis for natural selection and the selection itself results from pressures originating in the environment (Allaby 1986).

Biodiversity

Biodiversity

All living things on earth from microbes to the largest mammal, from algae to the largest tree. It is usually considered at three levels: genetic diversity, species diversity and ecosystem diversity.

The term **biodiversity** is used to describe the great variety (diversity) of species and refers to all living things on earth from microbes to the largest mammal, from algae to the largest tree. It is usually considered at three levels: genetic diversity, species diversity and ecosystem diversity.

Australia's biodiversity is considered exceptional because of its species richness and the very high proportion of species and families that are unique to this country and its waters. However, there has been a severe decline in biodiversity, and there is a danger of more losses. The Commonwealth Government's Environment Protection and Biodiversity Conservation Act 1999 seeks to promote the conservation of biodiversity and triggers Commonwealth involvement in decision making when matters are defined as being of national environmental significance. If they do not meet this threshold of significance they are dealt with at the state or local government level (Australian Bureau of Statistics 2000b).

Ecosystem

A system, as noted in Chapter 2, is a group of component items that are interdependent and may be identified and treated as an entity. An **ecosystem** is a discrete biological community of interacting organisms and their physical environment. Physically, it is an area which can be defined because it is different from the area around it.

Ecosystems are self-regulating by means of 'feedback' relationships. Allaby (1986) illustrates the principle with the example of an ecosystem containing grass, rabbits and foxes. If the rabbits increase in numbers there can be more foxes to hunt them, so fox numbers will also increase and rabbit numbers will be checked. However, while the rabbits are more numerous, they will eat more grass. This may reduce the amount of grass, so limiting further increase in the number of rabbits because there is insufficient food for more of them. These are feedback mechanisms, in which increases at one point in the system act to restore it to its former value.

An ecosystem need not be large but it can be. A forest might by studied as an ecosystem, because it has a definite edge, and the area surrounding it is not forest, so it is different. A single tree may also be regarded as an ecosystem.

Ecosystem
A discrete biological community of interacting organisms and their physical environment. Physically, it is an area which can be defined because it is different from the area around it.

Climate change

This refers to **climate change** over time, but international bodies use two different versions of the causes because of their different roles. Usage of the term by the Intergovernmental Panel on Climate Change (IPCC), a scientific body, refers to any change whether due to natural variability or as a result of human activity.

The United Nations Framework Convention on Climate Change (UNFCC), which is concerned with policy in regard to human-induced change, restricts the meaning of the term to fit its specific role, i.e. it uses it in relation to a change in climate that is attributed directly or indirectly to human activity (Intergovernmental Panel on Climate Change 2001c).

Climate change
Change in climate over time due to natural variability or as a result of human activity.

Cleaner production

This means improving the environmental efficiency of goods and services and thereby reducing the environmental impact of the production process. '**Eco-efficiency**' has a similar meaning. Achieving cleaner production requires the continuous application of an integrated strategy to reduce risks to humans and the environment.

For production processes it includes conserving raw materials and energy, eliminating toxic raw materials and reducing the quantity and toxicity of all emissions and wastes before they leave the process.

For products, the strategy focuses on reducing impacts along the entire lifecycle of the

Cleaner production (eco-efficiency)
Improving the environmental efficiency of goods and services and thereby reducing the environmental impact of the production process, from system design and use, to the consumption of resources required to provide the service.

DEFINITIONS

product, from raw materials extraction to ultimate disposal of the product.

For services, it reduces the environmental impact of a service provided over the entire lifecycle, from system design and use, to the consumption of resources required to provide the service (Vernon 1999).

GLOBAL PROBLEMS AND TOURISM

The variety and extent of specific environmental threats vary from region to region, country to country. Three global problems have specific relevance to this chapter because of tourism's involvement with them: they are global warming, air pollution and deforestation.

▓ Global warming

Global warming
A rise in temperatures at the earth's surface as the result of human beings changing the way energy from the sun interacts with and escapes from the earth's atmosphere.

Global warming is caused mainly by human beings changing the way energy from the sun interacts with and escapes from the earth's atmosphere. The result is a rise in temperatures at the earth's surface. The average surface temperature of the earth increased over the 20th century by about 0.6 degrees centigrade, probably the largest increase of any century during the past 1,000 years. These calculations were made by the Intergovernmental Panel on Climate Change (2001a), the international body assembled to assess the scientific information related to human-induced climate change. In predicting what is likely to happen in this century, it has modelled no fewer than 35 scenarios to reach a range of forecasts of rises in the temperature on earth of between 1.4 and 5.8 degrees centigrade in the period 1990 to 2100.[2]

Climate change can occur naturally as the result of such factors as variations in the amount of energy the sun sends us or because of volcanic activity. But human activities causing emissions of greenhouse gases are the chief cause of change. The concentration in the atmosphere of carbon dioxide, a prominent greenhouse gas, indicates the kind of thing that has occurred – it has increased by 31 per cent since 1750, roughly when the Industrial Revolution began. That may not appear too dramatic considering it has happened over a long time, but the current rate of increase is unprecedented during at least the past 20,000 years.

The Kyoto Protocol (www.unfccc.int), intended to be an agreement between nations to limit emissions, covers the following six gases:

Carbon dioxide	CO_2
Methane	CH_4
Nitrous oxide	N_2O
Hydrofluorocarbons	HFCs
Perfluorocarbons	PFCs
Sulphur hexafluoride	SF_6

The atmosphere consists mostly of oxygen (21 per cent) and nitrogen (78 per cent).

Proportionately, the greenhouse gases are only a tiny part of it, but they play a vital role in our lives. Energy comes from the sun, passing through the atmosphere to warm the earth's surface. Then the earth gets rid of the energy by sending it back towards space in the form of infra-red radiation. Most of this is absorbed initially in the atmosphere by the greenhouse gases and only after a complicated series of interactions does it escape into space. If the greenhouse gases did not slow the progress of the energy through the atmosphere, retaining its warmth, the earth would be 30 degrees centigrade colder than it is now. It would be a miserable, lifeless place.

The problem is that human beings are increasing the volume of greenhouse gases, slowing the process of escape of infra-red radiation from the atmosphere, and increasing temperatures on earth. The main culprit is carbon dioxide, which people keep sending into the atmosphere in huge quantities by burning fossil fuels – wood, oil, coal, peat and natural gas.

Over the last two decades of the 20th century, fossil fuel burning accounted for about three-quarters of the carbon dioxide released into the atmosphere as the result of human activity. The rest was mainly due to land-use change, especially deforestation. When forests are destroyed the carbon dioxide stored in the trees and their root systems escapes into the air.

Australian annual carbon dioxide production is about 14 tonnes per person. It can be estimated in terms of activities which are integral to our daily lives and which indicate the scale of the changes necessary to reduce production. For example, the average Australian car releases more than 4 tonnes of the gas each year and a fossil-fuel burning power station about 1 kilogram of carbon dioxide in supplying energy to light a 100 watt globe for eight hours (Intergovernmental Panel on Climate Control 2001a and 2001b, United Nations Environment Program 1997, UNEP/WMO Information Unit on Climate Change 1994, Allaby 1986, Shearman & Sauer-Thompson 1997).

Serious consequences predicted

Scientists are warning of serious consequences from the warming of the earth. Among them:

- There will be a shortage of food if farming systems are unable to adapt.
- Some species will become endangered, and entire forest types may disappear.
- Malaria and other diseases could spread to regions which are temperate at present.
- Heavier rains and tropical cyclones are expected to alter the risks to life in some parts of the world while droughts, especially in poorer countries, could reduce supplies of fresh, clean water to the point where there are major threats to public health.
- Melting glaciers and thermal expansion of sea water will raise sea levels, threatening low-lying coastal areas and small islands.

CSIRO scientists think some sections of the Australian travel and tourism industry will be wiped out in two or three decades because of the withdrawal of snow levels up the sides of mountains and the raising of shoreline water levels. The CSIRO's Division of Atmospheric Research has predicted that by 2030 there will be insufficient natural snow for viable ski operations at low Australian resorts (such as Mount Baw Baw) and by 2070 at most Australian resorts. It also expects destruction of much of the Great Barrier Reef by 2040 because of coral bleaching (CSIRO 2000). Northern coastal regions of Australia are expected to have average temperatures of 1 degree centigrade higher than today by 2030 and southern coastal regions may warm up by 1.5 degrees. As the earth warms so do the upper layers of the oceans. Higher temperatures kill corals, although some scientists think the biodiversity of coral reefs may lead hardy types to survive.[3]

Coral bleaching is only one possible consequence from warmer waters. Water expands when heated and expansion will raise sea levels, as will melting of land-based ice in the temperate regions of the world (floating sea ice does not change sea levels when it melts). Coastal and island resorts will be threatened by rising waters.

IPCC's assessment reports

The Intergovernmental Panel on Climate Change (IPCC) was established by the World Meteorological Organisation (WMO) and the United Nations Environment Program (UNEP)[4] in 1988. It has produced a series of comprehensive assessment reports on the state of understanding of causes of climate change, its potential impacts and options for response strategies.

Its First Assessment Report, issued in 1990, was the basis for establishing the United Nations Framework Convention on Climate Change (UNFCC). The UNFCC was adopted in 1992 by the UN General Assembly and took effect in 1994. It provides the overall policy framework for addressing the climate change issue. More than 170 nations have signed it.

The UNFCC has set an ultimate objective of stabilising greenhouse gas concentrations in the atmosphere at a level that would prevent dangerous human-induced interference with the climate system. As at the time no one knew with scientific certainty what levels were dangerous, it does not specify what the concentrations should be, only that they be not dangerous. It directs that stabilisation should occur within a time frame sufficient to allow ecosystems to adapt naturally to climate change, to ensure that food production is not threatened and to enable economic development to proceed in a sustainable manner.

The IPCC's Second Assessment Report in 1995 provided key information for the negotiations which led to the adoption of the Kyoto Protocol to the UNFCC in 1997. At Kyoto, 39 developed countries agreed in principle to a collective target of a 5.2 per cent reduction in greenhouse gas emissions below 1990 levels by between 2008 and 2012.[5]

In 2001, the United States announced it would not implement the Kyoto Protocol on the grounds that it exempted developing nations and was not in the United States' economic best interest.[6] The US, which produces 25 per cent of the world's greenhouse gases, would have been required to lower its emissions by 7 per cent below 1990 levels by 2012. At the time of writing, Australia also has not agreed to implement the Protocol because of associated costs. For example, the Bureau of Agriculture and Resource Economics forecast that implementation of the Protocol would result in a one-third rise in electricity prices. This led to the belief that most aluminium producers would move to countries that do not face greenhouse penalties (Howarth 2003).

Although the fate of the Kyoto Protocol was uncertain at the time of writing, nations including Australia and the United States were still working to reduce greenhouse gas emissions. These take the form of voluntary programs as well as the imposition of mandatory limits. In addition, a great deal of scientific work is underway. In Australia, this is led by the CSIRO which cooperates with a number of other scientific agencies, including the Bureau of Meteorology and Cooperative Research Centres.

Implementation of action programs is being overseen by the Australian Greenhouse Gas Office, the lead Commonwealth Government agency responsible for implementing the National Greenhouse Strategy, which was developed by the Commonwealth, state and territory governments.

Air pollution

Air pollution has caused enormous damage to the natural and built environment – most notably the effect of acid rain on forests, lakes, rivers and city buildings – and to people's health: pollutants affect the throat and lungs in particular and cause respiratory and other diseases.

The problem is worldwide, but worse in the northern hemisphere. In a relative sense, Australia's problems are minor. It has a small population, is surrounded by oceans and does not receive masses of polluted air from other countries. Its oil and coal contain less sulphur than much of the oil and coal produced in other countries.

That having been said, air pollution still gives Australians plenty to worry about. Sydney, Melbourne and the other large Australian cities experience days of high air pollution, especially in summer and autumn. The causes and effects are shown in Table 6.1.

The main exposure to air pollutants for many people occurs when they are indoors – at home, where they work or in entertainment venues. Open fires, kerosene fires, and gas fires can all cause problems if they are not properly ventilated. Air conditioning systems which recirculate the same air retain pollutants. The dangers of smoking are intensified indoors for non-smokers.

The effect of indoor air pollution on human health varies, depending on the level

Table 6.1 Major air pollutants in Australia

POLLUTANT	SOURCES	HEALTH EFFECTS
Carbon monoxide	Motor vehicles, burning of fossil fuels	Blood absorbs carbon monoxide more readily than oxygen, reducing the amount of oxygen being carried through the body. Carbon monoxide can produce tiredness and headaches. People with heart problems are particularly at risk.
Sulphur dioxide	Coal and oil burning power stations, mineral ore processing, chemical manufacture	Attacks the throat and lungs. People with breathing problems can suffer severe illness.
Nitrogen dioxide	Fuel combustion	Affects the throat and lungs.
Volatile organic compounds	Motor vehicles, fuel combustion, solvent use	Some VOCs cause eye and skin irritation, headaches or nausea, while some are classed as carcinogens.
Ozone	From nitrogen oxides and hydrocarbons released by motor vehicles and industry	Ozone attacks the tissue of the throat and lungs and irritates the eyes.
Lead	Exhaust gases from motor vehicles that use leaded petrol, smelters	Particles containing lead in the air can enter the lungs and the lead can then be absorbed into the blood stream. Eventually it can affect the nervous system and the body's ability to produce blood.
Particles	Motor vehicles, burning of plant materials, bushfires	May cause breathing difficulties and worsen respiratory diseases. Some particles contain cancer-producing materials.

(Source: © CSIRO Atmospheric Research.)

of exposure and individual health. Common ailments attributed to poor indoor air quality include respiratory problems (e.g. asthma and bronchitis), skin irritations (e.g. rashes and eczema), ear, eye and throat irritations, headaches, nervous disorders and disrupted sleep.

▓ Deforestation

The destruction of forests has been pursued with vigor throughout history for a variety of reasons. A few examples: in Australia there were once tax incentives to clear land for agriculture; long before that, the Vikings, with murder on their minds, burned large areas of Scottish forests to flush out the local inhabitants, and during the 16th century some of what was left was cut down for smelting; the Romans removed forests around the Mediterranean to make way for crops.

Now there is incontestable evidence of the danger removing trees has brought upon the human race. Vegetation has a unique role in stabilising the atmosphere so that there is sufficient oxygen in it and not too much carbon dioxide. Instead of rewarding Australians for cutting down trees, these days the Commonwealth Government urges them to preserve those that exist and plant more of them.[7]

But of the forests that existed before colonisation, the best Australia can aim for now is to retain 15 per cent of them.[8] The focus is now on the tropical rainforests, which not only continue to exist but have a special role in keeping human beings healthy. Every hectare of rainforest takes from the atmosphere annually one tonne of carbon dioxide, the chief cause of global warming. But the forests are being depleted at the rate of about 2 per cent annually and this has the effect of putting 2 billion tonnes of carbon dioxide into the air each year (Shearman & Sauer-Thompson 1997).

Another reason for preserving tropical rainforests is that they act as a powerhouse for evolution of species and contain half of all species on earth. A small plot of rainforest will have 700 species of trees compared with the handful of species to be found in other woodlands of the world, and thousands and thousands of insect species, many of which are unidentified.

Australia has 3.6 million hectares of rainforests, which is 2 per cent of its native forest area. Twenty-three per cent of rainforests are set aside in conservation reserves (Department of Agriculture, Fisheries and Forestry, www.affa.gov.au).[9]

The health of forests is a direct benefit to tourism, but badly managed tourism can cause them severe harm. Careless use of fire in parks has caused major bushfires in Australian forests in the past. Other dangerous practices include the chopping of trees for tent poles and firewood, excessive dumping of rubbish and uncontrolled pedestrian and vehicular traffic damaging vegetation.

DIRECT TOURISM EFFECTS ON THE ENVIRONMENT

The effect of tourism activities on the natural environment is discussed under the following headings:
1. the impact of passenger vehicles
2. the impact of tourism development
3. the impact of tourism operations.

DEFINITIONS

▓ The impact of passenger vehicles

Noise pollution

Unwanted or offensive sounds that unreasonably intrude into our daily lives.

Worldwide the transport sector is responsible for 20 to 25 per cent of all fossil fuel consumption. As a result, vehicles essential to tourism – cars, coaches, planes, trains and ships – produce a significant proportion of the gases which pollute the air and cause global warming. They are also major causes of **noise pollution**. The main problems occur with road vehicles and aircraft; the contribution of ships and trains to air and noise pollution is much less significant.

Greenhouse gas emissions from the transport sector in Australia are rising and are expected to be 47 per cent above 1990 emission levels by 2010. A 2003 report by the Bureau of Transport and Regional Economics said growth from aviation was about 4.4 per cent a year and that from passenger cars about 2 per cent. However, the passenger car sector is much the larger ('Today's transcripts and stories', ABC Online, www.abc.net.au, 17 February 2003).

Worldwide, road transport consumes about three-quarters of fossil fuels used by the transport sector as against 12 per cent for the aviation industry (Air Transport Action Group 2000).[10] Motor vehicles produce more atmospheric pollutants in Australia than anything else, including those pollutants that endanger health (Table 6.1). They also are responsible for most of transport's contribution to the greenhouse gas problem, including 80 per cent of the carbon dioxide released by transport vehicles of all modes (air, sea and land). Emissions of carbon dioxide by aircraft are small by comparison.[11]

Passenger cars, the most popular form of tourism transport in Australia, cause more pollution problems than other motor vehicles. They release about 65 per cent of carbon dioxide from road vehicles and also 65 per cent of nitrogen oxides. By contrast, heavy duty trucks are responsible for only about 15 per cent of carbon dioxide emissions.

Air transport

While the aeroplane does not have the same impact on the chemical quality of the air as the motor car, its influence is considerable and its numbers are growing. At the beginning of the 21st century about 2 billion people were travelling by air annually; by 2020 that figure is expected to have tripled.[12]

More aircraft will be required and as a result more emissions of greenhouse and other gases will enter the atmosphere. Continuing improvements in technology and operational procedures have reduced emissions, but increased demand for more air transport has outpaced the reductions.

Aircraft emissions include carbon dioxide and water vapour (both greenhouse gases), nitric oxide, nitrogen dioxide, sulphur oxides and soot. Aircraft were responsible for about 2 per cent of all human-induced carbon dioxide emissions in 1992. They produce 2–3 per cent of global man-made nitrogen dioxide emissions. The improvements in modern aircraft engines have almost eliminated emissions of carbon monoxide, unburned hydro-carbons and smoke (Air Transport Action Group 2000).[13]

Noise pollution

Transport – road, rail and air – is also a major cause of noise pollution, another of the abiding environmental problems. It can be defined as unwanted or offensive sounds that unreasonably intrude into our daily lives (New South Wales Environment Protection Authority 1997).

Australians rated road traffic the number one cause of noise problems in a survey by the Australian Environmental Council in 1986 and the situation has steadily become worse since then as the number of vehicles on the roads increases. Railways were ranked ninth in the same survey behind such irritants as barking dogs, lawn mowers and noisy neighbours.

Aircraft came fifth. But noise from commercial airliners is an emotive subject for those affected and it has led to protest groups being formed in various parts of the world. The Aviation Environment Federation is made up of 25 environment and citizen groups from more than 20 countries. It coordinates the 'Green Skies' campaign and in 2000 launched a 'Save Our Sleep' initiative, taking the issue to the European Court in Strasbourg.

Following the opening of a third runway at Sydney's Kingsford Smith Airport in 1994, residents in some areas suffered from aircraft noise even though it had been predicted they would not hear the planes at all. The new flight paths were said to affect 31,000 house-holds, as well as schools, hospitals and nursing homes (Richardson 1999). Community concern has been forcefully expressed and has included mounting airport blockades.

However, road traffic noise affects far more people. In 1991 it was estimated that more than 40 per cent of the residents of Sydney, 1.5 million, were exposed to outdoor noise levels defined as 'undesirable', where sleep and amenity were affected. It was worse for 350,000 of those residents, who experienced noise levels considered 'unacceptable', where behaviour patterns were constrained and health effects were demonstrable (New South Wales Environment Protection Authority 1997). While the problem may be worse in Sydney than some other Australian cities it exists in all urban areas. How much tourism traffic contributes to the problem is difficult to determine, probably not a great deal in major centres, though in smaller places of tourism significance such as coastal resorts it could be the major cause of noise pollution.

Factors that affect road traffic noise include the location and design of roads, land use planning measures, the design of buildings, vehicle standards and driver behaviour. A number of these have implications for tourism planners and operators.

The impact of tourism development

Tourism development can cause major damage to ecosystems and be visually disturbing. In mountain regions problems have included sedimentation and emissions from construction of tourism facilities, and from erosion and landslides linked to trails and skiing/snowmobiling. The building of access roads has altered drainage patterns and streams have been polluted as a result. Wildlife habitats have been damaged during resort construction and use. The disruptions to mountain vegetation, soil stability and wildlife are particularly important because they induce snowballing effects.

Coastlines are vulnerable. Human pressure often leads to ecological disturbance, disfigurement of the coastline and a reduction in the attraction of the resource. Eyesores include skyscrapers, unsightly hotel developments, concrete walls and waste-water processing stations (Mathieson & Wall 1982).

The buildings

Tourism buildings include built attractions, terminals, convention centres and entertainment venues, but the majority are constructed to accommodate tourists. The principal environmental problems of hotels and other accommodation businesses are energy use and waste disposal. In Australia, the commercial sector, of which the accommodation industry is part, is responsible for about 12 per cent of energy-related greenhouse gas emissions. Most of the energy it uses is in the form of electricity, which is produced from burning coal and therefore has a very high greenhouse gas intensity (Deer 1999).

The location, design and construction of a building has a lot to do with its energy efficiency and in the late 1990s the building industry recognised that changes in the building code of Australia were necessary to eliminate practices that had led to some bad examples of building energy performance.

Solid waste is a by-product of all accommodation establishments, both in the construction phase and in day-to-day operations. It comes from building materials during construction and later includes kitchen scraps, glass, metal and plastic containers, packaging (cardboard, paper, plastic and foam), paper, and miscellaneous waste such as tissues and cigarette butts. There may also be toxic waste such as chemical containers from cleaning or gardening products.

▨ The impact of tourism operations

Tourism operations put pressure on the environment in a number of ways.

(1) **Pressure on natural resources** For example, tourists and/or their vehicles can destroy vegetation and fragile shorelines (e.g. sand dunes); recreation (scuba diving, snorkelling, sport fishing) can damage coral reefs with subsequent impacts on coastal protection and fisheries.

(2) **Harm to wildlife and habitats** Problems can include destruction of habitats by clearance of vegetation for tourism developments, preparing camping sites, gathering firewood. Tourists doing nothing more dangerous than sightseeing can disrupt feeding and breeding of birds and animals. Hunting animals has not been actively promoted as

a tourism activity by Australian destination marketing organisations, although it does take place in this country.

In the Maldives, a ban on shark hunting has proven that protection of marine life can be more profitable than exploitation. Many tourists visit the island nation on diving holidays and in the mid-1990s made day trips to see and photograph a colony of some 20 sharks. The tourism ministry estimated at the time that excursions to that single attraction were earning US$670,000 a year or $33,500 a shark while the value of one shark sold to a fish market was only US$32 (World Tourism Organisation 1997a).

(3) **Pollution and wastes** Sewage is the main danger to fresh water and is also a threat to marine waters and coastal areas. Other concerns in coastal areas include sediment run-off, pollution from land-based hotels and marinas; waste and litter linked with marine sports and cruises. Roads and gutters contribute oil, grease, litter, sediment and heavy metals to urban run-off, which forms a major pollutant of the coastal environment (www.unep.org).[14]

THE RESPONSE TO THE DANGERS AND PROBLEMS

The response of governments, organisations and companies concerned with tourism to alleviate dangers to the natural environment is discussed under the headings:

1. Increase in Australian tourism research
2. The quest for sustainable transport
3. Protection of special areas
4. Performance improvement commitment programs
5. Company-initiated best practice programs
6. Codes of conduct.

Increase in Australian tourism research

The knowledge produced by research is essential to Australia's ability to manage the complex problems as tourism grows in the future. The amount of research into tourism-related subjects in Australia has grown enormously since the mid-1990s. This is because of the widening interests of the Bureau of Tourism Research, the burgeoning university interest in tourism in the 1990s and very largely because the Cooperative Research Centre for Sustainable Tourism (CRC Tourism) has attracted the funds and expertise to initiate and coordinate a many-sided program which is already having an influence throughout the country. A high proportion of that effort is related to the natural environment.

The Commonwealth Government set up the Cooperative Research Centres program in 1990. It brings together researchers from universities, CSIRO and other government research organisations, and private industry. CRCs cover long-term, collaborative research and development efforts in many areas. They are part-funded by the Commonwealth Government and also attract money and resources from participants.

The work of a number of CRCs is related to the environment and their work has a bearing on tourism's relationship with it. In particular, three CRCs (CRC Tourism, CRC Reef and CRC Rainforest) have significant interests in tourism and are supported by travel and tourism industry organisations.

The CSIRO – Commonwealth Scientific and Industrial Research Organisation – is one of the world's largest scientific research institutions, with 6,500 staff. Its activities cover a wide range of areas, including the environment and tourism, often in related programs.

Reference has already been made to CSIRO research into general environmental problems such as global warming and pollution. The organisation also has its own tourism research program launched with 14 projects in 1997. They included innovative ways to plan and locate sustainable resorts, dispose of effluent and waste, enhance nature tourism and evaluate its impact, protect against the increase in storm surges and cyclones expected under global warming.

Other programs include sustainable tourism in the Snowy Mountains and development of a Tourism Futures Simulator, a model for regional development taking into account the environment, both natural and social, and the economy (Chapter 9).

▓ The quest for sustainable transport

Sustainable transport

That which does not harm the environment or use resources that cannot be replaced.

Sustainable transport is that which does not harm the environment or use resources that cannot be replaced. The world is a long way from reaching that goal. To achieve it – according to an Organisation for Economic Cooperation and Development (OECD) group which looked at the issue in 2000 – does not mean that we have to do with less transport than we have today, but it means using different transport.

It concluded that half the effort required to ensure transport was sustainable would come from technological improvements of cars, coaches and trucks, fuels and infrastructure. The other half would come from making transport smarter by using vehicles more efficiently (e.g. fewer cars carrying just one person) and by shortening journeys (more compact towns and cities and more local production) (Air Transport Action Group 2000).[15]

Attempts have been under way for several decades to reduce the emissions of vehicles by introducing laws and regulations to change the way their engines and exhaust systems operate. Since 1986 in Australia new cars have had catalytic converters in their exhaust systems which reduce the amounts of oxides of nitrogen, carbon monoxide and unburnt petrol escaping into the air. Use of unleaded petrol is lowering the amount of lead in the urban environment.

The Commonwealth Government has sponsored research and devised strategies to reduce energy consumption and greenhouse emissions. These actions have resulted in the Sustainable Energy Policy and the National Greenhouse Strategy. Their applications affect transport.

State and territory governments are responsible for developing and implementing their own policies and programs in planning transport systems, urban design and the integration of modes of transport. Local government has the major responsibility for managing rural and minor roads and verges.

State and territory governments have established environmental protection agencies to develop policies and strategies to deal with a wide range of concerns. Transport-related issues such as noise control, reduction of waste oil and tyres going to landfill, and roadside revegetation are managed by those agencies (Australian Bureau of Statistics 1997b). In Europe, politicians and economists are looking more and more at a 'polluter-pays' system, putting a price on the impact on the environment of different forms of transport to encourage travellers to use the form that makes the least impact.

The European Commission's 1998 White Paper on 'Fair Payment for Infrastructure Use' recommended a strategy that would evaluate the external effects of growing traffic volumes (air pollution, climate change, accidents, noise, and congestion). The Commission believes that such a strategy could adequately implement the polluter-pays principle and also increase system efficiency (Air Transport Action Group 2000).

London introduced a Congestion Charge scheme in 2003 to reduce traffic in the heart of the city between 7 am and 6.30 pm on weekdays. Motorists are required to pay a fee to drive inside a 21 sq km zone stretching from the financial district to Hyde Park. The revenues were to be spent on providing a better public transport system for the city (*MX*, 18 February 2003, p. 8).

Cleaner cars and trucks

Research aimed at reducing the environmental impact of motor vehicles has focused on engines and fuels. Alternative engines being tested include new combustion systems (e.g. two-stroke engine, hydrogen, gas turbine) and non-combustion systems (electric vehicles, solar vehicles). Alternative fuels being evaluated include reformulated petrol, liquified petroleum gas, natural gas, ethanol and methanol.

One possibility that has attracted industry and CSIRO research is the fuel cell. Within it hydrogen and oxygen react to create water, generating an electrical flow. Although some big name companies, such as Ford, Daimler–Chrysler and Renault–Nissan, are involved in their development, it will be years before fuel cells will be powering cars on a regular basis (Lamb 2001).[16]

The Australian Concept Car, known as the aXcessaustralia Low Emission Vehicle, is an industry project designed to demonstrate capabilities in design and component production. The aXcessaustralia LEV has a remarkable powertrain developed by several divisions of the CSIRO. It consists of an electric traction engine (ETM), a powerpack made of batteries and supercapacitors and a 1.4 litre petrol engine. The latter never directly drives the wheels, power is always harnessed through the ETM. Much of the time the petrol engine is switched off.

DEFINITIONS

It can recharge the batteries on the move, but the batteries also have been designed to be charged overnight on low tariff electricity. The battery pack provides enough storage without recharging to allow the car to complete an urban drive cycle, about 20 minutes, under electric power only. Drivers can, say, commute to the city outskirts from outer suburban areas with the assistance of the petrol engine. In city centres, or other areas that are particularly environmentally sensitive, the driver can switch to electric-only mode and run with zero emissions. Overall the car has the range of a conventional vehicle, but with very much lower emissions (Lamb 2001, and www.axcessaustralia.com).

Two petrol-electric hybrid vehicles, the Toyota Prius and Honda Insight, went on sale in Australia in 2001. These have petrol and electric motors, which operate at different times according to driving conditions. Their fuel consumption is much less than that of ordinary cars.

Reducing aircraft emissions

Although total emissions from aircraft will increase in the future because there will be more aircraft, there are several ways in which they can be minimised – by technology advances, by regulations and by improvements in **air traffic management**.

Air traffic management
Systems for the guidance, separation, coordination, and control of aircraft movements.

Subsonic aircraft being produced today are about 70 per cent more fuel efficient per passenger kilometre than planes of 40 years ago. Most of this is the result of engine improvements and the rest has come from better airframe design. Improvement is a continuing process. Compared with today's aircraft, a 20 per cent improvement in fuel efficiency has been projected by 2015. But with the extra planes in the air, it is expected that total aviation fuel use – including passenger, freight, and military – will increase by 3 per cent a year over the same period, as against the projected annual passenger traffic growth rate of nearly 5 per cent.

Regulations of the International Civil Aviation Organisation (ICAO) set technical limits for emissions of nitrogen oxides, carbon monoxide, unburned hydrocarbons and smoke. Efforts are being made to address emissions of greenhouse gases at all phases of flight, including climb and cruise (Air Transport Action Group 2000).

Congestion on the ground and in the air is another major cause of excess emissions from aircraft. Planes flying on inefficient routings or in holding patterns waiting to land not only infuriate passengers but also waste fuel. Planes lined up at airports with their engines burning fuel as they wait to take off have a similar effect. British Airways alone reported that its aircraft wasted 45,500 tonnes of aviation fuel in a single year during delays at just two airports – Gatwick and Heathrow (*Jane's Airport Review*, May 1994, p. 13).

The solution is in improved air traffic management systems, used for the guidance, separation, coordination, and control of aircraft movements. It has been estimated that with today's fleet and operations, better air traffic management could reduce fuel consumption by from 6 to 12 per cent.

Dealing with noise

Today's aircraft have quieter engines, which have significantly reduced the number of people affected by aircraft noise. On take-off, a 1960s Boeing 727 created a 'footprint' of noise which covered an area of more than 14 square km. In contrast, a modern commercial jet of similar capacity but with greater take-off power, such as the Airbus A-320, creates a 'noise footprint' covering only 1.5 square km. Noise annoyance has been reduced by up to 75 per cent (Air Transport Action Group 2000). International regulations call for the phasing out of older aircraft and for new aircraft to meet strict standards in respect to noise. At some airports – it depends on the physical layout of the airport and its surroundings – noise can be reduced by instituting favourable procedures for take-off, approach and landing.

All this may be gratifying news, but the number of planes using airports keeps increasing, and as the Sydney experience has shown, the noise from a major airport can discomfort many thousands of people. Its impact has been shown to decrease the value of affected houses in Australia by between 6–23 per cent (New South Wales Environment Protection Authority 1997).

The only real answer seems to deter people from living near airports. The Air Transport Action Group says control of land use near airports is vital if the noise reductions already achieved are not to be offset by people moving closer to airports – and to the noise. Improvements to the noise problem will depend to a great extent on maintaining a quiet buffer zone which is kept free of residential, or other noise-sensitive, development.

▓ Protection of special areas

Areas such as national parks, state forests and world heritage areas are protected by legislation, which places controls on commercial and recreational activity within them. Tourism is often looked upon favourably, to the extent it is allowed to continue, perhaps encouraged, where other uses such as logging and mining are banned or severely restricted. Tourism income from entry fees and permits provides money for conservation. In a number of Australian world heritage areas tourism is the chief commercial user.

The National System of Reserves, incorporating the protected area networks of each state and territory, covers more than 60 million hectares. It includes protected areas ranging from small nature reserves to major national parks and world heritage areas (Environment Australia 1997).

World heritage listing provides significant statutory protection to an area's outstanding natural and cultural values, particularly provisions that require the development, funding and implementation of management plans (Australian Bureau of Statistics 2000c).

▨ Performance improvement commitment programs

A number of programs, worldwide and in Australia, aim to improve the performance of the travel and tourism industry in relation to the environment by setting benchmarks and then judging performance against them. Companies commit themselves to take part in the program so that criteria can be applied systematically.

Green Globe is the environmental program of the World Travel & Tourism Council. This is an industry body – its members are more than 100 chairmen, presidents and chief executive officers of leading travel and tourism companies. Its program, Green Globe 21, is a benchmarking and certification system. In 2001, the Green Globe 21 campaign focused on reducing greenhouse gases emitted by travel and tourism companies. The use of energy by each participating company was benchmarked, improvement targets set and performance measured.

The Green Globe 21 process was said to have had these benefits for companies: (a) savings achieved through reduced energy consumption, reduced waste generation, reduced use of potable water and enhanced efficiency; (b) improved competitiveness; (c) a marketing advantage aimed at consumers who are increasingly concerned about the environment; (d) electronic marketing through the Green Globe 21 website; (e) improved staff commitment to the company; and (f) enhanced knowledge which means sharper business practice, especially for marketing (Green Globe fact sheets).

Greenhouse Challenge

Australia has its own voluntary commitment program aimed at abating greenhouse gas emissions. It is the Commonwealth Government's Greenhouse Challenge, which began in 1995. It is not specifically aimed at tourism, although travel and tourism companies and trade associations make up nearly a quarter of the more than 400 organisations in the program in the early 2000s.

The biggest number were hotels and other accommodation facilities, and coach/bus companies. The list also includes casinos and token numbers of restaurant, attraction, tour, and rent-a-car companies. Despite the large overall number, the coverage in the industry was far less than that achieved for aluminium and cement production (100 per cent), oil and gas (98 per cent) and coal mining (91 per cent).

Companies and other organisations sign agreements with the government committing them to take specified action to abate emissions. The Australian Greenhouse Office, the Commonwealth agency overseeing the Greenhouse Challenge, believes that in the first five years it led to 16 per cent fewer greenhouse gas emissions than if no action had been taken.

Trade associations help increase the travel and tourism involvement. It is no accident that hotels and coach/bus companies predominate among travel and tourism members of the Greenhouse Challenge because their peak industry associations are Challenge members. The Australian Hotels Association (AHA), represents more than 7,000 hotels, casinos and resorts, and the Bus Industry Confederation (BIC), represents a sector operating about 21,700 vehicles (www.greenhouse.gov.au).

▦ Company-initiated best practice programs

Some individuals and companies take the initiative and institute best practice programs of their own. They are not influenced by regulations or the possibility of penalties; they recognise that good environmental practice is good management. There are two ways of doing this: (a) developing a set of guidelines for their operation, incorporating them in a policy statement and instituting an audit process to ensure the guidelines are followed; and (b) following best practice guidelines developed by a government agency or trade association.

An environmental policy can be formulated by identifying the principal issues facing the company and then devising a statement to meet them. Goodall (1994) says the policy statement should indicate the company's intention to:

- comply with the spirit as well as the letter of environmental legislation and develop reasonable and workable environmental regulations
- avoid any negative environmental impacts from their proposed developments and reduce/eliminate any negative impacts of current activities
- promote increased efficiency in resource use, including waste minimisation, and substitute environmentally benign inputs and equipment wherever feasible
- develop products which are environmentally friendly
- foster among staff, and also customers and the communities in which they function, an understanding of environmental issues.

Environmental auditing is then employed to assess the firm's progress toward achieving these goals. Goodall describes the auditing process as the systematic, regular and objective evaluation of the environmental performance of the company, its plant and buildings, its processes and its products.

Best practice guidelines

In Australia, industry associations, government bodies and the CRC for Sustainable Tourism have produced guidelines and examples of responsible and sometimes imaginative 'best practices' which advance the cause of sustainable tourism.

In 1998, the Office of National Tourism, part of the then-styled Commonwealth Department of Industry, Science and Tourism, published, on the Internet, guidelines for the designing, construction and operation of tourism accommodation.

The guidelines start with the proposition that the design of buildings should be ecologically sustainable, defined by the Royal Australian Institute of Architects as 'the use of design principles and strategies which help reduce the ecological impact of buildings by reducing the consumption of energy and resources, or by minimising disturbances to existing vegetation'.

According to the guidelines, the design of the building should take into account its cost and ecological impact over its life – from extraction and processing of the building materials to construction and occupation and its eventual demolition. Important factors to consider are running costs, energy efficiency, maintenance and durability of materials, pollution minimisation, the energy embodied in the materials during their manufacture, and the building's potential for refurbishment or other uses (Office of National Tourism 1998b, http://twinshare.crctourism.com.au).

Codes of conduct

Voluntary environmental codes of conduct became widespread in the 1990s as a tool for raising awareness of environmental issues and improving behaviour and practice. They were developed by governments and their agencies and non-governmental organisations, including industry associations.

The World Tourism Organisation incorporated environmental issues in its Global Code of Ethics. It aimed to balance the responsibilities of governments, private enterprise, travellers and the host community. Another example of an international general code is the Sustainable Tourism Charter, which was developed at the World Conference on Sustainable Tourism, an event sponsored by UNESCO and held on the Spanish island of Lanzarote in 1995.

Tourism industry associations' codes can be international, national or regional, and can also be sector-specific, such as hotel industry codes. The majority of codes are directed separately at the responsibilities of industry, tourists or the host populations. For businesses, codes of conduct are usually short documents summarising the main points of responsible practices.

A survey of codes of conduct around the world by the United Nations Environmental Program, published in 1995, found that most tourism industry codes address issues such as travel and tourism businesses':

- acceptance of responsibility for the environmental impact of tourism and the taking of corrective action where necessary
- ensuring positive visitor experience by effective visitor management, control, and education
- provision of environmental training for staff and effective motivation
- monitoring and reporting on environmental performance, including assessment of water and energy conservation, waste minimisation, and recycling
- support of the local economy
- support of local and national planning bodies
- encouragement of the participation of host communities in decision-making processes
- recognition that (a) tourism development must consider all aspects of the human and natural environment; (b) it should be sustainable; and (c) every part of the

environment has limits beyond which development should not take place, particularly in sensitive areas

- acceptance that sustainability concepts should be incorporated into design and construction of tourism developments
- understanding that these considerations should be widened into a full environmental impact assessment, with implementation monitored after development. (Mock & O'Neil 1996)

The first codes of conduct for tourists were directed at the behaviour of ecotourists. The use of high-value, fragile wild areas and contact with particular local cultures made it necessary to establish voluntary behaviour guidelines.

Codes have been written for particular activities such as mountain biking, climbing, whitewater rafting and kayaking, usually advising visitors to (a) avoid disturbing wildlife and damaging ecosystems; (b) dispose of waste properly; (c) respect the practices of the local community; and (d) respect local legislation.

Some codes address tourist behaviour in specific locations, such as national parks and protected areas. These often combine general guidelines with others that are particular to the location, e.g. dispose of waste properly; protect the natural and cultural environment; use energy efficiently; pay a fair price for goods and services.

Environmental codes of conduct for host communities address three major areas of interaction between host communities and tourism; the social and cultural norms of the host community; the economic development of the host community; and the protection and preservation of the local environment.

The codes are useful tools for focusing local communities' concerns and for informing tourists and tourism businesses about those concerns. Thus they often deal with such matters as the role of the local population in tourism development; safeguarding local cultures and traditions; educating the local population on the importance of maintaining a balance between conservation and economic development; and providing quality tourist products and experiences (Mock & O'Neil 1996).

CASE STUDY

Environmental practices in Australian tourism

In Australia, as with the rest of the world, it is usually the larger companies – airlines, hotel chains, big tour operators – that have environmental policies and they tend to be the leaders in developing better management practices for the environment.

There are some exceptions. For example, trade associations have had some success in recruiting smaller companies as members of the Greenhouse Challenge and the operator members of the Ecotourism Association of Australia are mostly small companies. However, management techniques such as environmental audits and impact assessments are more relevant to larger companies because of the cost. Larger companies also have more power to exercise significant influence on suppliers to provide environmentally clean technologies and products.

Qantas Airways demonstrates the big company attitude. It operates to a Group Environment Policy which commits the company to planning and conducting its activities in a manner that protects the environment and minimises environmental impact. At the time of writing, it was managing a number of major environmental projects, including waste reduction, land management, noise management, environmental reporting and community relations. It was also supporting a number of environmental organisations and activities including the respected Banksia Environmental Foundation and Clean-Up Australia Day. It was in the process of going further, of establishing an environmental management system (EMS) based on the international standard ISO 14001 (Todd 2001).

This uses the same fundamental systems as the better-known ISO 9000 series of quality management standards, such as documentation control, management system auditing, operational control, control of records, management policies, training, statistical techniques and corrective preventive action. ISO 14001 also incorporates the setting of objectives and quantified targets, emergency preparedness, considering the view of interested parties and public disclosure of the environmental policy (Fredericks & McCallum 1995).

Australia's biggest hotel group, Accor Asia Pacific, works to an Environment Charter which covers 15 types of action in four main areas: (1) waste management and recycling; (2) technical control; (3) architecture and landscape; and (4) raising awareness and training.

Large adventure tour operators subscribe to 'RT' – responsible travel (or tourism) – and have staff members assigned to monitor programs to see that sustainable tourism practices are adhered to. For example, Intrepid Travel has a full time 'Responsible Travel Coordinator' in Melbourne and four part-time coordinators in Asia. Peregrine Adventures has written responsible tourism practices into its mission statement which also covers allied brands Exodus and Gecko's. Their mission is to 'operate tourism that fosters understanding, appreciation and conservation of the cultures and environments we visit'. World Expeditions says it is committed to the principles of 'true sustainability' and minimal environmental impact. 'Wilderness tours should leave a minimal trace of their passing' (Power 2001, www.intrepidtravel.com, www.peregrine.net.au, www.worldexpeditions. com.au).

Nature-based accommodation

While big companies may have been prominent in adopting environmentally responsible practices, small companies throughout Australia have been in the forefront of innovative measures to improve environmental performance, often driven by an individual's conservation ethic. Here are examples of unusual accommodation establishments:

The Daintree Wilderness Lodge is located in the Cape Tribulation region about 120 km north of Cairns on freehold land surrounded by the Wet Tropics World Heritage Area. There is plenty to do: visits to Aboriginal sites, rainforest walks, horseriding, canoeing on the Daintree River and so on. The owner, Anna Graham (1999) says she recognises the setting as a living biological museum and the underlying reason for operating the business is her commitment to sustainable tourism, not just for the sake of the environment, but her children's children.

Crystal Creek Rainforest Retreat is a nature-based resort in the McPherson Ranges in northern New South Wales, about 20 km north-west of Murwillumbah. The 140-hectare property, a private valley under the escarpment of Mt Springbrook, is bounded on three sides by the Numinbah Nature Reserve. To get to the resort requires crossing four creek fords which certainly heightens the feeling of being in a wilderness.

Accommodation is in seven cabins which are sited within the rainforest to make the most of natural breezes and shade from surrounding trees. The cabins, well-equipped and comfortable (some with spas), are placed out of sight of each other. They are designed to encourage guests to look outwards in every direction, to feel at one with the natural beauty which surrounds them and is always visible. The car park is a long way away and transport from the main lodge and administrative area is by silent electric buggy. The only constant sound is from that of flowing water from a pristine creek (Southern Cross University 2000, notes for Tourism Executive Development Program, June).

Bay of Fires Lodge is located on a freehold site surrounded by the Mount William National Park in north-east Tasmania. It overlooks the Bay of Fires. It is the end point of two- to four-day camping hikes through the park for groups of 10 people and two guides.

Rather than provide a scattering of cabins for the hikers (they spend two nights there), the architect designed two long parallel pavilions with metal skillion roofs separated by an open central walkway. The Royal Australian Institute of Architects jury which gave the building an award ('Commercial Commendation') in 2000, commented that the Lodge program '. . . includes high environmental settings, ecological sustainability, "touch the ground lightly" tourism and architecture, financial viability and the employment of a young and dedicated staff' (*Architecture Australia*, November–December 2000, p. 66).

Projects funded

The Commonwealth Government has funded projects it believed promoted ecologically sustainable tourism and provided standards and directions for Australian tourism. While generally these were small-scale projects outside mainstream tourism they broadened the vision of what could be done. The following are examples from the government's booklet

'Developing Tourism: Projects in Profile' published by the Office of National Tourism in 1996.

Broome Bird Observatory at Roebuck Bay, Western Australia. Development of a computer-controlled solar-diesel hybrid power system, capable of being operated remotely via a modem and telephone line. Solar tracking rigs follow the sun from dawn to dusk and provide 25–40 per cent more energy than non-tracking units. Enough power is derived from the sun for essential items such as refrigerators, fans, lights and office equipment and also to charge the batteries for night use so that the diesel generator is used only for back-up.

Cradle Mountain National Park, Tasmania. Installation of toilets in two separate sites on the Overland Track, where the circumstances are difficult for composting waste because of cold, wet conditions in a high usage remote area. Before installation, the Centre for Environmental Studies at the University of Tasmania spent 14 months researching dry sanitation techniques in Australia and overseas.

Atal, a mulga forest at the base of the Mann Ranges, about 5 km from Angatja, the homeland of the Pitjantjatjara people in South Australia, and about 350 km from Uluru. Development of a bush eco-camp for clients of Desert Tracks, an Aboriginal-owned tour company. The design for the campsite incorporated traditional architecture using local materials and modern technologies to ensure minimal impact and meet basic needs for visitor comfort. Examples are noiseless, solar water heating units in the ablution blocks and solar-powered refrigeration in the storeroom.

Point Halloran, Brisbane. Development of an ecotourism destination from 78 hectares of highly significant koala habitat. Infrastructure includes a stand-alone interpretive centre with a fenced carpark at the entrance to the site, 300 metres of timber boardwalk and 1,000 metres of walking track meandering through the forest and estuarine tidal wetland. Signs are incorporated in the interpretive centre and on the walking track to guide people through the site and to highlight interesting facts and features. Signs on the walking track describe the impact of fire on the wetland, markings left by animals, a stand of melaleucas, and salt tolerance of mangroves.

Hamelin Pool, in the Shark Bay World Heritage Area, north-west of Perth. Protection of marine stromatolites, which are identical to the earliest forms of life that have been discovered in the fossil record. They are formed by microorganisms that build mushroom-like structures up to one metre high in the hyper-saline waters. They are links to a past that goes back 3.5 billion years and are extremely rare, living in only two places on earth. Hamelin Pool is the only site accessible to the public.

A boardwalk a metre and a half above the surface has been erected to give an interesting perspective as well as protecting the stromatolites. Preservation has also relied on interpretation. A comic character, 'Stumpy the stromatolite', was created to help people relate to stromatolites, in particular to emphasise that they are another type of community or 'family'. At each point where the public can gain access from the foreshore, a 'Caring for stromatolites' sign with a graphic of Stumpy was erected. Ten concepts of stromatolite life history were selected for the interpretation materials.

Naracoorte Caves Conservation Park, a World Heritage-listed 350-hectare reserve in the south-east of South Australia. Provision of an interpretive facility for a colony of common bent-wing bats. Visitors are not permitted in the bat cave because of the extreme sensitivity of the bats to human disturbance. The interpretive facility is a windowless building that resembles the rock in the caves. Four remote controlled video cameras have been set up in the cave. They use infra-red lighting and image enhancement technology to relay images of bat life back to the six large monitors in the interpretation facility. Visitors can manipulate the cameras to observe a range of bat behaviour, including roosting, flocking, birthing, and feeding.

INDUSTRY PROFILE

ANDREW K SIVIJS PROJECT MANAGER, QUEENSLAND HERITAGE TRAILS NETWORK (QHTN), ARTS QUEENSLAND

I coordinate and facilitate the delivery of major cultural heritage tourism infrastructure and development projects across regional Queensland. This requires extensive consultation and partnership development with key stakeholders such as local government authorities, regional tourism organisations, Tourism Queensland, regional interest groups and state government agencies. Projects vary enormously in nature and structure and include the development of capital infrastructure, such as interpretive facilities and integrated information programs, and 'soft' infrastructure elements including business planning and marketing support.

This role requires regular travel and interaction with local communities, industry leaders and special interest groups and offers the capacity to provide strong leadership, personal initiative and direction for regional tourism development. The QHTN has formed effective relationships with land management agencies to focus on a number of sustainable tourism initiatives in national parks and wet tropics rainforests in Far North Queensland.

In association with the resource managers, LGAs and the regional tourism industry, a comprehensive series of world-class walking trails is being established in FNQ and is expected to have significant appeal in both the domestic and international visitor markets. Collectively known as the *Misty Mountains Trails*, this product will rival some of the most famous long and short walk trails in other high quality nature-based destinations such as New Zealand and Canada. Importantly, a common vision and shared direction has enabled the project partners to implement a capital works program that is sustainable and supports the strict planning and management regimes for these protected areas.

How did I get here?

A broad background in regional tourism planning, development, strategic analysis and private sector consulting provided a solid grounding for my current focus.

What do I like about my job?

Gaining experience in front-line resort management, consulting to the regional tourism industry and in a planning and development role with a state tourism authority has provided exciting and satisfying exposure to many facets of the tourism industry.

SUMMARY

There is worldwide concern about the natural environment and what human beings are doing to it. The natural environment is of supreme importance to tourism. Tourism's relationship with it is complex and should be viewed in the context of how human beings relate to the environment generally.

By 2050 the population of the world will have increased by more than half of what it was at the beginning of the century. But the number of people travelling around the world is expected to increase at a much greater pace. Travel requires large quantities of energy and adding numbers of tourists at destinations brings pressure on local resources, sometimes at the expense of host communities.

Three global problems have specific relevance because of tourism's involvement with them. They are:

1. **Global warming** The Intergovernmental Panel on Climate Change is predicting rises between 1.4 and 5.8 degrees in the period 1990 to 2100. The main reason is that human activities are causing increased emissions of greenhouse gases which slow the escape of infra-red radiation from the atmosphere and increase temperatures. The chief culprit is carbon dioxide, which people keep sending into the atmosphere in huge quantities by burning fossil fuels – wood, oil, coal, peat and natural gas.

2. **Air pollution** This has caused enormous damage to the natural and built environment – most notably the effect of acid rain on forests, lakes, rivers and city buildings – and to people's health: pollutants affect the throat and lungs in particular and cause respiratory and other diseases. In a relative sense, Australia's problems are minor, but air pollution still causes a range of health problems, affecting the throat, lungs, heart and eyes. Motor vehicles are a major cause.

3. **Deforestation** of the forests that existed before colonisation, the best Australia can aim for now is to retain 15 per cent of them. The focus worldwide is now on the tropical rainforests, which have a special role in keeping human beings healthy. Every hectare of rainforest takes from the atmosphere annually one tonne of carbon dioxide, the chief cause of global warming.

Tourism activities do or can have a severe impact on the natural environment:

(a) vehicles essential to tourism – cars, coaches, planes, trains and ships – produce a significant proportion of the gases which pollute the air and cause global warming; (b) tourism requires built attractions, terminals, convention centres and entertainment venues, and especially buildings to accommodate tourists. The location, design and construction of a building has a lot to do with its energy efficiency. The principal environmental issues of hotels and other accommodation businesses are energy use and waste disposal; and (c) tourism operations puts pressure on the environment by affecting natural resources such as vegetation and coral reefs, harming wildlife and habitats and producing pollution and wastes.

The response of governments, organisations and companies concerned with tourism to alleviate dangers to the natural environment have included:

(1) an increase in Australian tourism research, especially as the result of the establishment of the Cooperative Research Centre for Sustainable Tourism (CRC Tourism).

(2) reduction in the emissions of vehicles by introducing laws and regulations to change the way their engines and exhaust systems operate. Research aimed at reducing the environmental impact of motor vehicles has focused on engines and fuels. Emissions from aircraft are being reduced by technological advances, by regulations and, hopefully, by improvements in air traffic management.

(3) the National System of Reserves, incorporating the protected area networks of each state and territory, covers over 60 million hectares. It includes protected areas ranging from small nature reserves to major national parks and world heritage areas. World heritage listing provides significant statutory protection to an area's outstanding natural and cultural values, particularly provisions that require the development, funding and implementation of management plans.

(4) a number of programs, worldwide and in Australia, aim to improve the performance of the travel and tourism industry in relation to the environment by setting benchmarks and then judging performance against them. Other programs have included voluntary environmental codes of conduct developed by governments, industry associations and other organisations.

QUESTIONS

1. Public awareness about the dangers to the planet has increased markedly in the past 30 years. What are some of the important issues? Discuss them.

2. How are concepts like ecology and biodiversity related to tourism?

QUESTIONS continued

3. What Australian tourism assets are in danger from global warming? Is it possible that others may be created, that somewhere somehow tourism can benefit from warmer temperatures?

4. How do dangers from air pollutants indoors concern tourism operators? How can the dangers be lessened?

5. What kind of tourism operators should be concerned about the state of our forests? What should they do about it?

6. What environmental issues should the developer of a tourism resort take into consideration before starting the project?

7. In what ways can tourism operators contribute to the quest for sustainable transport?

8. Do you think the Australian Government's Greenhouse Challenge is a better program for Australian tourism operators than a worldwide industry program like Green Globe?

9. Do you think voluntary codes of conduct are likely to work, in creating awareness of issues and/or as a guide to behaviour?

10. At the Crystal Brook nature-based resort, the carpark is sited well away from the cabins and transport to them is by a relatively quiet electric buggy. Can you think of other circumstances where this could be beneficial by reducing noise? In your review of the case study were there other ideas which you think could be applied advantageously elsewhere?

MANAGING TOURISM

THIS SECOND PART OF THE BOOK IS CONCERNED WITH THE MANAGEMENT issues involved in tourism, who is responsible for management and how it is undertaken. The chapter subjects reflect the evolving nature of Australian travel and tourism, the changing scene facing governments and business managements as tourism and competition both increase, as globalisation brings about steady and unrelenting change, and as the world reacts to economic and health crises, wars and acts of terror.

The first chapter (Chapter 7) describes the roles of the managers: three levels of government, industry associations and the individual businesses that belong to them. It discusses the importance of research in reaching decisions on an ever-growing range of issues affected by or affecting tourism.

The subject of Chapter 8 is marketing, a versatile tool for management, the most valuable open to managers to influence tourism and its impacts. This is illustrated in subsequent chapters, including Chapter 9, which discusses the requirements and methods for tourism to be developed.

The next two chapters are concerned with matters which have become increasingly relevant to Australian travel and tourism – 'quality' as it is applied to tourism products, and particularly the service elements, and the management of visitors at the destination. The last chapter deals with the management of change, both the gradual change that may occur almost unnoticed but permanently alters tourism and its industry, and change brought about by crises and disasters, which may be unexpected and sudden.

THE MANAGERS OF TOURISM

LEARNING OBJECTIVES

Appreciating that government and industry are both involved in the management of tourism and that government must take the lead role.

Identifying what is managed and the methods adopted.

Understanding the concept of policy and how tourism policy is formed in Australia.

Noting the legal framework within which Australian travel and tourism businesses function and the special legal requirements for some of those businesses. In particular, taking note of the competition and misleading conduct provisions of the Trade Practices Act.

Understanding the different tourism roles of the Commonwealth, state/territory and local governments and how they relate to each other.

Examining the main features of the public–private sector partnership in managing tourism and the industry associations involved.

Appreciating the importance of the research role.

Examining a case study of the challenges faced by local government in Byron Bay as the result of tourism.

**UNDERSTAND
THE MEANING OF:**

* *management*
* *PATA*
* *tourism stakeholder*
* *NTA*
* *decentralised system*
* *TMC*
* *ASCOT*
* *policy*
* *TCF*
* *principals and agents*
* *Warsaw Convention*
* *innkeeper*
* *market power abuse*
* *price fixing*
* *exclusive dealing*
* *tourism research*

DEFINITIONS

. . . .

Management

*'The specific tool,
the specific
function, the
specific instrument,
to make institutions
capable of
producing results'
(Drucker 1998).
The critical
functions in tourism
management are
planning,
coordination and
control.*

ROLES IN TOURISM MANAGEMENT

Tourism operations are largely a matter for private companies. Australian governments intervene when there is a need to fill a gap, for example to provide an essential service or develop a resource which may not at first be profitable. But tourism is an entrepreneurial activity – it involves risk-taking – and individuals and companies are usually better at it than governments. However, tourism is not simply operations. It involves many interests which spread throughout a community. As we have seen it can have a major effect on a nation's well-being. It needs to be managed and governments must be involved.

Drucker (1998) defines **management** as 'the specific tool, the specific function, the specific instrument, to make institutions capable of producing results'. The critical functions in tourism management are planning, coordination and control (Leiper 1990).

Governments and business enterprises are both involved in tourism management in Australia and work together on important aspects of it. However, it should be recognised the cultures are not the same – the way governments and businesses operate are different even when their objectives are in tune. Having them march to the same drumbeat is not always easy.

What is managed?

What has to be managed in tourism? The Pacific Asia Travel Association (PATA), an international non-governmental organisation, recognised the diversity of interests affected by tourism when it launched its Values Tourism concept in 1995. According to the concept, sustained growth of the travel and tourism industry depends upon the ability to manage these things:

* meeting the needs of customers
* growing the economic contribution to national economies
* minimising the impact of tourism on the environment
* accommodating the needs of host communities
* delivering adequate returns to those with a financial stake in the industry.

The 'values' considered were consumer, cultural, economic, ecological, financial, future, human resource, heritage, political and social.

The objective is the now familiar one of balancing economic return with service to the consumer and protection of the environment and preservation of cultural diversity. The method is to bring the needs of the stakeholder groups into an integrated management framework. Stakeholders are:

DEFINITIONS

- staff of the travel and tourism industry
- customers
- investors and developers
- environment
- heritage and culture of tourism areas
- host communities
- governments
- national and local economies (Pacific Asia Travel Association 1995).[1]

Stakeholders have differing expectations and values and they all need to be addressed in tourism planning, development and in operational values.

The role of governments

In the early 1990s, the World Tourism Organisation conducted a thorough examination of the involvement by governments in tourism around the world.[2] It found acceptance that governments had responsibilities, to a larger or lesser degree, for:

- establishing the framework within which tourism's public and private sectors operate
- providing legislation, regulations and controls applicable for tourism, the protection of the environment and the cultural heritage
- constructing infrastructure, land, sea, air transport facilities and communications
- developing human resources with appropriate education and training for tourism employment
- elaborating a tourism policy with concrete plans, which could include:
  - evaluating the tourism wealth and assets of the country, natural and cultural, and their protection
  - identifying categories of competitive tourist products with comparative advantages
  - presenting requirements for infrastructure and superstructure[3] which could affect tourism development
  - elaborating programs for the financing of tourism activities in the public and private sectors.

The WTO also found that while there was a need for a public body to be responsible to carry out tourism **policy**, there was not a single model of such an organisation. A 'national tourism administration' (NTA) could be a separate department, or a section in a larger department or a semi-governmental organisation or any other form of a public body exercising public authority (Raphael 1993).

Policy
A course of action adopted and pursued by a government, expressed as a broad statement of general intent which guides the actions of public servants and others in carrying out the government's wishes.

Table 7.1 Government responsibilities in tourism, Australia

RESPONSIBILITY	COMMONWEALTH	STATE/TERRITORY	LOCAL
Economic well-being	All levels of government encourage tourism for the economic benefits it brings (e.g. employment, regional development). Tourism as an export industry contributes foreign exchange to the balance of payments account.		
Transport	Regulates air and sea transport to and from Australia and interstate	Regulates land and some air transport within state/territory	
Provision of infrastructure	Major airports, national roads system	Funding for roads, bridges etc	Lesser roads, bridges, sewerage etc
Provision of tourism plant	Financial assistance programs, certain attractions in the ACT	Museums, art galleries, convention/exhibition centres	Similar to state/territory, but to a lesser extent
Land use	Control over Commonwealth lands, including national parks	Control over Crown lands, include state forests, national parks and other reserves	Right of approvals
Building regulations		Planning legislation	Planning approvals
Travel operations		Travel sales, tour operations through commissions	
Attraction operations	National Museum, Art Gallery, War Museum, national parks	Museums, art galleries, historic sites, zoos, national parks, caves	Parks and reserves, monuments, historic houses and other attractions
Events	Financial, security support for 'mega-events' (e.g. Olympic Games)	Attract, market and in some cases manage major events	Attract and support local events
Information provision	Australian Tourist Commission (ATC) Commonwealth Department literature, online information, interpretive centres (e.g. national parks)	Brochures, tourism commission's Internet sites, state information centre networks	Local information centres, brochures, online sites

Table 7.1 Continued

RESPONSIBILITY	COMMONWEALTH	STATE/TERRITORY	LOCAL
Investment incentives	Guarantee of repatriation of profits and dividends to foreign investors; facilitation of foreign investment through Invest Australia	Grants, subsidies, loans, tax exemptions to encourage the building of accommodation, attractions, tour operations, etc.	Similar to state/territory
Environmental protection	National heritage legislation, global warming policy, forest reserve system etc. Agencies include Australian Greenhouse Gas Office, Environment Australia, Great Barrier Reef Marine Park Authority	Legislation re national parks, noise, noxious emissions, environmental impact statements, forest reserve system etc. Agencies include environmental protection authorities	Local environmental protection measures, including regulation of burning off and use of incinerators
Border controls	Customs, immigration and quarantine laws		
International tourism relations	Representation on UN and other relevant international bodies (e.g. APEC)	Representation on some international tourism bodies (e.g. PATA)	
Public health	Funding for health system including public hospitals	Administration of health system	Health and hygiene enforcement, clean water, sewerage etc.
Law and order, emergencies	Defence against terrorism, international criminals	Policing, operation of emergency services	Public safety at local sites, events, licensing approvals
Marketing	Overseas marketing, ATC and Export Market Development Grants Scheme	Domestic/overseas marketing through commissions	Involvement through regional tourism organisations

Continued . . .

Table 7.1 Continued

RESPONSIBILITY	COMMONWEALTH	STATE/TERRITORY	LOCAL
Research	Bureau of Tourism Research, Tourism Forecasting Council, CSIRO, Cooperative Research Centres	Joint funding of Bureau of Tourism Research, extensive independent research on particular projects	Contributions to localised research (modest role)
Education and training	Funding for universities, TAFE colleges	Administration of the education system	
Employment conditions	Workplace relations legislation	State/territory industrial awards	
Consumer protection	Australian Competition & Consumer Commission	Licensing of travel agents	Enforcement of regulations on health, fire and safety

Levels of responsibility

Government in Australia is on three levels – Commonwealth, state/territory and local – and it is necessary to examine the roles of each. Some interests are shared. Table 7.1 shows tourism responsibilities of each level of government.

The table describes the functions of a decentralised system, which in Australia is the result of constitutional arrangements since federation in 1901. Some countries incorporate all essential functions in one administration – in tourism terms that would mean having the one government body responsible for policy and strategy, marketing, land use planning and associated legislation.

However, Australia's three-level government system does have advantages. It is reasonable to expect that regional autonomy, ensured by mechanisms of decentralised decision making, allows for government which is closer and more responsive to the demands of its citizens (Federal–State Relations Committee 1998). Spurr (1993) points out that it is easier for governments to be clear about their role if they are defined narrowly. A national government is not well placed to have the detailed local knowledge of social and environmental issues, or to conduct the consultative processes that are necessary for the community support for planning decisions.

Making the decentralised model work requires:

- good communication
- information and research to support decentralised decision making
- an overall strategy or sense of direction to support decentralised decision making.

Some communication is formalised. The Commonwealth, state and territory and New Zealand ministers responsible for tourism meet at least once a year – more often if required – in the Tourism Ministers Council (TMC) to facilitate inter-governmental cooperation and a coordinated approach to policy development. Representatives of the Australian Tourist Commission, Norfolk Island and Papua New Guinea attend as observers.[4]

Senior tourism officials meet twice a year as members of the Australian Standing Committee on Tourism (ASCOT). The meetings are attended by representatives of the departments of the ministers who are members of TMC, the Australian Tourist Commission and the Bureau of Tourism Research.[5] ASCOT's main objective is to improve cooperation and coordination of government policies and activities as they affect tourism.

The Commonwealth and state/territory tourism organisations also cooperate on a day-to-day working basis on operational matters such as rural and regional tourism and the Australian Tourist Commission's cooperative marketing programs.

Spurr's second requirement 'information and research to support decentralised decision making' is still something of a vexed question. One of the reasons why decentralisation is a good idea is that national governments usually do not have adequate data in respect to tourism demand and supply to tackle policy issues except at the macro level. State and territory governments now feel confident enough to rely on the National Visitor Survey but Foster (2000a) and Allcock (1999) point out the provision of reliable and consistent data is still a problem at the regional level, despite recent improvements.

The third requirement for an overall strategy or sense of direction is met by the coordinating activities of ministers and officials and the planning documents produced at all levels of tourism activity. Strategic planning improved noticeably during the 1990s. Much of the planning is best done by the states/territories because they have the key tourism development responsibility.

On the other hand the primary planning role for overseas marketing rests with the Commonwealth agency, the Australian Tourist Commission. And the Commonwealth is best placed to set a broad general direction to which other planning bodies, including regional and sub-regional tourism organisations, can relate.

Management methods

In broad terms the methods governments and their agencies adopt include the items listed by the WTO above and also involve:

(1) **Consulting with stakeholders** This is done in a number of ways: through formal, structured meetings with industry and advisory groups; through public consultation on specific subjects such as information for strategic planning; through public inquiries into aspects of tourism; through policy consultation with a variety of interest groups; and through interaction between government departments and agencies.

(2) **Identifying issues** The list has become longer as the scale of tourism has increased.

This is a list for 1997 at Commonwealth level:

- tourism yield and dispersal
- tourism infrastructure development, including transport, accommodation and attractions
- investment issues, including access to capital and foreign investment
- international competition and the need for market intelligence
- tourism promotion
- research and statistical issues
- education and training issues
- the impact of technological change
- government regulations, taxation and industrial relations, and
- the needs of particular sectors such as MICE, rural tourism, backpackers, cruise shipping, ecotourism and indigenous tourism (Office of National Tourism 1997).

(3) **Setting policies** which either impact directly or indirectly on tourism. These guide the actions of public servants and others in carrying out the government's wishes in regard to tourism. These are often outside the tourism portfolio, e.g. visa or transport issues.

(4) **Setting up and funding specialised tourism agencies** with the task of helping develop the travel and tourism industry. These agencies produce strategic plans which guide the marketing and physical development of the destination. They also undertake market research and destination marketing and encourage development of plant and facilities.

(5) **Providing facilities and operations** when business is unable to undertake them at the time. Governments provide seed money, subsidising essential facilities or services that are not economically self-sustaining but in the long run are in the national or community interest. As business expands it is usual for governments to withdraw.

(6) **Creating the appropriate fiscal, regulatory and social environment** within which private businesses may make a reasonable profit if they have the skills to do so.

(7) **Adjudicating between conflicting interests** in society. This is a difficult role but one that is becoming increasingly important in an era when concern for the environment, the conservation of recreational and wildlife resources, is a major issue.

The concept of policy

Policy is a course of action adopted and pursued by a government, expressed as a broad statement of general intent which guides the actions of public servants and others in carrying out the government's wishes. It is of supreme importance in the direction a nation takes in tourism or any other endeavour. As with other sectors, government policies establish the economic and social framework in which travel and tourism businesses exist. But some policies are directed at issues which are critical specifically to tourism and the businesses that service it.

Lobbying on behalf of interest groups is usually part of the policy-making process. (Stroud 2001) says the aim usually should be to influence a decision rather than to attempt to change it. Understanding the process and persistence are other essential elements of a favourable outcome. On major issues, widespread grass roots understanding and support for the desired outcome are important ingredients in making politicians more receptive. Stroud also points out that the Commonwealth tourism minister has little direct power except for a relatively small grants program and responsibility for the Australian Tourist Commission Act. The main areas of government activity that impact on the travel and tourism industry are controlled by other ministers.[6]

There is no all-knowing 'big brother' in government sorting things out for tourism in a benign and efficient way. Eventually, many of the right things may be put in place – and a list of them will read well. But to suggest they arose in the first place in the minds of policymakers as part of a cohesive tourism policy is still a pipedream in Australia.

Figure 7.1 shows typical influences on Commonwealth Government policy decisions on tourism.

LEGAL FRAMEWORK

Travel and tourism businesses operate, as do other businesses, within a general legal framework, derived from the common law and legislation passed by the Commonwealth, state and territory parliaments. Some, but not much, legislation refers specifically to tourism, principally the Acts that empower the Australian Tourist Commission and the state/territory tourism commissions and those relating to travel agency licensing. Examples of the legal framework are the law of contracts (rights under agreements), the law of agency (the liability of agents), Trade Practices Act (competition and misleading conduct), Corporations Law (conducting a company) and the Fair Trading Act (consumer protection) (Cordato 1993).

▓ Travel agents and the law

At common law an **agent** is a person who is authorised to represent or act on behalf of a second person, called a principal, to transact some business or affair between the principal and a third person. Travel agents act on behalf of a variety of principals, including airlines, tour operators, hotel and motel companies, cruise lines, coach companies and car rental companies.

A licensing system for travel agents has been established throughout the country under state and territory legislation. In addition the Travel Compensation Fund has been set up under a trust deed to protect the public's money where it has been lost through the default of a travel agent or tour operator.

Participation in the TCF is a condition of licensing except in the Northern Territory where agents have a choice: they can participate in a private territory insurance scheme or

DEFINITIONS

Agent
A person who is authorised to represent or act on behalf of a second person, called a principal, to transact some business or affair between the principal and a third person. Travel agents act on behalf of a variety of principals, including airlines, tour operators, hotel and motel companies, cruise lines, coach companies and car rental companies.

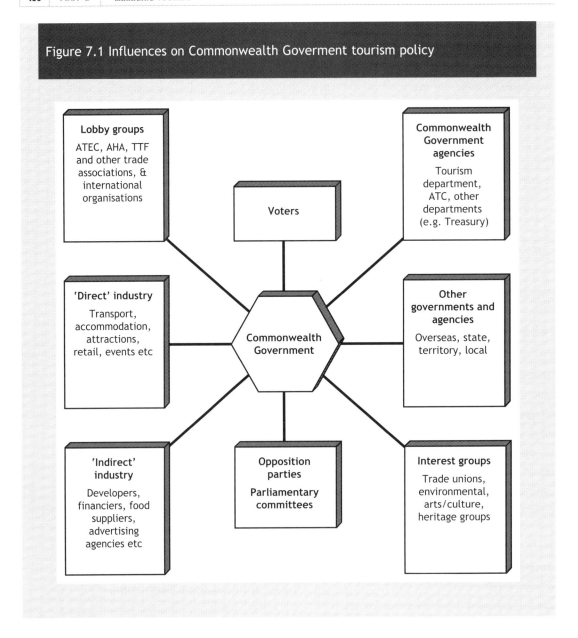

Figure 7.1 Influences on Commonwealth Goverment tourism policy

the TCF. Applicants for a licence elsewhere must be prepared to demonstrate adequate financial viability to become a member of the TCF and on being granted a licence pay a substantial levy. A more modest annual contribution is also required. Agents also pay an annual fee to the licensing authority.

It is compulsory for agents to be licensed. Anyone 'who carries on business as a travel agent' without a licence can be fined. In some states they can be sent to jail. Those carrying on 'business as a travel agent' are defined in each Act with variations from state to state.

Wholesale tour operators

Wholesalers may be regarded as both principals and agents – agents of the suppliers whose products they package, but principals to the travel agents who sell their packages. They are careful to state the limits of their liability in the extensive conditions they include in their brochures. For example, Tasmania's Temptations Holidays says that it sells services and tours 'solely as an agent for the persons providing these activities'. It continues (in part):

> Tasmania's Temptations Holidays, or its agents, finalise all arrangements for these tours upon the express condition that it shall not be liable for any injury, inadvertent errors in bookings, delays generally or irregularity which may be caused by any defect in vehicle, vessel or aircraft. Nor shall it be liable for any injury, damage or loss caused through the acts or default of any company or person engaged in conveying or accommodating passengers, or in the carrying out of any tours as per agreement (Tourism Tasmania 2001).

Liability of airlines

The liability of airlines is generally determined by an international agreement dating from 1929 and known as the Warsaw Convention. It has been ratified by 128 countries. It imposes limits of liability, originally because it was felt that otherwise a single disaster could bankrupt an airline and the cost of insurance would be too expensive for airlines or for passengers (if it were added to the price of a ticket). It was also feared that the capital needed to fund international airlines would be scared away by the fear of disaster.

The Warsaw Convention applies only to international carriage between contracting states.[7] Commonwealth and state legislation deal with liability on international flights to and from Australia and within Australia.[8] The Commonwealth's Transport Legislation Amendment Act of 1995 increased the Warsaw system limit per passenger and required carriers to hold insurance to cover compensation up to the limit for each passenger. These provisions include interstate flights (Cordato 1993, Atherton & Atherton 1998). Legislation also limits claims for injury/damage to third parties and property by airlines, e.g. if an engine falls off and lands on a house.

Accommodation

The Australian law on innkeepers is descended from ancient Roman law which prescribed special rights and duties for those providing travellers with essential services. In today's terms, an 'inn' includes most hotels, motels, backpacker hostels, serviced apartments, resorts and other establishments which provide accommodation for the travelling public.

The innkeeper is the proprietor or person carrying on the business and is usually the person in possession of the premises. Where the establishment is run by a hotel management company (such as Accor, Inter Continental or Hyatt) not as a lessee but as an agent of the owner, the owner as principal would be the real innkeeper at law.

The innkeeper has duties under the law:

- to receive and 'entertain' guests – entertainment meaning to supply them with accommodation, food and beverages. The innkeeper can refuse a guest on 'reasonable grounds', that is if the establishment is booked out or the traveller, for example has a contagious disease, is drunk or is otherwise unfit to be 'entertained'.
- to take reasonable care for guests. This includes a warranty that the premises are as safe for the personal use of guests as reasonable care and skill can make them.
- to look after the guests' means of transport. Originally, this was a duty to receive, stable and feed a guest's horse and receive a carriage. Atherton and Atherton (1998) question whether innkeepers would still be required to feed and stable a horse, and whether they have a common law duty to provide accommodation for a guest's car. In any case, planning laws now prescribe the minimum carparking space required and the innkeeper's self-interest dictates the facilities provided for coaches.
- to safeguard a guest's property. At common law, innkeepers are in effect insurers of their guests' property. In most cases, even if a guest's property is lost or damaged without their fault, innkeepers are liable.

Innkeepers also have rights under the law: principally to set reasonable 'rules of the house', which guests must follow once the rules have been brought to their notice. Innkeepers also have the right to a lien over property brought to the inn by guests. The lien gives the innkeeper the right to retain possession of the property until the guest's account is paid. It is only the right of retention; there is no power of sale except where it has been granted expressly by statute (Atherton & Atherton 1998).

Food standards

Australia and New Zealand are parties to a joint scheme on food standards overseen by the Australia New Zealand Food Authority (ANZFA). Food standards may relate to the composition, production, packaging, storing or handling of food as well as information about food, including labelling, promotion and advertising.

Liquor licensing

Although there are broad similarities in state and territory legislation on liquor licensing there is also considerable diversity in detail. The objectives of licensing, derived from the two most recent Acts (South Australia and Queensland), are to:

- encourage responsible attitudes towards the promotion, sale, supply and consumption of liquor

- minimise the harm associated with the consumption of liquor
- facilitate and regulate the optimum development of the tourism, liquor and hospitality industries having regard for the welfare, needs and interests of the community
- obtain revenue for the state to enable the attainment of the objectives of the legislation and for other purposes of government (Atherton & Atherton 1998).

Insurance

Insurance provides financial protection against risks and there are plenty of them for the traveller and the businesses which make up the travel and tourism industry. Baggage may go missing, flights may be delayed, accommodation or transportation may be cancelled. A tourist may be robbed, injured or take sick while travelling. Tourism operators incur risks in employing staff and giving customers professional advice. Their premises could be damaged by fire or flood or burgled. Equipment may break down.

Most of these risks can be protected under insurance policies which are designed for businesspeople generally – liability insurance, property insurance and commercial insurance. However, the Commonwealth's Insurance (Agents and Brokers) Act 1984 and the Insurance Contracts Regulations 1985 have particular relevance for travel agents and tour operators.

Arranging travel insurance is part of the normal activity of travel agents and has become part of most tour packages. Table 7.2 shows the risks covered under the standard contract as set out in the Insurance Contracts Regulations 1985.

Consumer protection – the Trade Practices Act

The Commonwealth Government's Trade Practices Act and the Fair Trading Acts of the states are designed to protect consumers from unethical, misleading or unfair business practices. The provisions in these Acts have pointed meaning for travel and tourism businesses which are tempted to offer their products in glowing terms.

The Trade Practices Act stipulates that the consumer must be able to do business with an organisation without being defrauded, must be able to make an informed choice, that there must be equality in dealing with the trader (that the relationship must be equally powerful) and that the product being sold must be safe.

It is illegal to make false representations about the quality, style and rating of goods sold. As McKercher (1998) observes, a tourism lodge cannot claim to have a four-star NRMA rating if, in fact, it has never been inspected by the organisation or if it were rated at two stars. Similarly, clients cannot be told in advertisements that they will travel in the newest, safest four-wheel drive vehicles and then be presented with a rusty 1963 mini-bus.

Businesses cannot claim sponsorships, approval or performance characteristics that do not exist. They break the law if they claim they are accredited by an industry organisation like the Ecotourism Association of Australia, if in fact they are not.

Table 7.2 Risks covered under standard travel insurance contract

TRAVEL RISK COVERED	TIME	MINIMUM AMOUNT PAYABLE

Financial loss
  fares for transport
  and accommodation
  expenses –
  cancellation through
  unforeseen
  circumstances
	Before or during journey	Recompense for money lost,
		i.e. indemnity

Personal belongings – loss or damage	During journey	Recompense for value – indemnity
Sickness or disease contracted, injury	During journey	Recompense for medical, surgical, hospital, ambulance and nursing home charges and other medical treatment during journey
Death	During journey	The reasonable cost of the funeral or cremation and transporting the remains to the former place of residence

(Source: *Australian Travel and Tourism Law* (3rd ed) (1999) pp. 341–2 by A. Cordato. Reproduced by permission of Lexis Nexis.)

Operators cannot make false or misleading statements about the prices charged and conditions of sale must be displayed clearly. They must be careful not to be misleading in their promotional campaigns or in wording the messages in their brochures. McKercher lists the following activities that are illegal:

- misleading claims or survey results ('100 per cent of our clients are satisfied' when clients have not been surveyed)
- misleading or false savings ('Book now and save $200' when in fact, if you booked three hours before the trip, you could save the same amount of money)
- undisclosed credit terms
- undisclosed payment schedule
- undisclosed reasonable or likely extra prices (such as the cost of mandatory safety equipment)
- misleading symbols
- 'exclusive' mail advertising when in fact every house in the neighbourhood got a letter
- unlimited or limited time offers when in fact that is not what is delivered

- classified ads that appear to be private sales
- 'like for like' comparisons when the items being compared are not similar (for instance ads that say 'Why pay $600 for a wildflower tour when you can have ours for $6?' – when the $600 tour is a fully escorted, luxury four-wheel drive with a world-renowned guide and the $6 product is a photocopied road map)
- use of similar brand names and logos
- false statements about the product or services to be delivered
- suggestions that goods are made in Australia when they are not.

Competition

Consumer interests are also promoted by the competition provisions of the Trade Practices Act and the Competition Policy Reform Acts of the states and territories passed in the mid-1990s, which together give legal force to the National Competition Policy.

Business practices prohibited include:

Agreements that affect competition This refers to entering into contracts, arrangements and understandings that are exclusionary or that have the effect of substantially lessening competition. A tour operating company was fined after admitting it tried to organise a ban on a travel agent who was discounting tour prices by rebating part of his commission.

Market power abuse This refers to a company with a substantial degree of power in a market taking advantage of that power for anti-competitive purposes. In 2002, when Ansett Australia's leaseholds on airport terminals were sold following its collapse, the Australian Competition and Consumer Commission blocked Qantas from bidding for them.

Price fixing This occurs when a company specifies a minimum retail price for its products. It is the most common method by which competitors can collude to control a market. The Act stipulates that any form of agreement between competitors that is likely to fix, control or maintain prices is prohibited. Price fixing does not occur if companies recommend retail prices, even if they recommend them strongly.

Exclusive dealing This is defined as supplying goods or services only on condition that the customer acquires other goods and services from a nominated supplier. Thus travel agents may recommend that clients take out travel insurance as a condition of travel, but they cannot insist on a particular insurer.

Mergers which would substantially lessen competition in a market The Australian Consumer and Competition Commission (ACCC) does have discretion in this instance. In 2001, it allowed negotiations for Qantas to acquire Ansett Australia to proceed even though such an acquisition would have reduced competition. However, the ACCC decided it would have been a preferable result than Ansett collapsing (in the event, Qantas did not proceed and Ansett did collapse) (Atherton & Atherton 1998, McKercher 1998).[9]

DEFINITIONS

Market power abuse
A company with a substantial degree of power in a market taking advantage of that power for anti-competitive purposes.

Price fixing
A company specifying a minimum retail price for its products, as prohibited under the Trade Practices Act. Price fixing does not occur if companies recommend retail prices, even if they recommend them strongly.

Exclusive dealing
Supplying goods or services only on condition that the customer acquires other goods and services from a nominated supplier.

IMPLEMENTING COMMONWEALTH TOURISM POLICY

The Commonwealth says it is working to develop a sustainable, internationally competitive and innovative tourism industry (Department of Industry, Tourism and Resources, www.industry.gov.au). However, the states and territories are responsible for the development of tourism in their areas. The Commonwealth has a primary responsibility for overseas marketing and has a modest product development role, mainly aimed at stimulating rural and regional tourism.

Another of its activities is preparing plans which give a national direction to tourism development. It produced a 'national tourism strategy' titled *Tourism: Australia's Passport to Growth* in 1992 and followed this with the more practical 'national action plan' called *Tourism: A ticket to the 21st Century* in 1998. It has produced plans on aspects of tourism such as ecotourism, indigenous tourism and the MICE sector. And it has prepared a number of publications on sustainable facility planning and best practice.

The Commonwealth administers its tourism interests through the department as specified in the Administrative Arrangements Order which simply refers to the 'tourism industry' as a matter dealt with by the department. The department also has responsibility for administering the Australian Tourist Commission, which is responsible for overseas marketing, and the Tourism Forecasting Council, which provides tourism forecasts. The Commonwealth shares the funding of the Bureau of Tourism Research with the states and territories.

The Department's role

In 2003 the public service area administering tourism was the tourism division of the Department of Industry, Tourism and Resources. The division operated within a framework of objectives or 'key result areas' identified for the department as a whole.[10] Significantly, the first of these is to improve the competitiveness of Australian business. Others relevant to tourism development related to research and innovation, investment, market access, technology and knowledge, ecologically sustainable development and economic growth (Department of Industry, Science and Resources 2000a).

One of the most important tourism roles of the department derives from its opportunity to comment on the tourism implications of every submission going to Cabinet. It is thus able to brief its minister on the line that might be taken when submissions are discussed in Cabinet. The importance of this function relates to the roles of other ministers in administering legislation, and having responsibilities, which impact on tourism (e.g. transport, immigration, environment).

Other roles can be gauged from the business plan of the tourism division for 2000–2001 (it was then the sport and tourism division)[11] which included items as diverse as preparing a national strategy to improving inbound operator standards, to implementing a national tourism investment strategy, to participating in a national accreditation scheme. Its priority goal was said to be advancing the economic benefits of regional tourism.

The Australian Tourist Commission

The Australian Tourist Commission is a statutory authority established in 1967 to promote Australia as an international tourism destination. Its Act has been revised on a number of occasions. Its principal objectives, in the words of the Act, are:

1. to increase the number of visitors to Australia from overseas
2. to maximise the benefits to Australia from overseas visitors
3. in meeting those objects, work with other relevant agencies to promote the principles of ecologically sustainable development and raise awareness of the social and cultural impacts of international tourism in Australia.

The ATC promotes Australia to consumers and the travel and tourism industry in more than 40 countries. Its head office is in Sydney and it has offices in Los Angeles, Hong Kong, Singapore, Taipei, Shanghai, Seoul, Tokyo, Osaka, London, Frankfurt and Auckland.

It has a reputation for working closely with the state and territory tourism organisations and especially the Australian travel and tourism industry. It provides the industry with targeted promotional opportunities in overseas markets through a cooperative marketing program, its online and database marketing, widely circulated publications and involvement in major tourism business exchanges. Its own Australian Tourism Exchange, held yearly in an Australian city, is one of the leading tourism business forums in the world.

The ATC has a high profile, but its role is limited within Australia. It no longer promotes tourism in this country[12] and it has minor influence on product development.

The Tourism Forecasting Council

The Tourism Forecasting Council was set up in 1993 as part of a move at that time to provide potential investors in tourism plant, particularly accommodation, with information that would indicate that tourism had a reliable future.

The council includes representatives of the Australian Bankers Association and Property Council of Australia as well as government and travel and tourism industry bodies. It prepares forecasts for domestic, inbound and outbound tourism and publishes them in a regular magazine called *Forecast* which is distributed widely electronically.

The Bureau of Tourism Research

The Commonwealth, states and territories share the funding of the Bureau of Tourism Research although the bureau operates within the Commonwealth public service system. Formed in 1987, the BTR's primary role is to provide tourism-related statistical and background information to the Australian travel and tourism industry and governments.

It conducts a variety of research activities including:

*   design, administration, management and analysis of ongoing surveys of international and domestic tourists. These include the major tracking studies, the International Visitor Survey and the National Visitor Survey
*   design, administration, management and analysis of one-off surveys
*   publication and marketing of results of research on current and emerging issues in tourism
*   publication and marketing of survey data and other tourism-related information.

The Bureau therefore provides a constant stream of information from regular surveys and research studies on a variety of subjects, which have relevance to the marketing of tourism, its economic evaluation and the development of tourism facilities. Its staff also produce papers for presentation at appropriate conferences and the bureau frequently publishes the proceedings of important research meetings.

Attractions

The Commonwealth administers some 18 sites under the National Park and Wildlife Conservation Act, among them the Uluru–Kata Tjuta National Park (Ayers Rock and the Olgas) and Kakadu National Park in the Northern Territory. The Great Barrier Reef Marine Park has been set up under its own Act of Parliament which provides for a Board of Management.

The Commonwealth Government is also responsible for some of the great attractions of Canberra – and the nation – including Parliament House, the Australian War Memorial, the National Gallery, the National Museum and the High Court.

Export Market Development Grants Scheme

Tourism representation and general marketing overseas has been greatly assisted by tourism operators having access to the Export Market Development Grants Scheme.[13] This reimburses eligible operators for up to 50 per cent of their marketing expenses overseas, less the first $15,000. The maximum grant for an individual applicant is $200,000 a year.

The scheme is the Commonwealth Government's principal financial assistance program for businesses seeking to develop export markets. It is administered through the Australian Trade Commission (Austrade).

THE ROLE OF THE STATES AND TERRITORIES

The states and territories are primarily responsible for the development of tourism in their areas. Under the Constitution, the states exist as autonomous entities and thus Commonwealth and state governments share sovereignty over the common territory of Australia. The Constitution also determines the way in which power is shared, specifying the powers of the Commonwealth and leaving the remainder to the states. Very few

Commonwealth powers are held by it exclusively and tourism is not one of them, except for international tourism. It does have a responsibility in that area because it has powers for 'international trade' (Federal–State Relations Committee 1998).[14]

The Northern Territory and the Australian Capital Territory have been established as self-governing territories under Commonwealth legislation. In respect to tourism development they operate in the same way as the states.

In broad outline the state and territory governments perform exactly as the Commonwealth does. They are responsible for managing public finances, for providing a policy and legislative framework in which business operates and they have specialist organisations to promote tourism development. However, they are at the operating end of government on most issues. For example, the Commonwealth determines national policy on the environment and runs a number of Australia-wide programs, but it is state/territory legislation which integrates environmental requirements into the planning system which developers must follow. The states and territories have authority over other matters which are of concern to tourism, e.g. crime and safety, health and hygiene.

They all have tourism commissions – statutory authorities governed by independent boards wholly or strongly representative of industry. However, like the Australian Tourist Commission, they are still government organisations, with a broader range of objectives than a business organisation and a hybrid culture which has some of the freedoms of business but still reflects public service disciplines.

Whatever their Acts say, the freedom of boards of statutory bodies is not absolute. Boards are responsible to ministers and some ministers are more 'hands on' than others. Governments expect tourism commissions to act in accordance with their policies and were a commission's board not prepared to do this it might feel constrained to offer its resignation. This has not happened in Australia.

Commissions prepare strategic plans for the development of tourism within their areas. These plans are usually particularly strong on the marketing side and the commissions have well-developed marketing departments which dispose of considerable funds. The tourism agencies, as a general rule, cannot exert the same leadership in the development of its tourism plant. Indeed, where state governments are directly involved in developmental activity – e.g. by taking an equity position, 'rescuing' a struggling enterprise, streamlining the development approvals process – it is normally done through the state's development authority, rather than the tourism authority. However, state/territory tourism authorities usually have small teams which work with appropriate departments to ensure tourism needs are taken into consideration in infrastructure planning and the development of tourism facilities. Aviation specialists have the task of trying to ensure adequate air linkages with major tourism markets. This involves attracting new services and ensuring that airline requirements are met.

On the marketing side, state/territory tourism authorities take part in the development of tour products by wholesaling themselves or by commissioning tour wholesalers to

Table 7.3 State/territory representation overseas, 2001

	QLD	NSW	VIC	TAS	SA	WA	NT
Auckland	X	X	X		X		X
London	X	· X	X	X	X	X	X
Munich	X	X			X	X	
Frankfurt			X	X			X
Paris					X		X
Rome							X
Stockholm							X
Los Angeles	X	X	X		X		X
Chicago				X			
New York				X			
Toronto				X			
Dubai							X
Tokyo	X	X	X		X	X	
Shanghai	X		X				
Hong Kong	X	X					
Taipei	X		X				
Seoul	X						
Singapore	X	X	X	X	X	X	
Kuala Lumpur						X	

(Source: Tourism Commissions.)

produce programs. Some have their own retail outlets, though in recent years there has been a cutting back on direct retail activity. Some commissions have withdrawn from it entirely. The state and territory commissions all maintain marketing offices or have representation overseas in what they perceive as their prime markets. Table 7.3 shows the distribution of offices/representation.

Links with regions

The state tourism organisations and the Northern Territory Tourist Commission have close links with the tourism regions in their areas. They maintain constant contact with regional tourism organisations, through managers especially appointed to the task. In some cases, these reside in the region. Regional managers often sit on regional tourism organisation boards.

The MICE industry

State governments have invested hundreds of millions of dollars in convention and exhibition centres in their capitals since the first purpose-built facility in Australia was opened in Adelaide in 1987. Since then others have been built in Sydney, Melbourne and Brisbane and in the early 2000s Perth was building a new complex.[15]

Governments either directly or through their tourism commissions subsidise capital city and some regional convention bureaus, which are primarily membership organisations designed to increase MICE business.

Most natural attractions

While some of Australia's great natural attractions are managed by the Commonwealth, most of those within the national park and reserves system are administered by state/territory government departments or authorities.

The same is true for historic sites. Some states have special departmental sections charged with the task. This is usually outside the official tourism organisation. In Victoria, for example, there is an Historic Places Section in the Department of Sustainability and Environment and in Tasmania the responsible section is in the Department of Natural Resources.

Zoos are another category of major attractions in which governments are involved. They typically set up organisations with their own legislation to manage major zoos under their control. As noted in Chapter 1, the Zoological Board of New South Wales manages the Taronga Park Zoo in Sydney and the Western Plains Zoo in Dubbo, the Royal Zoological Society of South Australia runs the Adelaide Zoo and the Monato Zoo, and the Zoological Parks and Gardens Board operates three Victorian zoos and parks – Melbourne Zoo, Healesville Sanctuary and the Victorian Open Range Zoo at Werribee.

Events

All the states and territories have organisations of some sort to attract events and sometimes to manage them. Western Australia set the trend when it established Eventscorp in the mid-1980s to develop, attract and manage events of economic importance to the state. These organisations have been discussed in Chapter 1.

LOCAL GOVERNMENT AND TOURISM

Australia's third tier of government – local government – plays a regulatory and service-delivery role at the community level. Local government is not an autonomous tier of government in the way that the Commonwealth and the states are. Local government is instituted by legislation enacted by state/territory parliaments and remains subject to the overriding control of state/territory governments and parliaments (Federal–State Relations Committee 1998).

Local government authorities are increasingly assuming important roles in tourism development in Australia – as part of regional tourism organisations, in their statutory roles in relation to planning, building and licensing regulations, in supplying tourism facilities and in supporting information and other marketing initiatives.

They have powerful tools which can determine the capacity and market positioning of the tourism product in their area. In summary these tools are:

- **Provision of infrastructure** Local councils are responsible for roads and bridges in their areas. Some of them are responsible for airports. They provide basic facilities such as parks and gardens, car and coach parking areas, public toilets, and in some cases swimming pools and conference centres.
- **Investment incentives** Councils raise most of their money by rates on land and buildings, which can be varied as an incentive if desired.
- **Land use planning and building regulations** are two very influential tools which eventually determine the importance or otherwise of tourism in the area. Policies and strategies leading to decisions on planning establish the relative priority to be given to tourism and exert a critical influence on the rate of new tourism development in the area. Planning mechanisms also allow local councils to preserve the natural and historical resources which sustain tourism (Charlton & Essex 1994).

Attractions and events

Local authorities maintain excellent art galleries and museums throughout the country. Tasmania provides two examples: in Launceston the Queen Victoria Museum is managed by the city council while in Devonport, the local council administers the Devonport Gallery and Arts Centre, which is housed in a converted church.

Local councils help economic development by encouraging local events. There are a great number of these in regional areas throughout the country. In one month in Victoria, for instance, 135 significant events were listed outside Melbourne, including a variety of carnivals, festivals and fairs, a number of art shows and one photography exhibition, several popular music concerts, horse race meetings, golf tournaments, tennis tournaments, regattas and a polo match, two hot rod car rallies, a bicycle rally, a kite-flying gathering and two rodeos, a fish tasting and wine festival, a balloon festival and a tractor pull (Richardson & Richardson 1998).

THE PUBLIC–PRIVATE SECTOR PARTNERSHIP

The history of tourism reflects the collective efforts of men and women in businesses whose imagination, enterprise and determination have brought about its advancement. Businesses develop the products which meet the changing needs and wants of tourists; they continue to drive industry growth.

Spurr (1993) contrasts the private sector and governments in tourism this way:

Businesses are well-suited to entrepreneurship. If they do not respond quickly and innovatively to market opportunities; and/or if they do not operate flexibly and efficiently and provide good customer service, they generally go out of business so that scarce resources can be redeployed to some other area of economic activity. On the other hand, governments are generally not good entrepreneurs. They respond slowly and without the disciplines of the market. They tend to continue with enterprises that should fail. Unlike private sector operators, they tend not to go bankrupt when they should.

Commonwealth, state/territory tourism organisations work with the 'big picture' vision of tourism, its effect on the economy, the environment and society of a state, territory or all-Australia. They produce plans to try to influence those impacts. On the other hand, business people are primarily interested in their own businesses and their fate; most of them have a very different viewpoint from the big picture view of the government planners. The activities of government agencies are only one factor in their marketing and operational opportunities.

The government organisations need a certain level of business cooperation – that is, a 'critical mass' of businesses following their plans – for them to succeed. But they cannot direct businesses to follow their lead. Governments and their agencies may influence the travel and tourism industry by the way they regulate, stimulate, encourage and tax it. But they do not manage it.

In general the promotional efforts of Australian government tourism agencies are strongly supported by the larger businesses. Small businesses simply have come to expect leadership from government. In Tasmania 87 per cent of tourism operators who responded to a survey in 1993 considered that the Tasmanian Department of Tourism, Sport and Recreation (later Tourism Tasmania) should take the lead in everything from destination advertising to research, training, regional development, tour wholesaling . . . there was not much left out (Richardson 1996). Considering the foregoing, it is not surprising that leadership in destination management has largely been a government affair in Australia, at least since the 1960s so far as the Commonwealth is concerned and long before that in the case of the states — before federation in some cases.

This is the way it is in much of the world. Middleton and Hawkins (1998) say that most large organisations – airlines and hotel companies – have no necessary commitment to individual places. Small individual businesses are more obviously committed to the destination areas in which they live and operate but they do not necessarily recognise or support sustainable goals.

Elected local governments and the public sector managers responsible for planning and regulatory matters in a destination are, at least in theory, the most obvious sources of destination management. But experience proves they cannot manage effectively in practice without the active support and participation of tourism businesses.

INDUSTRY ORGANISATIONS

Collectively, associations within the Australian travel and tourism industry play a significant role in the management of Australian travel and tourism because of their:

- influence on government policies relating to tourism
- concern with standards of performance
- emphasis on training and education
- information role in respect to their industry sector.

Given the diversity and number of businesses involved in travel and tourism there are many trade associations involved. The following is a selection of the best known of them:

Aboriginal Tourism Australia
Australian Airports Association
Australian Automobile Association
Association of Australian Convention
  Bureaux
Australian Bed and Breakfast Council
Australian Bus and Coach Association
Australian Camping Association
Australian Council of Tour Wholesalers
Australian Duty Free Association
Australian Farm and Country Tourism
Australian Federation of Travel Agents
Australian Gay and Lesbian Tourism
  Association
Australian Hotels Association
AustralAsian Incentive Association
Australasian Railway Association
Australian Retailers Association
Australian Road Federation
Australian Society of Travel Writers
Australian Society of Association
  Executives
Australian Tourism Accreditaiton
  Association
Australian Tourism Export Council[16]
Australian Tourism Operators Network
Australian Youth Hostels Association

Board of Airline Representatives of
  Australia
Bus Industry Confederation
Business Events Council of Australia
Camping and Motorhome Club of
  Australia
Caravan Industry Australia
Catering Institute of Australia
Club Managers Association Australia
Council of Australian Secondary Tourism
  Teachers
Council of Australian University Tourism
  and Hospitality Educators
Ecotourism Association of Australia
Exhibition Industry Association of
  Australia
Hotel Motel & Accommodation
  Association of Australia
Hospitality Sales and Marketing
  Association International
Institute of Australian Tour Guides
International Cruise Council Australia
Museums Australia
Meetings Industry Association of
  Australia
National Restaurant and Catering
  Association

National Tourism Alliance	Restaurant and Catering Association of
Outdoor Tour Operators Association	Australia
Professional Conference Management	Society of Incentive Travel Executives
Association of Australia	TTF Australia
Property Council of Australia	Tourism Attractions Association (NSW)
Regional Airlines Association of Australia	Tourism Training Australia
	Travel Industry Council

The organisation which claims to represents the industry as a whole is the National Tourism Alliance, set up to replace Tourism Council Australia (TCA), which failed financially early in 2001. At the beginning of 2003, however, it lacked strong industry support and had only a small budget.

The most effective lobbying organisation is TTF Australia, which makes public statements on behalf of the industry and attracts political and public interest. Its membership is by invitation only and limited to 200 chief executive officers of organisations representing investors, operators and regulators in the tourism, transport and leisure sectors. Its objectives are (a) to act as a lobby group in matters affecting the viability and profitability of tourism enterprises; (b) promote investment in viable, profitable and sustainable activities in the tourism industry; and (c) remain an elite group of senior executives, representing the major players in Australia's travel and tourism industry (TTF Australia information sheet).

Industry members are involved in management as members of the boards of:
- The Australian Tourist Commission
- Tourism Forecasting Council
- State/territory tourism organisations
- Regional tourism organisations
- Convention and visitor bureaus.

THE RESEARCH ROLE IN MANAGEMENT

Research is essential to the good management of tourism. Governments, their agencies and businesses cannot carry out their tourism roles without knowledge of what is happening in the markets and the destinations. Research is also needed on operational methodologies and results, on environmental and social impacts among other things – many other things. Tourism research is a broad field. A single planning document – the National Tourism Strategy published in 1992 – was found to have research requirements which could be classified under 38 headings (Faulkner et al 1995).

It has been said there are three 'cultures' involved in tourism research:
1. A government culture where research is part of the policy formulation process, used to evaluate and direct decision making. The focus is on mainstream issues and macro topics.

2. An industry culture which uses research principally for marketing purposes or for validating arguments for lobbying governments.

3. An academic culture where the emphasis is on understanding the tourism phenomenon. Academics see research as an opportunity to explore, test out ideas and add to the knowledge of tourism (Pearce 1993).

The Bureau of Tourism Research is the principal directional and coordinating body for tourism research. Its role and that of the Tourism Forecasting Council have already been discussed. The Australian Tourism Research Institute (ATR*i)* funded and took part with several universities in the successful proposal to the Commonwealth Government to establish the Cooperative Research Centre for Sustainable Tourism (CRC Tourism).

The advent of the CRC in 1997 was a very large step forward for tourism research because it produced not only much greater funding but also involved a much wider spectrum of organisations and individuals than ever before. By early 1999 13 universities were involved, as well as Government tourism organisations in most states and a number of companies including Qantas Airways and Warner Bros. Movieworld. CRC Tourism was expected to have total resources of $90 million over its seven-year life. Of that, $14.7 million will have come from the Commonwealth Government (CRC for Sustainable Tourism 1999a).

As noted in the previous chapter, the CSIRO, the research arm of the Commonwealth Government, has developed its own tourism research program 'which tends to be different from university, government and consultants. The intent is to develop projects which are applied, strategic, multi-disciplinary and collaborative' (Braithwaite 1998).

Although tourism research is still behind other industries in terms of expenditure,[17] it is a large and complex operation, unrecognisable by the meagre standards of previous eras. The Australian Tourism Research Institute plays a networking role linking the various strands of tourism research and aims to improve the interpretation, distribution and comprehension of the data produced.

CASE STUDY

Tourism challenge for Byron Bay Council

Tourism for some local governments is very much a hands-on affair. The experience of the Shire Council for Byron, in northern New South Wales, illustrates this. Byron Shire is largely rural but includes Byron Bay, a town of 7,000 people. It is the easternmost settlement in Australia, a place of rare beauty and attracts those interested in an alternative lifestyle as well as the wealthy. It is a place where artists and craftspeople flourish. One of its attractions is the Cape Byron Headland Reserve, which includes a lighthouse and is a focal point for recreational activities and for whalewatching.

The council had its first formidable test with tourism in the early 1990s, when it approved an application by the French leisure group Club Méditerranée SA to enlarge the 90-hectare Byron Bay Beach Resort and turn it into a Club Med. This aroused such protests – marches, letters to authorities, approaches to politicians including the prime minister and a well-orchestrated press campaign – that eventually the proposals were shelved (Richardson 1999). The issue was the impact of the proposed development on lifestyle and town character. But other issues for the council were also emerging.

Byron Bay is a place of notable events, like the Blues Festival at Easter, and a traditional New Year's Eve celebration that can bring more than 30,000 visitors to the town. This is too many people for not only the town's sewerage facilities but also the shire's – its two treatment plants have a capacity for 21,000 people. So the council has to provide portable toilets and hire seven pantechnicons to cart sewage from Byron Bay to a plant 10 km away at Ocean Shore. If that cannot cope they may have to move outside the shire as far away as Ballina, a distance of about 30 km.

The shire authorities have been putting money away in a special account for years to build a new plant which eventually will have capacity for the sewerage needs of 30,000 people. Many people fear the increase because they see it enabling a future council to allow the permanent population to grow to the number catered for. The council cannot raise rates to pay for infrastructure to cope with tourists unless the state government agrees. It does rate central business district property owners higher than those in rural areas of the shire on the basis that businesses benefit from tourists' spending. But with the government cap on the total amount of revenue that can be raised from rates this merely redistributes the rate burden in what is thought to be a more equitable way.

In common with other New South Wales councils which have to cope with large numbers of tourists – e.g. Manly, Blue Mountains – it would like to impose a modest tax on tourists (e.g. bed tax, arrival tax) to pay for needs like parking and sewerage. But it cannot do so without state government approval and that has not been forthcoming.

State government authorities do provide money to help pay for the work of the New Year's Eve safety committee, essential to keeping the council's liability for mishap within reasonable bounds, and to ensure public safety and environmental health standards are met (David Kanaley [shire director of environmental planning] 2001, pers. comm., 18 August).

The Byron Bay Community Safety Committee (BBCSC) was established by the shire authorities in January 1994, soon after a wild New Year's Eve in the town which resulted in personal injury and property damage. At the time Byron Bay was perceived as relatively 'lawless' as a result of constant growth in tourism numbers and limited ability to manage the crowds.

Strategies adopted by the BBCSC since 1994 to reduce drunkenness, anti-social and criminal behaviour on New Year's Eve have been:

- establishing a community parade to give 'ownership' of the event back to the resident community and to foster a 'sense of place' as integral to the celebrations
- promoting awareness of the Byron Bay commitment to cultural and environmental principles
- closing the northern, southern and western entrances to Byron Bay from 6 am on New Year's Eve to 2 am New Year's Day, except for vehicles with an entry sticker; and the town centre to vehicles from 4 pm on New Year's Eve to 4 am on New Year's Day. At least 3,500 vehicles were turned away on the night of New Year 2000–01
- engaging 40 traffic controllers and security staff to control the town centre, beachfront areas, access roads into Byron Bay and various entertainment venues. The security staff supported police
- providing entertainment to disperse revellers but keep them engaged. Community radio station BayFM managed a dance party in the town centre that continued until 5 am. This provided entertainment and crowd management during the after-midnight period that had been regarded high risk
- negotiating alcohol service arrangements with local licensees, conducting a public relations program encouraging responsible consumption of alcohol, staggering closing times for venues, closing bottle shops at 9 pm, and policing alcohol-free zones
- continually removing refuse, particularly bottles that have the potential to be used as missiles.

Another of the issues tackled by the BBCSC was to offset the excessive promotion of Byron Bay as a suitable place to celebrate New Year's Eve. Media coverage focused on the restricted access to Byron Bay by private vehicle and public transport, and characterised the celebrations as being low key. This was reinforced by the use of the theme 'community in unity'; it didn't sound as if a wild party could be expected. Within the local Byron community the public relations strategy was designed to give residents the confidence to cope with the influx of visitors and to create a safe celebration from their own substantial cultural and social resources.

The BBCSC estimate for managing the 2000–01 event was more than $100,000. Attempts at attracting corporate funding failed, but a number of state government departments contributed a total of $60,000. The deficit was made up by the council and other local sources. The BBCSC's report on the 2000–01 New Year's Eve celebrations said:

> Byron Bay continues to be promoted extensively and effectively by Tourism NSW. There continues to be a reluctance at a state government level to recognise the

negative impacts of tourism when it outstrips resources. Council and industry representatives are continuing to hold regular meetings with Tourism NSW to overcome these problems, however at this point in time there does not appear to be any resolution to this conflict in resources (Hickey 2001, p. 6).

INDUSTRY PROFILE

TANYA GREENWOOD MANAGER, RESEARCH (ACTING), TOURISM VICTORIA

The focus of my career has largely been on the tourism sector – I've studied it, researched it, marketed it and, most importantly, I enjoy it. It's an exciting and diverse industry, presenting many challenges and opportunities for those who choose to build their careers within it.

Currently a Senior Market Analyst with Victoria's state tourism organisation, Tourism Victoria, I'm part of a team who provide the market intelligence to inform tourism marketing and infrastructure development strategies for Victoria. Managing research projects, liaising with government and industry at the national, state and local levels, communicating, and applying strategic thinking are all part of the job.

Actually, I don't see my job as a 'job' per se. Rather, a fulfilling role in which I get to apply the knowledge and skills I have gathered along my path so far, and build these to new and greater levels each and every day. I like what I do and I am satisfied in the sense that I have achieved many of the career goals I set myself six years ago when making the student–professional transition.

How did I get here?

I grew up in Brisbane, I studied in North Queensland and Canada, then took my first 'real' job in tourism research for the CRC Reef – this marked the beginning of my six-year path to progressing my career to its current day status.

From the idyllic tropical North, I took an opportunity to broaden my experience and gain first-hand knowledge and understanding of the role government plays in industry, the policy process, and the programs delivered to support business, the community and the environment. I undertook a graduate program with the Commonwealth Department of Industry, Tourism and Resources in Canberra. This lead to various roles within the portfolio including a position in international tourism policy, national marketing of innovative business programs in AusIndustry, and managing tourism research projects for the Bureau of Tourism Research.

A couple of years on and eager to combine my tourism research skills with marketing, I moved to Melbourne to commence my role with Tourism Victoria.

My career so far has taken me across the globe and to many far reaching areas of metro and regional Australia. And why shouldn't it? After all, I work in tourism. The key to achieving a rewarding career within this industry is not just through perseverance and hard work, but through 'getting out there amongst it', taking opportunities, moving with it and talking to people. The tourism industry is anything but static. While the world changes and grows before our eyes, new destinations and new markets are shaping the industry. The information needed to effectively plan, develop, market and manage this industry is becoming more and more important – I enjoy being involved in providing it.

SUMMARY

Tourism operations are largely a matter for private companies, but tourism is not just operations. It can have a major effect on a nation's well-being and therefore it needs to be managed and governments must be involved. The critical functions in tourism management are planning, coordination and control. Governments have responsibilities, to a larger or lesser degree, for:

- establishing the framework within which tourism's public and private sectors operate
- providing legislation, regulations and controls applicable for tourism, the protection of the environment and the cultural heritage
- constructing infrastructure, land, sea, air transport facilities and communications
- developing human resources with appropriate education and training for tourism employment
- elaborating a tourism policy with concrete plans.

Australia has a decentralised governmental system, with three levels of government. All are involved in tourism, with many responsibilities. One of them is to provide the legal framework in which travel and tourism businesses operate. Some laws derived from the common law and legislation passed by the Commonwealth, state and territory parliaments affect some sectors of the travel and tourism industry specifically. These include licensing of travel agents and laws affecting the liability of airlines, the obligations of innkeepers, food standards, liquor licensing, insurance and the protection of consumers from unethical, misleading or unfair business practices.

In specific tourism terms, the Commonwealth Government has a primary responsibility for overseas marketing and has a modest product development role, mainly aimed at stimulating rural and regional tourism. It prepares plans which give a national direction to tourism development and publications on sustainable facility planning and best practice.

The Commonwealth administers its tourism interests through a department, which is responsible for the Australian Tourist Commission (which carries out overseas marketing) and the Tourism Forecasting Council (which provides tourism forecasts). It shares the funding of the Bureau of Tourism Research with the states and territories. It administers some of the nation's outstanding attractions, including national parks, Parliament House and the Australian War Memorial. It makes funds available for tourism operators to recoup some of their overseas marketing costs through the Export Market Development Grants Scheme.

The states and territories have specialist tourism commissions to promote tourism development; they are statutory authorities governed by independent boards wholly or strongly representative of industry. These have well-developed marketing departments which dispose of considerable funds. State/territory governments have invested hundreds of millions of dollars in convention and exhibition centres. They maintain close links with regional tourism organisations and they manage most natural attractions, historic sites and animal parks in Australia. They have set up organisations to attract, and sometimes manage, events.

Local government authorities are increasingly assuming important roles in tourism development in Australia, as part of regional tourism organisations, in their statutory roles in relation to planning, building and licensing regulations, in supplying tourism facilities and in supporting information and other marketing initiatives.

Most of the many associations within the Australian travel and tourism industry represent one aspect of tourism. They play a significant role in the management of Australian tourism because of their influence on government policies relating to tourism; their concern with standards of performance; their emphasis on training and education and their information role in respect to their industry sector.

Research is essential to the good management of tourism. There are three 'cultures' involved in tourism research: (1) a government culture where research is part of the policy formulation process; (2) an industry culture which uses research principally for marketing purposes or for validating arguments for lobbying governments; and (3) an academic culture where the emphasis is on understanding the tourism phenomenon.

The advent of the Cooperative Research Centre for Sustainable Tourism (CRC Tourism) in 1997 was a very large step forward for tourism research because it produced not only greater funding but also involved a much wider spectrum of organisations and individuals than ever before. CRC Tourism was expected to have total resources of $90 million over its seven-year life.

QUESTIONS

1. Describe the kind of management tourism needs in the macro or big picture sense. What are its main functions and who should be involved?

2. Who are tourism's stakeholders?

3. In the broad sense, what are government's responsibilities with respect to tourism?

4. Why is the private sector considered better at running travel and tourism businesses than governments?

5. What is policy and how does the Commonwealth Government formulate tourism policy? What part does the tourism section of the Commonwealth public service play?

QUESTIONS continued

6. Where does the basic law affecting the Australian accommodation sector originate from and what are its main points?

7. How does the Trade Practices Act protect customers from false representation in regard to tourism? Give examples.

8. What are the Commonwealth Government agencies concerned with tourism and what are their roles?

9. Why are the states/territories more 'hands on' in their tourism activities than the Commonwealth Government? How do they approach marketing tourism and what means do they have for advancing the development of infrastructure and facilities?

10. What are the tools local government bodies can use to determine the capacity and market positioning of the tourism product in their areas. Why are these tools considered powerful?

MANAGING DEMAND

Appreciate marketing as an instrument for managing people.

Understand the marketing concept which guides the practice of trying to satisfy customers' needs and wants.

Consider competitive theory in terms of customer expectations.

Examine the importance of image-making and the theory of positioning and branding.

Understand the elements of the marketing mix, the combination of 'tools' an organisation uses to pursue its marketing objectives.

Examine the features of the marketing plan and the detail of creating it to control the implementation process.

Review examples of marketing operations: sector variations in the marketing mix, MICE industry marketing, relationship and sponsorship marketing.

Examine a case study on the ATC's operations as a destination marketer.

**UNDERSTAND
THE MEANING OF:**

* *marketing*
* *tourism marketing*
* *marketing concept*
* *image*
* *positioning*
* *branding*
* *brand equity*
* *brand management*
* *Brand Australia*
* *marketing mix*
* *Four Ps*
* *product development*
* *pricing process*
* *promotional mix*
* *place = distribution*
* *advertising*
* *personal selling*
* *sales promotion*
* *public relations*
* *publicity*
* *situation analysis*
* *SWOT analysis*
* *mission statement*
* *objectives*
* *strategies*
* *action statement*
* *resource statement*
* *marketing audit*
* *bid-and-boost*
* *Visiting Journalists Program*
* *Destination Australia Marketing Alliance*
* *Australian Tourism Exchange*

AN INSTRUMENT FOR MANAGING PEOPLE

Marketing is the most powerful instrument available for managing tourism. This is because it influences people's actions and managing tourism is about managing people. The most obvious use of marketing is to increase business – the numbers of customers for an airline or hotel or coach company or attraction or a whole destination. But it can also influence the types of tourists attracted, how long they stay, what they do, what they spend, how they behave. It can be used to limit numbers, if that is desirable, through a process called demarketing.

This chapter discusses the theory of marketing, its techniques and operations in respect to tourism. But marketing cannot be confined to one chapter – its influence is pervasive and is part of a discussion on any aspect of managing tourism. Therefore, it has a role in the chapters that follow:

Chapter 9 Development There is little point in erecting buildings, providing transport linkages and devising new forms of tourism if what is being developed cannot be effectively marketed. The development process starts with a marketing assessment.

Chapter 10 Service quality Satisfying customers or, better still, exceeding their expectations, is a marketing objective.

Chapter 11 Visitor management Marketing is one of the most effective ways of preventing carrying-capacity problems. It is in this chapter that demarketing is discussed.

Chapter 12 Change Marketing is the basis for reaction as markets change for whatever reason. It is an essential part of risk management.

Drucker (1974) says marketing is so basic to a business that it cannot be considered a separate function (i.e. a separate skill or work, on a par with manufacturing or operations or personnel).

> *Marketing requires separate work, and a distinct group of activities. But it is, first, a central dimension of the entire business. It is the whole business seen from the point of view of its final result, that is, from the customer's point of view. Concern and responsibility for marketing must, therefore, permeate all areas of the enterprise* (p. 63).

MARKETING THEORY

Marketing is often thought of as what a company does to sell its products – especially promotion and selling – but that is only part of it. Marketing is directed at satisfying customers' needs and wants – at a profit, of course –

and embraces activities within the organisation from the conception of the product to after-sales service; in tourism terms the latter means determining the visitor's satisfaction, or lack of it, after a visit has been made. Marketing theory is based on the 'marketing concept', of which the core component is the customer orientation described.

> The **marketing concept** is the most fundamental precept in the discipline of marketing. It holds that firms should try to discover what consumers want and make products to satisfy those wants. It is based on the 'market-pull' model of marketing, a commonsensical notion that customers will demand products that meet their needs and pull them through the channels of distribution (Schnaars 1998, pp. 2–3).

At the other extreme is product orientation, where the production side of the business decides what is a 'good' product and the sales department is instructed to go out and sell it. However, as O'Shaughnessy (1984) notes, if products are developed in an 'observational vacuum', a company is likely to find itself trying to sell what too few people seek and competing against products having far greater appeal.

Definitions of marketing usually acknowledge its wide-ranging role and the validity of the marketing concept. Kotler (1999) defines marketing as 'the science and art of finding, keeping, and growing profitable customers' (p. 121). The American Marketing Association gives more emphasis to the product but still implies the need for understanding what the customer needs and wants. It calls marketing the process of planning and executing conception, pricing, promotion and distribution of ideas, goods and services to create exchanges that satisfy individual and organisational objectives (McCarthy & Perreault 1990).

Tourism marketing follows the same principles as other marketing. It has been defined as the management process by which organisations develop destinations, facilities and services as tourism products, identify potential travellers and their needs and wants, price their products, communicate their appeals to target markets and deliver them to their customers' satisfaction and in compliance with organisational goals (Richardson 1996).

▓ Competition

The marketing concept ignores competition. Yet customer orientation is a business precept appropriate to competitive markets. 'Satisfying' customers is not enough to outperform competitors, according to O'Shaughnessy, who says the term is too vague when undefined. A firm that merely satisfies loses out to the firm that pleases. 'Customer expectations' – what the customer believes is realisable – provide the competitive benchmark.

> The more competitive the market, the more a firm must meet or exceed customer expectations if it is to stay in business. Customer orientation in the sense of trying to meet or exceed customer expectations so as to beat competition is a key posture for any firm in a competitive economy (p. 9).

DEFINITIONS

Marketing
(1) The science and art of finding, keeping, and growing profitable customers; (2) The process of planning and executing conception, pricing, promotion and distribution of ideas, goods and services to create exchanges that satisfy individual and organisational objectives.

Marketing concept
Companies should try to discover what consumers want and make products to satisfy those wants.

Tourism marketing
The management process by which organisations develop destinations, facilities and services as tourism products, identify potential travellers and their needs and wants, price their products, communicate their appeals to target markets and deliver them to their customers' satisfaction and in compliance with organisational goals.

DEFINITIONS

....

Common approach

There are strong differences in the use of marketing tools (discussed later in the chapter), but the marketing processes followed by the travel and tourism companies in different sectors are not very different. As Petzinger (1995) says,

> *An airline, when one cuts through the romance and the technical vagaries of flight, (is) nothing more than a marketing company, selling its product to a customer base nearly identical to that of a hotel chain* (p. 69).

Image

An overall evaluation based upon a set of perceptions concerning an entity.

A product is a product. Whether it's an airline seat or a hotel bed or anything else, the marketer has to determine the target markets for it, the appropriate price, and how to get the message across so that the customer will perceive a way to satisfy a need or want and buy the product.

MARKETING TECHNIQUES

Destination image

An evaluation of a destination consisting of both positive and negative perceptions, which may or may not be factual.

The use of segmentation research to establish target markets was described in Chapter 2. It is central to the marketing process as are (1) positioning and branding, and (2) the marketing mix.

▨ Making images: positioning and branding

Positioning

The process of developing a distinctive image for a destination, a company or a product so that it can be distinguished from its competitors and their offerings.

Destination and corporate images are extremely important. **Image** is an overall evaluation based upon a set of perceptions concerning an entity (Wilkie & Pessimier cited in Dadgostar & Isotalo 1995). The image of a destination invariably consists of both positive and negative perceptions, which may or may not be factual (Ahmed 1994). Nevertheless, the image they make up represents truth to a tourist choosing a destination. **Destination image** is a critical factor in the destination-choice process.

A corporate image, as represented by its brand, is no less crucial. Some companies value their brands at millions of dollars. One could scarcely conceive continuing success for many of the world's leading companies (e.g. Coca-Cola) if they lost their image of quality and leadership.

Branding

The process of building a distinctive image in people's minds so that it will be recalled when the brand is encountered in the form of a name, design, symbol or slogan.

Images are often developed from information which may come from many sources: TV, radio, newspapers, books, films, hearsay etc. The information may be fleeting and fragmentary and an image may be formed over a long period. On the other hand destinations and companies can deliberately set out to create or modify images through positioning and branding.

- **Positioning** is what the marketer does to develop a distinctive image for a destination, a company or a product so that it can be distinguished from its competitors and their offerings.
- **Branding** is the process that follows positioning – building the distinctive image in people's minds so that it will be recalled when the brand is encountered in the form of a name, design, symbol or slogan.

An image in one market is not the same as in another. Qantas has been chosen a number of times as the company with the best corporate image in Australia in an annual survey of several hundred chief executives. But it has had to spend millions of dollars in overseas markets to position itself as an Australian airline. The brand name 'Qantas' is not enough by itself; many people overseas do not even connect it with Australia.

It is therefore fundamental to the positioning and branding process that it starts with an understanding of how the target market perceives the subject of the process – a destination or an organisation and/or its products in the marketplace. Obviously it is not possible to make a destination or product distinctive if the marketer doesn't know what the target markets think of it in the first place. That requires research. As a result, different positioning statements may have to be devised for different markets.

There are two elements that must be resolved and included in a positioning statement:

- The customers' perceived benefits in visiting the destination or in buying the product promoted. Benefits are what prompt customers to buy. Advertising messages that both promise the potential buyers a benefit and lead them to believe in the promise are often the most successful. Of course, the promise must be capable of being delivered.
- The creation of product differentiation in the minds of the customers. The destination or the product must be seen as different from others, i.e. to have unique features.

A hotel that advertises 'low price does not mean low quality' is making a positioning statement offering a benefit (low prices) and differentiation (high quality). It creates an image, combining both (low prices and high quality) (Coltman 1989).

Having produced the positioning statement, the next step is to produce the devices which give tangible effect to the image: the **brand** – the distinctive name, designs, symbols or colours (or combinations of these).

Brand
A collection of enduring intangible values in the mind of the tourist or user.

Brands do more than merely identify a destination, company or product. According to Clarke (2000), a 'true brand' exists as a collection of enduring intangible values in the mind of the user, but the resources, processes and management energy necessary to create those values are integrated into the marketing effort and are largely undetected by consumers.

> *The final brand is a composite that delivers to the consumer both functional or performance benefits and emotional benefits, the latter being harder for competitors to replicate* (p. 330).

Brand names with an image of quality abound in the travel and tourism industry – Qantas is one and Virgin Blue is the very effective brand of its domestic competitor. Others include Australian Pacific Touring, Avis Australia, P&O, American Express and so on.

Big hotel companies manage several chains of hotels aimed at different target markets and distinguish them by giving them different brand names. Thus Accor Asia Pacific's

Brand equity

The value of a brand consisting of brand awareness, preference, loyalty and distribution.

Brand management

The actions taken to ensure that the product is consistently delivered in accordance with the promotional promise. It is an important factor in brand equity.

Marketing mix

The combination of 'tools' a company uses to pursue its objectives in target markets. There are dozens of tools and they are often classified by using the 4P framework – product, price, place (meaning distribution) and promotion.

Price

What is paid for a product: its value expressed in dollars and cents.

five-star hotels are called Sofitel, its Novotel brand is aimed at the middle range of the market, Mercure hotels are distinctively reflective of the environment in which they operate, Ibis offer simplicity and value for money and the Formule 1 brand is for budget motels. Accor prefers branding to star ratings because it says the star system often does not reflect what the hotels are offering. Brands do. Brand names not only conjure up a level of product or service in a customer's mind, they assure a tourist of a recognisable quality.

This has led to the extension of brand names from country to country, assuring travellers of standards associated with the brand. This is, perhaps, most noticeable in the growth of international hotels. Hyatt, Hilton, Sheraton, Holiday Inn, Radisson, Ramada and Inter Continental, are among the international hotel brands prominent in Australia which are household words in many countries.

With major destinations the brand name is a given or it can be created. The marketer does not have to think of a new memorable name for Tasmania or New South Wales, nobody is likely to listen to a plea to change it to make it easier to attract tourists. However, names like the Gold Coast and Sunshine Coast were chosen for their appeal to visitors.

What is important to the destination marketer (and others) is '**brand equity**'. This consists of a number of elements, such as brand awareness, preference, loyalty and distribution. '**Brand management**' is important to brand equity, because its purpose is to ensure that the product is consistently delivered in accordance with the promotional promise. Brand equity expresses the success or otherwise of the entire marketing effort rather than a clever piece of advertising or sloganeering.

◼ The marketing mix

The **marketing mix** is the combination of 'tools' a company uses to pursue its objectives in target markets. It is the core of the marketing system. There are dozens of tools, ranging from those which affect the product (e.g. quality, brand name) to pricing (e.g. discounts, credit terms), to the variety of communication tools like advertising, telemarketing and online sales used to reach distribution channels and targeted consumers.

As a means of seeing more clearly the various elements which can be used in the mix, it is usual to classify them under different headings. A popular method, devised in the 1960s, is the use of the 4P framework – the four Ps standing for product, **price**, place (meaning distribution) and promotion. By these criteria, the marketing process calls on the marketer to decide on the product and its characteristics, set its price, decide how to distribute it and choose methods for promoting it.

Some writers think the 4P framework is inadequate because it omits or undervalues activities which they see as important. For instance, some tourism marketers would add a fifth P, for people, meaning the employees of travel and tourism businesses who come face to face with visitors, provide them with services and influence their behaviour. Morrison

(1989) goes further. He extends the number of Ps to eight – partnership, product, people, packaging, programming, place, promotion and price.

In adding Ps writers appear to be following particular fancies because the additions can usually be seen as subsets of the original four. Thus P for people is part of product. But as Kotler (1999) notes:

> *The issue is not whether there should be four, six, or ten Ps so much as what framework is most helpful in designing marketing strategy. Just as economists use two principal concepts for their framework of analysis, namely demand and supply, the marketer sees the four Ps as a filing cabinet of tools that could guide their marketing planning* (pp. 95–96).

The qualifications to the 4P 'filing cabinet of tools' should be borne in mind as the elements of the marketing mix are discussed in detail.

Product

On the commercial product level, companies, driven by competition, should be constantly examining their services (i.e. products) to ensure they are meeting their customers' needs. New products are devised or built with particular markets in mind, e.g. theme parks or casino complexes or a new menu in a restaurant, weekend package in a hotel, different routing and scheduling for an express coach service.

For a destination, the most appealing part of the product may seem natural and unalterable, like beaches, mountains or lakes. However, by referring back to the components of the overall destination product in Chapter 2, it can be seen there is always something that can be done to make a destination more appealing to a particular group of tourists. This may not necessarily be in tangible form. For instance, it may involve making the destination more friendly for tourists.

Replacing old products with new ones is essential to the growth and vitality of tourism organisations. Moutinho (1989) defines new products as those where the degree of change for customers is sufficient to require the design or redesign of marketing strategies. They are needed to provide growth and to offset the inevitable levelling or decline in sales of old products. New products can be found through acquisition or through new product development. The developmental process is shown in Figure 8.1.

New product development should be in accordance with the overall strategy of the business as laid out in its strategic plan.

Price

Price is what is paid for a product: its value expressed in dollars and cents. Obviously, price has a major effect on demand. People buy what they can afford, what they see as value for money, what they perceive is the best deal among competitive offerings. Price is sometimes the most critical factor in the marketing mix.

Figure 8.1 New product development

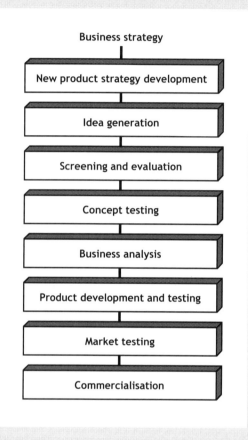

Business strategy

New product strategy development

Idea generation

Screening and evaluation

Concept testing

Business analysis

Product development and testing

Market testing

Commercialisation

(Source: Witt and Moutinho, *Tourism Marketing and Management Handbook* © 1989 Prentice Hall International (UK) Limited, reprinted by permission of Pearson Education Limited.)

But usually decisions on price have to be coordinated with decisions on product, promotion and distribution. The pricing process must start with the expectation of the customers who make up the chosen segment, or target market. It is their attributes and attitudes that give overall direction in determining the marketing mix.

Meidan (1989) has listed these cost structures as used by the travel and tourism industry:

- cost-plus
- rate of return
- backward pricing
- marginal pricing

- flexible pricing
- market penetration
- skimming
- yield and revenue.

These are discussed below.

Cost-plus

The price is arrived at on the basis of variable costs to which is added a certain percentage to cover fixed costs and a satisfactory profit margin. Typically, an operator will set this percentage on industry practice or by analysis and projection of the market conditions. This method is appropriate for cost-oriented businesses, but not for market-oriented ones because it does not take into account demand.

Rate of return

This method concentrates on the profits generated in relation to the capital invested. It ignores sales volume and while it may appeal to investors, it is regarded as mechanistic, rigid and unduly profit-oriented.

Backward pricing

This starts with a predetermined market price (often influenced by a competitor) and a specified profit and attempts to achieve the latter by adjusting variable service and qualitative aspects to reduce costs. This method should be used with care. An analysis of customer attitudes and competitive products should be made before selecting the price.

Marginal pricing

By estimating the demand curve for a particular product, it is possible to see what would happen to total profits if the selling price were raised or lowered. Marginal pricing permits a more aggressive policy by segmenting the market and using product differentiation to take advantage of the different layers of consumer demand and for selecting the most profitable pricing when capacity is limited – as, for example, at the peak season.

Flexible pricing

This approach takes into consideration market demand and enables discrimination according to time, place, version or volume. This is the most profitable way to price if it works because it is based on what the market will bear. But it is not always easy to find the right levels and some costly mistakes can be made. It is price discrimination based on segmenting the market and producing different prices for the different segments based on willingness and ability to pay. It is a familiar method used by airlines and hotels, among others.

DEFINITIONS

Market penetration

Prices are set below the competition to attract volume with the hope that prices may be raised later while retaining a high proportion of the custom that has been built up.

Skimming

This means setting a high price, well above production and marketing costs. Skimming can be applied to a very differentiated product, such as a new transport method or a new destination where premium prices may be charged. This policy can only work when there is a strong demand for the product.

Yield and revenue

This involves an attempt to increase the revenue from the existing level of demand. It is suitable (and used) as a short-term approach.

Meidan says some of these pricing methods are particularly suitable for small tourism enterprises. Examples are the cost-plus method, marginal pricing technique and market penetration pricing. However, before reaching a decision even small tourism businesses should research:

- its customers and the nature of demand
- the quality/quantity of the product required and its costing elements
- the nature of the competition
- the price customers are willing to pay for the product.

Place

'Place' means distribution. It is a complex subject in tourism and extremely important in influencing demand because if the tourist or their travel agent cannot book the services required easily then they may not be booked at all. For most larger suppliers the advent of computer reservation systems has meant their products are available from tens of thousands of outlets throughout the world. However, many smaller companies cannot afford to place their products in the big systems.

Most companies make at least some sales directly to the public, but the influence of electronics has not diminished the importance of middlemen in the distribution chain; indeed it has probably enhanced it. For example, airlines, hotels and rent-a-car companies become each other's middlemen by being associated in frequent flyer programs.

Distribution channel
A set of interdependent organisations involved in making a product available to the traveller.

A **distribution channel** is a set of interdependent organisations involved in making a product available to the traveller. There are three main industry channels of distribution in travel and tourism:

- tour packagers (wholesale or otherwise)
- retail travel sellers, including agencies, motoring organisations and government travel centres

- specialty companies, such as incentive travel companies, convention planners and general sales agencies.

DEFINITIONS

As an example, a hotel may use all of these, or choose only those which suit its particular market. The choice of a motel may be to rely on motoring organisations or the wider distribution obtained through joining a referral group such as Best Western or Budget.

Tour wholesalers can affect a range of suppliers by packaging not only transport and accommodation, but also meals, entertainment and attraction entrance fees. Shopping is not usually packaged, but some shops relying on tourists regard tour operators as their main distribution channel, paying them commission to bring groups to their shops.

Electronic systems have had a profound effect on distribution channels. For almost 30 years, travel agents have been in a very strong position, having almost exclusive access to Global Distribution Systems and providing the travel industry access and proximity to the customer. But with access to the Internet and the rapid spread of technological innovations such as electronic ticketing, the consumer is now able to communicate and transact directly with suppliers.

Promotion

Promotion is the most obvious way marketers attempt to influence demand. There are five main kinds of promotional activity, the combination of which is called the **promotional or communications mix**:

- advertising
- personal selling
- sales promotion
- public relations
- publicity.

They are employed either singly or in combination in a promotional campaign. Selling messages are developed and media aimed at target markets employed to convey them to likely prospects. A 'selling message' need not be an aggressive statement, but it should be designed to convey essential information to the tourist making decisions on a trip. Different methods appeal to different markets and segments within them; for example a travel journalist's article after a visit to a destination may be more persuasive than an expensive advertisement.

Advertising

Advertising is any paid form of non-personal presentation of destinations or products by an identified sponsor. Its task in tourism marketing is to attract the attention of potential travellers and cause them to visit a destination or use a particular product.

There are five major decisions in developing an advertising campaign.

Promotional or communications mix
The combination of promotional methods a company uses as part of its marketing effort. The elements are advertising, personal selling, sales promotion, public relations and publicity.

Advertising
Any paid form of non-personal presentation of destinations or products by an identified sponsor.

DEFINITIONS

1. **Setting objectives**, which are specific communication tasks to be accomplished with a specific target audience during a specific period of time. Objectives can be to inform (used when introducing a new product category), to persuade (to build selective demand), to compare (with competitors' offerings) or to remind (important for mature products).

2. **Setting the advertising budget** This will depend on the objectives, the stage of the product lifecycle and the circumstances in the market. For example, new products usually need heavy advertising. In a market with many competitors, it is necessary to spend considerable amounts of money on advertising to be heard above the clutter.

3. **Deciding on the message** Appeals used in advertising messages should be meaningful (pointing out benefits), distinctive and believable. Good advertising messages are not easy to create and the creative people must also find the best way of presenting them – the best style, tone and words.

4. **Selecting the media** that is, whether to use television, radio, newspapers, magazines, direct mail, outdoor billboards etc. Media selection is based on reach and frequency goals and the perceived impact of the various media. Reach is a measure of the percentage of people in the target market who will be exposed to the campaign in a given time. Frequency is the measure of how many times the average person in the target market will be exposed to the message.

   Media impact is judged on the suitability of each type of medium to present the message. As an example, the sight and sound of television may combine to create an attractive awareness message for a destination, whereas a newspaper travel section may offer a 'supermarket' effect where many small advertisements offer holidays at competitive prices.

5. **Measuring the communication effect** The best test of effectiveness is by sales results. However, this might mean waiting up to 18 months. Sometimes advertisers pre-test their advertising to see if it is communicating well and at other times they post-test it for an indication of how the message was noticed and retained (Kotler & Armstrong 1994, Coltman 1989).

Personal selling

Personal selling

The oral presentation of a product to one or more persons for the purpose of making sales.

Personal selling is the oral presentation of a product to one or more persons for the purpose of making sales. It is very common in the marketing of travel and tourism products, not only directly to the customer (e.g. by a travel agent) but also by a supplier to some other person or company in the distribution chain (e.g. a hotel representative to a tour wholesaler). It is conducted in a formal sense by well-disciplined sales teams and it is conducted informally by managers at all levels and owners of businesses; indeed, many who do not think of themselves as salespeople at all.

Personal selling takes place at great trade shows like the Australian Tourism Exchange, over a travel agency desk, more simply on the telephone, at lunch, and in many other circumstances. It can be a one-off interaction between two people or it can, as it sometimes does in travel and tourism marketing, lead to lasting relationships.

For training purposes the selling process can be broken down into several steps:

- **Prospecting** Identifying potential customers and qualifying them (identifying the good ones and screening out the poor ones).
- **Pre-approach** Learning as much about the prospect as possible before making the call.
- **Approach** Meeting the prospective buyer, introducing the salesperson and their company and perhaps learning more about the prospect's need with a few opening questions.
- **Presentation** Telling the story of the product. The idea is to show that it will satisfy the prospect's needs.
- **Handling objections** Most prospects will have objections and the salesperson should be trained to take a positive approach and provide more information.
- **Closing the sale** This means asking for the order.
- **Follow-up** The salesperson should schedule a follow-up call after the order has been fulfilled to see that everything is satisfactory.

Efficient management is essential and some companies have introduced computerised control systems, such as Accor Asia Pacific's Team Accor. Kotler and Armstrong (1994) define sales management as the analysis, planning, implementation and control of sales-force activities. It includes setting objectives for the salesforce and designing strategies as well as recruiting, training, supervising and evaluating the company's sales people.

Sales promotion

Sales promotion consists of activities which supplement and coordinate personal selling and advertising. A variety of tools are used including contests, discounts, 'two for the price of one' offers, redeemable coupons, free trials and so on. They are incentives designed to increase sales, usually in the short term.

Sales promotion
Activities designed to supplement and coordinate personal selling and advertising. They include incentives for travel agents, window and booth displays, contests, discounts, 'two for the price of one' offers, redeemable coupons, free trials, and so on.

Not all sales promotion activities are as active as the list above suggests. They include window displays aimed at boosting a destination or service, booth displays at trade shows and displays in tourism information centres. Familiarisation trips for travel agents are a sales promotion activity. Other incentive programs for agents include money prizes or other rewards for increasing sales.

Although they are often thought of as tactical responses to unanticipated situations, sales promotion methods are frequently used as part of strategic marketing; for example, to combat a predicted seasonal downturn or in support of a new media campaign.

DEFINITIONS

· ·

Public relations

The planned and sustained effort to communicate images and messages to influence a number of 'publics' or groups to take a favourable view of the organisation.

Public relations

Public relations is a planned and sustained effort to communicate images and messages to influence a number of 'publics' or groups to take a favourable view of the organisation.

Among the activities of the public relations department are: (a) financial reporting, which includes preparation of annual reports and publicity in the financial media; (b) presenting a favourable image to government, business and community interests; (c) speech-writing for senior executives; (d) internal communications, providing staff with the reasons for improving or maintaining a high level of customer service.

Publicity

This is information about the organisation or product as part of the marketing effort, but, unlike advertising, it is not paid for and therefore the organisation does not have the same control over whether or how it is published or broadcast.

Publicity

Information about the organisation or product as part of the marketing effort, but, unlike advertising, it is not paid for.

Despite this risk, **publicity** is a powerful marketing tool. It is very much cheaper than advertising and it can be more believable. Publicity usually takes the form of a favourable news presentation of a destination or product. It is achieved through a visit by a journalist or a sampling of a product – or by the provision of written or pictorial material. The standard tool of the publicity department is the press release, which is information presented in the form of a news story.

Publicity occasions can be made, for example, an event or incident created to attract the attention of the media. Virgin Blue and its founder Sir Richard Branson have demonstrated a masterful ability to do this.

Publicity is often regarded as one of the functions of the public relations department. However, public relations and publicity are different things.

THE MARKETING PLAN

Marketing plan

A system for developing objectives and setting out the marketing actions to achieve them over a short period, usually a year.

The **marketing plan** sets out objectives and the marketing actions to achieve them over a short period, usually a year. It is derived from the organisation's strategic plan (discussed in the next chapter) and is designed to contribute to its longer-term objectives. Marketing always plays a role in achieving strategic objectives; in many travel and tourism companies it is the major role. For them, marketing's role provides direction for the company.

The marketing plan represents the sharp end of the planning process. It has an immediacy about it that the strategic plan does not. Actions are planned to take place in a relatively short space of time.

A marketing plan is usually written in sections, as summarised in Table 8.1.

Situation analysis

This is an examination of the organisation and where it stands in its environment, its scale of operations, its market share and its relationship to its competitors. The current business

Table 8.1 Contents of a marketing plan

EXECUTIVE SUMMARY	A BRIEF OVERVIEW OF THE OBJECTIVES AND MAIN RECOMMENDATIONS IN THE PLAN
Situation analysis	(1) Examination of the organisation and where it stands in relation to the market and its competitors. Emphasis on marketing, operational and financial performance. (2) Analysis of marketing environment, including market size, industry trends, competition, regulatory and general economic situation affecting tourism.
SWOT analysis	Identifies the organisation's strengths and weaknesses and the external threats and opportunities which might impact on the year's marketing effort.
Business definition	Statement establishing the general boundaries of the business operation. It includes consumers or segments of the market to be served and a generic statement of the products/services to be offered.
Mission statement	Describes the type of organisation, general direction and underlying philosophy.
Objectives	Concise, specific, measurable performance criteria, usually related to market performance (e.g. market share, growth rate).
Marketing strategies	Statements in broad terms of how the objectives will be met.
Action program	The action program is made up of individual action plans which detail how each strategy will be carried out and the objectives achieved. Each action plan specifies its target market and the marketing mix to be employed.
Resource statement and budget	Forecast sales and profit. Budget established. Also resources – such as money and manpower – to implement action program.
Controls	How objectives will be measured to determine whether they are being achieved, who is responsible and when evaluation is to occur.

(Source: Zallocco (1989), Kotler (1991).)

definition, mission, marketing strategies and resources are examined critically. The **situation analysis** requires collection of information on:

The enterprise itself The starting points are its balance sheet and the profit and loss statement. What needs to be improved or is desirable? Are there sufficient resources to support the marketing program? This is followed by an examination of internal data, contrasting current results with past results, performance between different distributors, costs and sales trends.

The industry Its size, trends, outlook for the year and relevant characteristics. For example, airlines are intent on cutting costs of distribution – what will happen, what will

DEFINITIONS

Situation analysis
An examination of a company and where it stands in its environment, its scale of operations, its market share and its relationship to its competitors.

it mean? What will be the effect of international airline alliances? There is a shortage of accommodation here, a surplus there; what are the effects on tour operations?

Markets What are the trends? Which markets have the potential to grow? Which are emerging? What are the Tourism Forecasting Council's forecasts?

Economic conditions General outlook (boom, recession). What are the likely effects on household incomes, unemployment, interest rates, inflation and exchange rates, all of which affect travel? Are there likely changes to fuel costs, taxes affecting travel and tourism, regulations affecting the industry?

Travel trends Are there relevant changes in lifestyles, attitudes and social values of travellers? What effect will the trend towards nature tourism have? Will the building of big resorts, massive cruise ships and huge theme parks elsewhere in the world affect Australian tourism? There are more businesswomen travelling – what does that mean?

Political outlook This is assessed wherever politics is likely to affect the company's operations. What has been the effect of terrorism so far? And what is its influence likely to be in the period of the plan? Are there likely to be changes of policy towards tourism at home? Could elections change the outlook?

Technology What is analysed will depend on the organisation's activities. For example, How will electronics continue to change distribution? Where will it all be this time next year? What will be the costs? What will be the advantages?

Competitors The organisation needs to know who are its competitors and what are their market shares. There should be an assessment of their objectives (attitudes towards profitability, market share, technological leadership, customer service leadership etc.) and their strategies (product features, pricing policy, distribution, promotion etc.).

SWOT analysis

A technique for evaluating the strengths and weaknesses of a company and the opportunities and threats it faces.

The SWOT analysis

SWOT stands for 'strengths, weaknesses, opportunities and threats'. The SWOT analysis lists the organisation's internal strengths and weaknesses, and the external opportunities and threats facing the organisation.

The analysis should provide evidence about what the company should and should not try to set as marketing objectives. It should use strengths to exploit opportunities and minimise threats and weaknesses.

Mission statement

A statement that defines what business the organisation is in, in terms of what benefits it provides or what needs it satisfies rather than what it does or what it makes.

Mission statement

This would normally be developed during the strategic planning process. It should be assessed relative to the SWOT outcomes. The **mission statement** defines what business the organisation is in, in terms of what benefits it provides or the needs it satisfies rather than what it does or what it makes. It may reflect the organisation's essential skills or resources or direction. It should be motivating. For example: 'STA Travel aims to be the natural choice of all students and young travellers' (STA Travel, Corporate Profile, p. 6).

Objectives

Objectives are specific, measurable results (e.g. increasing sales by 33 per cent) that an organisation plans to achieve in a given period. In a company these are related to:

- markets (e.g. market share, sales in dollars and units)
- financial performance (profits, return on investment, costs, margins achieved etc.)
- other factors (e.g. marketplace image, consumer awareness, social responsibility).

While the conventional view is that objectives of companies are mostly financial, this may not be true of many small firms in tourism, particularly those run by their owners. British studies have shown that the underlying motivation of many owners of small businesses can be summarised as the 'need to attain and preserve independence'. This attitude sums up a wide range of highly personal gratifications provided by people working for themselves. These include personal supervision and control of staff, direct contact with customers, the opportunity to develop ideas, and a sense of personal achievement and pride. Lifestyle is frequently a consideration (Hughes 1986).

But companies big and small must make a profit. And pyschological objectives are much more difficult to include as objectives in a planning document than financial aims. Large companies with shareholders to satisfy do not have this dilemma. Shareholders expect the benefits of profit maximisation whether it is in the form of return on investment as expressed in dividends or for the financing of growth, which increases the value of their shares.

Destination marketing organisations like the Australian Tourist Commission, the state and territory tourism commissions and regional tourism associations have a different approach to objectives. A 1990s study to which 88 national tourism organisations responded concluded that the most important marketing objectives were:

- financial and volume-based (to increase tourism revenue, to increase average daily expenditure and to increase overall visitor numbers)
- market share-related (to increase market share in growing markets, to maintain market share in mature markets)
- image-related (to strengthen the image of the country as a tourist destination, to extend seasonal spread of visits if the seasonality problem is linked to its image) (Rita 1995).

Marketing strategies

What is meant here is not the 'grand strategy' which guides the overall fate of the company, but specific **strategies** to achieve the marketing objectives. The objectives are the *what* of the exercise, the strategies are the *how*. In a marketing plan they are expressed in broad terms as a guide to the detailed action planning. For example an objective of increasing market share by 3 per cent might be best accomplished by a strategy of promotion to a new market segment of experienced women travellers between the ages of 20 and 34.

DEFINITIONS

Objectives
Specific, measurable results that an organisation plans to achieve in a given period.

Strategies
The means of achieving objectives.

DEFINITIONS

The strategies usually flow from the situation and SWOT analyses, which provide selective identification of opportunities or problems.

Elements that need to be considered include:

- market segments to be targeted
- positioning relative to competitors
- development of an underlying thrust (e.g. low price).

Action program

An action plan is devised to achieve each objective according to the appropriate strategy. The sum of the action plans is the **action program**. An action plan specifies what will be done, who will do it, when it will be done and how much it will cost. The target market is defined in each action plan and the elements of the marketing mix – the four Ps – are brought into play to reach and influence it. Thus the selection of a target market and developing a marketing mix are interrelated; the characteristics of the target market dictates the appropriate marketing mix. There are many ways to approach the task. The product may be altered or a new one may be introduced. New brochures may be devised, various advertising media may be used, a sales blitz or a travel trade mission may be scheduled, a radical new pricing policy introduced or a new method of distribution launched.

Action program

The sum of the action plans devised to achieve objectives in accordance with the appropriate strategies. Whereas a strategy is a broad statement, the action plan specifies what will be done, who will do it, when it will be done and how much it will cost.

Resource statement and budgets

The resources required to carry out the action program should be stated. Depending on the circumstances, these can include not only funds to carry out the action plans, but also capital investment, people, marketing skills and organisational investments. Functional requirements such as team-building tasks, organisational integration and information system needs should be identified.

The budgeting of action plans combined with sales forecasting enables a projected profit and loss statement to be included in the plan. Expenditure is the cost of implementing the action program plus that of production and distribution. On the revenue side there are forecasts of sales, taking into the account the results of the action plans.

Controls

Controls are put in place to monitor progress. The action plans must be implemented on time and an evaluation made of their effectiveness in achieving objectives. The plan may allow assessments at regular periods – say a month or a quarter – or at the conclusion of a particular action plan. If necessary, corrective action should be taken to ensure that marketing objectives are attained.

▓ Marketing audit

This is an examination of the effectiveness of the whole marketing effort and is best carried out by people outside the organisation, or at least from a separate department, because it should be unbiased and critical. The **marketing audit** is a systematic review of the policies and objectives of the marketing function and of the organisation, people and procedures who carry it out.

The auditor works backwards to evaluate the plans that are being implemented, interviewing customers, competitors, distribution channel members and the company's own personnel. It is no small task.

MARKETING OPERATIONS

▓ Sector variations in marketing mix

The marketing mix employed by travel and tourism companies varies according to the sector. Branding is important, particularly to the bigger companies, either through advertising (e.g. Qantas) or publicity and association with other companies (e.g. Virgin Blue). Major airlines are by far the biggest advertisers, but they also rely on relationship marketing (i.e. loyalty programs), yield management, holiday packaging, sophisticated personal selling, and elaborate distribution systems.

The big hotel chains advertise, but not nearly to the extent of airlines. Their main marketing tools are personal selling, electronic distribution and loyalty programs. The hotel industry talks oddly about 'sales and marketing'. However, Kotler (1999) says it is no wonder they are thought to be the same by hotel people. The sales function is highly visible – sales managers provide prospective clients with tours and entertain them in the hotel's restaurants – whereas the non-promotional areas of the marketing function take place behind closed doors.

Media advertising, direct mail (including postbox drops) and sales promotion usually feature in the marketing mix of restaurants. Those appealing directly to tourists may make deals with tour operators, advertise in specific tourist literature and participate in tourism commission/convention bureau promotions.

Tour wholesalers often put more effort into making their distribution channels work for them than anything else. They also advertise directly to consumers, often in the 'supermarkets of travel' – newspaper travel sections where there are collections of competitive travel advertising (not awareness or simply motivating, but priced products ready to buy).

The theme park business is extremely marketing-sensitive. The important marketing tools are advertising, promotions and public relations. Pricing policy is important: the single all-in-one admission charge (pay one price) is what usually distinguishes theme parks from other kinds of tourist attractions. Once visitors are in the park, rides and facilities are free of additional charges.

Small operators in travel and tourism often spend very little on marketing, relying on word of mouth, brochures and help from a government tourism organisation. Tourism Queensland found in a survey published in 2000 that the most widely used marketing devices used by nature-based and ecotourism operators were:

DEFINITIONS

Marketing audit
A systematic review of the policies and objectives of the marketing function and of the organisation, people and procedures who carry it out.

- brochures
- editorial
- Internet
- trade events
- cooperative marketing
- newspaper advertising
- direct mail.

The Internet plays a key role in the marketing plans of environmental tourism businesses (77 per cent of all operators used this method to some degree) and evidence suggested effective usage would increase (Tourism Queensland 2000c).

Interdependence

The common distinguishing feature of tourism marketing is that while the services offered may differ radically, each company offering them is dependent on others who make up the travel and tourism industry. This is because they share the same customers who require a range of services and if one element is missing the customer may not make the trip.

Businesses often combine their marketing efforts for their mutual benefit. Hotels help sell sightseeing tours, airlines help sell hotels, coach companies sell theme parks, companies in different sectors engage together in database marketing such as frequent flyer programs.

MICE sector marketing

The MICE sector – the meetings, incentive travel, conventions and exhibitions sectors – represents forms of business travel, and uses a range of management, educational and marketing tools. Its components are especially valued for the economic benefits they bring to a country, city or region because they are 'high yield'; that is, the economic return from their expenditure and that associated with the events that cause them to travel is higher than from most other forms of travel.

Conventions

The theoretical basis of marketing conventions is simple – first attract the conventions you want and then promote attendance. It has been called the 'bid-and-boost business'. A variety of organisations might assist the bid but at the heart of the process is usually the Australian branch or affiliate of the international association holding the convention. Although the process is not difficult in outline, succeeding in the face of fierce competition is another matter; it is anything but simple. Every single convention, regardless of size, involves a massive amount of work to secure and organise. With international conventions, this may take place over four or five years.

Facilities count. Sydney and Melbourne are likely to attract big international conventions with exhibitions attached because they, among Australian cities, have the most capacious exhibition areas. Other cities highlight their own strengths. For example, Adelaide concentrates both nationally and internationally on fields in which it can demonstrate particular expertise – automotive, technology and medical. Service quality is also emphasised. The Adelaide Convention Centre has been described as a five-star hotel without rooms, with an emphasis on fine food and excellent service (van der Hoeven 1997).

Marketing a destination as an international convention venue is a cooperative effort. The Australian Tourist Commission participates in overseas marketing through an alliance with 13 convention bureaus called Team Australia. Convention centres join convention bureaus as major partners in the bidding process. Thus the Melbourne Convention and Exhibition Centre and the Melbourne Convention and Marketing Bureau jointly maintain representative offices overseas. Sometimes, private interests such as casinos or professional conference organisers play a significant role in convention bids.

Convention bureaus themselves are cooperative organisations with hundreds of members representing providers of a variety of services for MICE participants. The only exception is the Northern Territory Convention Bureau which is an administrative unit of the Northern Territory Tourist Commission. Important as the international convention business is, an estimated 80 per cent of the meetings in Australia are domestic (Department of Tourism 1995a).

Convention bureaus play a lesser role in bidding for national conventions. Many of these move from city to city on a rotational basis. When it is ordained that a particular association will meet in a particular city then the venues within that city compete for its business. The lead time for national conferences is shorter, usually within the 18–24 months range.

Corporate meetings

Corporate meetings come in considerable variety. They include corporate training seminars, management meetings, regional and national sales meetings, new product introduction meetings, professional and/or technical meetings and shareholder meetings. Annual general meetings are predictable and some companies with thousands of shareholders require large venues. Convention centres and hotels approach such companies for their business.

Direct mail and personal selling techniques are used to encourage likely prospects. There are a variety of ways to circulate information on facilities, ranging from convention bureaus' planners guides to specialist publications such as guides on websites.

DEFINITIONS

Incentive travel

Incentive travel is used by companies as a reward for reaching productivity levels. For example, a company will give its staff or dealers a trip for achieving sales targets. It is also used for corporate communication, employee education and product launches.

Incentive travel is handled by a variety of companies, some of them general travel companies which have divisions specialising in the arrangements at the destination only. Others specialise in selling a whole program to the client. Understanding what the company is seeking from the program is essential for those seeking the business, who can then design an appropriate program.

The Australian Tourist Commission runs an annual five-day incentive promotion for overseas incentive travel buyers called Dreamtime. In 2001, 130 buyers and eight corporate decision-makers from 20 countries, mainly from Asia, the United States, the United Kingdom and Europe, attended.

Convention bureaus also do their best to attract incentive travel. They help search out prospects, with programming and with promotional material. Among other activities, the Sydney Convention and Visitors Bureau includes a page on its website inviting incentive travel planners to seek information and offering options for experiencing Sydney (www.scvb.com.au).

The Melbourne Convention and Marketing Bureau hosts the nation's biggest incentive trade show, the annual AsiaPacific Incentives & Meetings Expo (AIME). In 2002 some 60 destinations were represented (www.aime.com.au).

Exhibitions

Some exhibitions are attached to conventions and convention centres aim to increase the number, either by persuading convention organisers to include an exhibition in their event or by encouraging exhibition organisers to arrange conferences at the same time.

The usual method of creating exhibitions is for an exhibition organiser to rent space from the exhibition centre and then sell booth space to exhibitors. There is a core of about 12 exhibition organisers operating in Australia.

The big exhibition centres try to attract business by identifying industry segments with the potential for attracting overseas exhibitions. They also try to link international and national exhibitions to special events which may be held in their city.

Relationship marketing

Activities designed to create a bond between an organisation and its customers. The motivation is the retention of customers.

▓ Relationship marketing

The term **relationship marketing** refers to activities designed to create a bond between an organisation and its customers. The basic motivation is the retention of customers. Some travellers like to stay with the familiar but many are often curious about trying new experiences, new airlines, new hotels, new restaurants, a different rent-a-car or touring company. They need good reasons to stick to companies when there is plenty of competition.

Companies therefore may have to go to considerable lengths to hold their customers and relationship marketing is often complex and expensive. However, many studies have shown it is more profitable to retain existing customers rather than constantly seek new customers to replace lapsed ones.

Database management is used tactically for such things as promotional offers, but the main thrust is strategic, to develop long-term relationships with customers. Loyalty programs are part of relationship marketing: they reward consumers for staying with a company and its products. Airlines have their loyalty programs – the frequent flyer programs and airport clubs – just as hotel chains have frequent guest programs, rent-a-car companies have frequent user programs and some restaurants have frequent dining programs.

Typically programs award points for use of the company's products – a flight, a hotel room etc. When points are accumulated to certain levels they can be cashed in for rewards. So many points will earn a designated free flight or a free night's accommodation and so on. Travel companies can also benefit from other businesses offering travel credits for their loyalty programs, e.g. 'FlyBuys' which is run for the benefit of a group of retailers, and jointly badged credit cards.

▓ Sponsorship marketing

Travel and tourism companies are heavily involved in sponsorship marketing. Sponsorship can be paid for in two ways: cash and 'kind', or the provision of services for which the organisers of events would otherwise have to pay. Travel and tourism companies, in providing a free or discounted seat or room or entry, are thus involved in sponsorship every day of the year all over the country.

There has to be a reason. Companies will sometimes take the view that they are 'giving something back to the industry' by providing, say, a free coach or free rooms for an industry conference, but generally they regard contributions of cash or kind as a marketing expense, a budget item, which has to be justified by the return it brings. Therefore they seek tangible benefits such as naming rights, signage, identification in printed and broadcast publicity.

In sponsoring an event, a company or other organisation agrees to pay for the right to use the image of the event for marketing communications purposes. Typically, the sponsor buys the sponsorship rights and then allocates further expenditure to draw further public attention to its involvement.

Sponsorship can have significant benefits over other forms of marketing. Some sponsors believe it is the best way to reach many potential customers, because of problems with the cost of traditional advertising and audience fragmentation. On the negative side, the benefit from sponsorship is often difficult to quantify.

CASE STUDY

Destination marketing and the ATC

Destination marketing is widely practised in Australia. From regional tourism association level up, there are some 80 destination marketing organisations and there are many more at local level.

Their role is, of course, to attract tourists to their destination; no small task considering the number of destinations in Australia and throughout the world. Competing for attention in any market requires skills and appropriate resources. In this case study, the role of Australia's national tourism organisation (NTO) overseas, the Australian Tourist Commission (ATC), is examined.

Target markets

The ATC competes in markets in most parts of the world. This is how it sees its main target markets.

Europe The United Kingdom is the dominant market in Europe; by itself it is Australia's third biggest after New Zealand and Japan. Other important markets are Germany, France, Switzerland, Italy, Ireland and the Netherlands.

Americas The United States is the major market in the region, with Canada as a secondary market. Emerging markets include Brazil, Argentina, Chile and Mexico.

Asia The ATC maintains a network of offices and representatives in the area. Target markets include China, Hong Kong, Taiwan, India, Singapore, Malaysia and Thailand.

Japan It is part of Asia of course, but it is singled out for special attention because of its importance. Despite ongoing economic uncertainties, Japan continues to be a vital source market for Australia.

New Zealand Australia's largest tourism source market as well as the most mature, driven by proximity, affordability and close cultural and sporting ties.

Additionally, the ATC sees **South Africa** and countries in the **Middle East** – Israel, the United Arab Emirates, Kuwait and Saudi Arabia – as emerging markets (www.atc.australia.com).

How the ATC spends its money

The ATC has a budget of well over $100 million a year. In the year ending 30 June 2001 its revenue totalled more than $122 million of which $92 million was from the Commonwealth Government and nearly $27 million was from industry contributions.

Table 8.2 shows how it allotted its operational funds.

Table 8.2 ATC's operational expenditure 2001–02

Advertising	$44.9 million
Promotion and publicity	$11.9 million
Films, publications and distribution	$10.7 million
Information systems and telecommunications	$6.2 million
Research, service fees and travel	$9.3 million

(Source: Australian Tourist Commission.)

Operational methods

In broad terms, the ATC operates as do many other NTOs around the world. Professor Peter Keller, director of Swiss Tourism, sees the primary role of NTOs as maintaining 'supreme authority' over a country's image. Other tasks include:

- defining a 'brand value' for their destinations, to expand awareness and attract new clients by offering a quality assurance for the products and services offered
- standardising information services to improve the quality of distribution and ensure the information is properly targeted
- investing in information-technology-supported product management to help rejuvenate products and services
- cooperating with the private sector in developing and marketing new products
- justifying the need for continuing government support by helping small- and medium-sized enterprises to innovate and cooperate (World Tourism Organisation 1999d).

All these tasks are covered in the description of ATC activities below.

Brand Australia

For all its achievements, Australia, a small nation, does not present a powerful image on the world stage. Images are the result of many influences, not just a tourism campaign. Economic and political influence, wartime activities, sporting prowess, films and other art forms all contribute to a nation's image.

In 1995, the ATC set out to build 'Brand Australia' as an international brand image for Australia as a travel destination. According to the Commission, it was an attempt to highlight the elements of the country and nation that distinguish us from the rest of the world and promote 'the personality of Australia as a free spirited, optimistic, fun and liberating destination offering a range of experiences' (www.atc.australia.com).

The Brand Australia logo features a stylised kangaroo, the design having been developed after consumer testing had confirmed that the animal was Australia's most recognisable symbol. The colours ochre and blue are said to represent the diversity of the

The Brand Australia logo

(Source: Australian Tourist Commission.)

coastal and interior climates of Australia. The logo is used in all ATC advertising campaigns, promotional publications, Internet and trade marketing activities to provide a unifying link and to promote the brand in travel markets.

Change of advertising emphasis

Throughout much of the 1980s and 1990s the ATC pursued a policy of heavy spending on brand (or image) advertising in its major markets. This was designed to create awareness of Australia as a tourism destination. Research consistently showed that Australia was rated as a preferred destination as a result, but this was not followed up by a proportionate number of people visiting Australia. In some markets where Australia was rated by research as the 'most preferred destination', it lost market share (Richardson 1999).

In mid-2001, the ATC announced a change. It appointed a new network of advertising agencies around the world to undertake 'tactical advertising' to convert interest in Australia into bookings. It would feature holiday packages and 'key messages to overcome barriers for travelling to Australia such as price and time constraint' (Ken Boundy, managing director, 2001, press release 29 June).

'Brand advertising' was to be continued in certain markets, including emerging markets. The ATC defined 'tactical advertising' as that based on special offers, prices, packages and destination and said 'brand advertising' related to generic image advertising.

Visiting journalists program

The ATC plays host to about 1,000 international print and broadcast journalists each year through its Visiting Journalists Program. The journalists are targeted in overseas markets and then invited to come to Australia. They write, film or otherwise tell their audiences back home about Australia as a country and what it's like as a place to visit. According to the ATC, they tend to focus on Australia's contemporary urban culture, food and wine, arts and cultural themes as well as showing a strong interest in the lifestyle and backgrounds of Australian people. It is said this information reaches more than a billion a people a year.

Standardising and distributing information

The ATC is a massive distributor of information on Australia overseas. No other government agency comes close to it. It does this through advertising, publicity and the distribution of literature – it distributes annually more than one million brochures a year in five languages in Europe alone – and it continues to increase its dissemination of information on the Internet.

The 2001–02 annual report gave a variety of instances illustrating how online marketing has become an integral part of the ATC's strategic and tactical activities. About 38 million pages were downloaded worldwide on the ATC's consumer site www.australia.com during the year and 4.2 million pages were delivered on the Japanese-language website www.australia.jp. In the US www.croc.australia.com was developed to coincide with the release of the film *The Crocodile Hunter: Collision Course*; in Italy the 'micro-site' www.occasioni.australia.com was launched with 21 partners and 80 deals, coinciding with a 14-page Australia supplement in major media and supported by advertising.

The ATC is a participant with the state/territory tourism organisations in the Australian Tourism Data Warehouse (ATDW), a standardised system for storing information on tourism products throughout Australia. It replaces a range of different formats and systems and is intended to make products accessible to local, state, national and international markets. The system is not a booking agency but a data storage facility, which can be used by wholesalers, inbound tour operators, travel agents and others to source products and tourism information and is also being used for material for the ATC's consumer site and the state/territory websites.

It is common for the larger destination marketing organisations to have more than one site – one for consumers with destination information and another for corporate matters and information which can help the home industry. In 2003 the ATC had six sites: its consumer site (which incorporates the media site www.media.australia.com), its corporate site (www.atc.australia.com) and separate sites for its film and video library, its image library, for trade events and the meetings industry.

Cooperation with industry

The ATC is acknowledged for the thoroughness with which it organises cooperative marketing opportunities with the Australian travel and tourism industry. Its prime cooperative program is the Destination Australia Marketing Alliance, which involves state and territory organisations and members of the industry in targeted promotional activity overseas.

The ATC has an extensive database of Australian suppliers and offers them a range of marketing opportunities, including attendance at the Australian Tourist Exchange, a forum held in Australia each year where overseas buyers and Australian sellers gather for one-on-one business talks.

The ATC also arranges industry participation in the leading overseas business exchanges and trade shows (25 in 2000–01), in travel missions, in the visits of overseas journalists to Australia, in advertising in overseas markets and in electronic marketing.

It maintains continual contact with members of the industry throughout the country, partly by its roadshows and attendance at industry functions, but also effectively by email. It distributes an online newsletter and also sends information – breaking news – when warranted.

It took a leadership role in informing the industry of events following the September 11 terrorist attacks on the United States in 2001 and was able to help other government initiatives at the time because of its effective industry information network.

INDUSTRY PROFILE

MARIO GIANNATTILIO MANAGING DIRECTOR, PERFORMANCE TRAVEL, AND MANAGING DIRECTOR, MARKET LINK AUSTRALIA

I have a multi-faceted role in tourism marketing. Performance Travel is a total travel solutions company. Its primary role is organising travel for the entertainment business, including specialised logistics, but it is also involved in corporate travel and the MICE sector and its retail department looks after holiday travel. Market Link is a representation company and, in particular, it is general sales agent for the European Sixt rent-a-car company. That function is part of a global enterprise because Sixt has an affiliation in the Americas with Dollar Rent-A-Car and marketing arrangements around the world. Part of my role here is to work with Australian tour operators on fly/drive programs.

How did I get here?

I started in Adelaide as a travel consultant with Sea–Air Travel. Later I had my first airline experience with Air New Guinea and saw much of the world in my sales position. I returned to Adelaide for jobs with Hilton hotels and World Aviation, a representation company. Next I helped set up Lan Chile's operations in Australia and then came a major involvement with Aerolineas Argentinis. Based in Melbourne, from scratch I set up a fully operational office responsible for sales in Victoria, South Australia and Tasmania. After that experience I concentrated on the MICE area with Market Link Australia. The GSA for Sixt and involvement with Performance Travel followed.

What do I like about my job?

No two days are the same. I get up in the morning and know that today is not going to be the same as yesterday. That's the excitement of it, that's what keeps me going in this business.

Marketing theory is based on the 'marketing concept', which states that firms should try to discover what consumers want and make products to satisfy those wants.

The marketing process

Central to the marketing process are (1) market segmentation (described in Chapter 2), (2) positioning and branding, and (3) the marketing mix.

The positioning and branding process, which is to do with image, starts with an understanding of how the target market perceives a destination or an organisation and/or its products. The positioning statement distinguishes the destination or product from its competitors. Branding involves producing devices which give tangible effect to the image: the distinctive name, designs, symbols or colours.

The marketing mix is the combination of 'tools' an organisation uses to pursue its objectives in target markets. They are often classified as the four Ps, meaning product, price, place and promotion. The five main kinds of promotional activity are advertising, personal selling, sales promotion, public relations and publicity.

The marketing plan sets out objectives and the marketing actions to achieve them over a short period, usually a year. It is usually written in sections: (1) executive summary, (2) situation analysis, (3) SWOT analysis, (4) business definition, (5) mission statement, (6) objectives, (7) strategies, (8) action program, (9) resource statement and budget, and (10) controls (monitoring and evaluation).

The marketing mix employed by travel and tourism companies varies. Major airlines are by far the biggest advertisers, but they also rely on relationship marketing, yield management, holiday packaging, sophisticated personal selling, and elaborate distribution systems. The main marketing tools of the big hotel chains are personal selling, electronic distribution and loyalty programs. Tour wholesalers often put most effort into distribution channels. Small operators usually spend comparatively little on marketing, relying on word of mouth, brochures and help from government tourism organisations.

Specialised marketing

The basis of marketing conventions is called 'bidding-and-boosting — bidding for the convention and then promoting it. The process may take four or five years for an international convention and involve the Australian association, the ATC, a convention bureau and convention centre as well as service providers. Convention bureaus play a lesser role in bidding for national conventions, many of which move from city to city on a rotational basis. The lead time is shorter, usually 18 to 24 months.

Incentive travel is often sought by specialist incentive travel houses or large companies with an incentive travel department, and convention bureaus. The ATC and the Melbourne Convention and Marketing Bureau run annual incentive trade shows.

SUMMARY

Exhibitions may be attached to conventions and convention centres aim to increase the number, either by persuading convention organisers to include an exhibition, or by trying to attract business independently of conventions, often by working with one of about a dozen exhibition organisers.

Relationship marketing is designed to create a bond between an organisation and its customers. The tactics include database management, for such things as promotional offers, and loyalty programs which reward consumers for staying with a company and its products.

Sponsorship marketing often attracts travel and tourism companies. Sponsorships can be paid for in cash or 'kind', the provision of services for which the organisers of events would otherwise have to pay, such as a free or discounted seat or room. From the sponsor's point of view, the contribution is a marketing expense, which has to be justified by the return it brings, e.g. naming rights, signage, identification in printed and broadcast publicity.

Destination marketing is widely practised in Australia. From regional tourism association level up there are some 80 destination marketing organisations and there are many more at local level. The chapter's case study examines the role of the Australian Tourist Commission.

QUESTIONS

1. Why is marketing the most powerful instrument available for managing tourism? Give examples.
2. What is the marketing concept? Contrast it with the production concept.
3. Positioning is often said to be the hardest part of destination marketing. Why do you think this should be?
4. How can a brand represent a 'collection of enduring intangible values in the mind of the user'?
5. Is there an advantage for most travel and tourism companies in flexible pricing as against cost-plus pricing? If so, why? If not, why not?
6. What are the constituents of the marketing mix and what influences marketers in choosing or not choosing each one as a tool?
7. What are marketing objectives and strategies and where do they fit into the marketing plan?
8. Big airlines put more emphasis on advertising than big hotels, which rely more on personal selling. Why do you think this is so?
9. What does 'bid-and-boost' mean? What kind of organisations are convention bureaus and what do they do?
10. What does relationship marketing set out to achieve and what are some of the methods employed?

MANAGING TOURISM DEVELOPMENT

LEARNING OBJECTIVES

Understand that development can apply to all parts of the tourism system.

Examine planning processes which apply to tourism: strategic planning, the Commonwealth Government system, long-range planning.

Appreciate the importance of infrastructure to tourism and some of the problems of providing it. Note some examples of identified infrastructure needs in different parts of Australia.

Understand the development process involved in providing tourism buildings and the principles of their design.

Consider the main points covered in environmental and social impact assessments.

Identify issues associated with attracting investment to tourism projects.

Review a case study of the Tourism Futures Simulator as it is applied in Queensland and Western Australia.

**UNDERSTAND
THE MEANING OF:**

* *tourism development*
* *strategic planning*
* *long-range planning*
* *overall goal*
* *planning horizon*
* *assumption*
* *outcomes*
* *outputs*
* *administered items*
* *structure plan*
* *land-use plan*
* *infrastructure*
* *development process*
* *feasibility study*
* *Environmental Impact Assessment (EIA)*
* *Social Impact Assessment (SIA)*
* *Tourism Futures Simulator*
* *simulation technology*

DEFINITIONS

`· · · · · · · · · · · · · · · · · · · · · ·`

Development

*(1) A process of
physical change or
its end product e.g.
a resort, an
accommodation
building or a whole
destination area;
(2) An expansion or
enhancement of any
or all elements of
the tourism system.*

'DEVELOPMENT' APPLIES TO WHOLE TOURISM SYSTEM

This chapter is concerned mainly with development of destinations. However, 'development' can mean an expansion or enhancement of any or all elements of the tourism system – the traveller generating region, the transit route region, the number of tourists and the travel and tourism industry (and its constituent businesses), as well as the tourism destination region.

This should be borne in mind as each section is read. For example, long-range destination planners may be thinking of expanding forms of tourism (e.g. wine and food tourism, surf tourism, ecotourism) as well as increasing accommodation and/or other physical structures. This would impact on other elements of the tourism system, e.g. it would require an expansion of the travel and tourism industry and would have an impact on marketing in traveller generating regions. The development of infrastructure is another subject discussed in this chapter. It is important to the transit process.

'Development' can also be defined as a process of physical change or its end product, e.g. a resort, an accommodation building or a whole destination area. It is used in this sense in the latter part of the chapter dealing with the development of tourism buildings. But even then the development process must look to other elements of the tourism system than the destination region. The process requires a marketing 'quick check' at the start to see if it is worth proceeding, then a marketing study as part of a full feasibility study and then a marketing plan as part of the operational plan. Always remember always that a change in one part of the system will bring about changes in the other parts – if that does not occur there will be a development failure.

TOURISM DEVELOPMENT PLANNING

Tourism **development** requires detailed and systematic planning in its own right. Tourism is also affected by planning which has a wider purpose. For example, governments at all levels are involved in infrastructure planning and local government has the task of land-use planning, within the bounds set by state/territory governments. This chapter is concerned with the theory and practice of planning carried out at national, state and regional/local levels in Australia in relation to tourism. Three types of planning are involved:

- strategic planning, with horizons of, say, three to ten years
- the Commonwealth Government planning system
- long-range planning, usually at a regional level, and looking ahead, say 20 years. This itself may not be concerned solely with tourism but our interest in the detail is confined to tourism.

DEFINITIONS

▨ The strategic planning process

Strategic planning is the managerial process of matching an organisation's resources and abilities with its business opportunities over the long term. It consists of defining the organisation's mission and determining an overall goal, acquiring relevant knowledge and analysing it, then setting objectives and the strategies to achieve them.

In Australia, strategic planning became a routine task for government tourism organisations and a good number of regional and local organisations over the last two decades of the 20th century. It is a process also favoured by companies, which produce strategic plans directed at developing their businesses, with objectives related to sales growth, market share, return on investment and so on. These plans usually are commercially sensitive and while some broad features may be announced, details are kept within the company. So it is easier to get examples from government organisations.

Strategic planners follow a basic formula. They:

- decide what *business* they are in
- aim to achieve an *overall goal*
- gather *knowledge* as the basis of decision making
- *analyse* the information, usually in terms of the organisation's strengths and weaknesses and external opportunities and threats
- set *objectives* which determine the activities designed to achieve the overall goal
- devise *strategies* to achieve the objectives
- allot resources to an *action program* to give effect to the strategies
- *implement* the plans
- put in place *controls* to monitor results and take corrective action if necessary.

Planners and managers do not expect that everything will work out exactly as planned. Inevitably, circumstances will change during the period of the plan. It is a working document which needs to be consulted as it is being implemented, the results monitored and adjustments made. But unless something of overriding importance or something catastrophic occurs, the overall goal remains the same.

The business we are in

The mission statement was described in the last chapter. It is derived from deciding what business the organisation is in. This may or may not be what might be expected at first

Strategic planning
The managerial process of matching an organisation's resources and abilities with its business opportunities over the long term. It consists of defining the organisation's mission and determining an overall goal, acquiring relevant knowledge and analysing it, then setting objectives and the strategies to achieve them.

sight. For instance the Grand Hotel Group does not mention hotels in its mission statement. It's in the business of making money for its shareholders. 'Our mission is to maximise returns from assets and create wealth on a sustained basis for our security holders' (annual report 1998). Government organisations, with a different audience to convince, are usually more directly descriptive. 'The role of the Western Australian Tourism Commission is to accelerate the sustainable growth of the tourism industry for the long-term social and economic benefit of the state' (annual report 1999–2000).

Overall goal

Overall goal

A single overriding objective such as market leadership or change of direction involving new products and/or new markets.

A strategic plan usually works towards an **overall goal**, a single overriding objective such as market leadership or change of direction involving new products and/or new markets.

Goal setting involves answering these questions:

- Where are you?
- Where do you want to go?
- When do you want to arrive?

For a destination, answering those questions may lead to a development program involving all facets of the tourism system. For a business, it sets in motion a process so powerful that, according to Drucker (1974), the business itself will have changed by the end of the period of the plan.

The overall goal should have a horizon year, indicating when it is to be realised. This provides a time framework for making projections, setting objectives and strategies and carrying out the work necessary. The timing may be a good number of years ahead, particularly if it involves building tourism plant like a new accommodation complex or a complicated theme park.

Gathering knowledge

Judgment and creativity are important attributes in planning, but it takes more than flair. The quality of decision making depends upon the quality of the information gathered. A company or other organisation will have a great deal of knowledge in its internal systems, but it will also need external sources for a large proportion of what will be required. Some of this will come from government authorities at various levels; considerable information is available on tourism matters. Other information can be gathered from industry sources. Knowledge-gathering should be carried out in a systematic way with a clear idea of what is required. It is often a time-consuming task.

Analysis and assumptions

Broadly, the information gathered is classified into two classes of information for analysis: (a) information about the current state of affairs – about the organisation itself and the external environment which affects it; (b) information which can help planners make reasonable judgments about the future. The SWOT analysis has been described as a technique for use in marketing planning. It is often used also as part of the strategic planning process to examine an organisation in terms of its internal and external environments.

DEFINITIONS

Planners need to gather as much relevant information as they can about the likely future. They must tap the most knowledgeable sources available on political, economic, technological and social trends and expected developments. On specific tourism matters, they should turn to the work of the Tourism Forecasting Council and the Bureau of Tourism Research or, if relevant, examine results from specific reseach undertakings, e.g. the Tapestry Region Tourism Futures modelling project in Western Australia, described in this chapter's case study.

The planners know they cannot predict the future with accuracy, but they must estimate some facets of it. They make **assumptions**, which are not forecasts but can be defined for this purpose as temporary estimates or hypotheses of important, probable developments (Green 1970). If later there is a significant deviation to an assumption, the area of the plan based on it must be reviewed. But it is impossible to plan without assumptions.

Assumption
A temporary estimate or hypothesis of an important, probable development.

Objectives, strategies, action program, implementation and controls

Reference can be made to the marketing plan in the previous chapter for a description of the other items in the structure of the strategic plan – objectives, strategies, action program, implementation and controls. The description does not differ from that outlined previously. However, the content of each section will be markedly different because strategic planning is guided by the overall goal and the time horizon is not immediate, but usually three to ten years ahead.

Shorter-term plans, like year-long marketing plans, are derived from the strategic plan, with their objectives, strategies and action plans in tune with those of the strategic plan and designed to contribute to a stage in its fulfilment. If they are directed at one development role such as marketing, then they should be synchronised with strategic plan activity in different areas, such as facility development.

Terminology

The intention in the description above has been to explain the process rather than provide a format. Planners do not use the word 'knowledge' as a heading. They present summaries of information gathered under a variety of headings (e.g. 'situation analysis'). Also, there are fashions in planning presentation and terminology. More stages in the process may be introduced and a number of techniques may be used to aid the planning process (in the outline above, the SWOT analysis is a 'technique').

The overall goal may become the 'business mission', or may not be stated publicly at

DEFINITIONS

all. However, there has to be one. Even if the starting point is as vague as 'to do better than last time', questions are posed which lead to the formulation of an overall goal, putting the planning process in motion.

State and territory planning

State and territory tourism organisations produce a variety of strategic plans, some for or in association with regions, others for specific forms of tourism including wine and food, nature-based tourism, cultural tourism, indigenous tourism. Each state/territory has a principal plan which guides the organisation as a whole. Tourism Tasmania produces its plan in association with the state industry body, Tourism Council Tasmania, which also has a role in its implementation.

South Australia has a 'state tourism plan' which implies a 'whole of government' approach. This recognises that the tourism organisation itself can achieve only so much; other government agencies (e.g. those responsible for state development and roads) have far-reaching impacts on tourism development and planning is on the basis that all their policies and efforts must be coordinated. Other states – New South Wales, Western Australia, Tasmania – take the same view.

The Northern Territory Masterplan is a five-year strategic plan which is oriented towards marketing. However, most state/territory strategic plans now include strategies in relation to infrastructure and other physical development.

Outcomes and outputs framework
The basis of the Commonwealth Government's planning system, consisting of three essential elements: outcomes (impacts of the Government's actions on the community), outputs (goods and services produced by Commonwealth agencies) and administered items (resources administered by the agency on behalf of the Government – such as grants and benefits – to contribute to a specific outcome).

The Western Australian Tourism Commission developed a separate development strategic plan in the mid-1990s to examine the requirements for infrastructure and supporting facilities against a perception of market needs and expectations. The main features of its strategic plan, Partnership 21, launched in 2000, were marketing initiatives, but the plan also called for the development of regional tourism infrastructure and product development plans.

A three-year horizon is favoured by most state/territory planners, but there are variations. New South Wales' three-year plans are produced within the framework of a Masterplan which has a life of 15 years – from 1995 to 2010. Tasmania produces three-year strategic plans, designed to cumulatively achieve 10-year targets of tourist expenditure and employment.

The Commonwealth Government planning framework

Governments in Australia have become more rigorous in the last decade in developing systems relating results to what they want done and have budgeted for. Thus the planning of Commonwealth Government agencies, including the tourism division of the Department of Industry, Tourism and Resources and the Australian Tourist Commission, is accomplished within an '**outcomes and outputs framework**'.

There are three essential elements:

- **Outcomes** The results, impacts or consequences of actions by the Commonwealth Government on the Australian community, including influences from outside the Government.

- **Outputs** The goods and services produced by Commonwealth agencies on behalf of the Government for external organisations or individuals. Outputs include goods and services produced for other areas of government external to the agency.

- **Administered items** These are resources administered by the agency on behalf of the Government (such as transfer payments to the states, grants and benefits) to contribute to a specific outcome. They are identified separately from departmental outputs because they involve different accountability requirements. About 80 per cent of the Commonwealth budget is made up of administered items, the balance being made up of departmental outputs.

The process begins when agencies apply inputs (e.g. finances, human resources, capital equipment) to the activities that generate the products and services that generate their outputs. These inputs include the funds appropriated to them from the Budget or received through purchaser/provider arrangements, as well as revenue raised through other means, such as sales, levies and industry contributions.

The framework is designed to help answer these questions:

1. What does government want to achieve? (outcomes)
2. How does it achieve this? (outputs and administered items)
3. How does it know if it is succeeding? (performance reporting)

Information in the form of outcomes and output indicators provide feedback to help in organisation learning and redesign of the system as a whole. They also provide the basis for reporting in such documents as annual reports.

The Commonwealth Government management system allows for three types of plans:

1. **Corporate plan** A plan introduced by the agency providing the framework for the agency's operation and direction over a number of years.
2. **Strategic plan** Similar to a corporate plan, but not restricted to organisational boundaries. A strategic plan is intended to give direction and cohesion to activities over a specified timeframe, for example, three to five years. It may set out planned outcomes and the ways in which they may be achieved.
3. **Operational plan** A plan, usually covering a limited period (e.g. one year), which details the strategies, activities, outputs and resources that will be used in achieving planned outcomes over the period. Such plans often include specific performance targets such as deadlines, number and type of beneficiaries (Department of Finance and Administration, www.finance.gov.au).

DEFINITIONS

....

Long-range planning

A comprehensive process designed to guide development of usually a large area over a long period, say 20 years. It is concerned with tourism as one of a number of activities which have economic, social and environmental impacts on an area.

▦ Long-range planning

Long-range planning is more comprehensive in its approach than strategic planning. Its recommendations are designed to guide development over a long period, say 20 years or more. Public and private sector organisations either initiate projects as a result of the planners' recommendations or use them as a guide in carrying out projects initiated for other reasons.

Long-range planning is less common in Australia than strategic planning, but it is becoming more frequent. Usually it is concerned with tourism as one of a number of activities which have economic, social and environmental impacts on an area, often a large area. Planners aim to integrate tourism into the overall development policies of the region or other area and to establish linkages between tourism and other economic sectors.

The planning process brings together national, state/territory and local interests in the determination of how land is to be used for tourism (and other purposes) and what kind of physical developments will be built, allowed or encouraged. It may be carried out in a city or at regional or local government level.

The planners will examine the economic impact of tourism development and the new levels of tourist expenditure it is anticipated will follow. This can be projected in income and jobs, but must also be reckoned against the costs; the rewards must be seen to be worth the sacrifices (e.g. in substituting tourism for other economic activity, in effects on the physical environment and in congestion and other possible social costs).

The process is shown in Figure 9.1.

The first step: study preparation

The first step in long-range planning for a destination is to work out the method of conducting the study and preparing the plan. Usually it starts with a preliminary review

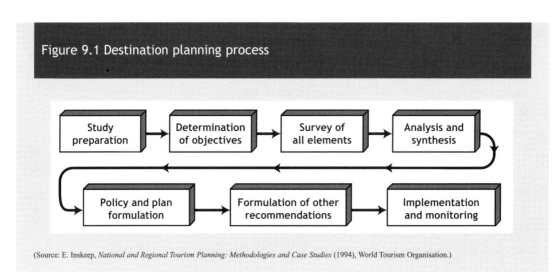

Figure 9.1 Destination planning process

Study preparation → Determination of objectives → Survey of all elements → Analysis and synthesis → Policy and plan formulation → Formulation of other recommendations → Implementation and monitoring

(Source: E. Inskeep, *National and Regional Tourism Planning: Methodologies and Case Studies* (1994), World Tourism Organisation.)

DEFINITIONS

of tourism resources in the destination area, the potential tourist markets and current linkages. The study terms of reference are written, setting objectives of the plan, detailing the range of the surveys to be undertaken and specifying the results required from them.

The terms of reference address specific issues affecting the area – economic, environmental and social – and also critical institutional elements. They set a horizon year when the plan and its targets and recommendations are to be realised. As this may be 20 or more years away, development staging – e.g. 3- or 5-year periods – should be specified. Personnel are selected – members of the steering committee who will oversee the process and the technical team which will carry it out.

The survey stage

During this stage information is gathered on (a) the overall size of the destination area's prospective market and the share of that market it can be expected to gain, and (b) the tourism resources which exist or can be developed to attract that potential market share. The survey includes all the elements in the tourism system. The early forecasts usually will be general estimates of numbers of tourists and their expenditure; but these will be sufficient to determine the way the rest of the survey – or indeed the entire plan – should proceed. In an extreme case, it might be decided not to proceed at all if it is shown that the potential scale of tourism to the destination area would not be enough to support further tourism development.

However, usually the forecast results in further studies to determine how best the destination area can be developed to attract and service the expected volume of tourists. It gives planners an idea of the magnitude of investments and commitments that will be required.

Following this stage, the survey work becomes much more detailed and technical. It assesses the tourism assets of the destination area (and also identifies its deficiencies); the suitability of its climate, whether it has – or can have – natural or built attractions which distinguish it from other destination areas, whether its facilities are suitable for its markets, whether its prices are competitive, whether it is accessible, and whether it projects the right image.

Analysis and synthesis

The next step is to analyse the information from the surveys and 'synthesise' the result. **Synthesis** means combining and integrating the various components of the analysis, relating the attractions to markets in a form of 'product/market fit', a term for the process whereby destination tourism products are matched with the needs and wants of the market.

Synthesis also integrates the analysis of physical, social and economic factors, including the relevant carrying capacities. This gives information about the optimum development of tourism in the destination area. Another important result from synthesis is

Synthesis (as a step in long-range planning)

The combining and integrating of various components of analysis of survey information about markets and the area. In tourism, synthesis relates the types of tourist attractions to potential markets. Synthesis also integrates the analysis of physical, social and economic factors, including relevant carrying capacities, giving information about the optimum development of tourism.

DEFINITIONS
....

**Tourism
development policy**

*A set of statements
establishing the
basis for developing
and managing
tourism in a long-
term plan.*

Structure plan

*Part of a long-term
plan which provides
the physical
framework for the
type and location of
development. The
elements can be
shown on a map.*

the identification of the major opportunities and constraints for developing tourism in the area. These provide much of the basis for determining future tourism development.

Tourism policy and plan formulation

Two essential and linked elements are involved at this stage: tourism development policy and the structure plan.

Tourism development policy consists of a set of statements based on (a) the objectives of the plan; (b) the overall development policy of the destination area; (c) the survey and analysis of present tourism development patterns and infrastructure, attractions and activities and the tourism markets; and (d) relevant socio-economic and environmental factors.

The **structure plan** provides the physical framework for the type and location of development. It is composed of several elements: (a) the primary and secondary attractions; (b) the tourism development areas such as resorts or attraction complexes; (c) access points to the destination area; (d) internal transportation linkages. Tourist excursion routes may also be shown.

The tourism structure plan is part of a broader plan for the area showing settlements (cities, towns, villages), agricultural lands, greenbelts, industrial land, airports and seaports, access corridors. It can be presented on a map so that it can be seen how tourism fits into the overall picture. It guides the location, types and extent of attractions, facilities, services and infrastructure. These criteria might also be influenced by what the planners see as new directions for tourism in the area (e.g. ecotourism).

Recommendations

Based on the analysis and synthesis, tourism development policy and the structure plan outline selected, the plan can be finalised in detail and the relevant recommendations made.

Implementation and monitoring

The final step in the process is the implementation of the plan accompanied by monitoring to ensure that the objectives are being accomplished. This step bridges the gap between the acceptance of the development plans and the adjustments of the travel and tourism industry to incorporate the new developments in its operations. The drive that produced the plan up to this point must continue. Even when funding and other resources are committed, plans are not always carried out.

Land use plans

Tourism development areas designated for integrated tourist resorts, resort towns, urban tourism and tourist attractions require land use plans. This more detailed level of planning indicates the (a) specific areas for hotels and other types of accommodation, retail shops and other tourist facilities; (b) recreation, parks and conservation areas; (c) the transportation system of roads, walkways and other elements such as a local airport or railway line and station; and (d) the planning for other infrastructure such as water supply, electric power, sewerage and solid waste disposal and telecommunications.

Zoning regulations and specific architectural, landscaping and engineering design standards are often prepared at this level of planning. Planning for tourist attractions may include visitor use and flow analysis.

Involving the community

Community consultation during the planning process is essential. It not only serves as a guide to what the public want and don't want from tourism development but also makes more likely community support for the final plans and the development itself. It goes without saying that people living in the area have a vital stake in major decisions which affect their future lives. They deserve to be fully informed and given the opportunity to state their opinions. Some people who do not live in the area but have particular interests there – they may have businesses, be thinking of investing, or be regular visitors – may also be invited to take part in the consultation process (Inskeep 1991 and 1994, Mathieson & Wall 1982, Gunn 1994, Kaiser & Helber 1978, Office of National Tourism 1998b).

INFRASTRUCTURE: A PROBLEM OF COORDINATION

Infrastructure is a major concern for tourism planners. Some of it may be built just for tourists and other travellers – airports, tourist roads etc. – but generally it also serves the needs of the resident community and requires expansion or enhancement for tourists. In any case, decisions on major infrastructure projects are usually not based on tourism alone.

The ratio of tourist volume to the size of the resident community counts in discussions on infrastructure. One of Australia's large cities may not be overstrained by an influx of 30,000 visitors,[1] but, as we saw with the example of Byron Bay in Chapter 7 that number on one night caused a serious infrastructure overload in a town of 7,000.

Cities contain a basic infrastructure that is costly to develop at remote locations or enhance in smaller population centres – water supply, waste disposal, police protection, fire protection and power. This has become an important issue in Australia as tourism spreads into more smaller communities, putting strain on their ability to provide basic infrastructure to cope with large numbers of visitors.

Transportation infrastructure – roads, signs, terminals, air and sea ports – is obviously essential to tourism. So is the provision of drinkable water, the disposal of sewerage and the supply of energy. Tourism's dependence on social infrastructure – education, hospitals, health and community services – may not be so obvious. Nevertheless, all these services are important. Managers and employees of tourism businesses need schools for their children. At times, tourists require hospitals and the other services (e.g. medical, information centres, post offices) and like to know they are not far from where they are visiting.

All three levels of government fund infrastructure and the private sector provides the money for some individual projects. A number of states have a 'PPP (public/private partnerships) policy' intended to facilitate involvement of the private sector in major public infrastructure development.[2] According to the Australian Local Government Association current programs are effective in providing baseline services, but there are gaps and little coordination between the levels of government (Australian Local Government Association 1999).

Report card critical of roads

An 'infrastructure report card' produced in 2001 by a group representing major infrastructure users, owners, operators, investors and relevant industry groups gave a discouraging view of Australian infrastructure. Of particular concern to tourism interests was the low rating it gave roads. Calling itself the Australian Infrastructure Report Card Alliance,[3] the group commissioned consultants Gutteridge Haskins & Davey (2001) to produce a 'report card' on 10 infrastructure sectors on a national level: roads, railways, airports, ports, wastewater, potable water, stormwater, irrigation, electricity and gas.

Ratings were based on a consideration of asset condition, asset availability and reliability, asset management and sustainability, including economic, environmental and social issues. Its ratings for roads were C ('adequate' but major changes required) and D ('poor' critical changes needed). Table 9.1 shows the results.

Funding for roads is shared between the three levels of government, although there has been some private sector funding used to build high volume roads in capital cities. These have included the CityLink in Melbourne, the Eastern Distributor in Sydney and the Sydney Harbour Tunnel.

Otherwise governments share responsibility for the funding and management of the 810,000 km of public highways and roads in Australia.[4] The Commonwealth Government funds the national highways and roads of national importance (2.5 per cent by length) while the states fund the major arterial road system (13.5 per cent) and local government is responsible for the rest (84 per cent). The 'Roads To Recovery' program, announced in 2000, increased Commonwealth Government allocations for roads by $1.6 billion over four years. This is a considerable sum, but the need is great. It has been said that if that allocation were divided between every council in the country it would equate to the cost of about half a roundabout for each (Yates 2001).

The 'report card' gave airports a B grading, meaning only minor changes were required. It said Australia's airports were generally in a good to very good condition

Table 9.1 Australian roads rated in 2001

CATEGORY	GRADE	COMMENT
National roads	C	Despite some major upgrade works on the eastern seaboard, the overall quality of the national highway system is only average.
State roads	C–	State roads vary greatly in quality. Urban congestion is increasing and the overall quality of rural highways has not improved. State roads are rated as average to poor.
Local roads	D	The average age of the nation's local roads continues to increase. Lack of both capital and maintenance funding is an ongoing issue of concern. Urban congestion is worsening. Local roads are rated as poor. The 'Roads to Recovery' funding should improve this grading over time, if the funding becomes ongoing.

(Source: Gutteridge, Haskins & Davey (2001), p. iv.)

because they were maintained under an inspection and management regime required by the Commonwealth Air Safety Authority (CASA). Some improvements in infrastructure in 2001 were noted from the previous year. In rating wastewater disposal (e.g. sewerage) at C minus it noted this was a one-grade improvement in recognition of the increased investment in rehabilitation of existing infrastructure and the large number of treatment plant upgrades. This had resulted in reduced pollutants being discharged into Australia's waterways.

Linkages: needs of states

The importance of infrastructure in linking destination areas with their markets has been noted in Chapter 2. It is a matter constantly concerning state and territory tourism authorities.

Roads and signs

A report by consultants Coopers and Lybrand (1996) for the Western Australian Tourism Commission noted a need to develop regular passenger transport networks from the major gateways to the major regional hubs and between these regional hubs to the major natural assets of Western Australia. The report said road infrastructure in the state was a depreciating asset and unsealed roads were hampering the development of tourism attractions. It also called for better signage on many tourism routes, giving details of direction, attraction, location and related interpretation.

Road corridors

The New South Wales Masterplan has these comments about linkage infrastructure in that state:

- Attention had to be paid to linkage road corridors, particularly:
    - high speed/large capacity, freeway and highway-standard roads to facilitate access to major tourist destinations, e.g. the Hunter, North and South Coasts.
    - high capacity connections to facilitate access to/from major population centres, particularly Sydney, for day-tripping.
    - good quality inter-regional road links in semi-rural and rural locations.
- Also needed were tourist drives which provided alternative routes to the main traffic corridors and were of specific interest to tourists based on the attractions found en route.
- The application of Australian tourist sign standards was essential and coordinated signage programs were required throughout New South Wales for major tourist attractions, accommodation facilities and tourist information points (Tourism New South Wales 1996).

State intervention

The small town of Strahan in Tasmania provides an example of how a state can intervene to ensure infrastructure needs are met when tourism development is at stake. In 2000, the West Coast Council put a moratorium on further development in Strahan because the sewerage system had become inadequate. This meant that no building approvals were issued, effectively putting a stop to new construction. This was a serious matter because Strahan has a special role in the economy of the area. The council's rate base is shrinking as mining declines and a strategy has been developed to see how Zeehan, Queenstown, Roseberry and Tullah can 'hook on to' tourism interest focused on Strahan.

Although small (population about 800 permanent residents), Strahan is the main destination area in Tourism Tasmania's West Coast 'cluster', a vital element of the state's tourism development plan. The sewerage problem affected a lot more than the town's population, because of tourism. As a result, the state government took the initiative in organising funding for a new $4.5 million treatment plant. Some federal and council funds were included in the package, as well as those from the state budget.

The moratorium was lifted in early 2002, some months before the opening of the new treatment plant. Strahan also has a new $1.2 million water plant (Wardlaw 2001).

Outback infrastructure

Not surprisingly, the road and track network is considered the most important infrastructure requirement in the huge Flinders and Outback Region, which includes a significant proportion of South Australia. But the consultants who produced a

WELCOME TO THE DIAMANTINA SHIRE

THE ROADS WHICH YOU ARE ABOUT TO TRAVEL ARE EXTREMELY ISOLATED & FOR YOUR PROTECTION YOU ARE REQUESTED TO.....

❶ ENSURE THAT YOU ARE CARRYING SUFFICIENT QUANTITIES OF PETROL & WATER FOR YOUR JOURNEY.

❷ CALL AT ALL STATIONS & ADVISE OF YOUR PROGRESS & PLANS.

❸ THE EVENT OF MISHAP REMAIN IN YOUR CAR & IF YOU HAVE ..LLOWED REQUEST N°2 YOU WILL SOON HAVE ASSISTANCE.

– WE WISH YOU A PLEASANT TRIP –

DIAMANTINA SHIRE COUNCIL

The Outback is not a touring region to be taken lightly. Signage is an essential part of the infrastructure which not only helps travellers find where they want to go, but also offers essential advice for their safety. This battered sign is on the Birdsville Track, not far from the little Queensland town of Birdsville.

(Source: Aussie Outback Tours.)

development plan for the region recommended care should be taken not to over-develop the roads. They thought drivers out to enjoy the Outback would avoid them if they were too good. They pointed out that progressive upgrading of the Oodnadatta, Birdsville and Strzelecki Tracks was sound for transport reasons, but had reduced the driver challenge for visitors, who might seek more adventurous routes (Gutteridge, Haskins & Davey 1997).[5]

The region extends north from Crystal Brook and Peterborough in the east and Port Augusta and the Western Australian border in the west. It is a legendary part of Australia, including such features as the Flinders Ranges, Wilpena Pound, Arkaroola, and the opal town of Coober Pedy. It is not easy to develop such a vast, diverse and sparsely populated area for tourism. It includes local government areas, but there are large tracts of land which are unincorporated. However, it does not lack interest: the planners have divided the region into 12 tourism precincts, within which there are no fewer than 28 nodes.

It is not a region in which to get lost, but the consultants noted that it was poorly signposted and recommended this be rectified. Other infrastructure recommendations included the construction of more airstrips for commercial aircraft, the extension of electricity supplies to remote areas and the provision of cost-effective emergency communications.

DEVELOPING BUILT PROJECTS

Tourism requires special purpose buildings, mainly (a) accommodation establishments of various kinds (e.g. hotels, motels, guest houses, holiday homes), (b) built attractions, of which there are a great variety (e.g. amusement parks, theme parks, museums and galleries, entertainment centres), (c) convention, exhibition and function centres and (d) transport terminals. Some of these are usually provided by governments (e.g. convention centres, the major museums and galleries), but the majority are developed by private interests on the expectation that they will return a profit to those who paid for them.

Success in tourism development often requires understanding the other's point of view from both the government side, where there is a concern for the social and environmental costs of a project as well as its benefits, and from the business side, with its understandable concern for profits. Planners usually have government connections; they are either employed directly by government agencies or by groups of organisations in which government of one level or another has a large, usually decisive, role. But there are limitations in government's relationship with the private sector which affect the implementation of plans, particularly when they involve physical developments requiring big investment.

Governments cannot tell businesses what to do, but they can tell them what they cannot do. They impose on the private sector regulations about land use, construction of buildings, licensing, the constraints of the Trade Practices Act. Investors and developers often start work without worrying about anybody else's ideas. They perceive an opportunity and act on it. But if their schemes do not fit into what government – usually state development and planning departments and local government – thinks is right for the area they can be prevented from proceeding.

The other side of the coin is that governments cannot insist that businesses invest in projects simply because they are indicated as desirable in a plan of some kind. Government agencies in Australia have a good record in marshalling the travel and tourism industry for marketing purposes, but the development of tourism facilities involves a different set of businesses often with other kinds of property interests competing for their attention. The private sector evaluates opportunities for tourism development on a project basis. Clearly the vision described in a plan is important to that evaluation because if all the components of the plan are implemented it will affect the prospects of each project.

The plan then is a factor in the potential project, but overall the evaluation is made to determine whether the project is considered viable, whether the risk of investing the money required is justified by the expected return on the investment.

One step at a time

The project development process is usually structured so that commitments are undertaken one step at a time. Commitment of time and funds are kept to a minimum at each step, so that the process can be stopped or altered before proceeding to the next step. The process is thus driven by the requirement to justify funding and the order of events may differ from that detailed below because of the funding circumstances. In some cases – e.g. apartment hotels or resorts with condominiums – the project will not proceed until a certain level of units are presold. It should be noted that some big developers (e.g. Mirvac Group) also operate hotels. The reason is that hotels provide the company with continuing cashflow, whereas receipts from developing them are intermittent. Some developers are operators as well because they are wary of the level of fees charged by big international hotel management companies.

The development process

A typical development process follows the following steps:

Step 1: Evaluate the potential market This is a 'quick-check' investigation to identify potential target markets and satisfy the developer that there are likely to be enough customers to make it worth proceeding to the next step.

Step 2: Choose a location The site for the building or buildings needs to be selected with care, with consideration for relationships to transport, existing attractions, services and competitors. Architects and other design professionals can identify special features such as visual amenity, drainage courses and other landscape elements that make a parcel of land unique. Buildings can then be optimally sited to take advantage of their locale, to create a special place, and to minimise their dependence on technology.

Step 3: Identify key players (e.g. architects, real estate brokers, lawyers and competitors) and work out the role each might have in the development of the project. The developer should make contact with planning officials (state/territory and local government) and any others concerned with planning controls and discuss what is likely to be approved and what is not. If there are public issues at stake, it may be wise to consult property owners or the community through public meetings. The aim would be to rally support for the project.

Step 4: Conduct a market and financial feasibility study This study is intended to test the viability of the project, so that it can be decided whether or not the market is likely to support the new facility sufficiently for the financial return to justify the investment. A feasibility study has two parts – the market or demand study and the financial viability study. It is a lengthy process taking into account national trends such as the strength of the economy, the performance and prospects of the tourism sector as a whole, as well as local information and projections relevant to the type of project.

The market study attempts to determine what type of tourist is likely to visit the

Feasibility study
A study intended to test the viability of a project. It has two parts – the market or demand study and the financial viability study.

project, how many, where they will come from, and when they will come, taking into consideration seasonality factors. For an accommodation facility, an estimate of how long they are likely to stay will be made. The study should help clarify costs: (a) the likely capital costs because it will have calculated capacity, and (b) the operational costs because it will have calculated patronage and income and taken into consideration issues such as staffing. The financial study will estimate income on a yearly basis, usually for three to five years, and also the costs for the same period. As well as operating costs, these will include finance charges, depreciation and taxes.

A note of caution needs to be sounded about feasibility studies. They should be what Swanbrooke (1995) calls a 'systematic, logical, neutral tool for rational decision-making (p. 103)', but in fact they often carry a degree of bias. In some cases the study is designed to reinforce a decision that has already been taken. Necessarily there are key assumptions on which viability turns and these can be made on the basis of a desired result instead of on a neutral basis.[6]

Step 5: Plan and design the concept This step is influenced by the market evaluation, which indicates the type of tourist the facility can be expected to attract; it helps with the positioning of the project. Therefore, the hotel, resort, attraction or other facility can be designed specifically to suit its target markets.

Step 6: Document the proposal An information document is prepared, describing the project in detail, estimating demand for at least three years and including financial projections for the same period. It is usual to illustrate this document to give people an idea what the project will look like when it is finished.

Step 7: Consult the community Whether or not the community was consulted earlier about the idea of the project, steps should now be taken to inform it of the details of the project, and the concerns of the developer for the environment and local opinion. Community interests should be given the opportunity to comment.

Step 8: Comply with the approvals process Continuing liaison with the appropriate planning regulatory body should have been maintained so that it fully understands the proposal. Now formal approval of the plan is sought.

Step 9: Complete the investment process Financial planning will have been in the developer's mind from the beginning, but the formal process of arranging finance must be completed at this stage. These negotiations will determine the owner of the project. The developer may have sufficient equity to retain ownership or may have to surrender control to the major investor, whether it be an individual, a company or a financial institution.

Step 10: The architects prepare the building documentation In effect, this guides the builders during construction. It is not necessarily complete before building begins. These days, because of fast-tracking, it is not uncommon for some documentation to be prepared during construction.

Step 11: The construction phase Before construction begins, there is a preliminary period involving clearing land, building access roads, developing utilities and so on. A

DEFINITIONS

project manager is appointed to manage the project within budget and time constraints. The task is basically to coordinate and manage people and there are lot of them – architects, designers, surveyors, builders, tradespeople, decorators, landscape gardeners, utility managers, local authority regulators. The suppliers of materials are a group on their own. They supply everything from building materials like bricks and glass, to wastebins and shop equipment. Poor management can cause delays and increase costs.

Step 12: Produce operational plan It is not unusual for a chief executive to be appointed soon after the decision to proceed is made or after construction begins. Sometimes the chief executive is the project manager. In any case operational planning necessarily takes place well ahead of completion. Personnel requirements must be worked out and recruiting and training programs planned in detail. An in-depth marketing study will be necessary. The demand section of the feasibility study will have indicated that a certain type and number of tourists can be attracted. The detailed plan must go further and identify the media for reaching them and include specific advertising and public relations programs (de Keijzer 2001).

Designing tourism buildings

A tourism site which includes purpose-built buildings has to look the part as well as suiting the function for which it is constructed. The design guides the people like builders and landscape gardeners who turn ideas into physical reality, ensures the best use of resources and is important in attracting investors and obtaining planning approvals. It also is a major influence on the visitor experience. A tourism building should be identifiable for its purpose (e.g. some form of accommodation, an attraction, an exhibition centre), be aesthetically pleasing and be efficient functionally. Theming in hotels and resorts is often an integrating design feature. The Palazzo Versace hotel on the Gold Coast is perhaps the most spectacular example in Australia, but there are many others. The 72 condominiums adjacent to the hotel have also been fitted out 'in all things Versace – from plates to the last tile' (MacDermott 2000, p. 52).

Not all efforts to give a complex a special flavour are so elaborate or costly,[7] but in any case the architect must have the consumer in mind when designing a tourism building or complex. Tourism experiences are out-of-the-ordinary experiences. Therefore design should reflect the market's values. The development should fit the physical and cultural landscape in which it is set. It should not be a copy of tourism architecture from somewhere else without regard for the special character of the setting.

Environmental impact assessment

Environmental impact assessment (EIA) is a procedure for protecting the environment accepted in one form or another by all governments throughout Australia. It provides a structured analysis of a proposed development, identifying the potential environmental

Environmental impact assessment (EIA)
A structured analysis of a proposed development, identifying the potential environmental effects of undertaking it and presenting those effects alongside the other advantages and disadvantages of the proposal to the decision makers.

effects of undertaking it and presenting those effects alongside the other advantages and disadvantages of the proposal to the decision makers. The EIA is thus used to decide whether development should be allowed to proceed and on what conditions.

Thomas (1996) points to the underlying political nature of the process. While EIA may seem purely technical it can only provide advice to decision makers and cannot veto a proposal. Decisions which are unsatisfactory from an environmental point of view may still be made, but that occurs with the full knowledge of the environmental consequences.

Most projects do not need an EIA. It is only required if the development is likely to produce some substantial adverse environmental effects. If the project is planned with one of its objectives being to minimise environmental effects, it is unlikely to need an EIA. Major infrastructure projects such as creation of a new airport or extension of an existing one usually do require an EIA.

The difference between an Environmental Impact Statement (EIS) and an EIA should be noted. The EIA is a two-step process, and the EIS is the product of the first step. It is a document which provides information on the existing environmental situation and the expected effects of a decision to proceed with the proposal (or a recommended alternative to the proposal). The second step in the EIA process is a review of the EIS by government officials and the public to consider the accuracy of the EIS, and in view of the predicted effects recommend whether/how the proposal should proceed. This review is reported to the authority that will make a decision on the proposal.

Social impact assessment

Social impact assessment (SIA) is a process for evaluating the probable effects of a development on the community. It is sometimes made part of the EIA process and at other times undertaken as a separate process. Barrow (2000) says integration of the two has not been effective in the United States where a study of impact assessments had shown that usually little social component had been included. In practice SIA has not had the same level of support, especially legislative support, and official acceptance as EIA.

SIA provides information on social institutions, social capital and social change, which may be of great importance in assessing whether or not the development is sustainable. Like EIA, SIA should go beyond anticipating possible impacts to suggest development alternatives to avoid, reduce or mitigate problems and maximise benefits. The SIA procedure uses a combination of objective and subjective assessment and ethical judgments, and considers external and internal changes. It is not a precise science and cannot rely only on quantifiable data. Qualitative measurements are useful and arriving at them requires the professional judgment of researchers. There is also flexibility in the way SIA is applied. The focus may change with circumstances. Sometimes the focus is on social systems affected by 'external' forces of change, at other times it is on 'internal' factors as a cause of impacts – for example, alterations of perception or aspiration. Sometimes the focus is social, sometimes more socioeconomic or sociocultural.

**Social impact
assessment (SIA)**

*A process for
evaluating the
probable effects of a
development on the
community. It uses a
combination of
objective and
subjective
assessment and
ethical judgments,
and considers
external and
internal changes.*

▓ Attracting investment

Tourism developments usually need big money, sometimes hundreds of millions of dollars for a single development. It comes from governments and private investors, both foreign and Australian. Many projects arise from developers' entrepreneurial instincts, but governments often play an important role in larger developments even when they do not invest taxpayers' funds – by planning, illustrating the benefits of private investment in particular projects and offering incentives for financiers and developers to put their money into the projects.

Many institutional investors in Australia are sceptical of tourism because:

- Tourism is subject to fluctuations which cannot be foreseen and which upset it more than other businesses. The events of 2001–2002 – the terrorist attacks in the US and Bali and the collapse of Ansett Australia – had a huge effect on travel. So did the Asian economic crisis and the SARS health crisis. The weather affects some kinds of tourism; fashions change and a destination's appeal may decline for no obvious reason.
- The accommodation sector has a reputation of profit inconsistency, partly because of a failure to manage yield from overseas tourists in the first half of the 1990s.
- International tourism is very sensitive to currency fluctuations.

The big accommodation building boom of the 1980s was largely financed by Japanese investors. To try to stimulate Australian investor interest, the Commonwealth Government set up the Tourism Forecasting Council in 1993 to provide tourism-related businesses and the government with relevant forecasts so that tourism investment decisions can be made with some confidence.

Interest in hotel investment in Australia has waxed and waned since the 1980s, depending on the conditions prevailing at the time. There has been little evidence of long-term thinking apart from the hotel building which occurred in Sydney in anticipation of the 2000 Olympic Games. It is easier to attract investment in projects where there are established markets – such as cities and well-known resorts – than in projects in regional Australia. This is partly due to past failures, and partly due to a general reluctance to step into unknown territory when there are opportunities for other types of property investment with returns which are more easily calculated with confidence.

A Tasmanian Government tourism development strategy paper has noted that the availability of capital both in terms of loan funds and equity is a significant impediment to development in Tasmania. It said most Tasmanian projects were too small for large equity investors such as superannuation funds. Experience had shown that major lending institutions were reluctant to provide loan funds and when they did they were likely to add significant risk premiums on loan facilities. Government agencies had provided a number of loans in the tourism sector in the past with mixed results. But some funding support was inevitable if tourism investment were to be encouraged (Sproule 2001).

CASE STUDY

The Tourism Futures Simulator: regional studies in Queensland and WA

T he CSIRO has developed a complex model called the **Tourism Futures Simulator** to help regional planners understand the forces that could shape the future of tourism in their areas. The prototype was formulated and successfully tested in the Douglas Shire and the Cairns section of the Great Barrier Reef Marine Park in Tropical North Queensland from 1997 to 2000. The Douglas Shire now maintains the system.

A new, larger, more complex model is being developed in the Tapestry Region of Western Australia and the system is being evaluated in other parts of the country.

Tropical North Queensland, numbering among its attractions the reef, the rainforest, its climate and culture, is one of Australia's most popular destination areas. In developing the Tourism Futures Simulator, CSIRO ecologists with expertise in the modelling of complex systems, set out to explore the level of tourism development that could be accommodated in the study area. They worked with a range of agencies.

The challenge was to protect the environment and the economy of the area in the future. The best way to do this was believed to be to develop a Tourism Futures Simulator which would provide a tool for planners and managers to understand what was likely to happen in the future – to tourism demand and its impact on the community and environment of the area.

A simulator can emulate the performance of complex systems and be used to explore future developments and scenarios. A model is created in which the key factors and their interdependencies are recorded and then used to simulate possible responses of the system to small or large changes in any of the factors.

The Tourism Futures Simulator was designed initially as a tool to assist tourism planners and other authorities to identify, monitor and manage the impacts of nature-based tourism on Douglas Shire's environment, economy and social structure. With this information they can plan to deal with problems before they cause a negative effect on demand or have an adverse effect on the community or the environment. Issues addressed in the modelling process were concerned with the land and marine environments, infrastructure, economic activities, possible patterns of tourism and cultural and economic factors.

The work began with the identification of a range of key indicators necessary to (a) quantify the benefits and impacts of nature-based tourism; (b) establish a framework for identifying the relationships between the indicators; (c) show how they affect future demand for nature-based tourism; and (d) establish a simulation system for impact and benefits of nature-based tourism opportunities.

DEFINITIONS

....

Tourism Futures Simulator

A model designed by the CSIRO to help regional planners understand the forces that could shape the future of tourism in their areas. Key factors affecting tourism in the area, and their interdependencies, are recorded and then used to simulate possible responses of the system to small or large changes in any of the factors.

The next step was to identify how various factors such as tourism markets, infrastructure and tourism facilities, the environment and regional development interact with each other. This involved examining each factor and identifying how it has developed in the past and how it is thought it might respond in the future. The simulator becomes increasingly complex as layers of information are added and as links between factors are developed. But it is relatively simple for planners and managers to use to test proposals and assess the likely impacts (Walker, 2001, CSIRO fact sheets *Tourism Futures Simulator* and *Exploring the Future of Tourism*).

The Tapestry Regional Model

A Tourism Futures Simulator is being developed in the Tapestry Region of Western Australia in a much larger and more complex setting than the Queensland project. The Tapestry Region embraces the city of Bunbury, 140 km south of Perth, and five adjoining shires. This group of local government areas, with a combined population of 75,000, formed an alliance in 1997 to promote tourism to the region and called it the South West Tapestry Group.

Physically, the Tapestry Region consists of 201,000 ha of state forests and national parks, coastal stretches and hinterland. It is off the regular tourism track and outside the major developments of Margaret River, the South West forests and the Busselton coastal area. Nevertheless, local stakeholders considered tourism, both actual and potential, a key sector of a varied economy which includes agriculture, dairying, fishing, forestry, mining and energy.

The modelling project is designed to help that process. It will deliver the Tapestry Tourism Futures Simulator as an aid to evaluating policy impacts and forming decisions about the development and marketing of tourism.

As with the Queensland model, the Tapestry TFS will use 'simulation technology' – a set of mathematical equations strongly inter-connected that can be used to help predict future occurrences. For example, the simulator might contain an equation that calculates the number of overnight visitors. Given this number, it is possible to calculate a range of environmental and economic impacts. These impacts in turn affect the number of visitors in the next time period.

The CSIRO is again involved. The work is being carried out with the support of the Cooperative Research Centre for Sustainable Tourism, with the involvement of Murdoch and Edith Cowan Universities, and the Commonwealth Department of Employment, Workplace Relations and Small Business.

The host organisation is the Bunbury Tourism Board, and the project manager, a former officer of the board, is located in the area. In the first year, the research team began a program to maintain community awareness of the project, solicit support from influence leaders, both individuals and organisations, and harness the resources of the six local government authorities.

Stakeholders include the region's more than 200 tourism operators, the other businesses that benefit from tourism, local government councils and agencies and community interest groups. They also include non-residents such as tour operators from Perth undertaking activities within the designated boundaries of the region, the State Government, its departments and agencies and potential investors and developers.

The project's formal objectives are to:

1. research and document all data and assets pertaining to the Tapestry Region, including social, economic and environmental factors. This information is to be used in determining future tourism infrastructure and development needs, opportunities and tourism employment prospects.

2. raise awareness of potential economic, social and environmental benefits of tourism through community consultations.

3. gain an understanding of the region's target markets over the whole year.

4. identify the key factors determining the pattern of tourism including social, economic and environmental factors.

5. identify and explore the inter-relationship between key factors/agencies and tourism, using a systems approach to record and analyse the dynamics of regional tourism.

6. develop the Tapestry Tourism Futures Simulator – a planning tool to enable local government authorities, tourism agencies and other stakeholders to explore and compare development scenarios based around increased visitation (especially their economic, social and environmental impacts, and employment generation).

As the complexity of the project became apparent, additional aims were added. These included the objectives to:

7. identify impediments to regional tourism development in the Tapestry Region.

8. develop strategies, including institution building, for enhancing tourism's contribution to planning in the region.

9. assess, analyse and where appropriate, refine and adjust the CSIRO systems analysis methodology to scope the future of tourism development in the region.

10. assess the value of tourism to the region, including the potential for employment generation.

One of the benefits of the project will be a regional umbrella strategy for tourism development in the Tapestry Region. It will provide enhanced understanding of the value of tourism to the region and encompass a shared vision for the future.

The project will also provide individual local government areas with the means to devise their own strategies to reflect distinctive characteristics consistent with the framework of the umbrella strategy. There will also be an implementation plan for each shire to transfer strategy principles to its policies, planning and regulations (Sofield & Pedersen 2000).

INDUSTRY PROFILE

MICHAEL 'MAX' ROCHE TOURISM DEVELOPER

I am in the process of creating an exclusive, hosted, wilderness beach house complex on the east coast of New South Wales. I have been lucky enough to travel the globe as part of the travel industry and I am incorporating many special discoveries I've made on those travels into the design of my new project.

How did I get here?

I began my career in tourism with a one-way ticket to London in 1983 and a stint with Top Deck Travel driving double-decker buses and leading tours around Europe and across Asia from London to Kathmandu. After returning from overseas I took a job as a sales representative with Access Tours, a small adventure tour operator and wholesaler. When it merged with Peregrine it led to various jobs in marketing and, in 1994, a directorship and part-ownership. I was able to help Peregrine to reach its position as a world leader in the adventure industry, with ships in Antarctica and the Arctic and operations across the globe.

What do I like about my job?

I have found a career in travel to be immensely rewarding in every sense. I feel a sense of privilege to have touched the world at a time when we can all reach into its far corners yet it remains richly diverse and surprising.

'Development' is used to describe an expansion or enhancement of any or all elements of the tourism system. It requires detailed and systematic planning. The three types of relevant planning discussed are (1) strategic planning, (2) the Commonwealth Government planning system, and (3) long-range planning.

In strategic planning, which usually looks ahead three to five years, government agencies and companies decide what *business* they are in; they aim to achieve an *overall goal*; they gather *knowledge* as the basis of decision making; they *analyse* the information, usually in terms of the organisation's strengths and weaknesses and external opportunities and threats; they set *objectives* which determine the activities designed to achieve the overall goal; they devise *strategies* to achieve the objectives.

State and territory tourism organisations produce a variety of strategic plans, some for or in association with regions, others for specific forms of tourism – e.g. wine and food, nature-based tourism, cultural tourism, indigenous tourism. Each state/territory has a principal plan which guides the organisation as a whole.

Planning of Commonwealth Government agencies, including the tourism division of the Department of Industry, Tourism and Resources and the Australian Tourist Commission, is

SUMMARY

accomplished within an 'outcomes and outputs framework'. The process begins when agencies apply inputs (e.g. finances, human resources, capital equipment) to the activities that generate the products and services that produce their outputs. Inputs include the funds appropriated to them from the Budget as well as revenue raised through other means, such as sales, levies and industry contributions.

The process for long-range planning, which may have a 20-year horizon, brings together national, state/territory and local interests in the determination of how land is to be used for tourism (and other purposes) and what kind of physical developments to cater for tourism will be built, allowed or encouraged. It may be carried out in a city or at regional or local government level.

Infrastructure is a major concern of tourism planners. A 'report card' produced in 2001 by a group representing major infrastructure users, owners, operators, investors and relevant industry groups gave a discouraging view of Australian infrastructure. Of particular concern to tourism interests was the low rating it gave roads.

Tourism requires special purpose buildings, such as accommodation establishments of various kinds, attractions (e.g. museums and galleries), convention centres and transport terminals. The project development process is usually structured so that commitments are undertaken one step at a time so that the developer and other decision makers invest their financial and other resources on the basis of proven results as they progress.

A typical development process first evaluates the potential market to see if there appear to be enough customers if the project goes ahead. Further steps are to choose the location and the professionals like architects and lawyers, conduct a full market and financial feasibility study, ensure that planning requirements are met, complete the design, consult the community and build the project. The design is extremely important. A tourism site which includes purpose-built buildings has to look the part as well as suiting the function for which it is constructed.

Projects which may produce some substantial environmenal impact will require an environmental impact assessment (EIA), which provides a structured analysis of a proposed development and is used to decide whether it should be allowed to proceed and on what conditions. In some cases a social impact assessment (SIA) may be required to evaluate the probable effects of a development on the community.

Although tourism developments may need big money to build, even hundreds of millions of dollars for a single project, many institutional investors are sceptical of tourism. Therefore, governments often play an important role in larger developments even when they do not invest taxpayers' funds – by planning, illustrating the benefits of private investment in particular projects and offering incentives for financiers and developers to put their money into the projects. The Commonwealth Government set up the Tourism Forecasting Council in 1993 to provide reliable forecasts to help investors make sound decisions.

QUESTIONS

1. What are the two meanings of development used in the text and which is more appropriate to the planning process? Who is most likely to use the other meaning?
2. How would you describe the form and the power of the overall goal in a strategic plan?
3. What are the essential elements of the Commonwealth Government's planning system and how are they linked in the process?
4. What are the main differences between strategic planning and long-range planning?
5. How would you describe the analysis and synthesis step in long-range planning?
6. How are some states tackling the development of specified destination areas and their linkages?
7. What are some of the problems of infrastructure development in the Outback?
8. What part does marketing play in the project development process?
9. What design features should be included in a tourism building?
10. What is the role of the Tourism Futures Simulator?

MANAGING QUALITY

CHAPTER 10

LEARNING OBJECTIVES

Understand what the term 'quality' means in tourism.

Examine the links between quality service and customer satisfaction, the criteria for success and the process for meeting customers' expectations.

Appreciate the contribution of education and training to the provision of quality service.

Note the widespread nature of the AussieHost program.

Understand the role of the Australian Quality Council and Standards Australia, the 'quality progression' in Australia and the influence of international standards on travel and tourism business practices.

Examine the national tourism·accreditation program, a number of independent programs and in-house quality assurance programs.

Appreciate the lessons in a case study of the change to a service mentality in British Airways.

| UNDERSTAND
THE MEANING OF:

- *quality*
- *customer satisfaction*
- *customer expectations*
- *internal marketing*
- *interactive marketing*
- *tourism expenditure*
- *perception*
- *quality circle*
- *empowerment*
- *quality audit*
- *competency standards*
- *Australian Quality Training Framework*
- *quality control*
- *quality assurance*
- *quality management*
- *standard*
- *ISO 9002*
- *accreditation*
- *performance indicators*

THE MEANING OF TOURISM QUALITY

This chapter is concerned with the quality of tourism products. It is a matter of great importance in a competitive world and there have been continuing improvement and extension of techniques devised to ensure that standards are achieved or exceeded. The chapter therefore deals with such technical subjects as the quality movement and accreditation as well as a first essential in delivering quality service – the training and motivation of the people who deliver it. The people who provide services directly to tourists can be the secret of the success of a tourism product or destination. They can also be the cause of failure, because nothing turns a visitor off more than poor service, whether it be because of lack of efficiency or because of the attitude of the person involved.

The key word in assessing service is 'quality'. Its relevant dictionary meaning is related to a peculiar excellence and superiority, especially when compared with other things of the same kind (The Oxford English Dictionary, 1989, Vol XII p. 974). As such, it is an everyday word but it has also been given special importance in management. Even without studying the subject, terms like TQC (Total Quality Control) and TQM (Total Quality Management) may not be unfamiliar. There are Australian Quality Awards to be competed for. And there is 'quality tourism'.

This has a wider reference than the service element already alluded to. Tourists' perceptions of quality will be conditioned by the amount of money they are paying for what is offered and by comparisons with other products in the same price range. A visitor may never intend to stay in a hotel which provides the ultimate in excellence because of the cost, but judge an inferior hotel as offering high quality because expectations were exceeded for the money paid.

On the other hand, a tourist may pay an outrageous price for a room because of the perception that the hotel is exclusive; in other words the customer is paying for snob value. The perceived approval or envy of others constitutes part of what quality means to that person.

'Quality' can be applied to the physical attributes of a tourism product. It is sometimes called the 'technical quality'. This can take the form of something relatively simple – a hotel room and its furnishings, for example. Or it can be complex. In 1999, when researchers Reisinger and Turner (2000) set out to survey Japanese tourists' satisfaction with the Gold Coast product they came up with 27 'elements of satisfaction', ranging from safety to the opportunity to visit national parks.

A few years earlier Braithwaite, Reynolds and Pongracz (1996) found there were four major variable factors influencing customer satisfaction for a tour operation on Yellow Waters in Kakadu National Park in the Northern Territory:

- biodiversity, measured by the number and importance rating of species able to be seen
- climatic comfort, measured by a relative stress index (temperature and humidity)
- vastness, the sense of enormity and spaciousness derived from being with a few people in a large open wilderness area. This is especially prevalent during the wet season when the area is in flood
- personal space, defined by the number of other people on the boat (loading factor) and the number of other boats.

But there is another dimension of product quality with which this chapter is primarily concerned. It is called 'functional quality' which refers to the process of how the technical elements of the service are transferred. Functional quality consists of elements such as attitudes, behaviour and general service-mindedness of personnel, all of which can be influenced by management (Gronroos cited in Gilbert & Joshi 1992).

Thus a customer in a restaurant will not only evaluate the quality of the food consumed but also the way in which it is delivered – the style, manner and appearance of the waiter and/or the ambience of the restaurant. The overriding principle is that the evaluation of **quality** in travel and tourism is always made by the customer.

QUALITY SERVICE AND CUSTOMER SATISFACTION

Quality service and **customer satisfaction** are inextricably linked. This has marketing importance, particularly when determining how to gain a competitive advantage. According to Schnaars (1998), the recognition of the role of customer satisfaction in this respect evolved from the TQM movement of the 1980s. Towards the end of that decade, it became clear that merely providing customers with products that were reliable and durable was not enough. The search for quality then turned into the search for 'total' customer satisfaction.

In travel and tourism the linking of customer satisfaction, quality service and competition has reached the point where competitiveness has been described as a constant 'race for service' for which there is no finishing line (World Tourism Organisation 2001, p14). The customer satisfaction movement is also directly related to the marketing concept, which calls for companies to define customer needs from the customer's point of view not their own – to give customers what they want. Now they try to 'completely' satisfy them.

The competitive aspect of customer satisfaction – and quality service by inference when travel and tourism is involved – is often referred to by marketing writers. In Chapter 8, it was noted that O'Shaughnessy (1984) believed that a firm that merely 'satisfies' would lose out to one that 'pleases'. It was necessary to meet or exceed

The guests in this hotel lobby scene look happy. They will remain so only if the staff offers service which meets their expectations. This requires quality-conscious management, well-trained staff and an understanding by both of what level of customer satisfaction to aim for.

(Source: Accor Asia Pacific.)

'customer expectations', defined as what the customer believes is realisable. This concept is discussed in more detail later in the chapter.

Kotler and Armstrong (1994) see the performance of quality service in marketing terms, saying it requires more than external marketing relying on the four Ps: it also needs both 'internal marketing' and 'interactive marketing'.

Internal marketing requires a service company to effectively train and motivate its customer-contact employees and all the supporting service people to work as a team to provide customer satisfaction. It is not enough to have a marketing department doing traditional marketing while the rest of the company goes its own way. Everyone else in the organisation must also practise marketing.

Interactive marketing refers to how they do it: to the skills and/or functions staff must learn to ensure the buyer–seller interaction during the service encounter is positive; in other words the 'how' and 'what' of providing service which leads to customer satisfaction.

THE DANGERS OF NOT PROVIDING QUALITY SERVICE

Satisfied customers talking warmly about their visit on their return to their homes and offices can be the best advertisement of all. But people tend to talk more about bad experiences than good ones. Bad word of mouth travels further and faster than good word of mouth and is a good enough reason in itself for a customer satisfaction program.[1]

A summary released by the United States of Consumer Affairs demonstrates the importance of satisfying customers.

- In the average business, for every customer who bothers to complain, there are 20 others who remain silent.

- The average 'wronged' customer will tell 8 to 16 people. More than 10 per cent tell more than 20 people.
- Ninety-one per cent of unhappy customers will never purchase goods and services from the offending company again.
- If the company makes an effort to remedy customers' complaints 82 to 95 per cent of them will stay on with it.
- It costs five times as much to attract a new customer as it costs to keep an old one (Soin 1992).

A marketable item

Quality itself is one of the most marketable of items and the formal significations of quality accreditation such as certificates and logos are regarded as marketing tools to be displayed prominently.

Quality comes at a cost, which must be compared to the advantage gained from quality management programs. Generally there are three types of expenses:

1. **A preventative cost** The expenses involved in preventing a mistake from happening – in succeeding first time. This can include material, training charges and audit charges.
2. **An insurance cost** Costs of covering any breakdowns and accidents in the service or duty.
3. **A failure cost** Covering the loss of earnings due to the dissatisfaction of the customer (Lanquar 1989).

CRITERIA FOR SUCCESS

Whether or not a company or other organisation takes part in some formal program, such as accreditation, or institutes its own program to improve service and customer satisfaction, there are similar criteria for success.

The first is leadership. Zeithmal et al. (1990) say that without leadership from managers, service excellence is a pipe dream. Redirecting an organisation's paths of habit and convenience is hard work and senior managers cannot delegate responsibility for it. They themselves must 'lead the charge' or nothing will happen.

The second is time. Quality service is almost always a 'slow fix'. It usually takes longer to materially improve service than the sponsors of such change realise, and then it takes longer still for the customers to notice.

The third criterion is knowing what level of customer satisfaction to aim for. Some companies set out to 'delight' their customers, going beyond meeting expectations of the customer. Setting goals requires relevant data, measuring product performance against customer expectations. If the product's performance falls short of customer expectations, the customer is disappointed; if it meets expectations, the customer is satisfied; if it exceeds expectations, the customer is delighted.

DEFINITIONS

There is a significant difference in providing a customer service improvement program for a service industry like travel and tourism and an industry that produces a manufactured product, like a car, which may meet specifications which can be described precisely.

On the other hand the products consumed by a tourist in a day will consist mostly of services delivered by people, sometimes a large number of people, whose training, temperaments and motivations will vary, resulting in behaviour much less predictable than that of a machine. It sometimes takes only the default of one person providing one of those services to undo all the goodwill created by the others.

The importance of perception

Perception

The process by which people select, organise and interpret information to form a meaningful picture of the world or a situation.

One of the psychological factors in tourism demand is **perception** – the process by which people select, organise and interpret information to form a meaningful picture of the world or a situation. Two people in the same situation may act differently because they perceive that situation differently or their expectations are different. However, there are fundamentals which make it possible to generalise in some cases.

> . . . *people will tolerate many sacrifices to fly, but they will not tolerate surprise. They may sit with their knees to their chest for a low fare, but they will not stand for a lost bag. They may spend all night in the boarding area waiting to clear a standby list, but they will display no patience for a 30-minute rain delay. Predictability – the fulfilment of expectations – is the most important factor in whether an airplane flight is a pleasantly efficient experience or one of modern life's worst travails* (Petzinger 1995, p. 381).

The importance of predictability as one of the principal factors in customer satisfaction applies not only to the airline industry, but all businesses.

▨ Process to meet customers' expectations

A process to match actual performance with customers' expectations can be broken into stages.

First stage – determine expectations

Market segmentation is important. For example, the needs and expectations of business and leisure travellers are different in many ways. The business traveller is usually much more concerned with communication facilities than the average leisure traveller and appreciates amenities such as airport clubs, hotel business centres and rapid transfer facilities.

Research, both in the target markets and after the travel experience, can produce detail on expectations and, in the case of post-experience travel surveys, whether or not they were fulfilled. Customer satisfaction with products and destination attributes can be measured. Managers also learn directly about needs and expectations from their customers and from employees in constant contact with travellers.

Second stage – design the product

For a start, it is necessary to determine the product characteristics that will satisfy the target markets. Products are made up of a combination of tangible and intangible elements relating both to the physical characteristics and interpersonal contact that occurs during a tourism experience. Table 10.1 shows characteristics of the experience in useful categories.

Table 10.1 Characteristics of the product experience		
NATURE OF THE CONTACT	**TANGIBLE**	**INTANGIBLE**
PHYSICAL	The product	Atmosphere
	Facilitating goods	Aesthetics
	Information processes	Feelings
		Comfort
INTERPERSONAL	Actions	Warmth
	Process	Friendliness
	Speed	Care
	Script	Service
	Corrective action	

(Source: Adapted from AJ Lockwood and PLM Jones, *The Management of Hotel Operations*, Thomson Publishing Services (1988).)

All aspects of the matrix need to be considered when designing a tourism product. There are relative importances. According to Lockwood (1989) the evidence suggests:
- the physical/tangible component is more significant than the physical/intangible component
- the interpersonal/intangible component is more significant than the interpersonal/tangible component
- the interpersonal/intangible component is usually the more difficult to control, but it is also the component that quality assurance programs concentrate on and with which programs like AussieHost are principally concerned.

The next step is to design the product, taking into consideration the characteristics of the experience. Part of this will be concerned with the physical attributes – the design of aircraft or coach seats, in-flight entertainment, the design and decor of rooms and menus. Procedures are then devised for providing the service, which includes recruitment, training of staff and development of operations systems.

Third stage – set standards of performance

There must be standards against which service performance can be measured and these are often put into manuals for each activity. These may take the form of key performance indicators as in the British Airways example described in the case study or in requirements as set out in accreditation and certification programs.

Benchmarking sets standards in relation to a company's leading competitors. It is thus an external focus on internal activities, functions or operations in order to achieve continuous improvement. The objective is to be 'better than the best – to attain a competitive edge' (Liebried & McNair 1992).

Fourth stage – implementation

This is the stage where all the policies, the setting of standards, the intention to pursue excellence and satisfy customers are put to the test. It is a test of leadership – because all levels of management must be involved. It is a test of training – because employees must have not only a thorough understanding of the functional side of their roles, but also of what is necessary to achieve a quality performance in their jobs. It is a test of management–employee relationships because employees must want to deliver quality service and this requires good morale and a belief in the company and its products.

Biech (1994) lists these key components for a successful quality program which results in customer satisfaction:

- it has a customer focus – internal and external
- emphasis is on continuous process improvement in a systems approach
- it is based on data
- teamwork is essential
- employees must be involved
- a vision must be developed, communicated and applied
- senior management must be involved and lead the effort
- managers must coach and guide the organisation through changes
- training is imperative at all levels.

Conformance can be ensured by supervision and monitoring (quality control), but the quality assurance method which is more suited to travel and tourism companies is to engender an enthusiasm as the result of leadership, training and involvement.

Typically a quality program will include:

A training program for all managers and employees This is a continuous process, necessary not only to ensure people know how to do their jobs in the technical sense, but to produce the attitudes essential to quality service delivery. As part of a quality program, Australian Pacific Touring's staff throughout the world received some 25 hours of training and then specialised courses were devised for different areas of the company on an on-going basis.

Organisation of employees into teams for quality circle activity Quality circles are groups of employees meeting on a regular basis to solve problems and improve quality in their area. They are often structured by an overseeing committee which sets projects, reviews progress and rewards those teams which make significant contributions. In a large organisation, management and cross-functional teams can be formed. Quality circle conferences allow teams to present their projects to their peers and projects can be graded by a panel of judges.

Employee empowerment This means giving employees the authority to make decisions which directly affect their work without the need for management approval. It enables employees to show initiative, take responsibility, anticipate needs and solve problems. For managers, empowerment means trusting subordinates and respecting their judgment, giving up some control, training and encouraging multiskilling, delegating, information sharing and involving staff in planning and goal setting (Sheraton Towers Southgate, Melbourne 1997, Australian Quality Council team study course notes).

Institution of an employee suggestion system Employees are at the 'coal face' of the operation, use its equipment, see the reaction of customers, know when there are deficiencies. A system for gathering their suggestions includes the setting out of objectives and guidelines, the method for making suggestions (e.g. a form) and a reward scheme.

A customer relations program Every organisation can expect to get customer complaints. Some try to ignore them as much as possible, but those with a well-educated workforce try to satisfy their complaining customers and keep track of all complaints and compliments in an effort to improve service.

Customer satisfaction surveys These take a number of forms in the travel and tourism industry, from cards found in hotel rooms and aircraft seat pockets to research programs carried out by specialist companies.

Internal promotion of the scheme Employees need to be reminded of the quality management program through bulletins, achievements, display of employee-of-the-month photographs and so on.

A reward program for employees Whole teams or individuals should be rewarded for significant contributions. Companies vary the form of rewards, but they may include things like plaques, trips or dinner vouchers.

Fifth stage – assess the operation

The final stage in the quality management process is to evaluate the success of the operation in matching the customer's expectations. There are two main approaches: (1) monitoring the satisfaction level of tourists after they have sampled the product. This is best done by surveys. Unsolicited comments – complaints or compliments – can be a useful guide, particularly in alerting management to problems. Paying attention to individual comments is always useful for an experienced manager. But such comments

DEFINITIONS

Quality circle
A group of employees meeting on a regular basis to solve problems and improve quality in their area.

Empowerment
Giving employees the authority to make decisions which directly affect their work without the need for management approval.

may be unreliable as an indication of overall quality performance. Some guests like to grumble, others gush; but the majority are probably not motivated to say anything unless asked and their reactions are just as important as the others.

Quality audit

An objective assessment of the company's performance by outside consultants or internal specialist staff.

(2) The **quality audit**, an objective assessment of the company's performance by outside consultants or internal specialist staff. Those conducting a quality audit do not have an easy job. They need to understand the target markets involved and try to put themselves in the customers' place, adopting their attitudes. Their report should identify the issues affecting quality performance which can form the basis of corrective action, if necessary (Lockwood 1989).

PROVIDING QUALITY SERVICE IN AUSTRALIA

Education and training

The provision of quality service begins with education and training. Quality management is a pre-requisite for quality service and management education is a sound foundation for it. A seasoned traveller can usually comment accurately about the quality of general management of a hotel after a few minutes in the lobby. Similarly, the effectiveness of management is usually obvious in other tourism situations.

Staff who are well-managed are usually happy and efficient. Staff who are well-trained, conscious of their responsibilities and their own value, are usually confident in their abilities and keen to deliver quality service. Workplace training is essential for those who have contact with customers and who have not had formal training. For those who have, workplace training on service quality is fine-tuning: for them the substance of the training process has been delivered in public and private institutions.

In Australia the education and training of the workforce responsible for management and service in travel and tourism businesses has changed out of sight since the first university course in hospitality management was introduced in 1971 (Richardson 1999).

Thirty years later nearly three-quarters of Australian universities offered management courses in tourism and/or hospitality. There was a growing tendency to cater for specialist roles in tourism subsectors – e.g. management of events, of meetings and conventions, of clubs and so on.

Vocational training of people with specialist skills, particularly in the hospitality industry, has a much longer history.[2] In recent years, the range of courses available in the Training and Further Education (TAFE) system and in other training organisations throughout Australia has been progressively increased and now includes tourism and hospitality management.

Hospitality students can choose, with combinations, from 100 courses, while the range of tourism courses on offer is also impressively varied – for example, travel consultancy, Aboriginal and Torres Strait Islander tour guiding, and specialist training in management of events, meetings, attractions and theme parks.

The development, delivery and assessment of vocational training is highly structured in Australia. While TAFE plays the most prominent part in delivering it, registered training organisations (RTOs) can be private, public, community, industry or enterprise-based training, so long as they meet prescribed standards. Quality and assessment is regulated by the Australian Quality Training Framework (AQTF). It operates through state and territory bodies which register organisations to deliver and/or assess national qualifications.

National training packages, including one for the travel and tourism industry, are developed by National Industry Training Advisory Bodies (ITABs) in association with industry. Tourism Training Australia is the travel and tourism ITAB and has a network of state- and territory-based branches which consider issues of local concern. It also advises the Commonwealth Government on the training needs of the industry.

National training packages are funded by the Commonwealth Government and include competency standards, national qualifications and assessment guidelines. Registered training organisations must use these three components as the basis of their training products.

Competency standards are statements about the skills and knowledge that people need to perform their jobs to the required industry standard. They are the nationally agreed benchmarks for effective workplace performance in particular jobs in the travel and tourism industry (Homersham 2000).

The AussieHost program

AussieHost is a 'grass roots' program which has improved customer service and communication skills of tens of thousands of Australians since it was launched in June 1993. It is suitable for helping train people in thinly populated areas or in crowded cities and everything in between.

The program was established by the Inbound Tourism Organisation of Australia (now Australian Tourism Export Council) for the travel and tourism industry, but has since spread into other sectors of the business community and is now run by the Retail Traders Association.

Among those who have trained as AussieHosts are retailers, solicitors, bakers, moteliers, resort personnel, police, taxi drivers, bankers, dentists, hairdressers, restaurateurs, politicians, farmers, fishermen, students, government employees, supermarket and laundry employees.

The training program is delivered by organisations such as Business Enterprise Centres, Chambers of Commerce, councils, tourist associations and a range of private and public training providers. More than 180 organisations are involved.

The program also encompasses businesses. Those companies which train more than half their employees as AussieHosts qualify as AussieHost Businesses and receive special certificates, door decals and advertising logos.

Communities where 60 per cent or more of businesses have qualified as AussieHost

DEFINITIONS

Businesses can earn AussieHost town status. This entitles them to a special plaque and the right to promote themselves using the AussieHost symbol.

The basic AusseHost program is delivered through a one-day program, which deals with the principles of service in a class of up to 20 people. It is designed to develop new skills and build confidence and pride in the delivery of service excellence. Participants receive a nationally recognised accreditation and lapel pin.

▓ The quality progression

Quality programs administered within the Australian travel and tourism industry are related to the quality movement in industry generally and take the form of accrediting companies which meet and maintain certain standards. Understanding them requires some discussion of the quality movement – the 'quality progression' – and the system of standards in Australia. The development of the current approach to quality in Australia in industry generally can be seen as a progression from quality control to quality assurance to quality management.

Quality control

Quality control consists of the operational techniques and activities that are used to fulfil requirements for quality (British Standards Institution cited by Dale & Oakland 1994). It emerged in the early days of the 20th century from attempts to control the quality of goods produced in factories. Specialists were employed to inspect finished products made by others to see if they met customers' requirements or specifications. Later it led to the development of sophisticated sampling, measuring and testing techniques and is still employed in industry.

The term is used in travel and tourism to describe the activities of monitoring both the actual outcomes in relation to performance standards and the process or working practices employed. Lockwood (1989) cites the example of hotel housekeepers checking on each room that the maid cleans, monitoring the technical way the bed is made and the bath is cleaned and also behavioral aspects such as smoking on duty or playing the radio in bedrooms while cleaning.

The final stage of the control approach is to correct non-standard output, which means that if the housekeeper finds a room is not up to standard then it is put in order before the guest arrives. Deviations should be investigated so that action can be taken to see they do not occur again. Action may vary from correcting poor staff selection to better training to changing the operating procedures.

Quality assurance

Quality assurance is defined as all those planned actions necessary to provide adequate confidence that a product or service will satisfy given requirements for quality (British

---

Quality control

The operational techniques and activities that are used to fulfil requirements for quality. The term is used in travel and tourism to describe the activities of monitoring both the actual outcomes in relation to performance standards and the process or working practices employed.

Quality assurance

The planned actions necessary to provide adequate confidence that a product or service will satisfy given requirements for quality. It is directed more at the interpersonal aspects of the product than is quality control; it is not so concerned at monitoring outputs and correcting faults as it is with ensuring there are not any faults in the first place.

Standards Institution cited by Dale & Oakland 1994). It emerged in the 1950s because quality control, with its emphasis on final inspection, could not satisfy all the demands of business and technology for increasingly high levels of quality and reliability. Quality assurance introduced procedures that 'assured' the manufacturer that the final product would meet requirements and greatly reduced the need for final inspection. It demanded standardisation and documentation of procedures and achieved new levels of consistency, helping to enhance the quality of the finished product and reducing costs.

DEFINITIONS

It also laid the foundation for the development of a system of International Standards against which the quality of a product or the effectiveness of an organisation's quality systems could be assessed. Certification by an independent body that a company meets a required standard has become a condition for doing business with some government purchasing agencies and large firms (Wider Quality Movement 1995).

As applied to travel and tourism companies, quality assurance is directed more at the interpersonal aspects of the product than is quality control. It is not so concerned at monitoring outputs and correcting faults as it is with ensuring there are no faults in the first place. The assurance approach is particularly important where there is face-to-face contact with tourists – and there are few tourism businesses where this does not occur. Quality assurance relies on planned actions but it is as much a philosophy as a system. Management needs to think quality all the time and make sure that staff do too. Thus it is an important factor in staff recruitment and training.

Quality management

In the early 1980s, a broader approach to quality, initially called total quality control, then total quality management and increasingly just **quality management** began to attract considerable attention in the United States and Australian business and institutions followed suit. Its principles and practices are embodied in the Australian Quality Awards and the Australian Quality Prize.

> *Quality management saw Quality as the outcome of a process of continuous improvement and innovation, not only in products and services but in every aspect of work. It provided a holistic model that focused on pleasing customers, improving the systems and processes of the business to eliminate waste, managing with facts and data, involving and empowering people to improve their work, aligning the organisation around well-founded policies and plans, and committed leadership from management* (Wider Quality Movement 1995).

Quality management
A broader approach which embraces quality assurance and also the encouragement of innovation and improvement of systems and processes. It involves empowerment of employees and committed leadership.

While there is general agreement that today quality management embraces quality assurance and the encouragement of innovation and improvement, there is not total agreement on terminology. The acronyms TQC (for Total Quality Control) and TQM (for Total Quality Management) – particularly the latter – are used in reference works written in recent years often with meanings which are interchangeable.

Objectives may include customer satisfaction, a level of profit or market share, or the provision of services to the community.

'Customer' is interpreted broadly, meaning not only the company's external customers, but also those within the organisation served by someone else in the company. In every department or office there are processes with suppliers and customers, e.g. the suppliers of secretarial services to executives, who are the customers.

▓ Management's role

The Australian Quality Council (1997) says the key aspects of management's role, identified through the experience of many organisations, include but are not restricted to:

* leadership that creates and deploys clear values to the organisation
* a level of community and environmental responsibility appropriate to the organisation's activities
* a planned and structured approach to setting and achieving goals and objectives
* an understanding of variation and management of appropriate facts and data
* the full involvement and development of the organisation's people
* customers who play the central role in the definition of product and service quality
* the organisation, its suppliers and its customers all working in partnership
* quality derived from well planned and managed processes
* standardisation as part of process management
* continual improvement as part of process management
* innovation recognised as an essential driver of continual improvement
* management emphasis on prevention and improvement rather than reaction.

The Australian Quality Council was formed in 1993[3] and is recognised by the Commonwealth Government as the peak advisory body on quality, productivity and best practice. It is a membership organisation with more than 1,500 corporate members. They have access to a range of services which include help in achieving best management practice through the application of quality principles and practice. Members can also call on help in preparing for International Organisation for Standardisation (ISO) certification.

Standards Australia

Another organisation that plays a part on quality management is Standards Australia, the trading name of the Standards Association of Australia, a non-government, not-for-profit association, which prepares and publishes voluntary technical standards and conformity assessment programs. Founded in 1922, it has more than 14,000 Australian organisations and individuals as subscribing members.

Standards Australia is the Australian representative on the two major international standardising bodies, the International Organisation for Standardisation (ISO) and the International Electrotechnical Commission (IEC).

It defines a **standard** as 'a published document which sets out technical specifications or other criteria necessary to ensure that a material or method will consistently do the job it is intended to do' (Standards Australia 1997, p. xvi).

There are 5,700 Australian standards, developed by technical committees, most of them technical, many relating to manufacturing. More than 20 per cent are applicable to building and construction. However, the international ISO 9000 series of quality management standards has had a major influence in Australia as elsewhere in the world and, in particular, ISO 9002 has influenced travel and tourism quality systems.

The ISO 9000 series is not related specifically to any industry or product group, but offers a set of 'good practice' rules for manufacturing a product or delivering a service which can be applied to any business. ISO 9002 is issued by Standards Australia with an 'AS/NZS' prefix, a designation which reflects the close links it has with Standards New Zealand. The standard is regarded as a model for quality assurance in production, installation and servicing.

Few travel and tourism companies have applied for ISO 9002 accreditation, but the national tourism accreditation program developed in Western Australia has been derived from it. Elements are incorporated in the national tourism accreditation program and it takes little extra effort for companies which meet its requirements through all levels to qualify for the ISO 9002 certification.

One company certified under ISO 9002 is the Melbourne Convention and Exhibition Centre, the first meetings and exhibition venue in Australia and New Zealand to receive accreditation. To achieve this it had to comply with requirements affecting:

- management responsibility
- training
- servicing
- corrective and preventative action
- control of customer-supplied product
- purchasing.

It was also required to adopt methods aimed at continually developing and improving procedures to stay abreast of market trends. To ensure the effectiveness of the system, an audit by a third party (e.g. a major accounting firm) takes place every six months of at least one departmental process and a full system audit is carried out every three years.

▧ National tourism accreditation program

Tourism accreditation is a process designed to establish and continually improve industry standards for conducting travel and tourism businesses. Accreditation provides consumers and the industry with an assurance that a tourism operator is committed to quality business practices and professionalism in all aspects of the enterprise (Australian Tourism Accreditation Association 2001).

DEFINITIONS

Standard
A published document which sets out technical specifications or other criteria necessary to ensure that a material or method will consistently do the job it is intended to do.

Accreditation (tourism)
A process designed to establish and continually improve industry standards for conducting tourism businesses.

(Source: Australian Tourism Accreditation Association.)

Although the need for a national approach to accreditation seems obvious, the practice began in Australia with several unrelated moves. The Victorian Tour Operators Association introduced a program in 1988 and Victoria later established a Tourism Accreditation Board. A program developed by the Western Australian Tourism Commission was later operated in several other states by Tourism Council Australia (TCA) and is the basis of the present Australian Tourism Accreditation Standard. Two important measures adopted in that period were a national framework using a national logo and the establishment of a national accreditation organisation, the Australian Tourism Accreditation Authority.

When TCA went into administration in December 2000, steps were taken to establish an independent body to continue the task of implementing and maintaining a national system. Australian Tourism Accreditation Association Ltd (ATAA) was registered in January 2001 and is operated from the offices of Tourism Council Western Australia. The Western Australian Tourism Commission retains the rights to the intellectual property of the current program.

By the end of 2001, six states and territories – Victoria, Western Australia, Tasmania, South Australia, the Northern Territory and the Australian Capital Territory – were operating accreditation programs endorsed by ATAA. Additionally, Caravan Industry Australia, Museums Australia, and Camping Association of Victoria were operating endorsed industry sector programs under the umbrella of the national scheme.

These programs involved more than 1,750 travel and tourism businesses, from bed and breakfast establishments to regional airlines. They met the Australian Tourism Accreditation Standard and displayed the national logo.

Understanding accreditation in Australia requires familiarity with a set of definitions:

- The **Australian tourism accreditation standard** is the generic set of principles established by the ATAA to apply to all programs. It is a checklist of the features found to be essential for a viable tourism business.

- An **Australian tourism accreditation program manager** is a person, company, association or group of associations licensed by the ATAA to implement an approved program, usually customised to meet the needs of a particular tourism sector.

- An **Australian tourism accreditation program** is a formulation of requirements and documentation prepared by a program manager to be followed by businesses seeking accreditation.

- The **Australian tourism accreditation logo** is the registered symbol that may be used by tourism businesses to indicate that they have achieved accreditation. The logo shows a yellow tick on a green background and contains the words 'Accredited Tourism Business' and 'Australia'.

- The **Australian tourism accreditation system** is the coordinated operation of programs throughout Australia approved by the Australian Tourism Accreditation Association.

- A **verification audit** is the process employed by program managers to ensure that tourism businesses continue to operate within documented and approved programs, thereby meeting the standard.

DEFINITIONS
. . . .

Verification audit
The process employed by program managers to ensure that tourism businesses continue to operate within documented and approved programs, thereby meeting the standard.

It has always been a tenet of accreditation that it should be run by industry rather than government, though governments have supported the concept and at times provided some concept development funding. Therefore the ATAA, the organisation overseeing tourism accreditation, is an industry body. It includes representatives of state and territory accreditation committees and up to seven other members with particular expertise, experience and/or industry interests.

The ATAA's charter is to provide leadership and coordination in the development and implementation of accreditation programs for the industry. It owns the logo and applies a range of processes to ensure the consistency and rigour of the standard. Thus it evaluates and approves accreditation programs and licenses use of the logo. It also oversees state and territory accreditation committees to ensure consistent practice and standards. It has a technical advisory committee made up of people with experience in the development and administration of accreditation standards and programs.

The programs operated in Tasmania, Northern Territory, South Australia and the Australian Capital Territory originated from the Western Australian model and Victoria rewrote its program to bring it into line with the Standard.

At the end of 2001 Tasmania led the way with 665 businesses accredited, followed by Western Australia (480), Victoria (357), South Australia (220) and Northern Territory (13).

Figure 10.1 shows how the system is structured.

A tourism business seeking accreditation begins the process by applying to a licensed program manager and preparing the documentation necessary to show that the business meets all requirements of the standard. Once the business is accredited, it must continue to maintain the standard and strive for excellence in its operation (Australian Tourism Accreditation Association 2001; Hollis 2001).

Table 10.2 shows what it takes to become accredited.

Accreditation research results

Taylor, Rosemann and Prosser (2000) say that, generally speaking, accreditation processes give businesses the opportunity to:

- clarify and document their policies, management systems and procedures
- improve control over operations and increase consistency in performance of functions
- enable a better understanding of expectations, roles and responsibilities within the business

Figure 10.1 The Australian tourism accreditation framework

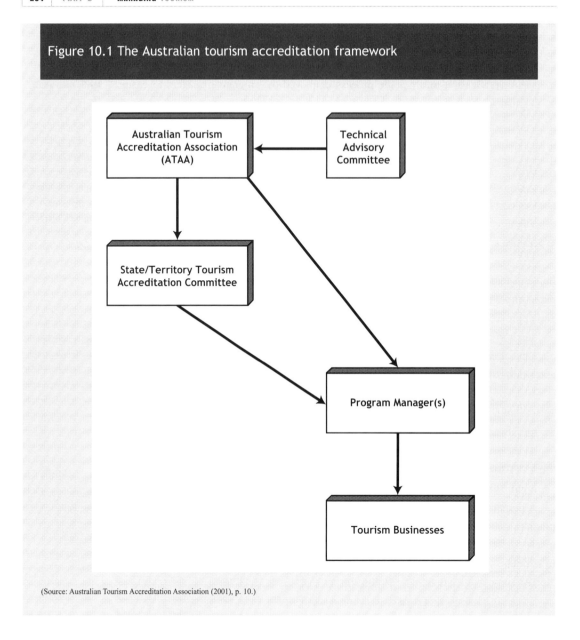

(Source: Australian Tourism Accreditation Association (2001), p. 10.)

- receive recognition for their quality status, and be able to maximise the competitive advantage from the recognition
- develop a framework for continuous improvement.

Research among accredited businesses suggests that the benefits so far are in business efficiency rather than in impact on the customer. The findings indicate that more needs to be done to tell the travelling public that an accreditation logo is a sign of quality.

Table 10.2 Principles and guidelines of the standard

REQUIREMENT	ELEMENTS	GENERAL INTERPRETATION GUIDELINES
Legal compliance	• Business registration/ certificate of incorporation • Australian Company Number • Licences and permits	Table listing pertinent details of regulatory compliance including licence, permit nos., issuing authority, issue and expiry dates
	• Insurance appropriate to the business, including $5 million minimum cover for public liability	Table listing pertinent details of insurance coverage including insurer, policy numbers, issue and expiry dates
	• Food safety compliance (if applicable)	Evidence of food safety compliance
	• Compliance with relevant codes of conduct/ethics	Sign-off on compliance with the national code of conduct or sectoral code, if it exists
Strategic/business planning	Corporate, strategic and/or business plans incorporating, as applicable:	
	• business description and product/service range	Provide a brief (50 words) description of the business
	• SWOT analysis	Complete a SWOT analysis and incorporate, as a minimum, the key headings of: customers competitors, environment and company
	• overview and statement of objectives	Evidence of documented objectives and supporting strategies
	• market research and competitive positioning	Evidence of market/customer research
	• marketing plan • budget and action plan to support the above	Provide basic template for plan including objectives and strategies, action program and budget
Human resource management	Policy and procedures for:	
	• staff recruitment (including job descriptions, organisation chart, roles and responsibilities)	Evidence of documented organisation chart, job descriptions, roles and responsibilities
	• staff rostering	Evidence of staff rostering

Cont . . .

Table 10.2 continued

REQUIREMENT	ELEMENTS	GENERAL INTERPRETATION GUIDELINES
	• training program for staff (including an induction program, customer service training and on-going professional development initiatives)	Evidence of a planned training program, and documented procedures for induction, customer service, training, and professional development completed
	• maintenance of personnel records	Evidence of personnel records
	• procedures to ensure occupational health and safety	
Environmental management	Documented policy and practices for sustainable environmental protection (e.g. Code of Sustainable Practice, National Ecotourism Accreditation Program or other sectoral codes)	Evidence of documented planning and application of procedures for environmental sustainability, and sign-off on the relevant code
Administration and operations	Sound, consistent procedures for day-to-day administration and operations, including: • financial management processes (banking and record documentation) • purchasing and storage (incl. preferred suppliers, purchasing, storage and sales procedures)	Evidence of a procedures/operations manual including all elements listed and evidence that procedures are being followed
Customer service	• Printed, available code of conduct for delivery of quality customer service • Procedures for how the promised product/service quality will be delivered (e.g. telephone answering)	Evidence of documentation related to service delivery and service standards provided to all staff Documented procedures to support all areas of customer service

Table 10.2 continued

REQUIREMENT	ELEMENTS	GENERAL INTERPRETATION GUIDELINES
	• Fair, equitable and publicised terms and conditions for bookings and cancellations	Evidence of documented terms and conditions
	• Periodic evaluation of customer feedback, and follow-through mechanisms to ensure customer views are noted and acted upon	Evidence that feedback is collected
	• Complaints handling	Documented complaints handling procedures
	• Truth in advertising and marketing	Evidence that advertising, collateral, images and claims are a true representation of the product offered
Risk management	Policies, procedures and planning to minimise the likelihood of risk to human, physical and/or informational resources, to include: • internal controls that ensure products, equipment and food are safe and 'fit for purpose' • known hazard management procedures in the workplace (physical, chemical and biological) • maintenance of safe storage of goods, plant and equipment, particularly of perishables • workplace safety procedures known by all employees • prominently displayed emergency and evacuation procedure guides	Evidence of documented risk management plan incorporating policies and procedures relevant to the industry sector, and evidence that procedures are being followed Emergency and evacuation procedures documented and accessible to staff and customers

Cont . . .

Table 10.2 continued

REQUIREMENT	ELEMENTS	GENERAL INTERPRETATION GUIDELINES
Maintenance	Documented procedures, records and schedules for cleaning, inspection, servicing, repair and replacement of equipment, buildings, transport and signage	Evidence of documented maintenance and cleaning procedures for equipment, buildings, transport and signage

(Source: Australian Tourism Accreditation Association (2001), pp. 12–14.)

Research carried out by the authors for the Centre for Regional Tourism Research involved interviews with 21 accredited tourism businesses from a range of different industry sectors. The results showed positive effects on business operations, including improved health, safety and risk management, increased business esteem and staff morale and streamlining of procedural systems.

Among the negative perceptions were some criticisms of the accreditation programs themselves, e.g. inadequate entry standards and program monitoring. And, significantly, there were negative comments about the lack of customer and industry awareness of accreditation and the lack of increased customer numbers and profitability resulting from it.

The thrust of the findings was supported by independent research carried out in Victoria, commissioned by the Tourism Accreditation Board of that state. A survey of accredited operators found that most operators considered the impact of accreditation had been fairly neutral. However, there was a noticeable variance in reaction to different items in the questionnaire. The areas of staff turnover and morale, overall business operations and health and safety standards were considered to have been most positively impacted upon while overall profitability and customer turnover (level of repeat business) were thought to have experienced the least positive impact.

A five-point scale was used in the survey, with 1 indicating a negative impact, 5 a positive impact and 3 neutral. Table 10.3 shows the results.

The survey showed a perceived general improvement in the way businesses were performing as a result of accreditation. Foster (2000b) commented that while the figures did not indicate a huge increase it was a step in the right direction. There was some concern about the awareness and acceptance of accreditation by consumers and so another

Table 10.3 Level of impact accreditation, Victoria

	NEGATIVE		NEUTRAL		POSITIVE	MEAN
	1	2	3	4	5	SCORE
Market positioning	14.1	8.2	47.1	17.6	12.9	3.61
Staff turnover & morale	17.4	1.4	68.1	7.2	5.8	4.09
Overall profitability	18.1	13.3	63.9	2.4	2.4	3.11
Customer turnover	18.3	3.7	65.9	9.8	2.4	3.35
Health & safety standards	4.7	2.4	43.5	30.6	18.8	4.19
Overall business operations	8.2	4.9	37.6	32.9	15.3	4.01
Customer satisfaction	10.7	6	57.1	17.9	8.3	3.66

(Source: Foster (2000b), p. 8.)

survey was undertaken representing all major sources of visitors to Victoria. One quarter (25.2 per cent) were from interstate, 23.2 per cent were from overseas and the remainder were from Victoria.

Foster (2001) summarised the findings by saying that there was a generally low level of awareness among consumers in Victoria about the accreditation logo. This demonstrated that accreditation played a minor part in the purchasing decision for both accommodation and tours. However, he pointed out that the absence or presence of many of the things associated with accreditation (e.g. appropriate booking systems, safety procedures) could determine whether tourists made the purchase, and if they did, influence the level of satisfaction that they experienced.

Indigenous tourism accreditation

The *Respecting Our Culture* Indigenous Accreditation Program, developed by Aboriginal Tourism Australia, has been designed not only to provide a set of professional tools and assure standards are met, but also as a means of controlling cultural exploitation and misrepresentation.

Applicants can be indigenous community members or non-indigenous tourism businesses. The program has been developed in conformity with the national accreditation program and is designed to enhance development opportunities by assisting operators to achieve sustainable businesses. Training and skills development are part of the program.

It also offers a guide to operators to implement sound cultural interpretation sensitive to the needs of local communities. Accredited businesses implement protocols so that indigenous communities welcome visitors to their land. The communities have formal processes for the authentication of tourism products that are recognised by the industry.

During the process of accreditation consultants liaise with local communities for the purpose of cultural authentication. Consultants may assist operators, if required, to complete the program. The consultants' recommendation goes to an independent nationally representative assessment board for approval. Once approved, a certificate of accreditation, the logo and other marketing collateral are sent to the operator. Operators are accredited for three years (Wine Food Strategies 2002).

Victorian accreditation

The Victorian interest in accreditation began when the Victorian Tourism Operators Association (VTOA) developed a program because the Department of Conservation and Natural Resources was considering regulation of tourism businesses on public land (Kayler-Thompson 1995). While the first program was produced solely for operators accessing public land – to avoid having departmental regulations imposed upon them – it was soon extended to other sectors. The VTOA accreditation program was essentially a compliance-based model administered by the association, developed with financial support from Tourism Victoria.

In 1994 VTOA and Victoria's Host Farms Association (HFA), again with support from Tourism Victoria, undertook a project for the Commonwealth Department of Tourism to develop an accreditation program for hosted accommodation (such as host farms and Bed and Breakfasts). This model moved from a compliance-based program to a quality journey approach based on the internationally recognised total quality management model.

As other organisations became interested, Tourism Victoria agreed to establish the Tourism Accreditation Board of Victoria to provide independent industry leadership. By 1997 the board was overseeing the accreditation programs of 14 associations.

The Victorian system now conforms to the national program.

Independent programs

Some associations run their own accreditation programs without reference to wider systems. Thus the Meetings Industry Association of Australia offers accreditation to individuals, which, it says, confers particular status on them and provides recognition of their personal achievements in the industry. There are two accreditation designations, which can be used after the accredited person's name:

(1) AMIAA – Accredited Member of the Meetings Industry Association of Australia. Anyone working in the industry for a minimum of three years is eligible. Candidates must then meet a range of criteria including continuous training and confidential assessment by referees. AMIAA members come from all fields of the industry, e.g. conference organisers, tour operators, venue staff, audio-visual personnel.

(2) AMM – Accredited Meetings Manager. AMM is meant for professional conference organisers and meeting planners working with organisations such as associations,

corporations or government bodies. Applicants must meet minimum criteria required for AMM candidacy, then successfully complete an assessment test to determine an acceptable level of skill in the major aspects of meetings management. Assessment includes personal interviews.

The Ecotourism Association of Australia and the Australian Tourism Operators Network jointly administer the Nature and Ecotourism Accreditation Program (NEAP), which has been developed with the aim of identifying genuine ecotourism and nature tourism products in Australia. Three types of products may be accredited: tours, attractions and accommodation. As would be expected, the principles on which ecotourism products are considered eligible for accreditation are more extensive than those for nature tourism.

Eligibility for nature tourism accreditation has been based upon the following principles in relation to the product. It should:

- focus on personally experiencing nature in ways that lead to greater understanding and appreciation
- represent best practice for environmentally sustainable tourism
- consistently meet customer expectations
- be marketed accurately and lead to realistic expectations.

In addition to the four requirements above, eligibility for ecotourism accreditation requires that the product:

- integrates opportunities to understand nature into each experience
- positively contributes to the conservation of natural areas
- provides constructive ongoing contributions to local communities
- is sensitive to, interprets and involves different cultures, particularly indigenous culture.

In-house quality assurance programs

Some of the larger travel and tourism companies conduct their own quality assurance programs, with or without the help of outside consultants. Thus hotel companies (e.g. Hilton, Sheraton) use consultants to conduct a quality audit of designated business processes without necessarily examining everything that would be required for formal accreditation.

In the mid-1990s, Australian Pacific Tours invested more than $500,000 in a quality improvement program, which was designed to ensure that everyone in the company, in overseas offices as well as in Australia, was skilled in quality service and committed to the delivery of what was promised in the APT brochures. This meant about 25 hours of training for all members of staff. At the end of the course each staff member received a certificate.

Avis Australia does not use outside consultants for its ongoing quality assurance program. One of the devices it does use is a version of the 'quality circle', where groups of people working in the same area meet on a regular basis to see how customer service can be improved or problems solved. Avis introduced its Employee Participation Groups (EPGs) in 1991. Employees meet monthly to discuss how they can be more productive and improve customer service.

■ Tourist guides standards

The Institute of Australian Tourist Guides (IATG) does not run a formal accreditation program but is involved with professional development and maintaining professional standards. Its stated purpose is to ensure that international visitors see 'the best possible face of Australian tourism' (Information sheet accompanying IATG application form).

The Institute aims to 'promote and maintain throughout Australia the highest standards of competence, integrity and professional conduct of those involved in the profession of Tourist Guide'.

It encourages adherence to a code of ethics and principles and arranges lectures and workshops to help the professional development of members. Membership is not taken lightly. Those applying for active membership must have:

- at least 12 months experience as a tourist guide
- a current first aid certificate
- Australian citizenship or permanent residency status in Australia
- language proficiency certificate, or equivalent, if they wish to be listed in the membership directory for languages other than their mother tongue
- a positive reference from their employer or client (IATG contacts the nominated referee)
- successfully demonstrated guiding skills and knowledge at an interview.

Prospective members are subject to a six-month probationary period, after which they may be offered full active membership.

CASE STUDY

The British Airways service metamorphosis

British Airways has provided one of the best documented examples of quality management following its conversion to a customer satisfaction culture, beginning in the early 1980s. Before the changes it employed 50,000 people, more than any other airline in the world, while ranking seventh in terms of number of passengers carried. Its service was such that its airline code BA was said to stand for 'Bloody Awful' (Petzinger 1995).

But as privatisation approached (it took place in 1987), and afterwards, it undertook a 'metamorphosis from a company that seemed to disdain customers to one that strives to please them' (Prokesch 1995, p. 102). The changes were driven by the chairman, Sir Colin Marshall, who had worked previously for service-oriented companies such as Hertz, Avis and non-travel companies in food and retailing.

Under Lord King, his predecessor as chairman, and Marshall, everything about the airline changed: its fleet, pricing, schedules and advertising. But most significant of all was the change in philosophy towards service. They recognised that a majority of people would buy an airline seat on price, but some were willing to pay a slight premium for superior service (in British Airways' case 'slight' meant an average of 5 per cent). British Airways set out to attract and retain those who were willing to pay a premium 'not to be treated like cattle'.

The British Airways' approach at that time has been summarised in the stages of management related to customer satisfaction discussed earlier in the chapter.

First stage – determine customers' expectations

Marshall believed that an airline must provide five basic services: (1) transporting people where they want to go, (2) doing so safely, (3) flying when they want to go, (4) providing some nourishment, and (5) allowing them to accrue frequent flyer points. Research had shown that customers took the basics for granted and many wanted a company to desire to help them, to treat them in a personal caring way. However, not everyone valued a particular service so it was important to identify and attract those who did, and then to retain them as customers and win the largest possible share of their lifetime business.

British Airways studied the market to pinpoint the segments that offered the possibility of generating a higher profit margin – segments such as businesswomen, unaccompanied minors and consultants. It created extensive lifestyle profiles of each type of customer, which it used to both increase ticket purchases and to sell other products and services. It tracked broader purchasing behaviour, lifestyles, the ability to influence other people's purchasing decisions, and their value needs.

Second stage – design the product

Identifying customers is one thing, learning from them is another; it was essential that the airline learned from them so that services could be designed and improved. Senior managers talked to passengers when they moved around the world. The airline conducted customer forums to help it continually improve products and services and to help it identify services that it should consider developing over the longer term. In designing its services, the airline tried to think of the impression or feeling each interaction between the company and a customer would generate. For instance, it had asked crews not to load up passengers with food and drinks and then disappear. It was better that passengers asked for more. This created additional personal contacts with the customer. Research had shown just seeing crew members creates higher customer satisfaction levels.

Third stage – set standards of performance

Key performance indicators were established, based on research on the level of perform-ances which must be achieved to remain efficient and to win repeat business. They ensured a focus on facts as opposed to personal perceptions.

Some 350 measures of performance were created, including aircraft cleanliness, punctuality, technical defects on aircraft, customers' opinions on check-in performance, the time it takes for a customer to get through when telephoning a reservations agent, customer satisfaction with in-flight and ground services, and the number of involuntary downgrades that had occurred in a given time period.

Fourth stage – implement the program

Delivering long-term and consistent value in a service business depends on employees and how they are trained and led. The company had a rigorous process for selecting new employees, which included résumé screening, psychological testing, group exercises and one-on-one interviews in which were probed areas of concern.

Managers were trained in leadership and in techniques to provide high-quality service. Marshall believed employees must understand their role in delivering superior service and must have the power and ability to deal with customer problems. According to Petzinger, they were trained to think of themselves as 'emotional labourers', no different from nurses or welfare workers.

They were told that among the 450 passengers checking in for a fully booked 747 flight,

> there will be a businessman, tired and obsessed by a particular problem; a woman with two children joining her husband abroad, anxious about going to a new country, worried about the house, schools, and so on. There will be a granny who has never flown before . . . Every human or emotional state you can think of will be there: euphoric, depressed, anxious, happy, excited. And all will be suffused by a level of preflight anxiety (Petzinger 1995 p. 391).

Teams received constant feedback on their service interactions. Information was sought from passengers on every flight through survey cards and a sample of passengers who had just finished their flights were asked to comment on service quality. This information was used to assess performance and to identify training needs.

Employees were given the freedom to act within specified boundaries. The customer does not expect everything to go right all the time; when something goes wrong employees should react quickly and in the most positive way. They should respond to customers on the spot – before a customer writes a letter or makes a phone call.

Fifth stage – assess the operation

British Airways formed a 'marketplace performance unit' to measure results relative to its key performance indicators, relative to the way customers expected the airline to perform, and relative to competitors' performances. The unit was charged with representing the customer's point of view; it was separate from, and therefore independent of, the marketing and operating side of the business.

It issued a monthly report which went to the chairman, the managing director and other senior members of the management team. Besides reporting on the key performance indicators, it usually focused on a particular problem or issue (e.g. in-flight food, performance on a particular route or the effectiveness of a marketing campaign).

The unit tried to use the customer's viewpoint rather than a management viewpoint in making its judgments. For example in examining waiting queues at check-in desks, management might measure the number of minutes it took for customers to get to the front of the line. But when the marketplace performance unit asked customers, it found they were more concerned with the length of the queues and the rate at which they moved.

The unit was not the only means the airline used to assess performance. Its senior managers were expected to attend customer-listening forums regularly, to take calls or at least to listen in on calls that came into the customer relations department's Care Line and to discuss with the customer relations staff the causes of and possible solutions to customer-service issues.[4]

INDUSTRY PROFILE

PETER HOPGOOD GENERAL MANAGER, GRAND HOTEL, MELBOURNE

A building such as the Grand Hotel demands quality service and presentation. Over the past three years it has been my role to develop a friendly and professional team, capable of delivering a quality experience at the 'Grand'. At the end of the day it is the staff who make the difference to a guest's stay. We have developed our own 'Credo Card' which reinforces the service culture we live by. All employees must carry the Credo Card at all times. It states, 'The Grand is a Hotel where Old World grandeur is complemented by genuine care for our guests'. It also says that 'Quality only happens when you care enough to do your best'.

How did I get here?

One of my former employers, Keith Williams (Hamilton Island Resort), once quoted to me, 'The harder I work the luckier I get'. This has been apparent throughout my career. I started as a pot scrubber in 1980 on

South Molle Island in the Whitsunday Group. After stints as a public area cleaner and barperson, I had my first taste of management as beverage supervisor. Twelve months later I was poached by the owners of Daydream Island to manage their bars. Several years later I ventured to Perth for the America's Cup. I started with the All Seasons group as a food and beverage cost controller but after 12 months I was given the opportunity to open the Tradewinds Hotel in Fremantle as administration manager. I eventually moved back to Queensland where I was appointed duty manager on Hamilton Island Resort. After 18 months, I was promoted to Assistant General Manager responsible for rooms division, concessionaires and on-island sales and marketing. I stayed on Hamilton Island for six-and-a-half years and then managed resorts and hotels in Cairns, the Sunshine Coast and finally Melbourne.

What do I like about my job?

The best part is meeting people (guests) and the development of people (staff). I have found that it doesn't matter where I go, I either run into previous work colleagues or past guests. The hotel business is all about people.

SUMMARY

The key word in assessing service is 'quality', but the term also includes the physical attributes of a tourism product, which may be the furnishings of a hotel room or the setting of a restaurant. Examples show this 'technical quality' can be complex, including elements like safety on the Gold Coast or biodiversity during a visit to Kakadu National Park.

Quality service and customer satisfaction are inextricably linked, a matter of marketing importance, particularly when determining how to gain a competitive advantage. Customer satisfaction is about meeting customers' expectations. Criteria for success in achieving quality service include: (1) leadership from senior managers; (2) time, as quality is almost always a 'slow fix'; and (3) deciding on what level of satisfaction to aim for. Some set out to 'delight' their customers, going beyond meeting their expectations.

The provision of quality service in Australia begins with education and training, including management education, vocational training and workplace training. Most Australian universities offer management courses in tourism and/or hospitality. In recent years the range of tourism-related courses available in the TAFE system and in other training organisations throughout Australia has been progressively increased. AussieHost is a 'grass roots' training program which has improved customer service and communication skills since it was launched in June 1993.

Important organisations in the pursuit of quality in industry in general are the Australian Quality Council which is recognised by the Commonwealth Government as the peak advisory body on quality, productivity and best practice; and Standards Australia, a non-government, not-for-profit association, which prepares and publishes voluntary technical standards and conformity assessment programs. The standard most relevant to travel and tourism is ISO 9002. The national tourism accreditation program has been derived from it.

Accreditation provides consumers and the industry with an assurance that a tourism operator is committed to quality business practices and professionalism. The national program is operated under the authority of the Australian Tourism Accreditation Association, an industry body. A tourism business seeking accreditation begins the process by applying to a licensed program manager and preparing the documentation necessary to show that the business meets all requirements of the standard. This covers a variety of subjects in the following categories: legal compliance, strategic/business planning, human resource management, environmental management, administration and operations, customer service, risk management and maintenance. Research among accredited businesses suggests that the benefits so far are in business efficiency rather than in impact on the customer.

An accreditation program for indigenous tourism operators has been designed not only to provide a set of professional tools to assure standards are met, but also as a means of controlling cultural exploitation and misrepresentation. Applicants can be indigenous community members or non-indigenous tourism businesses.

Victoria developed its own accreditation program from the early 1990s, started because the Department of Conservation and Natural Resources was considering regulation of tourism businesses on public land. The first program was produced so that operators could avoid having departmental regulations imposed upon them. Accreditation was soon extended to other sectors and the Tourism Accreditation Board of Victoria was set up to provide independent industry leadership. The Victorian system now conforms to the national program.

Some associations run their own accreditation programs without reference to wider systems, among them the Meetings Industry Association of Australia. The Ecotourism Association of Australia and the Australian Tourism Operators Network jointly administer the Nature and Ecotourism Accreditation Program (NEAP), which has been developed with the aim of identifying genuine ecotourism and nature tourism products in Australia.

Some of the larger travel and tourism companies conduct their own quality assurance programs. Thus hotel companies (e.g. Hilton, Sheraton) use consultants to conduct a quality audit of designated business processes without necessarily examining everything that would be required for formal accreditation. Australian Pacific Tours and Avis Australia are among those which have conducted quality programs.

QUESTIONS

1. How can a tourist's perception of quality be influenced by what they pay for what is offered?
2. What is customer satisfaction and how is it linked to the concepts of quality and competitiveness?
3. What are the criteria for a company's success in improving quality and customer satisfaction?
4. What form can standards of performance take?
5. What does employee empowerment mean?
6. What is meant by the quality progression?
7. How are standards (as issued by Standards Australia) important to the delivery of quality in Australian travel and tourism?
8. What is accreditation and what are the main features of the national tourism program?
9. Research indicates the benefits of tourism accreditation are in business efficiency rather than impact on the customer. Why is this so and what can be done about it?
10. What are some of the independent accreditation programs and how do they operate?

MANAGING VISITORS

LEARNING OBJECTIVES

Appreciate the need for visitor management and the broad issues with which it is concerned.

Understand that visitor management has two dimensions:
(1) management of the site, and (2) management of people.

Examine the strategies and techniques developed to manage tourists.

Assess key concepts involved – carrying capacity and demarketing.

Understand what is involved in visitor management in:

- an area managed by a single authority (includes pricing and regulatory issues and the functions of visitor impact management models)

- a destination area (includes the roles of governments and marketers and an examination of the Tourism Optimisation Management
Model)

- in cities (includes an appreciation of the impact of conferences and events and the fast-tracking of facilities).

Consider a case study of the consequences of tourism and visitor management in two cities: Venice and Tamworth.

**UNDERSTAND
THE MEANING OF:**

- *visitor management*
- *hard and soft management techniques*
- *carrying capacity*
- *demarketing*
- *timed entry system*
- *zoning*
- *Recreation Carrying Capacity Model*
- *Recreation Opportunity Spectrum*
- *Limits of Acceptable Change*
- *Visitor Impact Management Model*
- *Visitor Experience and Resource Protection Model*
- *Visitor Activity Management Program*
- *Tourism Optimisation Management Model*
- *Country Music Festival*

TOURISM ASSETS MUST BE PROTECTED

Earlier chapters have shown how tourism can endanger some of the environments in which it exists. Part of the management task is to limit its adverse impacts. One of the most pressing problems for managers is to ensure that their tourism assets are protected from over-use or abuse; that too many feet don't tramp over the same piece of a national park before it has a chance to recover, that a historic site is not damaged by visitors, or that the way of life of a whole city or town or destination area is not despoiled by having too many visitors there at the one time.

There have been examples of this happening in Australia – Byron Bay's problems have been related in the case study for Chapter 7 – and this chapter will examine some of the significant effects tourism has had overseas, including contributing to the halving of the permanent population in the Italian city of Venice over 50 years.

In most cases, it is neither possible nor desirable to stop tourism altogether. But it can be managed. Techniques for doing this have been developed in different parts of the world and marketing is increasingly seen as a powerful strategic tool.

Visitor management deals with the reality of visitors reaching an attraction, a local government area, a region, a town or a city with expect-ations they want fulfilled and being about to make an impact on the local community and its environment. Here tourists become more than numbers filling seats or adding to statistics collections; they are people in different but familiar hues, charming or boorish, appreciative or complaining, know-it-alls or receptive to learning, caring or careless.

For businesses and residents it is the time when the destination suc-ceeds or fails in a competitive world, because the most brilliant marketing will not sustain it in the long run if the majority of visitors leave dis-satisfied with what they have experienced. It is also the time that many of the problems are encountered – the possibility of damage to precious assets like rare vegetation or historic sites and monuments; the littering of a mountain trail or the fouling of a beach; the overwhelming of local culture, or stifling traffic congestion, or the number of visitors simply exceeding the point where local residents tolerate them with equanimity.

Too many people in the one location over a period or too many people at one time can cause severe problems for both the local community and visitors themselves. Overcrowding can occur without any sophisticated tourism activity, like an extensive marketing campaign or some noteworthy physical development. Getting in their cars and going for a drive is something Australians like to do, especially when the weather suits or if there is something special to attract them, like a New Year's Eve party. They may stop at a beach or a park or a sporting venue or a museum – one of any number of attractions – and they like to park as close as they can get. They can cause a crowd without anybody taking action to provoke it. They can be influenced by habit, the weather, the nature of an event or attraction, and fashion.

On the other hand, organised tourism, by its nature, is designed to direct numbers of people to attractions and destination areas. Further, it is usually intended to promote growth, e.g. trends are eagerly charted to see that there are more people than last year or last week. Growth is the measure of success.

The combination of the two factors – the unstructured travel by locals and organised tourism – creates the circumstances that call for visitor management. With the continual growth of tourism, the problem is bound to spread to more and more destination areas.

Yet the key message in this chapter is that the number of people may be only part of the problem. Increased tourism does often increase impact, of course, but it is not necessarily so. As Williams (1992) observes, what increased tourism does for certain is create the need for more management. A single example – experience at Kakadu National Park in the Northern Territory – effectively illustrates the point. In one period in the 1980s, visitor numbers increased fivefold. However, as a result of improved visitor management, which involved better facilities and more staffing, environmental damage was reduced (Industries Assistance Commission 1989).

VISITOR MANAGEMENT DEFINED

Visitor management is defined in different ways depending on whether strategies or tactics are appropriate. For a regional or larger destination authority taking a strategic approach, visitor management is the strategies and action programs used to control and influence tourism supply and demand to achieve defined policy goals (Middleton & Hawkins 1998). For an attraction operating under a single authority taking a tactical view, visitor management is the planning and operational techniques designed to protect valued resources and make visits by tourists more satisfactory. Visitor management at this level can be broadly divided into (1) site management and (2) people management.

Marketing to influence demand and activity at the location to minimise visitor impact is a people management tool and used at both the strategic and tactical levels. In Chapter 6 examples of site management were discussed, including an ecotourism site at Point Halloran, Brisbane (boardwalk, walking track and signs); Hamelin Pool, at Shark Bay, Western Australia (the only place in the world where marine stromatolites are accessible to the public); and Naracoorte Caves Conservation Park, South Australia (where a colony of common bent-wing bats can be seen via remote controlled video cameras).

Boardwalks are an effective way of protecting vulnerable plantlife while allowing walkers to experience the pleasures of the environment. This picture was taken in Tasmania's Evercreech Forest Reserve.

(Source: Photographer: Geoffrey Lea, Tourism Tasmania.)

STRATEGIES AND TECHNIQUES

DEFINITIONS

In broad terms the strategic choices open to planners fall into supply and demand categories. Supply includes the provision of infrastructure to facilitate access (airports, roads, bridges), the natural and/or built attractions and the facilities (accommodation, local transport, entertainment shopping) which make visiting possible. Demand is adjusted by marketing, which includes the methods used to attract target groups whose personal characteristics (age, sex, capacity to spend, motivations, attitudes and expectations, length of stay, type of activity desired) have visitor management implications.

Selective marketing

Targeting visitors who are socially and economically more attractive to the attraction or destination than others.

Selective marketing means targeting visitors who are socially and economically more attractive to the attraction or destination area than others. Australian cities, for example, make very considerable efforts to attract conference business because delegates spend far beyond the average visitor and also are relatively easy to manage. Selective marketing means more than promotion to target groups – the relevant product (e.g. attractions and facilities) must be provided and must be competitively priced.

Tourism demand usually reflects seasonal patterns that are dependent on weather, school holiday periods or events. Some overseas destination areas leave their tourism concentrated in specific zones and periods to allow areas that are not yet 'contaminated' and allow the periods of the year that are still quiet to be maintained as such. This gives residents the choice of being involved with visitors or not being bothered with them.

While Australian cities do have tourism precincts, most destination areas would prefer to spread the visitors around their territory and to even out the seasonal troughs. This is better for businesses and also enables visitor numbers to be maintained without the social costs of excess demand.

The implementation of strategies uses techniques which can be put into two categories – 'hard' or 'soft'. **Hard measures** include the physical restrictions on visiting attractions or destination areas, such as closure at certain times, the declaration of no-go zones, requirement for permits, selective parking, prohibition of vehicles in certain streets or areas. Financial restrictions are included in this category, including entrance fees, discrimination between residents and visitors, prices for parking and so on.

Soft measures are persuasive. They may offer incentives for taking some action or sometimes act as a deterrent without the need for actual prohibition. Thus an access road may not be widened or even left in need of repair to reduce demand. A simple measure like directional signage ensures that traffic flows proceed according to the management plan. Marketing is often employed as a soft measure to attract and guide people whose behaviour is likely to reduce negative impacts (Glasson, Godfrey & Goodey 1995).

Hard measures are usually more effective at an attraction governed by a single authority, although they may be employed temporarily in a city – usually in relation to traffic management – during times of tourism pressure, such as the staging of a major event.

DEFINITIONS

Hard measures (to manage visitors)
Physical and/or financial restrictions on visiting attractions or destinations.

Soft measures (to manage visitors)
Persuasive means, such as marketing, directional signage or incentives for taking some action.

▨ Management tools

Visitor management tools, hard and soft, can take many forms. Table 11.1 shows some of the techniques available for managing visitors.

Table 11.1 Visitor management techniques

OBJECTIVES	METHODS
Control size and capacity of facilities in order to limit numbers and distribution	(1) Consider carrying capacity in product design (2) Use local government regulations (e.g. land-use and building codes) to ensure size of facilities is appropriate
Build a reputation that matches visitor needs with destination opportunities	Use marketing images that do not create high-impact expectations
Attract groups that can be expected to respect the natural and social environments	Promote only to target markets likely to meet this requirement
Limit numbers to minimise impacts	(1) Increase prices (2) Limit access to particular times (3) Impose quotas

Cont . . .

Table 11.1 continued

	(4) Make access difficult (e.g. don't mend potholes) (5) Limit parking space (6) Impose bed limits (7) Require tour operators to have permits (8) Demarket
Welcome visitors and encourage them to act responsibly	(1) Arrange community-based activities which have specific visitor appeal (2) Make available signage or brochures on appropriate behaviour (code of conduct)
Encourage positive attitudes about the attraction and/or area	Ensure tour guides are trained and able to assist transfer of knowledge from other staff and local residents
Help tourists discover the significance of places they visit	Organise quality on-site interpretation; encourage use of local knowledge in interpretation
If a destination area, develop relationships between nature, history and the community	Develop self-guiding interpretation, e.g., car tours with numbered stops on brochure signifying pull-off areas, signage, picnic areas and short interpreted walks
Encourage choices and desired behaviour patterns among visitors	(1) Use appropriate signage (2) Make guided activities to highly resilient sites cheaper (3) Seal roads/paths to encourage use, leave them unsealed to discourage excess use (4) Construct short, wide paths for elderly to increase social contact (5) Rotate camping sites (6) Demarket
Create selective differences between visitor settings and help avoid conflict between groups of users	Use signage, interpretation, walkways etc. to separate groups of users, e.g. walkers and cyclists
Create different degrees of challenge and adventure or create particular images that enhance natural values	Grade guided tours, e.g. adventure, abseiling, rock climbing, bush biking
Clearly designate access routes and heavy use areas and keep impacts within acceptable limits	Site walking, bicycling, horse pathways along 'desire lines' (comfort zones); develop uncomfortable areas off-path at entrances to

Table 11.1 continued

	pathways (e.g. unstable rock mulch, prickly bushes) to discourage wandering
Protect wildlife, prevent interference with natural processes, protect natural values	(1) Designate 'no-go areas' during breeding seasons (2) Designate zones for specific activities (3) Remove signs and information from tourism maps
Prevent incremental impact by visitors in areas of heavy use	(1) Add appropriate infrastructure – hardstand areas, boardwalks, toilets etc. (2) Supply campers with firewood
Manage potentially high-impact visitors	(1) Provide infrastructure specifically for high-impact visitors (e.g. mobile skateboard ramps during school holidays) (2) Plan adventure experiences to reduce bored behaviour
Enhance the visitor experience	(1) Provide an information centre with architectural themes which reflect the area's history and spirit (2) An interpretation program (3) Slides of sites that are difficult to photograph (4) Mementos consistent with valuable experiences
Research the number, derivation and attitudes of visitors	Set up a program to monitor visitor numbers and behaviour

(Sources: Williams (1992); Middleton & Hawkins (1998); Garrod & Fyall (2000); Beeton & Benfield (2001); Glasson, Godfrey & Goodey (1995).)

▓ Carrying capacity

Carrying capacity can be defined as the level of human activity an area can accommodate without it deteriorating, the resident community being adversely affected or the quality of visitor experience declining (Chamberlain 1996b).

While it is common to measure capacity by the number of people or vehicles, there are other measures which should be applied, including those related to economic and social qualities; these too can be disrupted by too many visitors. Five dimensions of carrying capacity have been identified:

- **Physical (or design) capacity** – the maximum volume of visitor use that can be accommodated on a site

DEFINITIONS
....

Carrying capacity
The level of human activity an area can accommodate without it deteriorating, the resident community being adversely affected or the quality of visitor experience declining.

- **Ecological capacity** – the maximum level of use that can be sustained before the decline in ecological values becomes unacceptable or irreversible
- **Social capacity** – the maximum number of visitors that can be sustained before the host community's level of tolerance for their presence and behaviour is surpassed
- **Psychological (or perceptual) capacity** – the maximum level of use that can be sustained before there is a decline in the quality of the visitor's experience
- **Economic capacity** – the maximum level of use that can be sustained before other desirable local economic activities are squeezed out. For example, souvenir shops, restaurants, hotels and car parks may take land previously occupied by shops and specialist functions catering primarily for the local market (Prosser 1986, O'Reilly 1991, Mathieson & Wall 1982).

Capacity levels are influenced by two groups of factors. The first group, which has marketing implications, involves the tourist. It includes visitor characteristics such as age, sex, income; motivations, attitudes and expectations; racial and ethnic backgrounds and behaviour patterns. Other factors in this group are the level of use of the facility, visitor density, lengths of stay, types of tourist activity and levels of tourist satisfaction.

The second group of factors describes the local scene: the natural environmental features and processes; economic structure and development; social structure and organisation; political organisation; and level of tourist development (O'Reilly 1991).

There are limitations to carrying capacity as a management tool. Glasson, Godfrey and Goodey call it a relative management concept, or framework; it is not a scientific theory. It is difficult to define in a particular context and when it is so defined it is hard to measure; it cannot be used as an absolute limit.

Demarketing

Demarketing

That aspect of marketing that deals with discouraging customers in general or a certain class of customers in particular on a temporary or permanent basis.

Marketing is usually employed to increase demand, but it can be adjusted to reduce or regulate the number of people visiting a location. This is called **demarketing**. To a marketer it is a bit like turning the world upside down, although Kotler (1999) puts it as a matter of logic.

> *What if the current demand for a product is too strong? Shouldn't the marketer raise the price, cut advertising and promotion spending, and take other steps to bring demand more in line with supply?* (p. xiii).

Beeton and Benfield (2001) see the concept in visitor management terms, suggesting that in periods of excess demand the tourism supplier has the responsibility to produce promotional material that discourages visits or at least creates awareness of excess demand and a need for reservations, higher prices and so on.

The term demarketing was introduced by Kotler and Levy in a 1971 paper not as the opposite of marketing but as part of it. They called it 'that aspect of marketing that deals with discouraging customers in general or a certain class of customers in particular on a temporary or permanent basis' (cited in Beeton & Benfield, p. 4).

They described three types of demarketing:

- general demarketing when a company wishes to reduce level of total demand
- selective demarketing where demand from certain market segments is discouraged
- ostensible demarketing in which marketing management gives the appearance of wishing a reduction in demand as a result of scarcity, which in turn stimulates greater demand for the desired and increasingly scarce product.

In the 1970s, the Australian Tourist Commission practised selective demarketing, discouraging sex tours from Japan and mass tourism from Germany. The most common method employed was to discourage particular tour wholesalers. Demarketing has been used prominently in Australia more recently in a number of social programs to influence demand. Examples are campaigns to discourage smoking and drink driving.

Kotler and Levy listed a range of demarketing actions, including:

- curtailing advertising expenditure
- reducing sales promotion expenditure
- reducing sales representatives' actual selling time
- increasing prices and/or eliminating trade discounts
- adding to the time and expense of the purchaser
- reducing product quality or content
- reducing the number of distribution outlets.

According to Beeton and Benfield, academic writers include policy instruments like regulation and permits in demarketing.

MANAGING AN AREA: ADVANTAGES OF A SINGLE AUTHORITY

Management approaches vary widely according to the area – whether it is a city or region or an attraction. No matter how large the area is, management is simplified if it is governed by a single authority. This may take the form of a company, a local government, a statutory authority or something else. Management still may take into consideration the views of a range of stakeholders – the local residents, tourism businesses and tourists themselves – and consult them in preparing a management plan. Once that plan is accepted the manager of the area can administer the visitor management measures included in it as part of its normal activities, usually without need to further explain the measures.

A variety of management methods are open to an authority, including:

- marketing, especially pricing and promotion
- physical changes to the access and the area itself
- denying access to part of the area
- limiting access to the whole area of part of it
- interpretation and education.

The pricing debate

There is no argument about commercial enterprises charging entry fees to attractions; they are expected to make a profit. But it is a different story when public properties, such as national parks, are involved. Some argue that to charge fees disadvantages part of the community which either does not have the means to pay or finds it much harder to pay than others. And publicly-owned properties should be open to any member of the public.

These points were made in submissions to the Industries Assistance Commission inquiry into travel and tourism in 1989. The Australian National Parks and Wildlife Service suggested that instead of charging entrance fees a quota be set and access be allowed on a first-come first-served basis. In its report, the commission came out strongly in favour of charging fees, saying this would result in more efficient use of national parks. Managers should set fees to cover, at a minimum, the full cost of management of visitor use. Otherwise visitors were effectively subsidised by the rest of the community.

Nearly a decade later Garrod and Fyall (2000) found that managers of British heritage sites generally remained unconvinced by the logic of the user pays principle. Two reasons were suggested. Firstly, managers associated the pricing of access to heritage with its commodification. The argument is that heritage has a value far beyond the price that can be put on it, a cultural value to society, both present and future, which must not be compromised by base commercial values. Secondly, if potential visitors are prevented from experiencing the heritage property because it is too expensive, then it can be questioned whose heritage the property represents and for whom is it being preserved. Therefore many managers surveyed by Garrod and Fyall were 'intensely uncomfortable' with the thought of charging anything more than a token price for admission.

Cape Byron Trust which administers the Cape Byron Headland Reserve, in Northern New South Wales, makes an annual charge for its boat ramp in accord with the view that fees should be used to ration scarce resources. The fees enable the trust to employ a warden who has contributed to the safety of boating operations and has also helped resolve conflicts. The trust took a different approach to its hang-gliding site. It required those who use it to become paid-up members of the local club. The club is responsible for the safety, insurance, maintenance and traffic control of the launch site (Brown & Essex 1997).

Timed entry system

A timed entry system has been used since 1992 to regulate visits at Sissinghurst Garden in Kent, perhaps the most famous public garden in England. Visitors are granted immediate access if capacity has not been reached, but if it has they are given times at which they are allowed to enter the garden. Usually, entry is delayed no more than half an hour, but the wait could be as long as one hour. The wait time is calculated on the basis of studies showing that visitors spent an average of one-and-a-half hours in the garden. Thus the number of visitors leaving in any half hour period can be predicted accurately. This is seen by Beeton and Benfield as an example of demarketing, where the concept is widened to include regulatory methods.

DEFINITIONS

The trust that runs the gardens also employed demarketing by stopping advertising in 1997 to reduce environmental and social pressures, though it said there was a significant reduction in operating income as a result. Where possible, magazine articles were edited to stress the sensitivity of the garden and restrictions that were in place.

Zoning – a delineating tool

Zoning controls tourism by delineating where it is excluded and where it is an allowed activity. It is a primary management tool in both the Great Barrier Reef Marine Park and the Wet Tropics World Heritage Areas, important North Queensland tourism attractions which adjoin in parts. The Reef WHA is managed by a Commonwealth Government agency, the Great Barrier Reef Marine Park Authority, and a Queensland government agency, the Wet Tropics Management Authority, administers the Wet Tropics WHA in association with the state Department of the Environment and Heritage and the Department of Primary Industries.

Zoning
A control system that delineates where tourism is excluded and where it is an allowed activity.

Some areas of the Great Barrier Reef Marine Park are set aside as Preservation and Scientific Research Zones and cannot be entered for general tourism and recreation. Some areas are closed on a seasonal basis to protect nesting birds and turtles. In other zones commercial or recreational fishing is not allowed although they are open for tourism and recreation of the 'look but don't take' variety. In some areas, tourist infrastructure such as permanently moored pontoons is allowed; in others it is not.

The four zones of the Wet Tropics WHA have different physical criteria: Zone A is remote from disturbance and in a mostly natural state; Zone B is not remote from disturbance but still in a mostly natural state; Zone C is land on which or adjacent to which there is infrastructure needed for community services; and Zone D is land on which there are, or are proposed to be, significant developed facilities to enable visitors to appreciate and enjoy the area.

Visitor impact management models
Methods of managing recreational impacts in parks which identify strengths and weaknesses against previously established criteria and allow for management responses to achieve desired outcomes.

Tourism operators must have permits to operate in both WHAs. This requirement provides the managing authorities with the means of exercising precise control over sites of operation, numbers of people visiting sites and conditions of operation (Driml & Common 1996, Environment Australia 1997, Kelleher & Craik 1991).

Visitor impact management models

Visitor impact management models, beginning with recreational carrying capacity, have been extensively applied in Australia to national parks, state forests and other nature reserves. They have these general criteria:

- they are ongoing, continuously operating over a number of years
- they identify strengths and weaknesses against previously established criteria and allow for management responses to achieve desired outcomes.

Recreational Carrying Capacity Model

A management method based on the level of recreational use that an area can sustain without an unacceptable degree of deterioration of the resource or of the recreation experience.

By the mid-1970s the **Recreational Carrying Capacity Model** was regarded as the major model for managing visitor impact in parks. Recreation carrying capacity is generally defined as the level of recreational use that an area can sustain without an unacceptable degree of deterioration of the resource or of the recreation experience.

The effects of growth – type, location and quality – on the natural and man-made environment are studied to identify critical thresholds beyond which public health, safety or welfare will be threatened by serious environmental problems unless changes are made in public investment, governmental regulation, or human behaviour.

Typically, a capacity figure is produced referring to the number of visits per annum or per day, or the number of visitors at any one time. In addition, an optimum number, usually 10 to 20 per cent below the maximum number, may be established to represent the desired capacity limit. The method has strengths as a best guess for basic management decisions and as a yardstick for regulations based on resource use controls and performance standards.

Examples of applications can be found in such well-known Australian locations as Daintree National Park and Green Island in Queensland; Sydney Harbour National Park in New South Wales; Point Nepean National Park in Victoria; and Seal Bay, Kangaroo Island in South Australia. It has also been used extensively overseas.

However, it can be argued that any capacity put forward is highly subjective. Prosser (1986) says it is misleading to talk of *the* recreational carrying capacity for an area because of the different potential capacities, e.g. physical, ecological, social, psychological and economic. The travel and tourism industry came to regard recreational carrying capacity as a major impediment to sustainable tourism, because it treated all tourism operations as equally threatening. Ecotourism and indigenous tourism operators in particular objected to it (McArthur 2000). By the mid-1990s recreational carrying capacity was generally out of favour.

But long before then other models had come into use, at first still with the emphasis on conservation of natural areas and then broadening the scope to take in other issues, as well as being concerned with regional areas rather than single locations.

Five models which followed the Recreational Carrying Capacity Model are discussed roughly in chronological order of their introduction.

Recreation opportunity spectrum (ROS)

A range of opportunities that the public or private sectors can provide to meet a diversity of visitor activity in a park. It requires identification of different settings and matching them with the recreational opportunities that generate the best benefits to users and the environment.

Recreation opportunity spectrum (ROS)

The **ROS** established the technique of identifying characteristics of different settings and matching them with the recreational opportunities that generated the best benefits to users and the environment. It has been defined as a range of opportunities that the public or private sectors can provide to meet a diversity of visitor activity (Buist & Hoots, cited in McArthur 2000).

The characteristics of the site are established first. They may vary considerably. For example, the spectrum of settings of a national park may range from easily accessible, highly developed areas and facilities, to remote, undeveloped areas with no facilities. Once a ROS has been established as a form of inventory, management can evaluate recreational demand against supply.

Australian examples of applications include Kakadu National Park in the Northern Territory, Queensland state forests, Split Rock Dam and Newcastle's urban parklands in New South Wales, Tidbinbilla Nature Reserve in the Australian Capital Territory and the Southern Forests of Tasmania. One of the most interesting applications has been in Brisbane Forest Park in southern Queensland, where the ROS has been converted into a zoning system and integrated into the park's strategic plan.

Limits of acceptable change (LAC)

The **LAC** rejects the idea that more use equals more impact. The thinking behind it is that change is an inevitable consequence of resource use and a framework is required to tackle management problems on the basis of how much change is acceptable. When the limits of acceptable change are reached the area's capacity under current management practices has also been reached. Management then has a logical and defensible case to implement strategic actions before any more use can be accommodated. One action may be to limit use.

The validity of the LAC approach rests on the proposition that it is possible to predetermine acceptable limits of change ('standards') in the indicators of resource or social conditions. Indicators are 'specific attributes of resources and social settings which reflect the overall condition of different areas and enable change to be detected before it reaches unacceptable levels and threatens park values' (Prosser 1986, p. 9). Standards are acceptable limits which must be formulated for each indicator in each recreation setting.

Choosing indicators and selecting standards requires substantial data on the state of the resource, the nature of the visitor experience, and the interrelationship between the two. This data is usually lacking in Australia or expensive to acquire. There are other problems. According to Prosser, it is difficult to even identify reasonable base levels for some indicators. Resource indicators are unlikely to be stable, even in pristine natural environments, because of variations due to weather conditions, seasonal changes and other factors.

The LAC model has been variously employed and documented at approximately 20 sites across the world, most by the US Parks Service. The four or five pilots established in Australia were not fully implemented and ceased operating after some two years.

DEFINITIONS

Limits of acceptable change (LAC)
A technique for determining when the area's capacity under current management practices has been reached. The proposition behind it is that change is an inevitable consequence of resource use and a framework is required to tackle management problems on the basis of how much change is acceptable.

Visitor impact management model (VIMM)

The **VIMM** evolved in the United States in the late 1980s as a simpler version of the LAC. Managers continued to reject carrying capacity and focus on linking planning, monitoring and decision making, but narrowed the focus from managing broad-scale preferred scenarios.

The VIMM recognised visitors were not the only cause of impacts. Effective management had to go beyond recreational carrying capacities and limits on use to involve both scientific and judgmental considerations. This was considered a significant advance (Loomis & Graete cited by McArthur 2000).

The VIMM encourages explicit statements of management objectives, research and monitoring to determine environmental and social conditions, then generates a range of management strategies to deal with the impacts. It is attractive to managers who want a model suitable for smaller, localised sites. It has been pilot tested in the United States and Canada as well as Australia (Snowy Mountain region, parks and reserves in Victoria, the Tasmanian Wilderness World Heritage Area).

Australia also offers an example of a VIMM being fully implemented. This is being undertaken by the Jenolan Caves Management Trust at the Jenolan Caves Historic Reserve in New South Wales. Initially, the notion of a model was rooted in carrying capacity, but eventually switched to a visitor impact management model when a capacity was found to be impossible to define and agree upon (McArthur 2000).

Visitor experience and resource protection model (VERP)

The **VERP** adds to the VIMM approach zoning and legislative links with the region's management plan. Its starting point is determining (1) the range of visitor experiences that can be offered in a park, and (2) specific objectives for the condition of park resources. It uses zoning to prescribe appropriate uses and management strategies for different areas within a park. The process draws on experience with other models, but avoids specific carrying capacities and limits on the number of visitors in favour of determining desired ecological and social conditions. Measurement of the appropriate conditions replaces the measurement of maximum sustainable use.

Based on those conditions, the VERP identifies and documents the kinds and levels of use that are appropriate, as well as where and when such uses should occur. The prescriptions, coupled with a monitoring program, are intended to give park managers the information and the rationale needed to make sound decisions about visitor use and gain the public and agency support needed to implement those decisions.

The first application in Australia was by the Queensland National Parks and Wildlife Services and the University of Queensland on Fraser Island in 1994. This was followed by its use in the Snowy River region of the Australian Alps in 1997. In both cases elements of other models were incorporated.

Visitor activity management program (VAMP)

The **VAMP** was a bold attempt to change the orientation away from the product – the park itself and the visitor experience – to marketing, with its emphasis on fulfilling the needs and wants of the consumer. This required a fundamental change in the culture of heritage management organisations. Experience so far suggests it is too much to expect.

The model was developed in Canada in the early 1990s with an emphasis on deciding what people want in a park, then developing and marketing specific experiences to match the wants. The process included setting objectives for visitor activities, identifying visitor management issues against the objectives, analysis of current visitation characteristics, development of options for visitor activities and services.

The setting of clear objectives for visitor management helps to predetermine the type of experiences and benefits to be offered and the visitor markets in which the offer will be made.

Despite promise at first, the application of the VAMP has not been greatly successful. In 1992 Australian heritage managers seriously considered it but it has never been fully implemented in this country. While there were doubts about the theoretical underpinnings of the model, the main problem was trying to move park managers to a marketing-led approach (McArthur 2000).

VISITOR MANAGEMENT OF A DESTINATION AREA

Visitor management for a destination area up to the size of a tourism region uses broader-based measures for an attraction or an area managed by a single authority. It may well have within its borders a number of attractions and recreational areas; it will involve at least one but perhaps a number of local government bodies, a regional tourism organisation or some other body representing the travel and tourism industry, and other organisations representing community and business interests. Its population may be both urban and rural based.

The approach is a step towards the broader thinking of national and state bodies, but is still rooted in local needs, capacities, social and economic structures and attitudes. Governments, particularly local councils, play a leading role and there is a need for considerable consultation if contentious issues arise or tourism developments are planned.

Managers of attractions and facilities within the destination area may use the range of measures already discussed to meet their individual needs in managing visitor activity; those responsible for the sustainability of the destination area in the overall have to think in terms which are less specific. Nevertheless they have a range of instruments in two categories – regulatory and marketing – which can be very powerful.

Two different types of organisations are primarily involved in visitor management of a destination area: government and the travel and tourism industry.[1] Government is largely responsible for supply (e.g. infrastructure and the regulation of tourism facilities) while

DEFINITIONS

Visitor activity management program (VAMP)

A management system with an emphasis on marketing, deciding what people want in a park, then developing and marketing specific experiences to match the wants.

demand (stimulated by marketing) is mostly in the hands of the industry. They have different cultures, different ways of doing things, but if visitor management is to be successful, they must work together.

▓ The role of governments

Middleton and Hawkins (1998) note that local government has long been concerned with capacity issues. They cite housing as an example. There are well-developed methods for establishing how many houses can be built to meet demand on a particular area of land based on an acceptable number of houses per hectare.

The number of existing houses, plus any new ones to be built, determines the number of residents and all else follows from there – the provision for shopping, local transport, recreation facilities, capacity of schools and so on. Concepts of capacity, based on known area densities and easily quantified standards of provision per thousand head of population, are the basis for strategic decisions and comparisons with other areas.

Local councils have considerable powers – such as land-use and building regulations, car parking and licensing procedures – to control this capacity. These powers can also be used to control capacity of the facilities, accommodation and attractions required by tourists.

The principal regulatory/management tools available to governments are be discussed in the next section and include the following:

- provision of infrastructure
- investment incentives
- land use planning
- building regulations
- marketing.

Provision of infrastructure

Traditionally governments plan, fund and provide most of the infrastructure required by a destination area and, in particular, the means of access: the roads and bridges, airports, seaports, railway lines, public transport terminals. They also provide the publicly accessible parts of the built environment, tourism facilities such as marinas, and the provision of utilities.

Investment incentives

Governments of all levels in Australia have felt the need to encourage tourism development with financial incentives. These may include grants, loans either direct or through the public sector acting as guarantor, tax concessions, peppercorn rents, or preparing land for development.

Land use planning

Land use planning is essential. Tourism should not be allowed to grow in what Doswell (1997) calls an 'explosion of random development' (pp. 132-133). Competing uses for land must also be considered and, hopefully, the best use of different areas determined. Planning provides a framework for what can be built where, the form and style of buildings, their size and their height. Local council permission is required before a developer or operator can develop land for a resort, or build a motel or caravan park, or add more caravans or build an hotel extension. In some cases, the use of land is protected by state or Commonwealth legislation or by world heritage listing.

Building regulations

Local government controls cover buildings for all purposes, including tourism. They apply to the size of buildings, their height, the density of structures in relation to the site, plus access and car parking arrangements. There are some special cases which affect tourism. For example, existing buildings may be protected because of their heritage value. And governments of all levels may build, acquire or provide support for particular buildings and use them for tourism-related purposes, e.g. as convention centres, sports and entertainment complexes.

The measures discussed above – control of infrastructure, financial incentives, land-use and building regulations – add up to a powerful set of tools, or as Middleton and Hawkins express it, 'a public sector armoury for tourism management which is virtually impregnable' (p. 101).

Marketing

A principal task of the destination marketing organisation (a regional tourism organisation if the destination area is a tourism region) is to project a single image of the area and its overall tourism product. The marketing organisation must be part of the cooperative body which determines visitor management policy for the area. It can construct its promotion to include visitor management elements in line with the area's overall objectives, particularly in its awareness campaign in which the images used can include sustainable tourism messages.

Thus the programs can be designed to motivate particular groups of visitors and influence their behaviour, including the accommodation and activities they choose, the times of the year they visit, their length of stay and their expenditure patterns.

Governments and demand

The influence of governments on demand should not be overlooked and it should be used to further visitor management goals. Governments and their agencies charge fees to enter attractions such as some national parks and museums and for the use of facilities such as

DEFINITIONS
....

car parks. These fees have a direct effect on the level of patronage. If local governments are the owners of environmentally fragile sites, such as coastal dunes systems, they may control demand by a combination of both access limitations and price.

Demand can also be controlled by the application of licensing procedures to businesses that serve visitors, such as tourist coaches and taxis, bars and restaurants. Many councils run or support information centres. They also have a role in the production and general distribution of brochures and visitor information in other forms, including electronic distribution.

The tourism optimisation management model (TOMM)

Tourism optimisation management model (TOMM)

A long-term regional visitor management model which identifies desirable conditions for sustainable tourism activity to occur. Thus it focuses on optimising the tourism performance of a destination area rather than limiting use.

A long-term model with important implications for regional visitor management is being developed on Kangaroo Island, South Australia. Known as the '**tourism optimisation management model**' (TOMM), it focuses on optimising the tourism performance of a destination area rather than limiting use.

The TOMM approach is to shift the focus from a relationship between the levels of use and impact to identifying desirable conditions for sustainable tourism activity to occur in the first place. Although this approach differs from those of the park visitor management models, most of which were developed with a focus on maintaining the resource and quality of the visitor experience, it is their direct descendant. It was designed by Manidis Roberts Consultants who had been asked at first to develop a limits of acceptable change model for Kangaroo Island.

A range of stakeholders are involved including Tourism Kangaroo Island and individual travel and tourism businesses, local government and community organisations. The implementation committee includes representatives from state government agencies, including the South Australian Tourism Commission and the Conservation Commission. Specifically, the TOMM has been designed to:

- monitor and quantify the key economic, marketing, environmental, sociocultural and experiential benefits and impacts of tourism activity
- assist in the assessment of emerging issues and alternative future management options for the sustainable development and management of tourism activity (Manidis Roberts Consultants 1997).

It is not about setting limits, maximum levels or carrying capacities. It emphasises the best conditions for tourism to occur and sets acceptable ranges within which they should occur. It then indicates whether the various aspects of tourism are within the acceptable range or not. The trends that the TOMM creates can be used to predict change and help people to test and discuss new ideas.

The TOMM contains three main components: context analysis, a monitoring program and a management response system.

1. The **context analysis** identifies the current nature of community values, tourism

product, tourism growth, market trends and opportunities, and positioning and branding. It also identifies alternative scenarios for the future of tourism. This information is then used to define optimal conditions which tourism should create (rather than impacts it should avoid).

2. The **monitoring program** then measures how close the current situation is to the optimal conditions.

3. The **management response system** identifies problem areas and what needs to be done to address them.

There are methodological limitations. In company with the VIMM and LAC models, there is the problem of selecting the right indicator to suggest the state of the optimal condition. The TOMM also shares the potential for subjectivity when choosing the acceptable range and benchmark.

Nevertheless, the model has great potential for visitor management at a destination area and ensuring a better and sustainable result for the travel and tourism industry and for the host community.

VISITOR MANAGEMENT IN CITIES

Tourism changes the use of spaces in cities, the cultural life of their residents and, of course, their economic base. Attitudes within a community towards tourism phenomena vary considerably as we saw in Chapter 5 when examining the effect of the IndyCar race in the relatively small city of the Gold Coast. In a large city, the changes brought about by tourism will usually please some stakeholders and be against the interests of others. How this conflict is resolved is part of the management challenge and may become a political issue.

Tourism does not threaten the larger Australian cities in the same way as it does Venice, discussed in the case study later in the chapter. But there are pressure points. The cities compete fiercely for conferences and exhibitions, which can attract large numbers, and also for major events, of which the Olympic Games is the best example. Large events bring problems of managing people, usually for a short period.

Conferences and events

Conference delegates are considered relatively easy to manage, even when they arrive in great numbers, which does happen: there were more than 20,000 people at the five-day Rotary International Convention in Melbourne in 1993. There is time to plan because conferences are arranged years before they happen. Thus the number of delegates is known ahead of time, their program is arranged, transport organised and they use facilities which are chosen because they can cope with the numbers. Also, delegates have vocational similarities or some shared interest which helps management.

Events also can be planned well ahead of time. The Olympic Games in Sydney during

16 days in September 2000 presented formidable organising problems for the Sydney Organising Committee for the Olympic Games (SOCOG) and city authorities. They also put an enormous load on a working city. But there were years to plan and to test management theories.

One of these was that the 'mindset' of Sydney people in regard to public transport should be changed. Local people were accustomed to driving to big events; for example, about 70 per cent used their own cars to go the Royal Easter Show at Moore Park each year, with the rest taking public transport. Forecasts for travel during the Olympics were that 500,000 people would go to the main site at Homebush Bay each day and another 100,000 to Darling Harbour, 70,000 to venues around Blacktown and more to other venues. If anything like 70 per cent of them tried to drive themselves there would be chaos.

Public transport was the only answer. The Olympic Roads and Transport Authority was created to coordinate Sydney's rail network, ferries and an enhanced fleet of buses. It might be expected that a shift to public transport would not be popular with Sydney's drivers. However, the Royal Easter Show provided an opportunity to change their views and their ways. The Show was moved to Homebush three years before the Games and each year SOCOG encouraged visitors (about 180,000 a day) to use public transport rather than their own cars. They did this by restricting parking and making the cost of travel free with the entry ticket.

By the year of the Games, the proportion of visitors to the Show travelling by car and public transport had been reversed – 70 per cent travelled by public transport and only 30 per cent by car. The mindset remained after the Games, in 2001 the majority of people going to the Homebush stadium for events such as rugby games used public transport (Sloman 2001).

▓ Fast-tracking facilities

The other dimension of visitor management – the development of tourism plant, facilities and infrastructure – is usually the focus of continuing interest and often controversy. The 'successful urban tourist space' is described by Tyler and Guerrier (1999) as one which offers excitement, spectacle and stimulation at the same time as safety, security and familiarity. Developing it can change the city's image, attraction and physical carrying capacity. It can also cause a change in the distribution of tourists within a city.

Festivals, fairs and sporting events are held all over Australia. The mega events (also called major, hallmark or special events), such as the Olympic Games, the Formula One Grand Prix, Commonwealth Games, Expos and Bledisloe Cup matches are held in cities because only they have the infrastructure, accommodation and facilities which can support such large undertakings. They require large-scale professional management.

State governments are heavily involved. They have established special corporations to bid for and facilitate such events. Their agencies sometimes fund and organise events, at other times governments contribute to the necessary funding for infrastructure and promotion and sometimes management.

Hall (1999) notes that the significance of mega-events is not only related to their visitor component but also because of the impact they have on host communities, particularly of the large public expenditure, the construction of facilities and infrastructure, and the redevelopment and revitalisation of urban areas. He cites the redevelopment of Darling Harbour, a bay next to the central business district of Sydney, for which the catalyst was the 1988 Bicentennial Celebrations. One of most controversial aspects of the enabling Act was that it gave the Darling Harbour authority 'absolute planning control', exempting it from the Environmental Planning and Assessment Act 1979 as well as other Acts which covered such issues as subdivision approvals, heritage conservation and heights of buildings. This removed the authority from the jurisdiction of the City Council, the Department of Environment and Planning and the Land and Environment Court.

The government decided this was justified because the various approval and appeal processes within existing environmental legislation might have delayed the development process. There was public criticism, particularly over the construction of a raised monorail system designed to move people between the central city and Darling Harbour. The criticism had no effect, because as with the rest of the project, it was not subject to normal planning legislation. Hall comments that the establishment of special Acts and Regulations in respect to hallmark events may serve to reinforce the powerlessness of certain groups and individuals within the planning process. The law often acts to protect the integrity of the event and associated physical developments, but not the impact of the event on the host population. Governments elsewhere find themselves facing the problem of working to a deadline to stage an event (or approving a development) and risking alienating a section of the population if they fast-track the process.

Having reviewed a number of case studies of how cities in different parts of the world manage tourism, Tyler and Guerrier (1999) commented on a common schizophrenia about the role of tourism in a city economy: 'Tourism developed in a top-down manner, seeking prestige, often seems to forget the fact that the real problem to be addressed is local-level deprivation' (p. 231).

CASE STUDY

A tale of two cities: Venice and Tamworth

This examination of visitor management in two very different cities, Venice and Tamworth, does not attempt to compare them – not in character, nor measure of tourism, nor its challenges, are they comparable. They are linked in this case study merely to show how different cities tackle different problems and issues connected with tourism.

Venice

State governments and Australian city authorities have yet to deal with extremes from tourism by overseas standards. Venice is frequently cited as the supreme example of how tourism can impact on a city. It has brought in much money and wrought great changes, helping to drive out a large proportion of its population. Now, according to Van Der Borg (1999), Venice is at risk of losing its appeal to visitors because of its immense popularity.

Venice had 175,000 inhabitants in 1951, but fewer than 80,000 by the end of the century. Tourism-related activities, which have suffocated residential and other city functions, include overcrowding of streets, the production of excessive litter and other rubbish and destruction of monuments. Residents are still reported to be leaving Venice at the rate of 1,500 a year (TED – trade and environment database – Online Journal, www. american.edu/ted/VENICE.HTM).

While some see tourism as a 'menace for its continuity' (Van Der Borg 1999, p. 126), Venetians themselves are inclined to blame the poor management of the city by the municipality for the decreasing quality of life rather than excess tourism demand (Glasson, Godfrey & Goodey 1995).[2] However, it is clear that the municipal government's management problems substantially derive from tourism.

While the experience of Venice with tourism has lessons for others, it is, of course, a special case, a city like no other. The old historical heart of the city is 4 km from the Italian mainland on 118 small islands totalling about 700 hectares in the Venetian lagoon. It is criss-crossed by more than 150 canals and 400 bridges. Heritage buildings look on to hundreds of small squares, linked by narrow streets called *calli*. The municipal territory also includes the mainland centres of Mestre and Porto Marghera connected to the city by road and rail bridges. The lagoon centres of Burano, Murano, Lido, Cavallino, Malammocco, San Michele and Torcello are also administered by Venice.

Venice attracts a large number of overnight tourists (in the mid-1990s about 1.45 million a year who spent about 3.25 million bed-nights), but a much bigger number of day-trippers (about 7 million annually in the same period). The number of beds is limited and so the number of day-trippers continues to grow. They include people who travel from home, others who are touring around Italy and many who spend their holidays nearby, where it's cheaper. Day-trippers spend much less in Venice than those who stay there for one or more nights. Many come in tour buses and spend nothing in hotels or restaurants.

The city is ecologically sensitive. City officials opposed holding Expo 2000, a four-month world exposition welcoming the new century, after a feasibility study suggested the influx of visitors would cause irreparable damage. The Expo was held elsewhere.

From an everyday visitor management point of view, day-trippers are the problem. Residential demand is controlled by the number of beds available and information on bookings is available in advance, so that measures can be taken for peak periods. On the other hand, it is difficult to control day-trippers. There have been plenty of ideas, but not much action. For example, there were rumours in the 1990s that the city would put quotas on the number of visitors that could enter the city. Officials have considered issuing one-day passes valid for items such as car parks and canal transport. Another idea was to have computer hookups that allowed potential visitors to know how crowded the city was (TED – trade and environment database – Online Journal, www.american.edu/ted/VENICE.HTM).

Glasson, Godfrey and Goodey suggest several other options. A 'hard' (i.e. regulatory) solution would be to impose a combination of measures: (a) close the centre of the heritage city to private cars; (b) reserve the right to use central parking lots, and to stop at the relevant terminals, for inhabitants and commuters; and (c) ration public transport bringing visitors to the centre.[3]

'Soft' ideas (i.e. incentives) to ration excess demand would require an advance booking system:

1. When making a booking, day-trippers would be encouraged to buy a package of service items, such as meal vouchers, tickets for exhibitions and museums and discounts in souvenir shops. They also would be encouraged to visit Venice at specific periods. The system could be made mandatory, with the package documents serving as an entrance ticket. If optional, the system would serve only as an incentive for advanced booking.

2. A 'city currency card' could serve as a credit card, valid for the length of the visit, to pay for goods and services in the city. The card could be issued in different forms to different types of visitors, in numbers fixed in advance. The personal credit card furthermore could allow for price discrimination according to the hour or the day that it is used.

Tamworth knows what it wants

Tamworth is a small Australian city – it has about half the population of Venice – with a very different tourism profile, history and reason for existing. It has a successful record in image-building and in managing a tourism inflow which more or less doubles the population for 10 days each January. Most Australians know it as the home of the Country Music Festival.

In contrast to the large Australian cities, it has perfectly clear tourism objectives relating to its citizens and the city economy. It attracts and manages visitor inflow with the involvement of a range of business and community groups, and with professional leadership and substantial funds supplied by the city council. The city is firmly in control of the event; there are no ownership issues. This almost sounds too good to be true, but Tamworth has had 30 years to clarify its objectives and to fine-tune the management of the festival to the benefit of both visitors and the community.

Tamworth is an attractive city of 38,000 (50,000 in the 'greater Tamworth area' of Parry Shire) set in rich agricultural country about halfway between Sydney and Brisbane on the New England Highway. Its position on the highway, its role as a service centre for the north and northwest of New South Wales, and specialist attractions like gemstone hunting nearby, guarantee it a substantial number of visitors, annually about 300,000. However, it is the Country Music Festival which gives it prominence among Australian regional cities.

One of the objectives of the festival is to make it work year-round for Tamworth, to attract tourism and other business to benefit the city's economy. Some of this happens simply because the city's name is well known because of the festival – to travellers between Sydney and Brisbane, for instance, who are attracted to stop over. Other events naturally benefit from the Tamworth name; an example is Taste, a cooking festival held each year to promote the foods of the district.

The Tamworth Council actively courts media coverage of the Country Music Festival – television, radio and print – as a platform for promoting a 'clever image' of the city. For the 2001 festival the campaign began in December of the previous year when its major sponsor Carlton & United Breweries hosted boardroom lunches in Sydney and Melbourne at which the city honoured appropriate singers and songwriters. By the time the festival was over, coverage in national and regional media – television, radio and print – was valued at nearly $8 million.

Another objective is to spread the economic benefits from the festival to as many citizens and groups as possible. This is accomplished in a number of ways. Here are some examples.

1. Schools and sporting groups charge fees for use of temporary camps on their grounds. The council provides showers and toilets for the campers and generally supervises them to ensure health and safety. But the sporting groups, representing cricket, softball, netball and baseball interests in 2001, collect the fees before the campers enter the camping grounds and keep some of the proceeds to run their own affairs during the year. Schools also benefit financially from temporary camping on their grounds.

2. A six-day Countdown period, preceding the festival proper with a limited number of musical events, was introduced in 2000 to benefit accommodation and venue operators in an otherwise slack period.

3. Many Tamworth people have a holiday during the festival period. They rent their houses out and head for the coast with their holiday paid for because of the festival.

Visitor management issues

Accommodation

Besides regular commercial accommodation, there are home rentals, home hosting and camping. All camping is highly organised because of the council's dissatisfaction with ad hoc camping in early years of the festival.

Visitor spread

People attending the festival do not gather in one place, which can cause management problems. Country music has many genres with names like contemporary, bluegrass, bootscooting, bush poetry, country rock gospel, acoustic and new talent. The festival encompasses some 2,000 different events in 100 venues within a 4 km radius.

Transport

Some streets are closed to traffic. A 'customised' public transport system operates. This includes shuttle buses operating between the venues and also catering for home hosting.

Council patrols

Council staff carry out a multiplicity of regulatory activities during the festival. For example they regularly patrol camping sites to ensure compliance with regulations, they inspect mobile food vans to ensure operations are in accordance with food preparation regulations, they carry out sound monitoring of street buskers, using hand-held meters.

Expenditure

Much of the council's spending is on visitor management. Total expenditure in 2001 was $488,053 (income was $268,260, leaving a net cost of $219,793). Expenditure items included street cleaning, road closures and people safety, itinerant trading, erection of street signage, temporary camping facilities, portable toilets, publicity and promotion, operation of the media centre, opening and closing concerts.

Debriefing

A series of forums and debriefing sessions are held after the festival to assess it from as many points of view as possible. These include council staff debriefings and forums for councillors, the public, venue operators and moteliers, emergency services and police. The view of residents close to camping areas are also sought to identify any areas of concern (Smyth 2001).

(Source: Photographer: Shae Johnson, *The Advocate*.)

INDUSTRY PROFILE

CATHIE PLOWMAN INTERPRETATION OFFICER (TOURISM PROJECTS), PARKS AND WILDLIFE SERVICE, TASMANIA

I manage the two show caves at Mole Creek and interpretation at Cradle Mountain. At Mole Creek my focus is providing guides with training in interpretation and developing new ways for visitors to enjoy the beauty of the marvellous underground world, as well as helping them understand the links with the above-ground world. Caves are a fantastic environment and there are many possibilities for developing new ways for visitors to enjoy them. Some of the ideas I am pursuing are music and singing events, meditation and relaxation opportunities in a glow-worm-lit chamber, less energetic tours for the older-aged group and self-guided tours. I am also part of a team endeavouring to develop cave tourism on a statewide basis.

Cradle Mountain is one of Tasmania's key visitor destinations and I'm involved in the ongoing development and improvement of interpretation services. My goal is to match visitor needs with the opportunities available and to maximise the enjoyment of each visitor and add a little to their understanding of the national park.

How did I get here?

I've worked in several positions for the Parks and Wildlife Service, including ranger, track ranger, interpretation officer and caves manager. I also co-managed the implementation of the Great Short Walks project. But I didn't start out to work in national parks. On leaving school I trained as a psychiatric nurse. However, a keen love of bushwalking developed by my parents and a passion for conservation developed by two gifted high school teachers, gradually led me to increased involvement in these areas. In 1981 I left my nursing career to volunteer for the Wilderness Society's campaign to save the Franklin River. Ongoing work in conservation gradually led me to do volunteer work for the Parks and Wildlife Service. Experience, skills and interest eventually led to a permanent job. I've now completed a diploma in park management and am currently studying for a post-graduate certificate in cave and karst management.

What do I like about my job?

People love learning about the environment and it's a great privilege to share the fantastic environment of Tasmania's national parks with them. There are always challenges. It's hard work, but there's plenty of variety.

Part of the management task is to limit tourism's adverse impacts, to ensure that tourism assets are protected from over-use or abuse. In most cases, it is neither possible nor desirable to stop tourism altogether, but it can be managed.

Visitor management can be viewed strategically, with choices in supply and demand categories. Supply includes the provision of infrastructure, attractions and facilities. Demand is adjusted by selective marketing, that is, targeting visitors who are socially and economically more attractive than others. It can also be employed to reduce or regulate the number of people visiting a location. This is called demarketing.

Carrying capacity of an area is an important factor in visitor management. It can refer to physical, ecological, social, psychological or economic dimensions. Capacity levels are influenced by the characteristics of tourists and the local scene – the natural environment, economic and social structures, political organisation and level of tourism development.

Visitor management techniques vary widely according to the area – whether it is a city or region or an attraction. No matter how large the area is, management is simplified if it is governed by a single authority. This may take the form of a company, a local government, a statutory authority or something else. Among methods open to an authority are:

- marketing, especially pricing and promotion. Pricing can be controversial in respect to public properties, such as national parks. While one argument is that charging fees results in more efficient use of parks, another is that to charge fees disadvantages part of the community which either does not have the means to pay or finds it much harder to pay than others.
- denying access to part of the area. For example, zoning is used in the Great Barrier Reef Marine Park and the Wet Tropics World Heritage Areas in Queensland.

Other methods include physical changes to access and to the area itself and interpretation and education.

Visitor impact management models, beginning with the recreational carrying capacity model, have been extensively applied in Australia to national parks, state forests and other nature reserves. They identify strengths and weaknesses against previously established criteria and allow for management responses to achieve desired outcomes.

Visitor management for a destination area up to the size of a tourism region uses broader-based measures than for an attraction or an area managed by a single authority. The approach is a step towards the broader thinking of national and state bodies. However, local councils have considerable powers – such as land-use and building regulations, car parking and licensing procedures – to control capacity of the facilities, accommodation and attractions required by tourists. The destination marketing organisation can construct its promotion to include visitor management elements in line with the area's overall objectives, particularly in its awareness campaign in which the images used can include sustainable tourism messages.

Tourism changes the use of spaces in cities, the cultural life of their residents and their economic base. Cities compete fiercely for conferences and exhibitions, which can attract large numbers, and also for major events. Conference delegates are considered relatively easy to manage because the number of delegates is known ahead of time, their program is arranged, transport organised and they use facilities which are chosen because they can cope with the numbers. Events also can be planned well ahead of time. The Olympic Games in Sydney in September 2000 showed how the mindset of people towards public transport could be changed over a number of years ahead of the Games so that when they did occur traffic problems were avoided.

Development of tourism facilities in a city can be a big issue. The 'successful urban tourist space' is said to be one which offers excitement, spectacle and stimulation at the same time as safety, security and familiarity. Developing it can change the city's image, attraction and physical carrying capacity. It can also cause a change in the distribution of tourists within a city. Eagerness to develop has its dangers. Governments sometimes fast-track the development of facilities for major events by removing the checks and balances that are customary to protect all interests.

QUESTIONS

1. Why is visitor management defined in more than one way and what are the definitions?

2. What strategic choices in visitor management do planners have? Discuss them.

3. What are 'hard' and 'soft' visitor management techniques?

4. What is demarketing and how can it be applied to tourism?

5. Why does an area under a single authority have some advantages for visitor management? What are the methods the authority can use?

6. What are visitor impact models designed to do and what are their general criteria?

7. Local government has considerable powers to influence visitor management. What are they and to what purposes can they be used?

8. What are the main features of the 'tourism optimisation management model' (TOMM) and how does it differ from other visitor management models?

9. What are the issues faced by cities in managing conferences and events? Why are visitors to conferences and events usually easier to manage than general tourists? What are the potential dangers for residents?

10. What are the reasons Tamworth can manage a Country Music Festival each year and make it work for its citizens?

MANAGING CHANGE 12

CHAPTER 12

LEARNING OBJECTIVES

Recognise the differences between structural and temporary change.

Examine the causes of structural change, including globalisation, competition, social changes, customer preferences, wars and terrorism, and economic and health crises.

Appreciate the causes of temporary change, including cyclical changes and crises and disasters.

Understand the effects of both structural and temporary change on various sectors of the travel and tourism industry from the examples given.

Examine the means of mastering gradual change and how preparations are made to deal with crises and disasters, should they eventuate.

**| UNDERSTAND
THE MEANING OF:**

- *structural change*
- *temporary change*
- *cyclical change*
- *globalisation*
- *tourism dotcom*
- *business cycles*
- *demand–supply cycles*
- *crisis*
- *disaster*
- *disaster management
  team*

DEFINITIONS

....

Structural change

*A fundamental
transformation of
some activity or
institution which
brings about change
in its essential
quality, or
structure. It is
permanent; there is
no return to the
prior level or state.*

Temporary change

*An alteration in a
certain measure or
condition in an
activity or
institution to which
it is likely to return
later.*

STRUCTURAL AND TEMPORARY CHANGE

The travel and tourism industry is always in a state of change. There are many reasons both within the industry, such as competition, and outside it, such as the terrorist attacks on the United States in September 2001, the Bali bombings in 2002 and the SARS crisis in 2003. This chapter examines the causes of change and how it can be managed. Broadly, there are two kinds of change:

1. **Structural change** This involves a fundamental transformation of some activity or institution (e.g. the Australian travel and tourism industry). It is usually measurable because there is a considerable rise or decline over time in amount, size or range. This prompts other alterations which bring about change in the essential quality, or structure, of the activity or institution. Structural change is permanent; there is no return to the prior level or state. The adjustment to it must also be permanent.

2. **Temporary change** One form is cyclical change, another is brought about by a single event, a crisis or disaster. Cyclical change is a temporary alteration in a certain measure or condition from a level or state to which it is likely to return later. It can be almost overpowering at the time, but nevertheless follow a discernible pattern in its fluctuations while returning to a prior state (Martel 1988). A very severe crisis or a disaster can cause structural change, but the travel and tourism industry as a whole has proven very resilient and usually the change to it (as distinct from individual businesses) has proven temporary.

Structural change is more likely to be brought about over time and often to be recognisable only after a period of years. For example, in the 20 years 1979 to 1999, the scale of inbound tourism in Australia grew five times, from less than 900,000 to nearly 4.5 million.[1] Domestic tourism grew over the period as well. The travel and tourism industry underwent such fundamental structural change in the period that as the new century started much of it was unrecognisable from that of the previous era.

The structural changes discussed in this chapter have been caused mostly by alterations over time, brought about by such phenomena as globalisation, trends in customer preferences and social changes. Even when a sudden event has occurred, its reasons can sometimes be related to a longer-term occurrence. Thus the cause of the collapse of Ansett Australia may be traced to Air New Zealand's desire for market power to meet the challenges brought about by the trends towards larger airline groupings as part of globalisation. Ansett's demise caused structural change in several sectors of the Australian travel and tourism industry. Its effect was much more immediate and severe on the industry than the world event which preceded it by a few days, the terrorist attacks in the United States.[2] That event caused havoc with travel in the short term and severely affected the travel and tourism industry in most parts of the world. But it did not force immediate structural change on the Australian industry.

Some events, a crisis or disaster, will bring the industry in an area to a halt for a time. Generally its effect is not evenly spread; even when the industry appears to be severely damaged by an event or crisis of some kind it is common to find some part of it doing well. International travel to Australia was cut in the weeks that followed the terrorist attacks on New York and Washington, yet the backpacker market increased substantially. Low international air fares following the attacks helped attract young backpackers who were not afraid to fly (Strutt 2001). Australian travel to Bali was severely affected by the bombings of two bars packed with tourists in 2002, but travel to South Pacific destinations, particularly Fiji, increased as a result.

It is necessary to draw a distinction between the industry as a whole and individual businesses in discussing structural change. Businesses are not immune to significant events any more than they are to long-term forces of change. Businesses come and go as the external environment changes, there are mergers and takeovers, the influence of particular companies strengthens or wanes. Yet it can be shown that the industry as a whole is extremely resilient even in very severe adverse situations. Tourism has grown and the industry has flourished, albeit with some casualties, over the past two decades in the face of wars, terrorist attacks, economic crises, an unprecedented health crisis, interest rate fluctuations, energy shortages and a variety of natural disasters.

The industry has learned to expect quick changes in world conditions and, with the help of government agencies, to employ contingency planning and forecasting to help it respond creatively to problems that suddenly occur. Behind this is demand, the desire to travel. Through all sorts of travails, it has proved stronger than many forecasters thought:

> *the populations of the main generating countries now regard holidays as a near essential part of consumer expenditure and individuals protect their holidays even at the expense of many other forms of consumption* (Archer 1996, p. 94).

CAUSES OF STRUCTURAL CHANGE

These are discussed under seven main headings:
- globalisation
- competition
- economic crises
- health crises

DEFINITIONS
....

- social changes
- customer preferences
- wars, terrorism.

Globalisation – one big market

Globalisation

The process, accelerated by communication technologies, of turning the world into a single community, and, in particular, a single market. It has been described as 'boundarylessness'.

Globalisation is affecting all sectors of the industry largely because it is turning the world into one big travel market. It dates back at least to the late 19th century when telegraph cables provided, for the first time, an instant link between markets in Europe and North America (Gray 2002). It has been accelerated in more recent times by the building of a vast network of communication technologies which has drawn people from all nations into a single community; those technologies abolish or curtail time and distance. It is continuing and there are many threads to it. Cooper, Fayos-Sola and Pedro (2001) suggest it is possible to draw these threads together by considering globalisation as 'boundary-lessness' – 'a new paradigm characterised by speed, flexibility, integration and innovation' (p. 7).

They also suggest that radical thinking is necessary to adjust tourism policy to the reality of globalisation. They say the traditional tourism resources, the comparative advantages (climate, landscape, culture etc.) are becoming less and less important compared with new factors in tourism competitiveness: the strategic management of information, intelligence (the innovative capacity in teams within an organisation) and knowledge (know-how or a combination of technological skills, technology and organisational culture).

> *The major (most visited) destinations of the world are no longer the famous beaches or traditional cultural capitals, but rather man-made products, such as Orlando or Las Vegas. In fact, the greatest foreseeable competition to present tourism activity is not the appearance of exotic new resorts, but instead the massive use of the increasingly accessible and efficient information and communication technologies for new leisure products, including virtual travel and experiences* (p. 8).

The Internet has empowered consumers. Tourists have been given access to a vastly wider range of products from which to choose, resulting in much greater market segmentation and differentiation of products by industry sectors. It has led to an increasing desire to discover the differences in peoples and their cultures. This favours destinations that can clearly differentiate themselves.

Technology makes life different

The Internet makes life different for a variety of parties involved in travel and tourism, not just consumers. Table 12.1 shows who talks to whom on the Internet about travel and tourism matters.

Table 12.1 Online tourism communications

COMMUNICATIONS	FUNCTION
Government-Business	• Destination promotion • Destination information • Statistical data exchange • Regulations and standards information • Compliance procedures (*transaction*)
Government-Consumer	• Destination promotion • Regulations and standards information • Destination information • Passenger processing (*transaction*)
Business-Business	• Product promotion • Schedules, rates, availability information • Reports and analyses • Commission processing (*transaction*) • Settlement (*transaction*)
Business-Consumer	• Product promotion • Schedules, rates, availability information • Reports and analyses • Customer satisfaction procedures • Bookings (*transaction*) • Ticketing (*transaction*) • Settlement (*transaction*)
Consumer-Consumer	• Destination promotion • Destination information • Product promotion

(Source: Online Tourism Communications, *CRC for Sustainable Tourism*, National Online Scoping Study, Disk (1999b), p. 7. Copyright Commonwealth of Australia, reproduced by permission.)

Online bookings

Online bookings are taking hundreds of millions of dollars of business a year away from travel agencies, largely through airline reservations, but online travel agencies (for example travel.com.au) are also doing impressive business. The Internet has encouraged big non-travel organisations to enter the distribution sector. They include the Nine television network with its own travel site, building on the popularity of its *Getaway* television program, and Telstra, which has a comprehensive retail travel site.[3]

Tourism dotcom

There has been speculation over a number of years about whether the present 'bricks and mortar' travel agency system can survive as a result of the Internet. The Department of Industry, Science and Resources (2000b) addressed the issue in an online tourism strategy it produced called 'tourism dotcom'. It forecast a continuing role for intermediaries (e.g. travel agents, wholesalers, inbound tour operators), saying the Internet represented a 'tremendous opportunity' for them. They could:

- use it to seek the best possible products and prices, particularly those in regional areas. Competition engendered by the Internet meant better prices.
- cut costs by establishing their own websites to sell travel products online. This enabled them to reduce overheads, lower transaction costs and market more cost-effectively.
- demonstrate they were able to reduce uncertainty associated with online purchases from suppliers' sites, particularly in respect of product quality and security of transaction. Dealing with a variety of product suppliers online can carry a higher risk for consumers than purchasing through one large, well-known, secure intermediary.

Air transport transformed

Globalisation changed the rules of the game for governments in the last two decades of the 20th century. As a result of competition in the globalised markets, they resorted to economic disengagement, manifested by privatisation, liberalisation and deregulation.

The World Tourism Organisation (1994) noted: 'Governments around the world are privatising everything from airlines and airports to hotels and convention centres. In some cases even the tourism promotion office is being privatised' (p. 3).

Liberalisation of aviation policies was designed to increase visitor flows as competition increased. The (Australian) Industries Assistance Commission (1989, p. 102) stated:

> *Regulation of competition, government ownership of carriers, and infrastructure provision and pricing policies impose high costs on travellers, tourism, the airline industry itself, the economy, and the welfare of Australians. Fares and costs are higher than need be, capacity is constrained and even at these prices, Australia is turning away potential customers. Travellers are denied the range of fares and prices they would enjoy in a more competitive environment. The airlines and airport authorities are denied the opportunity to become efficient by international standards. In short, there is an overwhelming case for reform.*

The Commonwealth Government followed the IAC inquiry by deregulating domestic aviation (in 1990),[4] divesting itself of ownership of airlines (completed in 1995) and placing most of Australia's major airports in private hands (begun in 1997). Australia was not an innovator in privatising these assets. It rather belatedly caught up with overseas practice. The United States had deregulated domestic aviation in 1978. The European Union later instituted a staged introduction of liberalisation measures.

Larger airline groups

Privatisation was not enough in itself to advance the air transport industry. Larger airline groups were needed to take advantage of the new marketing realities – to control distribution to significant portions of the world's travelling population, to provide price leadership and competitive loyalty marketing programs and benefit from the power of large-scale advertising campaigns.

What came next were alliances of airlines forming worldwide networks by agreeing to follow common marketing and scheduling policies, blocking space for other members' passengers, sharing terminal facilities (Wheatcroft 1994). Qantas Airways is a member of the aptly named oneworld alliance, which includes (among others) British Airways and American Airlines. The other major alliances are called Star, Skyteam and Qualiflyer.

Ansett a casualty

Ansett Australia was a casualty of an attempt by Air New Zealand to better compete in the globalised environment. It had taken over the full ownership of Ansett in 2000[5] to give it access to the Australian market and to take advantage of the combined size of the two airlines in a world market where size matters.

However, problems began to occur for Ansett soon after the Air New Zealand takeover. On two occasions, some or all of its Boeing 767 aircraft were grounded by the Commonwealth Air Safety Authority (CASA) for problems related to maintenance shortcomings. There was fierce price-cutting as a result of new competitors Impulse Airlines (later absorbed by Qantas) and Virgin Blue entering the market.

On 12 September 2001, the day after the terrorist attacks in the United States, administrators were appointed to run Ansett and two days later its aircraft were grounded. At the time it was said to be losing $1.3 million a day. The administrators resumed Ansett flights between capital cities on a limited basis on 29 September, assisted by guarantees by the Commonwealth Government, but in late February 2002 it was clear their efforts to sell the airline had failed and operations ceased.

The reason for Ansett having been put into voluntary administration in the first place was to 'prevent its mounting losses and debt crippling parent Air New Zealand' (Boyle & Koutsoukis 2001). That airline was in such financial difficulties that it required the intervention of the New Zealand Government to save it.[6]

The Ansett collapse brought about immediate structural change in the Australian industry. It had been not only the second biggest domestic trunk carrier with about 40 per cent of the market, but also the second largest travel and tourism company in the country. It had run the biggest domestic wholesale tour business, Ansett Holidays, one of the largest travel retailers through its ownership of Traveland (a mixture of owned and franchised retail outlets), a small but significant international carrier through Ansett International and it was a power among regional airlines through subsidiaries Kendall Airlines, AeroPelican, Skyways and Hazelton. Overall it employed more than 16,000 people, about 12,000 in the core trunk airline.

The Ansett collapse therefore caused structural change in the:

- domestic airline sector, making Qantas the dominant force, with a much smaller competitor, Virgin Blue
- international airline sector, leaving Qantas as the only Australian international carrier
- regional airline sector, again making Qantas the major player
- domestic wholesaling sector, by taking out Ansett Holidays
- retailing sector, with the breakup of Traveland having a major effect on a restructure of the travel agency system which had already begun.

The collapse also affected other sectors, including accommodation and car rental.

Hotel scene changes

The expansion of international companies has changed the major hotel scene in Australia. Two companies, Accor Asia Pacific and Six Continents, which were not trading in Australia at the beginning of the 1990s, were the biggest hotel managers in this country by the early years of the new century. They are very big international operators, both rating in the top five multinational hotel groups in the world.

Accor, the leading company in Australia in 2002 measured by number of rooms under management, opened its first hotel here in 1991, at a time when Southern Pacific Hotel Corporation, founded in Australia, was the biggest in the country. Six Continents, a British company known as Bass Hotels and Resorts when it first came to Australia, bought most of Southern Pacific in 2000, taking over the management of 59 Centra and Parkroyal hotels.[7] Six Continents numbers among its brands the well-known American names Inter Continental and Holiday Inns.

Corporate travel sellers merge

Globalisation has changed the operation of the large corporate travel business. The bigger agencies specialising in this business took advantage of technology in the 1990s to build worldwide networks by merger and acquisition. The best known examples – though by no means the only ones – were (1) American Express's acquisition of Thomas Cook's international business travel operations and its US travel agencies and (2) a joint venture between Carlson, the second ranking travel group in the US, and Accor's Wagonlit Travel, one of the largest agency groups in Europe.

The benefits of concentration for the larger agency groups were enormous. Substantial economies of scale have been achieved through sharing technology; customers are provided with worldwide service; there is global reporting for accounts and of course the larger the company the greater its buying power when negotiating on behalf of corporate clients.

Globalising English

The Internet is helping to globalise the English language, which can only help the marketing of Australian tourism. In 2000 the English-speaking world accounted for more than 80 per cent of top-level Internet hosts and generated close to 80 per cent of Internet traffic.

Many websites based in non English-speaking countries are in English because it makes them more accessible around the world. A 1998 study found that the proportion of English tended to be highest where the local language had a relatively small number of speakers and where competence in English was high. In Holland and Scandinavia, English pages run as high as 30 per cent; in France and Germany they accounted for 15–20 per cent and in Latin America 10 per cent or less (Nunberg 2000).

Competition

Competition is one of the facts of business life and one of its driving forces. As such it can be seen in all facets of Australian travel and tourism, helping to reshape the industry, causing some companies to reduce their businesses, others to disappear, others to flourish, perhaps through mergers or acquisitions.

A case in point is the Australian express coach industry, in which there was intense competition in the 1980s and 1990s. The big names of the time – Pioneer and Greyhound – were under pressure from a raft of newcomers with names like De Luxe Express, VIP Express, Redline and Sunliner. In the end they all went out of business.

The Greyhound and Pioneer names were retained in Greyhound Pioneer Australia Ltd., a public company which in the early 1990s became the biggest express company in Australia. In 2000, it was put into receivership and its only national rival, McCafferty's, a Toowoomba express company, subsequently acquired control of the company.

Economic crises

Naturally, economic crises affect travel markets. But sometimes the effect is selective. The politically-induced oil crisis of the early 1970s brought on worldwide recession with devastating effects in some countries, but made little difference to Australia's inbound and outbound markets. On the other hand the Asian economic crisis of the late 1990s disrupted a number of Australia's most valuable markets.

The 1973 oil crisis

Travel and tourism need oil and its products to survive. An oil crisis in the early 1970s brought about a worldwide recession and caused severe problems for US airlines introducing wide-bodied jet aircraft, but did not stop the growth of world tourism.

The crisis began in October 1973 during the Arab–Israeli war when members of the Organisation of Petroleum Exporting Countries (OPEC) cut supplies of oil and increased their prices drastically. OPEC placed an embargo on selling oil to the United States because of its support in the conflict for Israel and this lasted from 16 October 1973 to 18 March 1974. The Netherlands was also included in the original embargo and it was later extended to Portugal, South Africa and Rhodesia.

Thus the oil shortage began as a short-run political weapon. But it revealed a potential for obtaining higher prices. OPEC discovered that by acting as a cartel it was able to maintain the higher prices without surpluses accumulating and a competitive price war occurring. Therefore after the war was over it continued to restrict production and oil prices rose four times above the initial level.

The impact was felt throughout the world. In the United States, the original target of the OPEC countries, there was higher inflation and rationing of oil products, but other countries suffered much more because they relied more on oil imports. Britain recorded its worst ever current account deficit in 1974, while the additional oil bill as a percentage of the total import bill in the same year for Uruguay was 39, Thailand 26, South Korea 20 and Turkey 19 (Cook 1981).

Airlines suffered with the big increases in fuel prices and the effects of recession. In the United States, the larger of them were already in trouble absorbing the extra capacity brought about by the introduction of wide-bodied aircraft.

> *Soon the Arab oil embargo made the gas-guzzling jumbo jets all the more uneconomical. National Airlines got rid of its first two 747s within a year. At least one airline parked a 747 and rented it out for business meetings, on the ground. Pan Am tried to borrow money from the Shah of Iran* (Petzinger 1995, p. 21).

At the other end of the size spectrum, in the islands of the South Pacific, the crisis brought great uncertainty about the future of tourism, which up to that time in the 1970s had appeared a promising way of bringing prosperity to the remote island communities. Polynesian Airlines, based in Pago Pago and flying to Fiji, Tonga, Nieue and American Samoa, had to make do with whatever fuel was left over after the American armed forces quarantined most of the fuel stored on Samoa for its B52 bombers. Petrol was so short on the island that one Polynesian Airlines captain contemplated buying a horse to get from his quarters to the RSL Club (Cahill 2000).

Despite the economic hardships, and the undermining of consumer confidence, international tourism continued unabated. Every year of the 1970s, including the years of the oil panic, was a year of growth. Although inflation was high – reaching 14.4 per cent in the 1973–74 financial year – Australia escaped the worst effects of the oil crisis because of its high level of self-sufficiency in oil, most of it coming from the Bass Strait oilfields (Wilkinson 1983). Arrival and departure figures show no discernible effect on travel to and from Australia. Both increased solidly: the number of Australians travelling overseas tripled during the decade and the number of visitors from overseas doubled.

Asia 1997–1998

The economic crisis of the late 1990s brought about structural changes in the industries of a number of Asian countries, not all of them bad. In 1996 all major Asian markets showed growth to Australia, ranging from 5 per cent for Taiwan to 36 per cent for Korea. In mid-1997 what was to become a multi-nation economic crisis began in Thailand; by the end of the year the Thai tourism market to Australia had fallen 23 per cent. The following year it fell another 28 per cent.

As the crisis spread to other countries in both South East and North East Asia, economies contracted, employment and incomes were reduced and currencies depreciated against the Australian dollar, making it more expensive to visit (Tourism Forecasting Council 1997). The effect on travel to Australia was considerable. The South Korean market registered negative growth in November 1997 and for the next 13 months the fall was continuous. The market was down 72 per cent in 1998 over 1997. The Indonesian travel market to Australia fell 42 per cent in 1998, and Malaysia was down 22 per cent. The Thai market, first to fall, was also the first to show signs of recovery, registering a return to positive growth in November 1998 (Australian Bureau of Statistics/*Impact* monthly fact sheets January 1996–October 1999).[8] The South Korean economy also began to strengthen in late 1998 and this was reflected in a return to growth in the tourism flow from South Korea to Australia from January 1999.

While the crisis period had been a worrying time in the industries in the affected countries and in Australia, the World Tourism Organisation (1999e) saw good in the crisis, saying it had helped weed out fly-by-night operators and exposed poor management, weak marketing and other bad business practices. Most large service providers, such as hotels and airlines, were forced to restructure with shakeups regarding ownership, management, operations and market orientation. In the Philippines, the national airline went bankrupt.

Health crises

Travellers have good reason to keep away from places where they are likely to get sick, although many of them do, most often from food or water which may be contaminated or may upset them because they are different from what they are used to. Usually they are protected by vaccination or preventative medicines from serious disease. Doctors have access to advice on what is required for each destination. However, in early 2003 an event occurred that has no precedent in the era of modern mass tourism – the SARS crisis. The World Health Organisation said it had never experienced a comparable event in its history (www.world-tourism.org).

The SARS threat

The disease which later became known as Severe Acute Respiratory Syndrome (SARS) was first recognised in China at the end of February 2003. It was spread to other countries by travellers. The World Tourism Organisation noted that cases of transmission during hotel stays, in restaurants, places of entertainment, or even during aeroplane trips, made it a phenomenon that was perceived to be linked with tourism itself – even though local transmission (close contact in households, hospitals and other contexts) was much more prevalent (www.world-tourism.org).

On 15 March, the World Health Organisation issued a press release saying SARS, an 'atypical pneumonia', was a worldwide health threat, adding that it had received reports of more than 150 cases. Three weeks later, the number of reported cases had risen to 2,353, more than half of them in China, Taiwan and Singapore (www.who.int and Webb 2003). The WHO advised all travellers to be aware of the main symptoms and gave special advice to airlines on disinfection procedures. Some airlines issued protective face masks to flight crew and passengers. Controls were put in place at airports in an attempt to identify and quarantine people suspected of having contracted the disease. Hotels in infected areas took precautions with room attendants and chefs wearing masks. In the coming weeks, there was a constant stream of reports of cases in various parts of the world, and deaths. The WHO and/or governments issued notices advising travellers to avoid places of possible infection, including Toronto and the popular Asian destinations of Singapore and Hong Kong.

By 3 June, the number of cases of probable SARS cases reported to the World Health Organisation had reached 8,398, of whom 774 had died. Table 12.2, which lists countries reporting 10 or more probable cases, shows where the disease was concentrated.

The WHO listed Australia with five probable cases and no deaths. All five recovered from their illnesses and there was no local transmission of the disease.

By early June the disease was being contained in most places and the WHO had

Table 12.2 SARS cases at 3 June 2003

COUNTRY	PROBABLE CASES	DEATHS
China	5,329	334
Hong Kong	1,747	283
Taiwan	679	81
Canada	213	31
Singapore	206	31
United States	68	0
Vietnam	63	5
Philippines	12	2
Germany	10	0

(Source: World Health Organisation, www.who.int.)

withdrawn its advice to travellers 'to consider postponing all but essential travel' to destinations such as Singapore, Hong Kong and Toronto. Three weeks later the last travel restraint advice – on Beijing – was lifted and on 5 July, the WHO said it appeared the outbreak had been contained. The airline industry, which had cancelled 1,150 flights in Asia since mid-March, had begun to recover in June. Bookings began to pick up as travel advisories were withdrawn and cancelled flights were restored. By early July, it was reported that on some routes there was already a scarcity of seats (www.who.int, www.atc.australia.com and Easdown 2003).

At the height of crisis, much of the world travel and tourism industry, however, particularly in Asia and Australia, was in disarray. The industry in Hong Kong was devastated. Its international airline Cathay Pacific carried 8,000 passengers over Easter when it normally carried 40,000 and had to dig deep into its reserves to keep going. When government and industry leaders met in Perth for the annual Australian Tourism Export Council (ATEC) conference in late May there was certainly a sense of crisis. It had been reported that tourism to Australia had sustained its biggest month-on-month decline in three decades in April, with 40,600 fewer international arrivals than the month before. A survey of operators by ATEC had showed there was likely to be a 25 per cent decrease in international visitors for the June quarter compared with the previous year. And ATEC estimated that the combined effects of the Iraq conflict and SARS would result in a loss of export earnings of $2 billion because of the decline in inbound tourism (Easdown 2003, Allen 2003 and www.australiantradecommunity.com).

Most sectors of the Australian industry were affected, as the following examples demonstrate. Qantas Airways announced a reduction in its workforce, cut international services by 20 per cent and deferred delivery of a number of new aircraft. It also cut fares from the United States by 42 per cent in an effort to boost demand. Australia's largest hotel company, Accor Asia Pacific, launched a promotional campaign in Australia and New Zealand to try to find a substitute for lost international business. A *Travelweek* sampling of a cross section of travel agents across the country found that many were struggling to find the cash flow to pay staff and keep doors open. Victoria's biggest international drawcard, Phillip Island's fairy penguin parade, showed a declining number of tourist numbers in the first half of 2003 compared with the same period the previous year. Revenue in March fell $100,000 (Allen & Strutt 2003, Simpson 2003, Galacho 2003).

In the wider sphere, the World Tourism Organisation noted that the outbreak of SARS chiefly concerned the East Asia Pacific region, the only region in the world that has recently seen strong, sustained growth in its tourism flows (8 per cent in 2002). Moreover, the reality of the epidemic had been compounded by its intense coverage by the media, which had led to a 'veritable wave of paranoia' in certain countries. Travel in some Asian destinations with no or few infections suffered almost as much as the areas at the heart of the crisis (www.world-tourism.org).

▓ Social changes

New kinds of travel are devised as the result of the amount of time people have to take a break, of ethnic and demographic changes in population and the rising of middle classes in large markets with specific travel needs. They all influence the make-up of the travel and tourism industry as it adapts to new needs and wants.

Decrease in leisure time

The amount of time people have to travel obviously affects tourism flows and choices of destinations and products, and hence the make-up of the industry. Contrary to expectations of a few years ago, the 21st century is starting out as a period of declining time for pleasure travel. It used to be thought that economic advances would lead to a new golden age of leisure, but the opposite has been occurring.

A study by the Business Council of the World Tourism Organisation (1998–99) found that because of intense global competition reductions in the working week in the 18 countries surveyed had slowed considerably in the 1990s; in fact, working hours had increased for many employees. It predicted that travellers in the foreseeable future will be poor in time and rich in money.

The countries included in the study, which was conducted by Horwath UK, represented 73 per cent of the world's tourism spending. It was found very few governments were considering reductions in the length of the working week, increases in paid holiday entitlements or additional public holidays. The demand for holidays was unlikely to weaken, but the trend towards shorter, more frequent holidays would continue at an even faster rate.

Population shifts

Changes in population have a big influence on travel and tourism. Until World War II, the focus of Australian outbound travel had been Britain and Ireland. Migration from other countries was a significant factor in altering that pattern. In 1950 31.5 per cent of Australian international travellers went to Britain; by 1965 the proportion was down to 10.6 per cent. On the other hand travel to Italy, the source of the second biggest ethnic group in the country at the time, rose from 5.4 per cent in 1950 to 8.3 per cent in 1965 (Richardson 1999).

The ageing of a population is significant to travel and tourism. Many people travel when they have retired or when their children leave home. In many countries the proportion of older people is growing. Thus seniors travel is a very important market segment. Another age group in a position to dictate travel trends is made up of baby boomers, those born in a period of unusual population growth in Western countries after World War II. In 2000 they were aged between 41 and 54 and controlled a good part of the wealth in countries of high tourism spending.

New middle classes

The rise of a middle class is also a sign of an emerging travel market. At a seminar in Melbourne in 1997 the size of the travel market in India was said to be at least 156 million – 6 million super rich and 150 million in the 'middle band' (Australian Centre for Tourism and Hospitality 1997). The World Tourism Organisation expects China, where the middle class is also growing in size and affluence, to be the fourth biggest tourist generating country in the world by 2020.

The attitudes of travellers from these countries have been affected by globalisation. The 'emerging Indian' has been described as being different in outlook to the Indian of the past who lived with his parents, to whom he gave part of his salary, and saved what he could for his children and grandchildren. Now the attitude was if he had money, spend it, the children will look after themselves.

> *The emerging Indian does not live with his parents, but is independent. He and his wife both earn money, they are integrated into the global village and their horizons have been expanded by films, television and, increasingly the Internet.* Santa Barbara *and* Baywatch *are the television favourites of millions. This high exposure to different destinations, cultures and lifestyles has brought about a breaking of barriers, of scaling new standards,* (Merzban Majoo [Vice President Holiday Tours, SOTC Kuoni Travel Corp., Mumbai] in Australian Centre for Tourism and Hospitality 1997).

Customer preferences

Changes in customer preferences alter patterns of demand, which affect tourism businesses, some of which find it impossible to adjust. Destinations can be in and out of fashion as markets mature with a consequential turning towards individual travel and less standardised itineraries. In Chapter 3 large-scale trends which have had a profound effect on the industry in many parts of the world were discussed, including 'new tourism' the name given to the trend in developed countries towards more individualised itineraries. It was also noted how the increase in concern for the environment had brought about an interest in nature tourism and ecotourism.

A more localised change has been in Australian dining habits. It has had profound effects on the restaurant industry. In the late 1980s, haute cuisine and fine dining rooms of five-star hotels were at the top of the restaurant hierarchy. But change was already discernible in independent restaurants with Asian influences and Australian innovation replacing French styles such as nouvelle cuisine and cuisine minceur.

Consumer preference and the innovation of Australian chefs has brought about the revolution in dining, which favours lighter food, informality and cheaper prices over the fine dining of the haute cuisine. The average Australian now dines at seven different types of restaurants in a year, including Italian, Asian, Mexican and Greek (Collier 2001).[9]

▓ Wars and terrorism

World wars cause the cessation of most pleasure travel, while smaller wars usually have local effects, notably in reducing non-military travel in the war area. However, some members of the industry may prosper because of the demand for rest and recreation facilities. Australia, particularly Sydney, benefited from additional 'arrivals' as a result of the Vietnam war – 277,000 American troops were on leave in Australia from October 1967 to December 1971 (Vamplew & McLean 1987). The Gulf War of 1991 caused a severe drop in American outbound travel because of the fear of terrorism, but overall Australian tourism was not notably affected.

11 September 2001

The immediate effects on the world industry of the terrorist attacks in the United States on 11 September 2001[10] were much more widespread, causing a sharp fall-off of tourism traffic in many parts of the world, and threatening the survival of some of the world's largest airlines, with a ripple effect to most tourism sectors.

The air traffic system in the United States was shut down following the attacks and airports did not begin to reopen until two days later. United States airlines promptly announced cuts to schedules and shed nearly 100,000 jobs. The US Government announced a US$15 billion package to help them through the crisis. In Europe and in other parts of the world airlines were also reporting financial troubles. As time went on, some airlines were bankrupted (e.g. Swissair and Sabena) and some sought legal protection from creditors under US law (e.g. United Airlines, US Airways). Generally, the reaction was to shrink, to take aircraft out of service and cut capacity from the market to try to keep load factors up despite a severe drop in demand. Airlines also tried to reduce internal costs, although some external costs (e.g. for security) increased.

A year after the 11 September crisis the International Air Transport Association (2002) said the impact of the terrorist attacks had been the most severe of any crisis the airline industry had faced in its history. It had occurred at a time of economic downturn, signs of which had been detected by October 2000 and which had become 'clearly evident' by June 2001. Particularly hard-hit was premium traffic on major long-haul routes such as the North Atlantic and Transpacific. Total losses on international scheduled traffic for 2001 were $US12 billion and, when domestic travel was added, the total was $18 billion. Job losses totalled 200,000.

According to the World Tourism Organisation (2002a) the 11 September attacks 'shook the entire global tourism industry' and the airlines' problems had a 'tremendous impact' on the hotel sector and the distribution networks. The International Labor Organisation reported in early 2003 that about 6.6 million jobs had been lost in the travel and tourism industry in the previous two years (McMahon 2003).

The Australian industry had a different experience, largely as the result of the Ansett collapse happening within days of the US terrorist attacks. Qantas was able to switch capacity from troubled international routes to take up the slack in Australia left by Ansett. Additionally, Virgin Blue was able to establish itself as the only competitor to Qantas on domestic trunk routes – and as a viable airline with an expanding future. Its low-cost approach was one which succeeded elsewhere, despite the general trend. IATA noted the 'unprecedented growth' of the low-cost sector of the industry and said it would continue to challenge the full-service carriers.

In Australia, some resort areas and hotels benefited from a desire by some people to holiday at home, but other sectors (e.g. city hotels, travel agencies) were hard hit by the effects of both the terrorist attacks and the Ansett collapse. A patchy inbound performance in the following year and a half could be put down at least partly to the effect of the crisis (the other big factor was the continuing economic downturn). The effects were not all adverse. As the Japanese market recovered from the crisis, Australia was one of the beneficiaries and by the end of 2002 was experiencing a growth rate of 6–7 per cent, something that had not occurred since the mid-1990s. The rapidly growing Chinese market also helped offset losses elsewhere, particularly from New Zealand.

Bali bombings

The next major terrorist episode after the US attacks occurred less than 13 months later and directly attacked tourism and Australians. Bombings in bars in the crowded Kuta Beach area on the holiday island of Bali on 12 October 2002 killed 202 people, 88 of them Australians. The immediate impact on the Bali travel and tourism industry was very severe; within a week of the attacks hotel occupancy fell from 75 per cent to 14 per cent. International airlines cut capacity to Indonesia and wholesalers removed Bali and other Indonesian resorts from their programs.

Australians did not stop travelling overseas. In fact, outbound travel in the month after the bombings – November – was up 10.4 per cent over the same month the previous year, a significant increase even allowing for the effect of 11 September in 2001. As might be expected travel patterns did alter. For the most part, Australians avoided Bali, and fewer visited Singapore. On the other hand Australian travel increased to other parts of the world – Fiji, New Zealand, Vietnam and the US. The increase in numbers, however, was in the visit friends and relatives (VFR) and business categories; in numerical terms holiday travel was static (McMahon 2003). At the end of 2002, the World Tourism Organisation (2002b) expected the Australian market to Bali to recover within six to 12 months and a full recovery of Bali's $12 billion tourism industry to take 18 months to two years.

Iraq war 2003

Coalition forces attacked Iraq on 20 March and by 15 April the war was virtually over. By then the regime of Saddam Hussein had been deposed and the United States had moved to set up a new civil authority. On 1 May major combat throughout the country was said to be concluded.

While the war was confined to a relatively small area of the world and was over quickly, the fear of terrorist attacks as a result had an impact on international travel and serious consequences for some airlines and other travel companies. Air Canada filed for bankruptcy protection as a result of fall in demand (Webb 2003).

The SARS outbreak overlapped the period of the war and had a much more severe effect on the Australian travel and tourism industry. The industry paper *Travelweek* reported that wholesalers believed at that time that if the war ended quickly losses incurred by the industry should be minimal. The start of the war actually resulted in increased bookings for 'many companies' contacted, though others reported market flatness (James & Kaye 2003). However, this optimism was soon deflated as the effects of the SARS threat took hold on the Australian and international markets.

Long-term outlook

The terrorist attacks of 2001 and 2002, combining with an economic downturn in some of the major tourism-generating parts of the world, caused a contraction in international tourism. Despite this the overall upward trend continued. The year 2000 was regarded as an exceptional year; international arrivals throughout the world increased by 45 million. In 2001, arrivals decreased by 0.6 per cent, the first year of negative growth since 1982. However, the World Tourism Organisation (2002a) commented that the results for 2001 would have been in line with the trend observed over the past decade had it not been for the magnitude of the increase in 2000, which was much larger than in previous years (6.9 per cent). In 2002, arrivals increased by 3.2 per cent, taking the number to more than 700 million for the first time.

Travel is expected to continue to increase despite the problems in the world. In a mid-2002 study, the Boeing aircraft manufacturing company conceded the powerful effect of terrorism on the airline business because of fear and the higher costs of security, but said the major driver of long-term air travel growth was economic growth. The globalisation of world economics and societies continued and over a 20-year period increasing numbers of people would travel. It predicted air passenger traffic growth would average 4.9 per cent a year. Traffic in the Asia Pacific region would grow above the world average and its market share would increase from 14 per cent to 19 per cent (Boeing Commercial Airplane Company 2002).

Despite the severe impact on international tourism of the events of the first half of 2003 – the Iraq war and particularly the SARS outbreak – the World Tourism Organisation predicted that growth would recover and did not foresee any substantial changes to WTO's previous forecasts (www.world-tourism.org).

CAUSES OF TEMPORARY CHANGES

Temporary changes are discussed under two headings:
*   trade cycles
*   crises and disasters.

▓ Trade cycles

Trade cycles are regular oscillations in the levels of business activities over a period of years (Bannock, Baxter & Rees 1977). Severe cyclical change in business activity can cause great damage to components of the travel and tourism industry, including putting some companies out of business, but it usually does not fundamentally or permanently alter the industry as a whole. And in that sense it requires only temporary adjustment.

Cyclical changes describe measurable movements, usually of up and down, or more and less. Economic indicators, for example, depict such changes. So does supply and demand of those in various professions and occupational skills. If there is a glut in the supply of chefs, demand will be low, salaries will weaken and the number of applicants to TAFE colleges and other training schools will drop. A shortage in supply – or a sudden increase in demand – will produce the opposite effects.

Most cyclical changes do not involve any changes in structure. They occur within the operation of institutions rather than in their form. The duration of cyclical changes is always limited. Adjustment to them is therefore temporary and not the permanent adjustment made to long-term structural changes.

Business cycles

A business cycle is a period when economic activity changes from a peak (when production, wages and profits are high and unemployment low) to a trough when (when unemployment is high and production and profits are low) and back to a peak again (French & Saward 1984).

The economies of free-market countries are inherently unstable. Among the measures of economic activity which exhibit cyclical patterns of change are the rate of growth of GDP (accounting for recessions and recoveries), prices and wages, interest rates, and the behaviour of various kinds of markets. All this gives rise to the cyclical changes we all know – consumer confidence waxing and waning, interest rates rising and falling, share prices soaring or dropping, inflation rates going up or down.

The Australian economy was in recession in the early 1990s and this had a profound effect on Australian tourism, particularly the accommodation sector. The recession began in 1991 and followed a stockmarket collapse in 1987. Then came 1989 with a strike of airline pilots and a rise in interest rates. In one year rates on some properties went from 12 per cent to 24 per cent. The early 1990s were desperate years for a large section of the accommodation sector, with much cutting of prices to attract tourists from the new Asian markets. One consequence was a change of ownership in hotels. A number of big Japanese investors withdrew from the market and a number of Australian developers defaulted. A new flock of overseas owners, particularly from South East Asia, appeared to buy up properties at bargain prices.

By 2001 Australian owners were well back in the hotel market, accounting for 55 per cent of it. There was renewed interest from Asian buyers at the end of the year because of

DEFINITIONS
....

Demand and supply cycle

Adjustments to increase or reduce supply in accordance with demand. Supply never precisely matches demand.

Crisis

A time of danger, suspense or catastrophic change caused by an event where the root cause is, to some extent, self-inflicted through such problems as inept management structures and practices or a failure to adapt to change (Faulkner 2000).

Disaster

A situation where a destination or enterprise is confronted with sudden unpredictable catastrophic changes over which it has little control. These are events such as floods, earthquakes, cyclones, wars and terrorist activities.

a perception that the Australian market was at the bottom of the hotel cycle and it was a good time to buy (Jones Lang LaSalle Hotels press release, 19 December 2001).

The air transportation business is cyclical. Boyle (2002) writes of the 'cyclical nature of earnings that is common to all airlines' and the Boeing company said in July 2002 the world airline industry is in the midst of a 'dramatic short-term cycle'. The chief reason, it said, was the largest world economic downturn in a decade, which was negatively impacting on air travel and airline profitability before the terrorism events of September 2001 (Boeing Commercial Airplane Company 2002).

Demand–supply cycles

A **demand and supply cycle** describes the oscillations that occur as the result of attempts to provide the right measure of supply to meet demand. Supply never precisely matches demand. Either it falls short or it exceeds demand. But those who provide supply are careful to watch signals indicating the size of demand, and when those signals show more supply is wanted they respond by supplying more. And sometimes when there is oversupply they reduce supply.

Again accommodation provides a good example. A hotel may take three years to plan and build, often much longer, and the demand situation may change in the meantime. It is not uncommon for an oversupply to be provided, followed by a period of reduced rates while the hotels or other accommodation establishments compete for market share until demand catches up. Then some situation or event will trigger another round of building.

There was a spate of hotel building for the Olympic Games in Sydney in 2000, but late in the next year hotels there were having a hard time. One of the consequences was an acceleration of a trend to reduce supply by converting eastern Sydney hotels into residential hotels. By December 2001, conversions had taken 2,013 hotel rooms out of the market in two years (Byrne 2002).

■ Crises and disasters

There are similarities between crises and disasters, but Faulkner (2000) makes a useful distinction. He uses '**crisis**' to describe a situation where the root cause of an event is, to some extent, self-inflicted through such problems as inept management structures and practices or a failure to adapt to change. For example, an aircraft accident may be traced back to some form of management failure. Crisis management in the airline sector specifically includes steps intended to prevent the crisis happening, be it a tragic accident or something else (Kilicarslan et al. 2000).

A '**disaster**' is a situation where a destination or enterprise is confronted with sudden unpredictable catastrophic changes over which it has little control (Faulkner 2000). These are events such as floods, earthquakes, cyclones, wars and terrorist activities. Although their timing and often their nature cannot be predicted with certainty, they should still be expected. Faulkner and Vikulov (2000) say that 'one of the certainties' in the evolution of a tourist destination is that, at some point in its history one of its visitors will be a disaster, triggered by some extreme natural event (e.g. flood, cyclone, earthquake) or malevolent human action (e.g. war, pathological behaviour). Disasters can be confined to a company or affect a destination, a country, a region or the world. They can occur at any time, in any industry.

Both crises and disasters have what Faulkner calls 'transformational connotations'. They may have extreme negative outcomes, but they also offer opportunities (e.g. stimulus to innovation, recognition of new markets). He has synthesised the work of other authors to produce this list of key ingredients of them both:

- a triggering event, which is so significant that it challenges the existing structure, routine operations or survival of the organisation
- high threat, short decision time and an element of surprise and urgency
- a perception of an inability to cope among those directly affected
- a turning point, when decisive change, which may have both positive and negative connotations, is imminent
- characterised by fluid, unstable, dynamic situations.

So a crisis might arise from a single incident such as beach pollution or a widely reported crime or the collapse of a plane's undercarriage or patrons at an attraction contracting legionnaires' disease. Natural disasters such as cyclones, floods or fires can lay waste a destination or part of it. Disasters also strike at the enterprise level.

Australians are familiar with all of these. Pollution on the beaches of Sydney and Melbourne and the massacre of 35 people at Tasmania's Port Arthur in 1996 are examples of widely reported incidents which can deter tourism. Similarly, with natural disasters. In 1998, the Northern Territory town of Katherine lost almost all its tourism assets and nearby Katherine Gorge was badly damaged in a catastrophic flood brought on by Cyclone Les. In 2000 another cyclone devastated Broome's Cable Beach and the nearby Eco Beach Wilderness Resort. Across the continent in the same year, drought almost drained Victoria's Lake Eildon, with a devastating effect on tourism.

Some crises and disasters do bring about structural change. Earlier, major economic crises which affected a good part of the world or a region were discussed. But this section deals with more localised problems and, as with most disasters, the recovery can usually be managed without the industry being permanently changed.

Thus Port Arthur has long been back in business as one of Tasmania's prime tourism attractions. The environmentally sensitive Eco Beach Wilderness Resort, which was completely wiped out by winds up to 300 km an hour, took several years to restore because of the painstaking work undertaken to ensure that it has a better chance of survival if there is a next time. Karl Plunkett, its creator, decided to do his best not to be caught napping again. So the new eco-cabins were designed to be dismantled before any future cyclone hits and research was conducted on the ability of other structures to withstand cyclones of specified force (Plunkett 2002).

On the other hand, Katherine made quite a quick recovery from its problems of January 1998. As the operators cleaned up, restored their plant and equipment and eventually resumed operations, the local tourist association, with substantial help from the Northern Territory Tourist Commission, mounted a 'Katherine Back on Track' campaign, designed to counter perceptions that Katherine had been 'washed off the map'. The campaign was 'reasonably effective', according to Faulkner and Vikulov (2000). Despite the flood, the Katherine region had nearly 60,000 more guest nights in 1998 than in 1997 – a 15 per cent increase.

> *It may well be that, in some perverse way, the media exposure Katherine received as a consequence of the flood, enhanced its appeal as a destination* (p. 9).

The Melbourne Aquarium also made a quick recovery from the outbreak of legionnaires' disease which threatened to cripple the attraction before it had made its mark. To the contrary, as the case study shows, its first year attendance almost reached the pre-set target and the following year, the Aquarium was named the number one attraction in Victoria.

MANAGING CHANGE

Mastering gradual change

A sudden event, a crisis or disaster, immediately absorbs interest and provokes action. But the most common causes of structural change occur gradually and can sometimes reach a critical point without being recognised. There are four things people involved in travel and tourism organisations should do to deal with gradual change: expect it, prepare for it, evaluate it and respond to it.

1. Expect

Recognise that change is occurring. Martel (1988) says the expectation of continuity breeds inactivity. The response to good news is often, 'We should do nothing to interfere'. The response to bad news is frequently, 'There is nothing we can do'. The natural bias in favour of continuity must be overcome, to be replaced by the more accurate view that continuity is rare and when it does occur it is usually short-lived. Change is the more common experience.

2. Prepare

Managers should try to anticipate changes and how they are likely to develop. This means keeping their management information systems finely tuned for information about changes in the business environment, e.g. economic, social and environmental factors, regulations, new competition or customer preferences.

3. Evaluate

This means assessing the direction, magnitude, pace and duration of change. These factors often can be difficult to evaluate at first, which means continuing to work on the problem. When the severity of the Asian economic crisis was first indicated, it took several tries for the Tourism Forecasting Council technical team to get right the scale of the effect on Australian tourism. Managers should remain cool. Even a worldwide event of great magnitude may not affect their destination or business very much. The oil crisis of the 1970s did not have a great effect on Australian tourism.

4. Respond

Martel warns against managers trying to 'ride out' changes. Instead, they should think of how to use them, how to exploit them, how to 'make them a partner'. Responses can take many forms. Changes in markets may cause a transport company, an airline or coach company, to switch vehicles to other markets and/or destinations. Qantas moved planes from international to domestic services in 2001 when international travel declined but the collapse of Ansett created more business for Qantas at home. This may seem an obvious response, but behind it was close monitoring of situations and good planning for whatever might occur.

Tour operators can switch their business, also. But accommodation establishments have less flexibility. They cannot easily change capacity or even their market positioning. They have to consider reducing staff if traditional markets decline and substitutes cannot be found. Competitive challenges may require price marketing or innovative product development. Technological change may well bring opportunities, but will require management effort and resources to exploit. Regulatory changes can alter the shape of the playing field, as happened with deregulation of air transport in the early 1990s, offering opportunities and dangers.

Those kind of responses take place in clear-cut cases where market changes are only too apparent. There are other cases where the results of change which has been coming for some time may manifest themselves in abrupt and emotional action, like the sudden collapse of Ansett. Another kind of change may not be abrupt although it may be obvious; the difficult part is assessing it properly, as in the early stages of the Asian economic crisis.

The need for mechanisms

Management needs mechanisms that can cope with the identification and evaluation of gradual change and also the completely unexpected. The first should be developed out of the planning process, the second from a structured method for preparing for crisis and disasters described below.

The planning process incorporates reviews which examine details and trends in the political and regulatory outlook, the economy, technology the industry, markets, consumer preferences, competitors and so on. They provide the indicators which, properly inter-preted, can alert managers that change is occurring. The collection of information on these topics should be ongoing and reviews made at regular intervals, not only for planning purposes. How this is done depends on management processes of the individual organisation. For example, it may be prudent to have prepared a monthly summary to be examined at a regular meeting of senior managers, who could then initiate responsive action if they saw fit. Executives in some Australian travel and tourism companies meet weekly to assess information which may lead to change.

Preparing for crises and disasters

When the crisis or disaster is on a national or international scale it is usual for the industry in Australia to look to governments, or their agencies, to produce information on which they can make decisions. The Tourism Forecasting Council worked very hard once the Asian economic crisis started to provide guidance to the travel and tourism industry and investors.

When the dual crisis of the terrorist attacks on the United States and the Ansett collapse occurred in September 2001, Commonwealth Government agencies again moved quickly to keep the industry informed. They were helped by having the Internet to reach industry managers and the Australian Tourist Commission's established expertise in com-municating with the industry via that medium.

However, although governments can offer guidance, the companies themselves must be prepared for crises and disasters. As a matter of course – and as a first step – they should have risk management procedures in place. These are required under accreditation programs discussed in Chapter 10 and include policies, procedures and planning to minimise the likelihood of risk to human, physical and/or informational resources.

They include:
- emergency procedures
- known hazard management procedures in the workplace (physical, chemical and biological)
- maintenance of safe storage of goods, plant and equipment, particularly of perishables
- workplace safety procedures known by all employees
- prominently displayed emergency and evacuation procedure guides.

Preparing for a crisis or disaster raises the level of risk to be provided for and requires more elaborate planning.

Disaster management model

Faulkner and Vikulov have developed a generic disaster management model for tourism destinations. It is reproduced in slightly adapted form in Table 12.3. This was produced following the Katherine floods in 1998.

Table 12.3 Tourism disaster management framework

PHASE IN DISASTER PROCESS	ELEMENTS OF THE DISASTER MANAGEMENT RESPONSE	PRINCIPAL INGREDIENTS OF THE DISASTER MANAGEMENT STRATEGIES
1. Pre-event When action can be taken to prevent or mitigate the effects of potential disasters	**Precursors** • Appoint a Disaster Management team (DMT) Leader and establish DMT • Identify relevant public/private sector agencies/organisations • Establish coordination/consultative framework and communication systems • Develop, document and communicate Disaster Management Strategy • Educate industry stakeholders, employees, customers and community • Agree on, and commit to, activation protocols	• Risk assessment • Assessment of potential disasters and their probability of occurrence • Development of scenarios on the genesis and impacts of potential disasters • Disaster contingency plans
2. Prodomal When it is apparent that a disaster is imminent	**Mobilisation** • Warning systems (including general mass media) • Establish disaster management command centre • Activate communication tree • Secure facilities and office files • Switch communication systems • Relocate mobile resources • Relocate perishable food stocks	**Disaster Contingency Plans** • Identify likely impacts and groups at risk • Assess community and visitor capabilities to cope with impacts • Articulate the objectives of individual (disaster specific) contingency plans • Identify actions necessary to avoid or minimise impacts at each stage
3. Emergency The effect of the disaster is felt and action is necessary to protect people and property	**Action** • Rescue/evacuation procedures • Emergency accommodations and food supplies • Medical/health services • Monitoring and communication systems	• Devise strategic priority (action) profiles for each phase • Ongoing review and revision in the light of a) experience b) changes in organisational structures and personnel c) changes in the environment Cont . . .

	Table 12.3 continued		
	PHASE IN DISASTER PROCESS	ELEMENTS OF THE DISASTER MANAGEMENT RESPONSE	PRINCIPAL INGREDIENTS OF THE DISASTER MANAGEMENT STRATEGIES
	4. Intermediate A point where the short-term needs of people have been addressed and the main focus of activity is to restore services and the community to normal	Recovery • Damage and audit/monitoring system • Clean-up and restoration • Office facilities and communication support • 'Buddy system'/task force for operator counselling/support • Media communication strategy	
	5. Long-term (recovery) Continuation of previous phase, but items that could not be attended to quickly are attended at this stage: post-mortem, self-analysis, healing	**Reconstruction and reassessment** • Repair of damaged infrastructure • Rehabilitation of environmentally damaged areas • Counselling victims • Restoration of business/consumer confidence and development of investment plans • Debriefing to promote input to revisions of disaster strategies	
	6. Resolution Routine restored or new improved state establishment	Review Reappraisal of marketing, planning and policy regime	

(Source: Faulkner and Vikulov (2000), p. 15.)

The role of the media

The media plays a critical role in crisis/disaster situations and needs to be managed. Sometimes this is not possible, at least for a time, because as Faulkner (2000) notes,

> . . . *disaster situations provide a fertile ground for misinformation, as disruptions to communications systems combine with publication deadlines to inhibit the verification of reports and the ratings game fosters sensationalism. Media reports*

have the potential to have a devastating impact on disaster affected destinations because pleasure travel is a discretionary item . . . (p. 12).

On the other hand the media often plays a central role providing important information to tourists during the emergency and in the recovery stage when other sectors of the industry and the public need to be informed about the restoration of services. Media management was an important part of the Melbourne Aquarium's recovery program during a crisis in 2000. It is described next.

CASE STUDY

The Melbourne Aquarium crisis

The Melbourne Aquarium, located on the northern bank of the Yarra River in a swirl of modern architecture, was an eye-catching addition to the Victorian capital's attractions when it opened on 17 January 2000. A few weeks later it had received enormous media exposure for the wrong reasons – an outbreak of legionnaires' disease spread from its water-cooling towers. The critical period was 13–27 April when more than 74,000 people attended the attraction. Of these about 100 were diagnosed with the disease.

A five-step crisis management plan was put into operation to control the situation and eventually get the aquarium back on track to attract some million visitors in its first year. The objective of the plan was to ensure that the danger to health was removed and then to convince staff and potential visitors that it was perfectly safe to visit the aquarium. Elements of the plan were to:

1. manage the problem
2. manage the message
3. manage the media
4. manage the staff
5. manage the management team.

Managing the problem

The company had to act decisively to fix the problem without any room for doubt – and to be seen to be doing so. First the towers were 'doused' and a new tower cleaning regime was introduced. This far exceeded the requirements of the existing regime which, in itself, exceeded government guidelines. The company offered to close the building, but the Department of Human Services advised that this was not necessary. Two of Australia's leading experts on legionnaires' disease were brought in to advise on appropriate action. They recommended removing the water cooling towers altogether and replacing the system with air cooling. The company did this at a cost of $500,000, thus removing any chance of a repetition of the disaster.

Managing the message

There was persistent media and public interest in this process and in everything associated with the tragedy. To ensure that the company's media policy was followed without a hint of inconsistency it decided there must be only one spokesperson. The policy was:

- the company accepted the blame for what had happened
- as soon as new information was available, it would call a press conference to ensure the general public knew all the facts
- its message was to be totally open and honest. All details would be made available.

Managing the media

The media was given access to the entire complex at any time. Requests for interviews were never refused.[11]

Managing the staff

Staff members were kept informed of events by senior management who spoke to each staff member informally three times a day. Staff knew of announcements before they were made public. They were also provided with medical advice and help in dealing with family, friends and the public.

Managing the management team

In hindsight, this is one area that Tom Smith (general manager, marketing and public affairs) felt could have been improved. A two-person team ran the public relations part of management plan, working together rather than in rotation. Among other things, they had to deal with eight death threats. In worrying about everyone else they did not worry about their own needs. The fatigue factor could have impacted on decision making. Smith says it did not but it would have been wiser for the two to have worked in rotation and had assistance.

The relaunch

The Aquarium was relaunched in July, after three months of great difficulty. The relaunch was delayed while people with legionnaires' disease were still in hospital. It involved:

- an open apology to the people of Victoria/Australia via full page letters in the press
- promotion by association, using high profile figures at the Aquarium, e.g. a press conference with a well-known footballer

- generic advertising mentioning the fact that there had been a problem and what had been done about it
- promotional advertising.

Results of the management process

The results of the program speak for themselves. The projected attendance for Year One was almost achieved – the projection was 980,000 and actual attendance was 950,000. At the 2001 Victorian tourism awards, the Melbourne Aquarium was named the number one attraction in the state (Smith 2002).

INDUSTRY PROFILE

GEOFF DIXON CHIEF EXECUTIVE OFFICER, QANTAS AIRWAYS

I am responsible for the operations of Qantas, Australia's largest domestic and international airline. Qantas was founded in 1920, employs about 35,000 people and operates a fleet of more than 180 aircraft across a network spanning about 142 destinations in 32 countries. Qantas carried about 27 million passengers in 2002.

How did I get here?

I was born and grew up in Wagga Wagga, a town that is half-way between Sydney and Melbourne. My first job was as a journalist on Wagga Wagga's newspaper, the *Daily Advertiser*. After several years in journalism, I worked in the mining industry in the Northern Territory before joining the Federal Government's Australian Information Service. I worked in Australia and then overseas, with postings to the Australian Missions in The Hague, New York and San Francisco.

I began my career in the aviation industry in 1987 when I joined Australian Airlines as General Manager Marketing and Corporate Affairs. Four years later, I moved to Ansett as Director Marketing and Industry Sales. I joined Qantas in 1994 and, over the next seven years, I had responsibility for all commercial activities, including worldwide sales and marketing, network development, revenue management, fleet planning, cabin crew, customer service, product development and airline alliances. I was appointed Chief Executive Officer of Qantas in March 2001.

What do I like about my job?

Aviation is one of the most complex, exciting and dynamic industries in the world. While this means there is a lot of pressure on airline executives, it also means that every day is fascinating. I take particular pride in working for Qantas, because – over the past 83 years – it has built a global reputation for excellence in safety, operational reliability, engineering and maintenance and customer service.

SUMMARY

The travel and tourism industry has to deal with two kinds of change – structural change which is permanent and temporary change which can be cyclical or the result of a one-off event. Structural change can be also result from an event but is more likely to be gradual, occurring over years. Businesses come and go as the external environment changes, there are mergers and takeovers, the influence of particular companies strengthens or wanes. Yet it can be shown that the industry as a whole is extremely resilient even in very severe adverse situations.

Seven causes of structural change are discussed:

1. **Globalisation** Communications technology is making the world one big marketplace, with effects on governments and businesses as well as consumers. In the 1990s, as a result of competition in the globalised markets, governments resorted to economic disengagement, manifested by privatisation, liberalisation and deregulation.

2. **Competition** It is constantly at work, helping to reshape the industry, causing some companies to reduce their businesses, others to disappear, others to flourish, perhaps through mergers or acquisitions. As an example, it has reduced the multi-state express coach industry in Australia to one major group.

3. **Economic crises** Their effect on travel markets is sometimes selective. The politically-induced oil crisis of the early 1970s brought on worldwide recession with devastating effects in some countries, but made little difference to Australia's inbound and outbound markets. On the other hand the Asian economic crisis of the late 1990s disrupted a number of Australia's most valuable markets.

4. **Health crises** The SARS outbreak of 2003 showed that health crises have the capacity to devastate the travel and tourism industry in a number of countries. SARS, described as an 'atypical pneumonia', was spread from China, where it originated, through travel and was described by the World Health Organisation as a worldwide health threat. It was contained after a little more than three months, but in that time threatened the existence of sections of the industry.

5. **Social changes** New kinds of travel are devised as the result of the amount of time people have to take a break, of ethnic and demographic changes in population and the rising of middle classes in large markets with specific travel needs. They all influence the make-up of the travel and tourism industry as it adapts to new needs and wants.

6. **Customer preferences** Changes in customer preferences alter patterns of demand, which affect tourism businesses, some of which find it impossible to adjust. Notable changes have resulted in 'new tourism' and the rising interest in nature tourism and ecotourism.

7. **Wars, terrorism** World wars cause the cessation of most pleasure travel, while smaller wars usually have local effects, notably in reducing non-military travel in the war area. Terrorist attacks in the US in 2001 and Bali in 2002 have had very severe effects on tourism and the industry. The World Tourism Organisation said the US attacks 'shook

the entire global tourism industry' and within a week of the Bali bombings hotel occupancy fell from 75 per cent to 14 per cent.

Causes of temporary changes are (1) cyclical change and (2) crises and disasters. Severe cyclical change can cause great damage to components of the travel and tourism industry, including putting some companies out of business, but it usually does not fundamentally or permanently alter the industry as a whole. Business and demand-supply cycles are familiar economic phenomena. Crises and disasters have 'transformational connotations'. They may have extreme negative outcomes, but they also offer opportunities (e.g. stimulus to innovation, recognition of new markets).

Change can be managed. There are four steps in mastering gradual change: expect change, prepare for change, evaluate change and respond to change. Temporary change can also be anticipated. A disaster management framework includes having a management team in place and procedures agreed to before any crisis or disaster occurs.

QUESTIONS

1. What are the essential differences between structural and temporary change?
2. How did globalisation influence the collapse of Ansett Australia?
3. In respect to tourism, how has the Internet affected (a) consumers, (b) government-to-business relationships, (c) business-to-business relationships?
4. Do you think that technology is more of a threat or an opportunity for the traditional travel agency system? Give reasons for your answer.
5. What are the main types of social changes that affect tourism? Give examples.
6. Is terrorism causing structural change in the world travel and tourism industry or are its effects likely to be temporary?
7. What were the causes of the oil crisis of the early 1970s? What were its effects on (a) the world, and (b) Australia?
8. What are trade cycles and how do they affect Australian travel and tourism?
9. How does Faulkner differentiate between crises and disasters?
10. What are the common factors in managing gradual change and crises/disasters? Provide details.

REFERENCES

Aboriginal and Torres Islander Commission (ATSIC) and Office of National Tourism 1997, *The National Aboriginal Tourism Industry Strategy – a summary*, Canberra.

Adams, PD & Parmenter, BR 1991, *The Medium Term Significance of International Tourism for the Australian Economy*, Bureau of Tourism Research, Canberra.

——1993, *The Medium Term Significance of International Tourism for the State Economies,* Bureau of Tourism Research, Canberra.

Agarwal, S 1994, 'The resort cycle revisited: implications for resorts', in *Progress in Tourism, Recreation and Hospitality Management*, vol. 5, eds CP Cooper and A Lockwood, John Wiley & Sons, Chichester, England, pp. 194–208.

Ahmed, ZU 1994, 'Determinants of the Components of a State's Tourist Image and Their Marketing Implications', *Journal of Hospitality & Leisure Marketing*, vol. 2(1), pp. 55–68.

Air Transport Action Group 2000, *Aviation & the Environment*, produced with the help of the International Air Transport Association, Geneva.

Allaby, M 1986, *Ecology Facts*, Hamlyn Publishing, Twickenham, England.

Allcock, A 1999, 'Introduction', in *Valuing Tourism, Methods and Techniques*, Occasional Paper No. 28, eds K Corcoran, A Allcock, T Frost, & L Johnson, Bureau of Tourism Research, Canberra.

Allen, L 2003, 'Journey into disarray', *The Australian Financial Review*, 23 May, p. 80.

Allen, L & Strutt, S 2003, 'Tourism contingency plans', *The Australian Financial Review*, 10 May, p. 22.

Archer, B 1996, 'Economic Impact Analysis', Research Notes and Reports, *Annals of Tourism Research* vol. 23(03), p. 704.

Atherton, TC & Atherton, TA 1998, *Tourism, Travel and Hospitality Law*, LBC Information Services, Sydney.

Australian Bureau of Statistics 1994, *A Guide to the Australian National Accounts*, Canberra.

——1997a, *Framework for the Collection and Publication of Tourism Statistics,* Canberra.

——1997b, *Australian Transport and the Environment*, Canberra.

——1999a, *Australian National Accounts, State Accounts*, Canberra.

——1999b, *Attendance at Selected Cultural Venues, Australia*, Canberra.

——2000a, *Australian National Accounts: Tourism Satellite Account, 1997–98*, Canberra.

——2000b, *Australia Now – A Statistical Profile: Conserving and protecting diversity*, Canberra.

——2000c, *Australia Now – A Statistical Profile: Protection of heritage places of national and international significance*, Canberra.

——2001, *Museums, Australia*, Canberra.

——2002, *Australian National Accounts: Tourism Satellite Account, 2000–01, Main Features*, Canberra.

Australian Centre for Tourism and Hospitality 1997, *Report of seminar 'India, the next tourism growth market for Australia'*, Melbourne, 26 August.

Australian Concise Oxford English of Current English 1987, ed. GW Turner, Oxford University Press, Melbourne, reprinted 1990.

Australian Heritage Commission 1994, *National Estate, National Parks, World Heritage, National Trust . . . What's The Difference?* Canberra.

——1998, *The National Estate . . . our special places*, Canberra.

Australian Local Government Association 1999, *Submission to the Inquiry into Infrastructure and the Development of Australia's Regional Areas*, prepared for the House of Representatives Standing Committee on Primary Industries and Regional Services, Canberra.

Australian Quality Council 1997, *Assessment Criteria Awards 1997*, Sydney.

Australian Tourism Accreditation Association 2001, *The Australian Tourism Accreditation System*, Perth.

Australian Tourist Commission 1997, *MICE Market Brief: Working Document*, Sydney.

Bannock, G Baxter, R & Rees, R 1977, *A Dictionary of Economics*, Penguin Books, Harmondsworth, England, first published 1972.

Barrow, C J 2000, *Social Impact Assessment. An introduction*, Arnold, a member of the Hodder Headline Group, London.

Beeton, S 1998, *Ecotourism: A practical guide for rural communities*, Landlinks Press, Melbourne.

Beeton, S & Benfield, R 2001, *Beyond Sustainability: Demarketing as an Environmental Policy Tool*, paper presented at 2001 CAUTHE Conference, Canberra.

Biech, E 1994, *TQM for Training*, McGraw-Hill Inc., New York.

Blank, U 1989, *The Community Tourism Industry Perspective*, Venture Publishing, State College, Pennsylvania.

Boeing Commercial Airplane Company 2002, *Current Market Outlook*, Seattle, July.

Bolin, R & Greenwood, T 2003, *Tourism Businesses in Australia,* Occasional Paper No. 34, Bureau of Tourism Research, Canberra.

Boyle, J 2002, 'Dixon revs up Qantas with $13bn expansion plan', *The Australian Financial Review*, 17 May, pp. 1, 80–81.

Boyle, J & Koutsoukis, J 2001, 'Ansett faces grim ride as lifelines take flight', *The Australian Financial Review*, 13 September, p. 21.

Brackenbury, M 1993, 'Trends and Challenges Beyond the Year 2000', in *Round Table on Beyond the Year 2000*, World Tourism Organisation, 10th General Assembly, Madrid, pp. 14–20.

Braithwaite, R 1998, 'Government Tourism Program in Australia', *Annals of Tourism Research*, vol. 25(4), October, pp. 976–978.

Braithwaite, R Reynolds, P & Pongracz, G 1996, *Wildlife Tourism at Yellow Waters*, Final report to the Federal Department of Tourism, Australian Nature Conservation Agency and Gagudju Association Inc., Darwin.

Brown, G & Essex, S 1997, 'Sustainable Tourism Management: Lessons from The Edge of Australia', *Journal of Sustainable Tourism*, vol. 5(4), pp. 284–306.

Brunt, P & Courtney, P 1999, 'Host Perceptions of Sociocultural Impacts', *Annals of Tourism Research*, vol. 26(3), pp. 315–493.

Buchanan, I 1999, *Tourism's Economic Contribution, 1996–97*, Research Paper No. 5, Bureau of Tourism Research, Canberra.

Buckby, M Burgan, B & Molloy, J 1993, *The Economic Significance of Alpine Resorts*, The Centre for South Australian Economic Studies, in association with Stephen McDonald, KMPG Peat Marwick Management Consulting Services.

Bull, A 1995, *The Economics of Travel and Tourism*, 2nd edn, Longman, Melbourne.

Bureau of Industry Economics 1979, *Economic Significance of Tourism in Australia*, Research Report No. 4, Australian Government Publishing Service, Canberra.

Bureau of Tourism Research 2000, *International Visitor Survey*, Canberra.

——2001, *Tourism's Indirect Effects 1997–98*, Canberra.

Byrne, M 2002, 'Hockey seeks tourism boost', *The Australian Financial Review*, 3 May, p. 17.

Cahill, D 2000, Aviation management consultant, former Polynesian Airlines pilot, pers. comm., 17 April.

Chamberlain, K 1996a, *Trends and Opportunities in Asia Pacific Tourism*, paper presented at Tourism Executive Development Program, Southern Cross University, Ballina (NSW), June.

——1996b, *Carrying Capacity*, paper presented at Tourism Executive Development Program, Southern Cross University, Ballina (NSW), June.

——1997, *International tourism: trends, opportunities and threats*, paper presented at Tourism Executive Development Program, Southern Cross University, Ballina (NSW), June.

Charlton, C & Essex, S 1994, 'Public Sector Policies', in *Tourism Marketing and Management Handbook*, 2nd edn, eds SF Witt & L Moutino, Prentice Hall International, Hemel Hempstead, pp. 46–59.

Chirgwin, S & Hughes, K 1997, 'Ecotourism: The participants' perceptions', *The Journal of Tourism Studies*, vol. 8(2), December.

Clark, I & Larrieu, L 1998, *Indigenous tourism in Victoria: products, markets and futures*, paper presented at 'Symbolic Souvenirs', a one-day conference on cultural tourism with the Centre for Cross-Cultural Research, ANU, Canberra.

Clark L 1988, 'Planning for Tourism in North Queensland: A local government response, *Frontiers of Australian tourism: The search for new perspectives in policy development and research*, Bureau of Tourism Research, Canberra, pp. 77–78.

Clarke, J 2000, 'Tourism brands: An exploratory study of the brands box model', *Journal of Vacation Marketing*, vol. 6(4), pp. 329–345.

Collier, K 2001, 'Variety of flavours on our plates: café culture brings lighter, more casual dining', *Herald Sun*, 27 November, p. 12.

Collins, C 1994, 'Lack of top-class resorts threatens Japanese tourism', *The Australian*, 19 October, p. 3.

Coltman, MM 1989, *Tourism Marketing*, Van Nostrand Reinhold, New York.

Cook, C 1981, ed., *Pears Cyclopaedia*, 89th Edition, London.

Cooper, C 1989, 'Tourist product life cycle', in *Tourism Marketing and Management Handbook*, eds SF Witt & L Moutino, Prentice Hall International, Hemel Hempstead, pp. 577–581.

Cooper, C Fayos-Sola, E & Pedro, A 2001, 'Globalization, Tourism Policy and Tourism Education', in *tedQual*, World Tourism Organisation and Themis, Madrid, No. 4, pp. 7–12.

Coopers & Lybrand 1996, *Western Australian Tourism Development Strategy Technical Report*, Western Australian Tourism Commission, Perth.

Cordato, A 1993, *Australian Travel & Tourism Law*, 2nd edn, Butterworths, Sydney.

CRC for Sustainable Tourism 1999a, Fact Sheet, March, Canberra.

—— 1999b, *National Online Scoping Study*, Department of Industry, Science and Resources, Canberra.

Crotts, JC 1996, 'Theoretical Perspectives on Tourist Criminal Victimisation', *The Journal of Tourism Studies*, vol. 7, no. 1, May.

CSIRO 2000, *Inquiry into Global Warming*, Submission to the Senate Environment, Communications, Information Technology and the Arts Reference Committee, Melbourne.

Dadgostar, B & Isotalo, RM 1995, 'Content of City Destination Images for Near-Home Tourists', *Journal of Hospitality & Leisure Marketing,* vol. 3(2), pp. 25–34.

Dale, D & Oakland, J 1994, *Quality Improvement Through Standards*, 2nd edn, Stanley Thornes (Publishers) Ltd, Cheltenham, England.

Davis, J Allen, J & Cosenza R 1988, 'Segmenting Local Residents by their Interests and Opinions towards Tourism', *Journal of Travel Research*, 27(2), pp. 2–8.

Deer, L 1999, *Benchmarking Energy Efficiency in the Hotel Industry*, Proceedings of Asia–Pacific Economic Cooperation (APEC) Tourism Working Group Seminar, April, Cairns, pp. 22–25.

de Keijzer, K 2001, dKO Architecture Pty Ltd, pers. comm., 18 November.

Department of Industry, Science and Resources 1999, *Cultural Tourism*, fact sheet, Canberra.

——2000a, *Leading the Way, Business Plan 2000–2001*, Sport and Tourism Division, Canberra.

——2000b, *tourism dotcom*, A National Online Tourism Strategy, Canberra.

Department of Tourism 1994, *National Ecotourism Strategy*, Canberra.

——1995a, *A National Strategy for the Meetings, Incentives, Conventions and Exhibitions Industry*, Canberra.

——1995b, *The Yield from Inbound Tourism*, Occasional Paper No. 3, Canberra.

Department of Tourism, Sport and Recreation (Tasmania) 1994, *Ecotourism: Adding value to tourism in natural areas*, A discussion paper on nature based tourism, July, Hobart.

Doswell, R 1997, *Tourism: How effective management makes the difference*, Butterworth-Heinemann, Oxford.

Dowling, J 1993, 'Honeymoon is over for Japanese tourists', *The Australian Financial Review*, 5 August, pp. 1 and 9.

Doxey, GV 1975, 'A Causation Theory of Visitor Resident Irritants: Methodology and Research Inferences' *Travel and Tourism Research Association, Sixth Annual Conference Proceedings*, San Diego, pp. 195–198.

Driml, S & Common, M 1996, 'Ecological Economics Criteria for Sustainable Tourism: Application to the Great Barrier Reef and Wet Tropics World Heritage Areas, Australia', *Journal of Sustainable Tourism*, vol. 4(1), pp. 3–16.

Drucker, Peter F 1974, *Management: Tasks, Responsibilities, Practices*, Harper & Row Publishers Inc, New York.

——1998, 'Management's new paradigms', in *Forbes Global Business & Finance,* 5 October, pp. 52–68.

Dwyer, L & Forsyth, P 1996, 'Economic Impacts of Cruise Tourism In Australia', *The Journal of Tourism Studies*, vol. 7(2), December, pp. 36–43.

Dwyer, L Forsyth, P Madden, J & Spurr, R 2000, 'Economic Impact of Inbound Tourism under Different Assumptions about the Macroeconomy', *Current Issues in Tourism*, vol. 3(4), pp. 325–363.

Easdown, G 2003. 'Travel bug bites back as SARS wanes', *Herald Sun*, 5 June, p. 47.

Echtner, C & Jamal, T 1997, 'The Disciplinary Dilemma of Tourism Studies', *Annals of Tourism Research*, vol. 21(1), pp. 868–883.

Edwards, S McLaughlin W & Ham, S 1998, *Comparative Study of Ecotourism Policy in the Americas*, Department of Resource Recreation and Tourism, University of Idaho in association with the Inter-Sectoral Unit for Tourism, Organization of American States.

Environment Australia 1997, *Incentives for the conservation of biological diversity–Australia*, Canberra.

Faulkner, W 2000, *Towards a Framework for Tourism Disaster Management*, companion paper to Faulkner & Vikulov 2000, paper presented at CAUTHE conference, LaTrobe University, Mt. Hotham, Victoria.

Faulkner, W Pearce, P Shaw, R & Weiler, B 1995, 'Tourism Research in Australia', in *Tourism Research and Education in Australia*, Proceedings from Tourism and Educators Conference, Gold Coast 1994, Bureau of Tourism Research, Canberra, pp. 3–25.

Faulkner, W & Vikulov, S. 2000, *Katherine Washed Out One Day, Back on Track the Next: A Post-Mortem of a Tourism Disaster*, paper presented at CAUTHE conference, LaTrobe University Mt. Hotham, Victoria.

Federal–State Relations Committee 1998, *Australian Federalism: The Role of the States*, Parliament of Victoria, Melbourne.

Fodness, D 1994, 'Measuring Tourist Motivation', *Annals of Tourism Research*, vol. 21(3), pp. 555–581.

Foster, DJ 2000a, *Monitoring Regional Tourism Activity*, paper presented at CAUTHE conference, LaTrobe University, Mt. Hotham, Victoria.

——2000b, 'Ensuring Service Excellence in the Australian Tourism Industry', in *Proceedings of the First International Research Conference of Organisational Excellence in the Third Millenium*, ed. RL Edgeman, Estees Park, Colorado.

——2001, 'The Customer's Perception of Tourism Accreditation', in *Proceedings of the Fifth International and Eighth National Conference on Quality Management*, February, Melbourne.

Fredericks, I & McCallum, D 1995, *International Standards for Environmental Management Systems, ISO14000*, Canadian Environmental Protection, August, www.mgmt14k.com/ems.htm.

Fredline, E & Faulkner, B 2000, 'Host Community Reactions, A Cluster Analysis', *Annals of Tourism Research*, vol. 27(3), pp. 763–784.

French, D & Saward, H 1984, *A Dictionary of Management*, revised edition, Pan Books, London.

Frew, E & Shaw, R 1996, *Profiling the Industrial Tourism Phenomenon*, Proceedings of the Australian Tourism and Hospitality Research Conference, ed. Garry Prosser, Bureau of Tourism Research.

Frost, T 1999, ' Economic Analysis and Tourism', in *Valuing Tourism: Methods and Techniques*, Occasional Paper No. 28, eds K Corcoran, A Allcock, T Frost, & L Johnson, Bureau of Tourism Research, Canberra.

Galacho, O 2003, 'Saddam and SARS take toll on tourism: Penguins left high and dry', *Herald Sun*, 9 May, p. 39.

Garrod, B & Fyall, A 2000, 'Managing Heritage Tourism', *Annals of Tourism Research*, vol. 27(3), pp. 682–708.

Gartner, W 1996, *Tourism Development: Principles, Processes and Policies*, John Wiley & Sons Inc, New York.

Geddes, M 2002, Manager, Tourism Development Group, South Australian Tourism Commission, pers. comm., 21 March.

Gee, CY Makens, JC & Choy, DJL 1989, *The Travel Industry*, 2nd edn, Van Nostrand Reinhold, New York.

Gilbert, DC & Joshi, I 1992, 'Quality management and the tourism and hospitality industry', in *Progress in Tourism, Recreation and Hospitality Management*, vol. 4, eds CP Cooper and R Lockwood, published in association with the University of Surrey, Belhaven Press, London, pp. 149–167.

Gillespie, R 1999, 'What do I need to know about benefit cost analysis?' in *Valuing Tourism, Methods and Techniques*, Occasional Paper No. 28, eds K Corcoran, A Allcock, T Frost & L Johnson, Bureau of Tourism Research, Canberra, pp. 63–76.

Glasson, J Godfrey, K & Goodey, B 1995, *Towards Visitor Impact Management. Visitor Impacts, Carrying Capacity and Management: Responses in Europe's Historic Towns & Cities*, Avebury, Ashgate Publishing Ltd, Aldershot, England.

Goodall, B 1994, 'Environmental auditing' in *Tourism Marketing and Management Handbook*, 2nd edn, eds SF Witt & L Moutinho, Prentice Hall International, Hemel Hempstead, pp. 113–119.

Goulding, P 1995, letter to Steve Noakes, general manager, Far North Queensland Promotion Bureau, dated 11 February.

Graham, A 1999, 'Daintree Wilderness Lodge', in *Proceedings of Asia–Pacific Economic Cooperation (APEC) Tourism Working Group Seminar*, April, Cairns, pp. 88–89.

Gray, J 2002, 'The decay of market power. Free trade will not survive the crises of a new era of war', *The Australian Financial Review*, 10 May, Review 3.

Green, E 1970, 'The Concept of Market Planning', in *Handbook of Modern Marketing*, eds V Buell & C Heyell, McGraw-Hill Book Company, New York, pp. 7–3 to 7–25.

Green, H & Hunter, C 1991, 'The Environmental Impact Assessment of Tourism Development', in *Perspectives of Tourism Policy*, eds P Johnson & B Thomas, Mansell Publishing Limited, London, pp. 29–47.

Griffith, DA & Albanese, PJ 1996, 'An Examination of Plog's Psychographic Travel Model within a Student Population', *Journal of Travel Research*, Spring, vol. XXXIV(4), pp. 47–51.

Gunn, CA 1994, *Tourism planning. Basics, concepts, cases*, 3rd edn, Taylor and Francis, Washington, DC.

Gutteridge Haskins & Davey 1997, *Flinders Ranges and Outback Tourism Development Strategy*, South Australian Tourism Commission, Adelaide.

——2001, *2001 Australian Infrastructure Report Card*, Australian Infrastructure Report Card Alliance, Sydney.

Hall, CM 1999, 'The politics of decision making and top-down planning: Darling Harbour, Sydney', in *Managing Tourism in Cities: Policy, Process and Practice*, eds D Tyler, Y Guerrier & M Robertson, John Wiley & Sons Ltd, Chichester, England, pp. 9–24.

Handszuh, H 1999, *Local Food In Tourism Policies*, paper based on research of the World Tourism Organisation secretariat and adapted from the author's original contribution to an international symposium entitled 'Sustainable Tourism, Health and Culture, Rural Tourism', Simrishamn, Sweden, September 1999. Distributed by the WTO, Madrid.

Ham, S 2000, Puffing Billy administration, pers. comm., 11 October.

Harris, P 1997, 'Limitations on the use of regional economic impact multipliers by practitioners: an application to the tourism industry', *The Journal of Tourism Studies*, vol. 8(2) December, pp. 50–61.

Heath, G 1991, 'Tourism and the Understanding of Environmental Issues', in *Proceedings of World Leisure and Recreation Association Congress,* Sydney, pp. 599–602.

Heilbroner, RL & Thurow, LC 1975, *The Economic Problem*, 4th edn, Prentice-Hall, Englewood Cliffs, New Jersey.

Heilbronn, G 1992, *Travel and Tourism Law in Australia and New Zealand*, The Federation Press, Sydney.

Hickey, P 2001, *Report on New Year's Eve 2000/01 Byron Bay*, Byron Bay Community Safety Committee.

Hill, N 1998, Associate Director Sales & Marketing, AAT-King's, pers. comm., 23 June.

Hobson, JS & Teaff, D 1994, 'Hospitality and Leisure/Recreation: Towards an Understanding of an Emerging Partnership Serving the Tourism Industry', *Journal of Hospitality & Leisure Marketing*, vol. 2(1), pp. 43–54.

Holper, P & Noonan, J 2000, *Urban and regional air pollution*, information sheet, CSIRO Division of Atmospheric Research, Melbourne.

Hollinshead, K 1990, 'Conference Reports: Cultural Tourism', Research Notes and Reports, *Annals of Tourism Research*, vol. 17(2), pp. 292–294.

Hollis, S 2001, executive officer, Australian Tourism Accreditation Association, pers. comm., 14 November.

Homersham, M 2000, principal, Project Profile, project management and consultancy services provider, pers. comm., 28 December.

Horne, D 1992, *The Intelligent Tourist*, Margaret Gee Publishing, Sydney.

Howarth, I 2003, 'Cost of Kyoto', *The Australian Financial Review*, 10 January, p. 48.

Hughes, HL 1986, *Economics for Hotel and Catering Students*, Hutchinson & Co (Publishers) Ltd., London.

——1996, 'Redefining Cultural Tourism', Research Notes and Reports, *Annals of Tourism Research*, vol. 23(03), pp. 707–708.

Hunn, C & Mangan, J 1999, 'Estimating the economic impact of tourism at the local, regional and state or territory level, including consideration of the multiplier effect', in *Valuing Tourism, Methods and Techniques*, Occasional Paper No. 28, eds K Corcoran, A Allcock, T Frost & L Johnson, Bureau of Tourism Research, Canberra, pp. 13–22.

Hvenegaard, GT 1994, 'Ecotourism: A Status Report and Conceptual Framework', *The Journal of Tourism Studies*, vol. 5(2), December.

Industries Assistance Commission 1989, *Travel and Tourism*, Report No. 423, Australian Government Publishing Service, Canberra.

Inskeep, E 1991, *Tourism planning: an integrated and sustainable development approach*, Van Nostrand Reinhold, New York.

——1994, *National & Regional Tourism Planning: Methodologies and Case Studies*, reprinted 1997, World Tourism Organisation and International Thomson Publishing Company, London.

Intergovernmental Panel on Climate Change 2001a, *Working Group I Third Assessment Report*, Summary for Policymakers, Geneva.

——2001b, *Working Group II Third Assessment Report*, Summary for Policymakers, Geneva.

——2001c, *Working Group III Third Assessment Report*, Summary for Policymakers, Geneva.

International Air Transport Association 2002, *A Review of Air Transport Following September 11*, Montreal.

Jackson, M 2000, 'Predicting Australian Mass Tourism Flow Using Hofstede's Cultural Model', in *Proceedings of Council for Australian University Tourism and Hospitality Education 2000 Conference*, LaTrobe University, Mt. Hotham, Victoria, CD-ROM, pp. 54–63.

Jafari, J 1977, Editorial, *Annals of Tourism Research*, vol. 5, pp. 6–11.

James, C & Kaye L 2003, 'Iraq war clouds industry future', *Travelweek*, 2 April, p. 1.

Jefferson, A & Lickorish, L 1988, *Marketing Tourism, A Practical Guide*, Longman, Harlow, United Kingdom.

Johnson, L 2000, 'Tourism Expenditure by Domestic Visitors in Regional Australia', paper presented at the CAUTHE conference, LaTrobe University, Mt. Hotham, Victoria.

Johnson, R 1999, 'Estimating the economic impact of a tourism accommodation development on my local government area, region, state or territory', in *Valuing Tourism, Methods and Techniques*, Occasional Paper No. 28, eds K Corcoran, A Allcock, T Frost & L Johnson, Bureau of Tourism Research, Canberra, pp. 23–32.

Johnson, W 1983, 'If it's Tuesday this must be ballet', *American Arts*, July, pp. 12–14.

Kaiser, C & Helber, L 1978, *Tourism Planning and Development*, CBI Publishing Company, Boston.

Kayler-Thompson, W 1995, *Tourism Accreditation and Quality Assurance: Strategic Directions for Victoria*, Tourism Victoria, Melbourne.

Kelleher, G & Craik, W 1991, 'How Much is the Great Barrier Reef Worth?', in *Proceedings of the World Leisure and Recreation Association Congress*, Sydney, pp. 96–103.

Kelly, I 1993, 'Tourist Destination Crime Rates: An examination of Cairns and the Gold Coast, Australia', *The Journal of Tourism Studies*, vol. 4(2), December.

Kilicarslan, A O'Connor, N Place, V Sharma, A Stewart, M & Reilly, A 2000, 'Effective Crisis Management in the Airline Industry During Air Incidents or Disasters', Loyola University of Chicago, in *This Week in Aviation*, weekly e-letter of *Aviation Today*, www.aviationtoday.com, 18 May.

King, B 1994, 'Bringing out the Authentic in Australian Hospitality Products for the International Tourist: A Service Management Approach', *Australian Journal of Hospitality Management*, vol. 1(1), pp. 1–7.

Kotler, P 1991, *Marketing Management: Analysis, Planning, Implementation and Control*, 7th edn, Prentice Hall Inc., Englewood Cliffs, New Jersey.

——1999, *Kotler on marketing: how to create, win and dominate markets*, The Free Press, New York.

Kotler, P & Armstrong, G 1994, *Principles of Marketing*, 6th edn, Prentice-Hall International Inc, Englewood Cliffs, New Jersey.

Lamb, D 2001, chief executive, Australian Automotive Technology Centre, CSIRO, pers. comm., 14 April.

Lanquar, R 1989, 'Quality control: the key to excellence in tourism', in *Tourism Marketing and Management Handbook*, eds SF Witt & L Moutinho, Prentice Hall International, Hemel Hempstead, United Kingdom, pp. 345–349.

Lawson, R 1994, 'Demographic segmentation', in *Tourism Marketing and Management Handbook*, 2nd edn, eds SF Witt & L Moutinho, Prentice Hall International, Hemel Hempstead, United Kingdom, pp. 311–315.

Lee Mei Foo 1998, *Cultural Tourism in Australia: Characteristics and Motivations*, paper presented at the Australian Tourism and Hospitality Research Conference, Gold Coast, February, Bureau of Tourism Research, Canberra.

Leiper, N 1990, *Tourism Systems: An Interdisciplinary Perspective,* Department of Management Systems, Business Studies Faculty, Massey University.

——1995, *Tourism Management*, TAFE Publications, Melbourne.

——1999, 'A conceptual analysis of tourism-supported employment which reduces the incidence of exaggerated, misleading statistics about jobs', *Tourism Management*, 20, pp. 605–613.

Liebried, KHJ & McNair, CJ 1992, *Benchmarking: A Tool for Continuous Improvement*, HarperCollins Publishers, New York.

Lockwood, A 1989, 'Quality management in hotels', in *Tourism Marketing and Management Handbook*, eds SF Witt & L Moutinho, Prentice Hall International Ltd., Hemel Hempstead, United Kingdom, pp. 352–355.

Lofting, C 2000, 'Cruise Vacations', advertising supplement to *The New York Times Magazine*, 23 January, pp. 41–52.

MacDermott, K 2000, 'Address Sense: One Gold Coast developer had a vision of an "haute culture theme park" – so he went out and got a label that speaks billions', *The Australian Financial Review Magazine*, 28 July, pp. 51–52.

Macquarie Dictionary 1997, eds A Delbridge, JRL Bernard, D Blair, S Butler, P Peters & C Yallop, 3rd edn, The Macquarie Library, Macquarie University, New South Wales.

Madrigal, R 1995, 'Residents' Perceptions and the Role of Government', *Annals of Tourism Research*, 22, pp. 86–102.

Manidis Roberts Consultants 1997, *Developing a Tourism Optimisation Management Model (TOMM), a model to monitor and manage tourism on Kangaroo Island*, final report, South Australian Tourism Commission, Adelaide.

Mansfield, Y 1992, 'From Motivation to Actual Travel,' *Annals of Tourism Research,* vol. 19, pp. 399–419.

Martel, L 1988, *Mastering Change: The Key to Business Success*, Grafton Books, London.

Mathieson, A & Wall, G 1982, *Tourism: economic, physical and social impacts,* Longman Scientific and Technical, Harlow, United Kingdom.

McArthur, S 2000, *Visitor Management in Action. An analysis of the development and implementation of visitor management models at Jenolan Caves and Kangaroo Island.* PhD thesis, University of Canberra.

McCarthy, EJ & Perreault Jr., WD 1990, *Basic Marketing: A Managerial Approach*, 10th edn, Irwin, Homewood, Illinois.

McIntosh, A & Prentice, R 1999, 'Affirming Authenticity, Consuming Cultural Heritage', *Annals of Tourism Research*, vol. 26(3), pp. 589–612.

McKercher, Bob 1996, 'Differences Between Tourism and Recreation in Parks', *Annals of Tourism Research*, vol. 23(3), pp. 563–575.

——1998, *The Business of Nature-based Tourism*, Hospitality Press, Melbourne.

McMahon, I 2003, 'Travel stats – encouraging or depressing?' *Travel Week Australia*, 5 February, p. 4.

Meidan, A 1989, 'Pricing in tourism', in *Tourism Marketing and Management Handbook*, eds SF Witt & L Moutinho, Prentice Hill International, Hemel Hempstead, United Kingdom, pp. 305–309.

Middleton, V 1989, 'Tourist product', in *Tourism Marketing and Management Handbook*, eds SF Witt & L Moutinho, Prentice Hall International, Hemel Hempstead, pp. 573–576.

Middleton, V & Hawkins, R 1998, *Sustainable Tourism: A Marketing Perspective*, Butterworth-Heinemann, Oxford.

Mock, J & O'Neil, K 1996, *Survey of Ecotourism Potential in the Biodiversity Project Area, Islamabad, Pakistan*, IUCN-Pakistan.

Morgan, M & C 2002, tour operators, Wundargoodie Aboriginal Safaris, pers. comm., 25 May–7 June.

Moore, K Cushman, G & Simmons, D 1995, 'Behavioral Conceptualization of Tourism and Leisure', *Annals of Tourism Research*, vol. 22(1), pp. 67–85.

Moore J 1999, Tasmanian Travel & Information Centre, pers. comm., 14 May.

Morley, CL 1990, 'What is Tourism? Definitions, Concepts and Characteristics', *Journal of Tourism Studies*, vol. 1(1), pp. 3–8.

Morrison, AS 1989, *Hospitality and Tourism Marketing*, Delmar Publishers, Inc, Albany, New York.

Morton, J 2000, Arts Victoria, pers. comm., 7 December.

Moscardo, G Morrison, A & Pearce, P 1996, 'Specialist Accommodation and Ecologically-Sustainable Tourism', *Journal of Sustainable Tourism*, vol. 4(1), pp. 29–52.

Moutinho, L 1989, 'New product development', in *Tourism Marketing and Management Handbook*, in SF Witt & L Moutinho, Prentice Hill International, Hemel Hempstead, United Kingdom, pp. 291–294.

Mules, T 1999, 'Events tourism and economic development in Australia', in *Managing Tourism in Cities: Policy, Process and Practice*, eds D Tyler, Y Guerrier, & M Robertson, John Wiley & Sons Ltd, Chichester, England, pp. 195–214.

New South Wales Environment Protection Authority 1997, *New South Wales State of the Environment 1997*, Sydney.

Nicholson, T 2000, 'The black man's lore', *The Age*, 7 October, News Extra p. 6.

Nunberg, G 2000, 'www.english.com', *The Australian Financial Review*, 31 March 2000, Review p. 2. Reprinted from *The American Prospect*.

O'Dea, D 1997a, *Tourism's Direct Economic Contribution 1995–96*, Research Paper No. 3, Bureau of Tourism Research, Canberra.

——1997b, *Tourism's Indirect Economic Effects, 1995–96*, Research Paper No. 4, Bureau of Tourism Research, Canberra.

Office of National Tourism 1996, *Developing Tourism: Projects in Profile*, Canberra.

——1997, *Terms of Reference for Development of National Tourism Plan*, Canberra.

——1998a, *Talking Tourism*, March, Canberra.

——1998b, *Twinshare: Tourism accommodation and the environment, Canberra*, posted to the Internet, June, http://twinshare.crctourism.com.au.

Organisation of American States 1997, *Sustaining Tourism by Managing its Natural and Heritage Resources*, paper presented at XVII Inter-American Travel Congress, San José, Costa Rica, 7–11 April, 1997.

O'Reilly, AM 1991, 'Tourism carrying capacity', in *Managing Tourism*, ed. S Medlick, Butternwork-Heinemann, Oxford.

O'Shaughnessy, J 1984, *Competitive Marketing: A Strategic Approach*, Allen & Unwin, Boston.

Oxford English Dictionary 1989, prepared by JA Simpson and ESC Weiner, 2nd edn, Clarendon Press, Oxford.

Pacific Asia Travel Association 1995, *Values Tourism: A simple revolution to protect the world's largest industry*, PATA Pacific Division, Sydney.

Pearce, D 1989, *Tourism Development*, Longman Scientific & Technical, Harlow, United Kingdom.

Pearce, P 1993, *World Tourism Trends to the Year 2000*, Research Catalyst Workshop, University of Western Sydney, Sydney, pp. 50–57.

Peterkin, L 1998, chairperson, Australian Bed and Breakfast Council, pers. comm., 2 August.

Petzinger, T 1995, *Hard Landing, The Epic Contest for Power and Profits That Plunged the Airlines into Chaos*, Times Business, a division of Random House, New York.

Plog, SC 1973, 'Why destinations rise and fall in popularity', *Cornell Hotel and Restaurant Administration Quarterly*, vol. 12(1), pp. 13–16.

——1990, 'A Carpenter's Tools: An Answer to Stephen L.J. Smith's Review of Psychocentrism/ Allocentrism', *Journal of Travel Research*, vol. XXVIII, no. 4, Spring, pp. 43–45.

Plunkett, K 2002, tourism developer/operator, Eco Beach Wilderness Resort, pers comm., 16–23 March.

Poole, M 1993, *CD-MOTA Users Guide*, Bureau of Tourism Research, Canberra.

Poon, A 1994, 'The "new tourism" revolution', *Travel Management*, vol. 15, no. 2.

Power, L 2001, Being Responsible, *The Sunday Age*, 29 July, Agenda p. 16.

Prokesch, SE 1995, 'Competing on Customer Service: An Interview with British Airways' Sir Colin Marshall', *Harvard Business Review*, November–December, pp. 101–112.

Prosser, GM 1986, 'Beyond Carrying Capacity: Establishing Limits of Acceptable Change for Park Planning, Developing Communities into the 21st Century', *Proceedings of the 59th National Conference of the Royal Australian Institute of Parks and Recreation*, Royal Australian Institute of Parks and Recreation, pp. 223–233.

——1997, 'The Development of Tourist Destinations in Australia: A Comparative Analysis of the Gold Coast and Coffs Harbour', in *Global Directions: New Strategies for Hospitality and Tourism*, eds R Teare, BF Canziani & G Brown, Cassell, London, pp. 305–332.

Raphael, M 1993, 'Conclusions of the Round Table', in *Proceedings of Round Table on Tourism Development and the Role of the State*, World Tourism Organisation, Madrid.

Reisinger, Y & Turner, L 2000, 'Japanese tourist satisfaction; Gold Coast versus Hawaii', *Journal of Vacation Marketing*, vol. 6(4), pp. 299–317.

Reynolds, P 1994, 'Culinary heritage in the face of tourism' in *Progress in Tourism, Recreation and Hospitality Management*, eds CP Cooper & A Lockwood, John Wiley & Sons, Chichester, vol. 6, pp. 189–194.

Richardson, B & Richardson, J 1998, *Victoria's Fantastic Festivals & Fun Events 1999*, Richworth Publishing, Melbourne.

Richardson, JI 1995, *Australian Travel & Tourism: An Economic Perspective*, Hospitality Press, Melbourne.

——1996, *Marketing Australian Travel & Tourism: Principles and Practice*, Hospitality Press, Melbourne.

——1999, *A History of Australian Travel & Tourism*, Hospitality Press, Melbourne.

Ringer, G 1996, 'Wilderness Images of Tourism and Community', Research Notes and Reports, *Annals of Tourism Research*, vol. 23, no. 4, pp. 950–953.

Rita, P 1995, 'International Marketing Objectives of National Tourist Offices', in *Proceedings of the World Marketing Congress, Melbourne*, vol. V11–1, pp. 3–57 to 3–70.

Ryan, C 1991, *Recreational Tourism, a Social Science Perspective*, Routledge, London and New York.

Salma, U 2002, principal economist, Bureau of Tourism Research, pers. comm., 22 January.

Schnaars, SP 1998, *Marketing Strategy: Customers & Competition*, 2nd edn, The Free Press, New York.

Shearman, D & Sauer-Thompson, G 1997, *Green or Gone: health, ecology, plagues, greed and our future*, Wakefield Press, Kent Town, South Australia.

Simmons, S 1996, 'The Protection of Heritage, Sites and Special Places. Australia's obligations under the World Heritage Convention. Current strategies and management issues', in *Proceedings from the Australian Tourism and Hospitality Research Conference*, ed. G Prosser, Bureau of Tourism Research.

Simpson, M 2003, 'Doing it tough: AFTA seeks emergency funds for embattled agents', *Travelweek*, 30 April, p. 1.

Sloman, J 2001, former deputy chief executive officer and chief operating officer of the Sydney Organising Committee for the Olympic Games (SOCOG), pers. comms., 18 August.

Smith, SLJ 1988, 'Defining Tourism, A Supply-Side View', *Annals of Tourism Research*, vol. 15, pp. 179–190.

——1990, 'A Test of Plog's Allocentric/Psychocentric Model: Evidence from Seven Nations', *Journal of Travel Research*, vol. XXVIII, no. 4, Spring, pp. 40–43.

Smith, T 2002, general manager, marketing and public affairs, Melbourne Aquarium, pers. comm., 3–8 March.

Smyth, J 2001, *'Traffic report – 2001 Carlton Tamworth Country Music Festival*, Item 1/2001, City Council, Tamworth.

Sofield, T & Pedersen, J 2000, *Tapestry Tourism Futures, Part B. Annual Report to CRC Against Deliverables, End Year 1–2000*, Bunbury.

Soin, SS 1992, *Total Quality Control Essentials: Key Elements, Methodologies and Managing for Success*, McGraw-Hill, New York.

Sproule, R 2001, *Planning Development for Tourism Infrastructure*, internal management paper, Tourism Tasmania.

Spurr, R 1993, 'The Role of Government in Tourism', in *Proceedings of Round Table on Tourism Development and the Role of the State*, 10th General Assembly, World Tourism Organisation, Bali, pp. 44–48.

Standards Australia 1997, *Catalogue of Australian Standards and Other Products*, Sydney.

Stroud, LG 2001, former Assistant Secretary, Department of Tourism, pers. comm., 24 June–10 September.

Strutt, S 2001, 'Tourism finds its saviour', *The Australian Financial Review*, 7 December, p. 13.

Stynes, DJ (n.d.), *Economic Impacts of Tourism*, Department of Park, Recreation and Tourism Resources, Michigan State University, www.msu.edu/course/prr/840/econimpact/.

Swanbrooke, J 1995, *The Development and Management of Visitor Attractions*, Butterworth-Heinemann, Oxford, reprinted 1998.

Taylor, D Rosemann I & Prosser, G 2000, *The Effect of Accreditation on Tourism Business Performance: An Evaluation*, prepared by the Centre for Regional Tourism Research for Australian Tourism Accreditation Authority.

Thomas, I 1996, *Environmental impact assessment in Australia: theory and practice,* The Federation Press, Sydney.

Timothy, DJ & Butler, RW 1995, 'Cross-Border Shopping: A North American Perspective', *Annals of Tourism Research*, vol. 22 no. 1, pp. 16–34.

Todd, G 2001, general manager environment, Qantas Airways, pers. comm., 18 June.

Tooman, LA 1997, 'Applications of the Life-Cycle Model in Tourism', *Annals of Tourism Research*, vol. 24(1), pp. 214–234.

Tourism Forecasting Council 1994, *Forecast*, August, Canberra.

——1995, *Forecast*, April, Canberra.

——1997, *Forecast*, June, Canberra.

——2002, *Forecast,* December, Canberra.

Tourism Queensland 1999a, *Ecotourism Consumer Research: A National Domestic Survey*, Brisbane.

——1999b, *Ecotourism, the Internet and Backpackers*, Brisbane.

——2000a, *Nature-based Tourism in Queensland*, Brisbane.

——2000b, *Ecotourism Consumer Research: International Leisure Market Survey*, Brisbane.

——2000c, *How Are We Tracking: Environmental tourism benchmarking study*, Brisbane.

Tourism New South Wales 1996, *New South Wales Masterplan to 2010*, Sydney.

Tourism Review Steering Committee 1997, *Review of the Marine Tourism Industry in the Great Barrier Reef World Heritage Area*, with assistance from the Great Barrier Reef Marine Park Authority and the Office of National Tourism, Townsville.

Tourism Tasmania 2001, *Tasmania's Temptations Holiday Book*, 2nd edn, Hobart.

Tribe, J 1999, *The Economics of Leisure and Tourism*, 2nd edn, Butterworth-Heinemann, Oxford.

Tyler, D & Guerrier, Y 1999, 'Conclusions: urban tourism – the politics and processes of change', in *Managing Tourism in Cities: Policy, Process and Practice*, D Tyler, V Guerrier, & M Robertson, John Wiley & Sons Ltd, Chichester, England.

UNEP/WMO Information Unit on Climate Change 1994, *Understanding Climate Change: A Beginner's Guide to the UN Framework Convention*, Geneva.

United Nations Environmental Program 1997, *Global Environment Outlook-1, Executive Summary*, Nairobi.

United Nations Environmental Program 1999, *Tourism*, Nairobi, www.unipie.org.

US Bureau of the Census 2000, *Total Midyear Population for the World: 1950–2050,* www.census.gov/impc/www.worldpop.html.

US Department of Commerce 1996, *Abstract of International Travel To and From the United States 1995*, Washington.

Vamplew, W & McLean, I 1987, 'Transport and Communications', in *Australian Historical Statistics*, eds W Vamplew, W Fairfax, Syme & Weldon Associates, Sydney.

Van Der Borg, J 1999, 'Tourism management in Venice, or how to deal with success', in *Managing Tourism in Cities: Policy, Process and Practice*, eds D Tyler, Y Guerrier, & M Robertson, John Wiley & Sons Ltd, Chichester, England, pp. 125–136.

van der Hoeven, P 1997, general manager, Adelaide Convention Centre, pers. comm., 30 March.

Vernon, D 1999, 'Greening Tourism – Governments' Role in Promoting Sustainability', in *Proceedings of Asia–Pacific Economic Cooperation (APEC) Tourism Working Group Seminar,* Cairns, April, pp. 44–51.

Walker, P 2001, CSIRO Wildlife and Ecology, pers. comm., 6 November.

Wardlaw, A 2001, general manager West Coast Council, pers. comm., 18 November.

Webb, R 2003, 'Panic infests airline industry', *The Sunday Age*, 6 May, p. 16.

Wheatcroft, S 1994, *Aviation and Tourism Policies: Balancing the Benefits*, World Tourism Organisation and Routledge, London and New York.

Wheeller, B 1992, 'Alternative tourism – a deceptive ploy, in *Progress in Tourism, Recreation and Hospitality Management*, vol. 4, eds CP Cooper & A Lockwood, John Wiley & Sons, Chichester, pp. 140–145.

Wider Quality Movement 1995, *Quality and Australia*, Sydney.

Wilkinson, R 1983, *A Thirst for Burning, the Story of Australia's Oil Industry*, David Ell Press, Sydney. New edition published 1988.

Williams, M 1992, 'Visitor Management', in *Meeting Visitor Expectations and Enhancing Visitor Enjoyment*, a compilation of papers given at tourism infrastructure seminars in Adelaide, Ballarat, Liverpool, Brisbane and Canberra, Department of Tourism, Canberra, pp. 25–36.

Wine Food Strategies Pty Ltd 2002, *Respecting Our Culture: Indigenous Accreditation Program*, Aboriginal Tourism Australia, Melbourne.

World Tourism Organisation 1994, *WTO News*, No. 3, May/June, Madrid.

——1995a, *WTO News*, January, Madrid.

——1995b, *Technical Manual No. 1, Concepts, Definitions and Classifications for Tourism Statistics*, Madrid.

——1995c, *Technical Manual No.2, Collection of Tourism Expenditure Statistics*, Madrid.

——1997a, *WTO News*, March, Madrid.

——1998, *WTO News*, March–April, Madrid.

——1998–99, *WTO News*, December 1998–January 1999, Madrid.

——1999a, *Recommendations on World Statistics*, Madrid.

——1999b, *Tourism Highlights 1999*, Madrid.

——1999c, *Global Code of Ethics for Tourism*, Madrid.

——1999d, *WTO News*, February–March, Madrid.

——1999e, *WTO News*, October–November–December, Madrid.

——2000, *Proposals of the World Tourism Organization Relating to Priority Issue Number 9: 'Clarify the Concepts of Sustainable Tourism and Ecotourism'*, paper presented to the United Nations Multi-stakeholder Working Group on Tourism, Madrid, January.

——2001, *WTO News*, 3rd quarter, Madrid.

——2002a, *WTO News*, 3rd quarter, Madrid.

——2002b, *WTO News*, 4th quarter, Madrid.

Yates, A 2001, senior policy analyst, Institution of Engineers, Australia, pers. comm., 8 December.

Zallocco, RL 1989, 'Marketing Plan', in *Tourism Marketing and Management Handbook*, eds SF Witt & L Moutinho, Prentice Hall International, Hemel Hempstead, pp. 265–267.

Zeppel, H & Hall, CM 1991, 'Selling Art and History: Cultural Heritage and Tourism', *The Journal of Tourism Studies*, vol. 2(1), pp. 29–45.

Ziethmal, VA Parasuraman, A & Berry, LL 1990, *Delivering Quality Service: Balancing Customer Perceptions and Expectations*, The Free Press, New York.

GLOSSARY

Aboriginal tourism product	A tourism experience or service which is majority owned by Aboriginal people. Ownership may include a partnership with non-Aboriginal people.
accessibility	(1) The relative ease with which a tourist can reach a destination. (2) The degree to which a target market can be reached and served.
accreditation	(1) Approval by companies, conferences or associations for allowing the sale of tickets and other travel services. (2) A process designed to establish and continually improve industry standards for conducting tourism businesses.
acculturation	A theory which assumes that when two cultures interact the dominant one overpowers the weaker one, bringing about changes within the weaker culture.
action program	The sum of the action plans devised to achieve objectives in accordance with the appropriate strategies. Whereas a strategy is a broad statement, the action plan specifies what will be done, who will do it, when it will be done and how much it will cost.
advertising	Any paid form of non-personal presentation and promotion of ideas, goods or services by an identified sponsor.
agent	A person who is authorised to represent or act on behalf of a second person, called a principal, to transact some business or affair between the principal and a third person. Travel agents act on behalf of a variety of principals, including airlines, tour operators, hotel and motel companies, cruise lines, coach companies and car rental companies.
airline codes	The system of abbreviations for airlines, airports and fares used by airlines and travel sellers throughout the world.
airline classes	F, P and A all designate first class, although P is the main code used in Australia. J or C designates business class and any coding from K to Y means economy. Y is usually a full-fare economy ticket code.
air traffic management	Systems for the guidance, separation, coordination, and control of aircraft movements.
architectural pollution	Inappropriate designs for hotels, terminals, theme parks and other attractions and facilities which disturb the social and cultural integrity of the landscape.
arrival and departure cards	Cards travellers are required to fill in before arriving in or leaving Australia. From the detail on the cards the Australian Bureau of Statistics gathers and analyses the statistics which allow it to quantify inbound and outbound tourism.

Asia Pacific Incentives and Meetings Expo (AIME)	An international MICE sector trade show held in Melbourne each year.
ASKs	An airline term meaning available seat kilometres. They are the number of seats available for sale multiplied by the distance between the points. See *load factor.*
assumption definition	A temporary estimate or hypothesis of an important, probable development.
attraction	(1) A natural wonder or man-made establishment which is managed and promoted. (2) Whatever provides the motivation for a tourist to go to a particular place.
Australian Standing Committee on Tourism (ASCOT)	A body consisting of senior tourism officials from the Commonwealth, state, territory and New Zealand governments, plus the Australian Tourist Commission and the Bureau of Tourism Research. ASCOT meets twice a year. Its main objective is to improve cooperation and coordination of government policies and activities as they affect tourism.
Australian tourism accreditation	A program that describes a minimum set of standards that organisations must meet in order to achieve membership of the program.
Australian Tourism Exchange (ATE)	A trade show held in Australia each year by the Australian Tourist Commission to enable overseas buyers of tourism products to meet and do business with Australian suppliers.
authenticity	The quality of being genuine, reliable and unspoiled as applied to a tourism experience. It is a central issue in cultural tourism.
average room rate	Total revenues from room sales in a hotel, or collective room revenues of a destination, divided by the total number of rooms available. Average room rates may be computed on a daily basis for an individual property or an annual or seasonal basis for a destination.
balance of payments	A statistical statement, linked to the National Accounts, which provides a systematic record of Australia's transactions with the rest of the world.
Bass Strait Passenger Equalisation Scheme	A Commonwealth Government program designed to reduce the cost of taking a vehicle across Bass Strait to the cost of driving the same vehicle the same distance on a mainland highway. It is applicable to vehicles carried on the ferries plying between Melbourne and Devonport.
benefit–cost analysis	A technique for calculating the social and environmental implications of expenditure as well as the economic factors. Thus it is concerned with valuing a tourism resource from society's point of view and the cost of funding tourism as against some other activity.
biodiversity	The biological diversity or variety of life forms, including the different plants, animals, fungi and micro-organisms, the genes they contain, and the ecosystems they form.
brand	A name, term, sign, symbol, or design or a combination of these intended to identify the goods or services of one seller or group of sellers and to differentiate them from those of competitors.

Brand Australia	An Australian Tourist Commission program intended to highlight the elements of the country and nation that distinguish Australia from the rest of the world and 'promote the personality of Australia as a free spirited, optimistic, fun and liberating destination offering a range of experiences'.
brand equity	The value of a brand, based on the extent to which it has high brand loyalty, name awareness, perceived quality, strong brand associations and other assets such as patents, trademarks and channel relationships.
brand image	The set of beliefs consumers hold about a particular brand.
branding	The process of building a distinctive image in people's minds so that it will be recalled when the brand is encountered in the form of a name, design, symbol or slogan.
brand management	The actions taken to ensure that the product is consistently delivered in accordance with the promotional promise. It is an important factor in brand equity.
building codes	Statutory codes enacted by local governments for the purpose of safeguarding public safety and health through the regulation of building construction, building use, and maintenance, and through the installation of certain types of services.
Bureau of Touring Research (BTR)	A joint state and federal government agency which collects, analyses and disseminates information about the Australian tourism industry to the general public, government and industry.
business cycles	Fluctuations in the patterns of business activity as the result of changes in the behaviour of the various kinds of markets, e.g. consumer confidence waxing and waning, interest rates rising and falling, share prices soaring or dropping, inflation rates going up or down.
cabotage	Restriction of the right to transport between two points within a country. It applies to both air and sea transportation. A cabotage fare is a special rate applicable to nationals only and within one country.
carrying capacity	The level of human activity an area can accommodate without the area deteriorating, the resident community being adversely affected or the quality of visitor experience declining.
charter service	Non-scheduled service whereby the party or parties obtain exclusive use of a vehicle. The term can be applied to an aircraft, coach, ship or train, where the entire capacity or a minimum number of seats are hired by contract for exclusive use.
cleaner production (eco-efficiency)	Improving the environmental efficiency of goods and services and thereby reducing the environmental impact of the production process, from system design and use, to the consumption of resources required to provide the service.
climate change	Change in climate over time due to natural variability or as a result of human activity.

code sharing	The sharing of an inventory between two or more airlines on the one aeroplane. Thus two or more airlines use the same designator (flight number) to provide allegedly seamless travel. It usually disguises a change of aircraft.
commission	Payment received by travel agents for the sale of air transportation, accommodation, tours, rental cars, and other products and services, usually computed as a percentage of sale made by the agent.
commodification	The process whereby something of intrinsic or cultural worth is turned into a commodity that has commercial value.
competency standards	Statements about the skills and knowledge that people need to perform their jobs to the required industry standard.
competitive advantage	An advantage over competitors gained by offering consumers greater value, either through lower prices or by providing more benefits that justify higher prices.
competitor	Someone or some company, organisation or destination satisfying the same customer need or serving the same customer group.
competitor analysis	The process of identifying key competitors – assessing their objectives, strategies, strengths and weaknesses and reaction patterns; and selecting which competitors to attack or avoid.
computable general equilibrium (CGE) model	A representation of the economy as a system of flows of goods and services between sectors, including industry sectors, household sectors, government and foreign sectors. CGE models provide the most detailed and informative modelling technique available for estimating the economic impact of tourism.
computer reservation system (CRS)	An electronic information system connecting individual travel agencies to a central computer, making possible immediate inquiries and reservations on an airline, accommodation, car rental or other travel-related services.
conference centre	A self-contained facility designed and staffed to handle conferences and business meetings as its primary function.
conservation	All the processes of looking after a place so as to retain its significance. In the wider sense, defined by the World Conservation Strategy as 'the management of human use of the biosphere so that it may yield the greatest sustainable benefit to present generations while maintaining its potential to meet the needs and aspirations of future generations'.
consolidator	A person or company acting between the airline company and travel agents, including issuing tickets to non-IATA accredited agents. The consolidator's role is that of a marketing arm of the airlines, particularly in discounting for volume – the consolidator contracts special rates with the airlines by providing volume sales.
convention	Business or professional meeting, usually organised by an association as distinct from a corporation.

Cooperative Research Centre	A research entity set up under a Commonwealth program to pursue a particular field of study. The principal CRC concerned with tourism is the Cooperative Research Centre for Sustainable Tourism.
corporate rate	A standard business traveller's hotel room rate which is usually about 20 per cent off the 'rack' or walk-in rate.
crisis	A time of danger, suspense or catastrophic change caused by an event where the root cause is, to some extent, self-inflicted through such problems as inept management structures and practices or a failure to adapt to change (Faulkner 2000).
culture	The set of basic values, perceptions, wants, and behaviour learned from family and other important institutions.
cultural commodification	Packaging cultural events for sale, fitting them into a tourist's time frame, or staging them in an area to suit tourists rather than the event itself. It also occurs when handicrafts are produced to sell to tourists, but traditional manufacturing methods are not used.
cultural tourism	Tourism that focuses on the heritage and culture of a country and its people, preserved and portrayed in monuments, historic sites, traditional architecture, artefacts, events and cultural attainments in the arts.
customer expectations	What the customer believes is realisable in a product.
customer satisfaction	The feeling a customer has when their expectations from a product are realised or exceeded.
cyclical change	A measurable movement, usually of up and down, or more and less. Economic indicators, for example, depict cyclical changes. So do supply and demand of those in various professions and occupational skills. Most cyclical changes do not involve any changes in structure and their duration is always limited.
day-tripper	In Australia, one who travels for a round-trip distance of at least 50 kilometres, is away from home for at least four hours, and who does not spend a night away from home as part of the travel. Same-day travel as part of overnight travel is excluded, as is routine travel such as commuting between work/school and home.
demand	Desire of would-be purchasers for products or services combined with the ability to pay for them. The demand for tourism is the total number of persons who travel, or wish to travel, to use tourist facilities and services away from their places of work and residence. They must be able to pay for such services.
demand–supply cycles	Business changes that occur because supply never precisely matches demand; either it falls short or it exceeds demand. When indicators show more supply is wanted business or other organisations will respond by supplying more. And sometimes when there is oversupply they will reduce supply.
demarketing	Marketing designed to reduce or regulate the number of people visiting a location.

demographic research	Dividing the market into groups based on variables such as age, income, family lifecycle, income, occupation, education, religion and race.
demographic segmentation	Dividing the market into groups based on demographic variables.
demographics	The description of a population in physical terms such as age, gender, occupation, income levels, marital status, ethnic origin and education level.
demonstration effect (acculturation)	A theory, relevant to tourism, which assumes that when two cultures interact the dominant one overpowers the weaker one, bringing about changes within the weaker culture.
deregulation	Cancelling by a government of regulations governing a commercial activity. Popularly applied to the process by which the Commonwealth Government withdrew from economic regulation over aircraft imports, capacity, air fares and routes within Australia on 3 October 1990.
destination	The place visited by a visitor. In the case of domestic visitors, the destination is an area within the same country. In the case of international visitors, the destination can refer to the country or to a region of that country. A destination is the basic geographic unit used for the production of tourism statistics.
destination area	Part of a destination. A homogeneous tourism region or a group of local government administrative regions.
Destination Australia Marketing Alliance	A program initiated by the Australian Tourist Commission designed to involve it, state and territory tourism commissions and the travel and tourism industry in cooperative tactical marketing projects in overseas markets.
destination image	An evaluation of a destination consisting of both positive and negative perceptions, which may or may not be factual.
destination lifecycle	Destinations (and destination areas and resort areas) go through a cycle of evolution which includes introduction, growth, maturity and decline and/or rejuvenation. Models characterising each stage have been produced as planning and marketing tools.
Destination Management System (DMS)	A computer-based system which enables a prospective tourist or agent access by means of telecommunications to a database carrying a destination's product inventory. The other essential feature is provision for online interrogation so that information of prospective tourists' needs and wants can be recorded. Optional, though desirable, is a booking system.
developer	A person who buys property and by improving it – through sub-division or construction, for instance – increases its value.
development (tourism)	(1) An expansion or enhancement of any part or all parts of the tourism system – markets, linkages and/or destinations. (2) A process of physical change or the product of that change, e.g. a resort, or an accommodation building or a different form of tourism or a whole destination area.
development process (built projects)	The series of steps undertaken in the development of a built project, such as a hotel or resort. The process is usually driven by the need to justify funding.

Therefore it is structured so that commitments are undertaken one step at a time and are kept to a minimum at each step, so that the process can be stopped or altered before proceeding to the next step.

direct marketing
: Marketing through various advertising media that interact directly with consumers, generally calling for the consumer to make a direct response. Marketing on the Internet is one form.

disaster
: A situation where a destination or enterprise is confronted with sudden unpredictable catastrophic changes over which it has little control. These are events such as floods, earthquakes, cyclones, wars and terrorist activities.

discretionary income
: What is left of disposable income after paying for necessities.

disposable income
: Income that is left after taxes.

distribution channel
: A set of interdependent organisations involved in the process of making a product available for use by the consumer.

Domestic Tourism Monitor (DTM)
: An annual household survey of domestic travel conducted by the BTR, replaced in 1997 by the National Visitor Survey. Details were collected on trips, visits, nights and people. Results are available from the Bureau of Tourism Research.

domestic visitor
: Any person residing in a country, who travels to a place within the country, outside their usual environment for a period not exceeding twelve months and whose main purpose of visit is other than the exercise of an activity remunerated from within the place visited.

duty-free stores
: Retail stores in which merchandise is sold only to travellers who are leaving the country. The merchandise is sold completely or partially free of the taxes or duties which would otherwise be imposed by the country in which the store is located.

East Asia & Pacific Region
: One of six regions into which the World Tourism Organisation divides the world so that it can track the movements of tourists and their expenditure. Australia is one of the 37 destinations within the region.

ecologically sustainable development (ESD)
: An ideal whereby human development and the use of natural resources is carried on in such a way as to preserve the planet's resources and biological diversity for future generations.

ecology
: A branch of biology concerned with relationships among species and between species and the physical and chemical environments they inhabit.

ecosystem
: A dynamic interdependent complex of living plant, animal, fungal and micro-organism communities, the non-living environment they inhabit and the interactions within and between the living and non-living components.

ecotourism
: Nature-based tourism that involves education about, and interpretation of, the natural environment within a management framework that supports the sustainability of the environmental, economic and social environments.

effects of tourism expenditure	(1) Direct effects are produced by initial spending by tourists. (2) Indirect effects are the production changes resulting from various rounds of re-spending of the direct expenditure, e.g. payments to suppliers as tourism establishments replenish their stocks. (3) Induced effects are the changes in economic activity resulting from household spending of income earned directly or indirectly as a result of tourism spending.
elasticity	A measure of the impact on demand from a change in price.
elements	(of a system) are the basic building blocks. They are essential, but need not be dissected for an understanding of the system and how it functions.
empowerment	Giving employees the authority to make decisions which directly affect their work without the need for management approval.
energy audit	A way of determining the amount of energy a building uses with a view to reducing the use of fossil fuels, so as to save money and preserve the environment.
environment	All aspects of the surroundings of humanity, affecting individuals and social groupings.
environment impact assessment (EIA)	A detailed study for a proposed development that should comprise four essential components: (1) description of the environment affected by the proposed development; (2) predictions of the likely changes in the environment as a result of the proposed development; (3) an assessment of the significance of the predicted changes in terms of health, social, aesthetic, ecological or economic implications; and (4) a detailed report on all of the above in the form of an environmental impact statement.
environment policy statement	A statement detailing the actions a company will take to implement its environmental policy, developed by identifying the principal issues facing it.
exclusive dealing	Supplying goods or services only on condition that the customer acquires other goods and services from a nominated supplier.
excursion	Usually a side trip out of a destination city; can be used interchangeably with 'tour' or 'sightseeing'.
excursionist	Temporary visitor staying less than 24 hours in a destination and not making an overnight stay. Includes travellers on cruises.
Export Market Development Grants Scheme (EMDG)	A Commonwealth Government program to assist exporters, including travel and tourism companies.
familiarisation tour	A tour offered to tour operators, travel agents, travel writers and other influence leaders to promote a new product or destination, usually at a discount price or free of charge.
family lifecycle	The stages through which families might pass as they mature over time. Each stage has different characteristics in terms of commercial behaviour and these affect the probability of travelling.
feasibility study	A study intended to test the viability of a project, e.g. a proposed new tourism

building, such as a hotel. It is in two parts – the market or demand study and the financial viability study.

flag carrier	The designated national airline of a country.
food cover	A unit of food service provided to a customer. It is not the same thing as a 'meal' because a food cover may be only a cup of coffee or a bowl of soup.
forecasting	The art of estimating future demand by anticipating what tourists are likely to do under a given set of conditions.
foreign independent tour (FIT)	An international trip where the itinerary has been prepared to an individual traveller's specifications. Some travel sellers refer to FIT as 'free and independent travellers' to denote those who have made independent arrangements.
fossil fuel	Any natural fuel such as coal, oil and natural gas, that is derived from the anaerobic (absence of oxygen) decomposition of organic matter in the earth's crust.
Four Ps	A method of classifying the main categories of elements in the marketing mix. The Four Ps stand for product, price, promotion and place (distribution).
franchise	The right to market a service or other product, often exclusive to a specified area, as granted by the manufacturer, developer, or distributor in return for a fee. It is common in the fast-food industry. Some Australian travel agency chains are franchises.
freedoms of the air	Basic traffic rights, as bilaterally arranged between nations or established by treaty. The five freedoms are: (1) the right to overfly a country; (2) the right to land for technical reasons only; (3) the right to carry from the home country to another country; (4) the right to carry from other countries back to the home country; (5) the right to carry between foreign countries.
frequent flyer program (FFP)	A program in which airlines offer bonuses to passengers who accumulate points by travelling.
globalisation	The process of drawing people of all nations into a single community. There are many threads to it, including tourism. It has been accelerated by the building of a vast network of communication technologies which abolish or curtail time and distance.
global warming	A rise in temperatures at the earth's surface as the result of human beings changing the way energy from the sun interacts with and escapes from the earth's atmosphere.
Green Globe	The environmental program of the World Travel & Tourism Council. It is directed at members of the travel and tourism industry and is a benchmarking and certification system designed to improve environmental performance.
Greenhouse Challenge	A Commonwealth Government program aimed at abating greenhouse gas emissions which cause global warming. It relies on voluntary commitment – that is, companies agree to take steps to reduce emissions. It is not aimed at tourism specifically, but travel and tourism companies and trade associations make up a substantial portion of those involved in the program.

greenhouse effect	The effect in which the earth's atmosphere behaves like a greenhouse. Certain gases (e.g. carbon dioxide, water vapour, methane, nitrous oxide) trap the sun's heat after it is re-emitted from the earth. The enhanced greenhouse effect, causing global warming, occurs as a result of additional greenhouse gases from human activities entering the atmosphere.
gross domestic product (GDP)	A measure of the total flow of goods and services produced by the economy over a particular time period, normally a year. It is obtained by valuing outputs of goods at market prices and then aggregating.
gross value added	The gross output of goods and services produced, less the value of intermediate inputs required to produce them. Unlike GDP, it is measured before net taxes on products are added to the value of industry gross output. Gross value added is the preferred National Accounts measure for the production of industries.
group inclusive tour (GIT)	Prepaid tour, with transportation, accommodation, sightseeing and other arrangements covered. Special air fares are provided for the group, requiring that all members must travel on the same flights to and from the destination.
hard measures (to manage visitors)	Physical and/or financial restrictions on visiting attractions or destinations.
heritage	Collectively, the things we have inherited and want to keep because some form of value has been ascribed to them. The term encompasses landscapes, historic places, sites and built environments, as well as biodiversity, collections, past and continuing cultural practices, knowledge and living experiences.
host community	The residents of a town, region or nation who are influenced by the presence of tourists and who serve officially or accidentally as hosts by sharing their land, facilities and culture with tourists.
IATA	International Air Transport Association.
ICOMOS	International Council on Monuments and Sites.
image	The set of beliefs, ideas and impressions that a person holds about an object, product, company or other organisation.
incentive travel	Travel provided as a reward for sales or work performed by employees, distributors, members of organisations etc. The Society of Incentive Travel Executives defines it as a 'global management tool that uses an exceptional travel experience to motivate and/or recognise participants for increased levels of performance in support of organisational goals'.
inclusive tour (IT)	A packaged tour that includes transportation, accommodation, transfers, sightseeing and, usually, some or all meals.
indigenous tourism	Tourism concerned with indigenous peoples and their cultures – in Australia, the various Aboriginal communities across Australia and the Torres Strait Islanders. In practice, indigenous tourism is mainly involved with Aboriginal people.
indulgent tourism	Tourism based on a search for luxury, glamour and name brands. It is provided for by large cruise ships, glamour resorts, casinos, theme parks and themed

	hotels. Indulgent tourists are not greatly concerned with the community and the natural environment in which they are staying.
industrial tourism	Tourism that involves organised visits by tourists to operational industrial sites where some facilities have been provided specifically for their use. It includes visits to factories, farms, vineyards and other places of work. It is usually considered as part of cultural tourism.
infrastructure	The basic physical structures which makes travel possible. It includes roads, bridges, airports, electricity and telephone services, water supply and sewerage.
input–output analysis	A tabular technique that statistically analyses how an economy's industries interact to provide measures of the economic activity generated by tourist spending in terms of four key variables: value added, output, employment and household incomes.
internal marketing	The actions taken by a company to train and motivate its customer-contact employees and all the supporting service people to work as a team to provide customer satisfaction.
internal tourism	Tourism that comprises domestic tourism and inbound tourism.
interline agreements	Agreements involving two or more air carriers to cooperate on specific actions, such as interline travel rights and privileges or to share airport facilities or other resources.
international tourism	Tourism that comprises inbound tourism and outbound tourism.
International Tourismus Böurse (ITB)	A major trade and retail travel show held annually in Berlin. It is considered by many to be the world's most influential trade show. The ATC coordinates a stand for the Australian industry and invites selected buyers from all over Europe to attend.
international visitor	A person who travels to a country other than that in which they usually reside but outside their usual environment for a period not exceeding twelve months and whose main purpose of visit is other than the exercise of an activity remunerated from within the country visited.
International Visitor Survey (IVS)	A survey of departing international visitors conducted annually by the Bureau of Tourism Research in airport departure lounges.
interpretation	A means of communicating ideas and feelings which helps people enrich their understanding and appreciation of their world, and their role within it.
Irridex	The short form of 'Irritation Index', a model produced by Doxey in 1975 as a guide to the likely reaction of residents as tourism increases. Doxey argued that as numbers increase, resident populations react with increasing hostility towards tourists, passing through stages from euphoria to antagonism.
ISO 9002	The international standard from which the Australian national tourism accreditation program has been derived. It is regarded as a model for quality assurance in production, installation and servicing.
IUCN	International Union for the Conservation of Nature and Natural Resources.

Kyoto Protocol	An in-principle agreement by 39 developed countries to reduce greenhouse gas emissions below 1990 levels formalised as a protocol to the United Nations Framework Convention on Climate Change in Kyoto, Japan, in 1997.
landscape	A place containing cultural features and values extending over a large area. Usually used to refer to rural landscapes, but may also include extensive places within urban areas such as parks or gardens.
land-use plan	A plan setting aside areas for tourism and other purposes such as residential, industrial use, agriculture. Zoning regulations and specific architectural, landscaping and engineering design standards are often prepared at this level of planning.
leakage	Money which 'escapes' from the destination area, reducing the income received by the community from tourism expenditure. It may be paid for imports of food, fuel, equipment or other goods necessary for servicing tourists. It may be paid to international hotel management companies operating within the destination area. It may be paid as dividends or profits to outside investors.
leisure	(1) The free time or discretionary time remaining after work, obligatory household and personal activities and sleep. (2) A state of mind, because some leisure activities (recreation) include both obligatory and discretionary components. Thus gardening can be both enjoyable and a chore.
lifestyle	A person's pattern of living as expressed in their activities, interests and opinions.
Limits of Acceptable Change Model (LAC)	A park management model based on the proposition that it is possible to predetermine acceptable limits of change in the indicators of resource or social conditions. When the limits of acceptable change are reached, the area's capacity under current management practices has also been reached.
load (or revenue seat) factor	The percentage of total passenger capacity on an aircraft actually used by paying passengers. Equals RPKs divided by ASKs (passenger revenue per kilometre divided by available seat kilometres).
long-range planning	A planning process designed to guide development over a long period, say 20 years. In Australia, such planning is usually concerned with tourism as one of a number of activities which have economic, social and environmental impacts on an area, often a large area.
management	(1) The organ of leadership, direction and decision in social institutions and, especially in business enterprise. (2) The process, activity or study of carrying out the task of ensuring a number of diverse activities in such a way that a defined objective is achieved.
management contract	An agreement between the owner(s) of a property such as a hotel, restaurant, convention centre or resort complex and a professional management company to develop and/or operate the property for a consideration, typically a set percentage of the gross operating profit.

marginal person	A member of a host community who has rejected his or her ordinary life as the result of trying to assimilate into the tourist culture.
market	(1) The set of all actual and potential buyers of a product or service. (2) A place where things are bought and sold.
market development	A strategy for company growth by identifying and developing new market segments for current company products.
market positioning	Arranging for a product to occupy a clear, distinctive and desirable place relative to competing products in the minds of target consumers.
market power abuse	A company with a substantial degree of power in a market taking advantage of that power for anti-competitive purposes.
market research	The systematic gathering and analysis of data which provides an overall picture, at a given point of time, of a market, its segments, or some aspect of buyer behaviour. It can be quantitative, based on numbers, or qualitative, based on opinions, attitudes, needs and motivations of people.
market segment	A group of consumers who respond in a similar way to a given set of marketing stimuli.
market segmentation	Dividing a market into distinct groups of buyers with different needs, characteristics, or behaviour. They may require different products or marketing mixes.
market targeting	The process of evaluating each market segment's attractiveness and selecting one or more segments to enter.
marketing	The performance of business activities that direct the flow of goods and services from producers to consumers or users.
marketing audit	A comprehensive, systematic, independent and periodic examination of a company's environment, objectives, strategies and activities to determine problem areas and opportunities and to recommend a plan of action to improve the company's marketing performance.
marketing concept	The idea that a company should aim all its efforts at satisfying its customers – at a profit. Companies should try to discover what consumers want and make products to satisfy those wants.
marketing information system (MkIS)	An organised way of continually gathering and analysing data to provide marketing managers with information they need to make decisions.
marketing intelligence	Everyday information about developments in the marketing environment that helps managers prepare and adjust marketing plans.
marketing mix	The 4 Ps – the set of controllable tactical marketing tools – product, price, promotion and place – that the company blends to produce the response it wants in the target market.
marketing plan	A system for developing objectives and setting out the marketing actions to achieve them over a short period, usually a year.

marketing process	The process of: (1) analysing marketing opportunities; (2) selecting target markets; (3) developing the marketing mix; and (4) managing the marketing effort.
marketing research	The systematic gathering, analysis and reporting of information relevant to a problem in marketing. The term has a broader application than market research, which it includes.
media	Non-personal communication channels including print media (newspapers, magazines, direct mail); broadcast media (radio, television, Internet); and display media (billboards, signs, posters).
meeting	The word is used in two ways in Australian tourism – as a generic term used to describe all types of off-site gatherings, such as conventions, congresses, conferences, seminars, workshops and symposiums; and as a specific term to refer to a gathering for the sharing of information organised by a company or other business organisation, as distinct from a convention which is usually organised by an association.
MICE	Meetings, incentives, conventions and exhibitions.
mission statement	A statement of an organisation's purpose – what it wants to accomplish in the larger environment.
model	A theoretical system of relationships which tries to capture the essential elements in a real-world situation.
motivation	A process of internal psychological factors (needs, wants and goals) generating an uncomfortable level of tension within the minds and bodies of individuals. This leads to actions to try to release tension and satisfy needs.
motive (or drive)	A need that is sufficiently pressing to direct the person to seek satisfaction of it.
multiplier (tourism)	A measure of the total effect on national or local income of tourist expenditure on transport, accommodation, food, sightseeing, souvenirs and whatever other goods and services they buy. It thus encompasses the direct and secondary effects of visitor expenditure.
National Accounts	An integrated framework of accounts which provides a systematic summary of national economic activity. See *System of National Accounts*.
National Estate	The National Estate is made up of places in Australia deemed of world, national, state/territory or local significance in three categories – natural environment, historical and indigeneous. Its register, administered by the Australian Heritage Council, had 13 000 entries in 2003.
National System of Reserves	This covers more than 60 million hectares of Australia, incorporating the protected area networks of each state and territory. It includes protected areas ranging from small nature reserves to major national parks and world heritage areas.
national tourism office or organisation (NTO)	The organisation charged with managing and/or promoting tourism on behalf of a nation. It may be a government department, part of a department

or a semi-autonomous body. The organisation, title and functions vary from country to country, but functions would typically include policy advice, promotion and research. In Australia the responsibilities of a national tourism organisation are divided. The Australian Tourist Commission is responsible for overseas promotion, while the Department of Industry, Tourism and Resources is responsible for policy advice and some development activities. A number of official bodies conduct research. This is not unusual. The WTO uses the term National Tourism Administration (NTA) for the body entrusted with the broad management of tourism and NTO for the national promotional body.

National Visitor Survey	A domestic survey introduced in Australia by the Bureau of Tourism Research in 1997 to replace the Domestic Tourism Monitor. It has a larger sample size and collects data on domestic tourism expenditure and outbound travel, neither of which were done by the DTM.
nature tourism	Tourism that is primarily concerned with the direct enjoyment of some relatively undisturbed phenomenon of nature. It does not necessarily have any explicit conservation motive.
needs	A person's innate feelings of deprivation. The basic forces that motivate a person to do something.
net rate	A wholesaler rate to be marked up for eventual resale to the consumer.
new tourism	A name given to the present era of tourism, the chief characteristic of which is that, from the mature markets at least, travellers want individual choices rather than buying a package of attractions and services determined by a tour operator.
noise pollution	Unwanted or offensive sounds that unreasonably intrude into our daily lives.
objectives	Specific, measurable results which an organisation plans to achieve in a given period.
occupancy rate	The proportion of the rooms or bed-places in a collective tourism establishment (e.g. hotel, motel) that is occupied over some period of time, such as night, month or year. Gross occupancy rate (GOR) refers to the use of the total accommodation in a given period, irrespective of whether or not part is closed for the season or for other reasons.
outbound tourism	Tourism that comprises the activities of residents of the given country travelling as visitors in other country.
outcomes and outputs framework	The basis of the Commonwealth Government's planning system, consisting of three essential elements: outcomes (impacts of the Government's actions on the community), outputs (goods and services produced by Commonwealth agencies) and administered items (resources administered by the agency on behalf of the Government – such as grants and benefits – to contribute to a specific outcome).

overall destination product	A bundle of tangible and intangible components, based on activity at a destination. The package is perceived by the tourist as an experience, available at a price.
overall goal	The single overriding objective of a strategic plan such as market leadership or change of direction involving new products and/or new markets. The goal should have a horizon year, indicating when it is to be realised.
override commission	Extra commission paid to travel agents by suppliers based on incremental volume of sales.
Pacific Asia Travel Association (PATA)	An international organisation dating from 1952 devoted to the development of travel in the Pacific-Asia region. In the early 2000s it had a membership of more than 2000 government and industry organisations.
package	The combination of pre-arranged elements of a trip such as transportation, hotel accommodation, meals, sightseeing and transfers. A package comprises two or more component products. Packages are sold to the consumer as a single product for a single price.
perception	The process by which people select, organise and interpret information to form a meaningful picture of the world or a situation.
performance indicators	Measures of performance which are suited to a particular company. Thus an airline might have performance indicators relating to aircraft cleanliness, punctuality, or the time it takes for a customer to get through when telephoning a reservations agent.
personal selling	Oral presentation with one or more prospective buyers for the purpose of making sales.
planning horizon	The time period, usually in years, in which the objectives of a plan are to be realised.
policy	A broad statement of a course of action. Public policy is the expression of the general intent of a government which guides the actions of public servants and others in carrying out the government's wishes.
positioning	The process of developing a distinctive image for a destination, a company or a product so that it can be distinguished from its competitors and their offerings.
price	What is paid for a product: its value expressed in dollars and cents.
price fixing	A company specifying a minimum retail price for its products, as prohibited under the Trade Practices Act. Price fixing does not occur if companies recommend retail prices, even if they recommend them strongly.
primary data	Information collected for the specific purpose at hand.
process	A series of steps taken in combination to produce a result.
product	(1) General: anything that can be offered to a market for attention, acquisition, use or consumption that might satisfy a want or need. It includes physical

objects, services, persons, places, organisations and ideas. (2) Tourism: any good or service, purchased by, or consumed by a person defined as a visitor.

product development
A strategy for company growth by offering modified or new products to current market segments.

product lifecycle
The course of a product's sales and profits over its lifetime. It involves five distinct stages: product development, introduction, growth, maturity and decline.

promotion
Communicating information between seller and potential buyer to influence attitudes and behaviour.

promotional mix
The specific mix of advertising, personal selling, sales promotion, and public relations/publicity a company uses to pursue its marketing objectives.

protected areas
Terrestial and/or marine areas reserved under Commonwealth, state or territory legislation, primarily for nature conservation purposes.

psychographics
The technique of measuring lifestyles and developing classifications of them. It involves measuring dimensions of activities, interests and opinions.

psychographic segmentation
Dividing a market into different groups based on lifestyle or personality characteristics.

public
Any group that has an actual or potential interest in or impact on an organiation's ability to achieve its objectives.

public relations
The means of building good relations with the company's various publics by obtaining favourable publicity, building up a good corporate image and handling or heading off unfavourable rumours and events. Major tools include press relations, corporate communications, lobbying and counselling.

publicity
Activities to promote a company or its products by obtaining news about it in media not paid for by the sponsor. Any form of unpaid non-personal presentation of ideas, goods and services.

purpose of visit
The reason in the absence of which a trip would not have taken place. The World Tourism Organisation recommends that data should be presented separately for: (1) leisure, recreation and holidays; (2) visiting friends and relatives; (3) business and professional; (4) health treatment; (5) religion/pilgrimages; and (6) other.

push and pull factors
Push factors are economic, social, demographic, technological and political forces that 'push' consumers away from their usual place of residence. Pull factors 'pull' consumers towards a particular destination (e.g. a positive image, safety, attractions, climate).

quality
The totality of features and characteristics of a product that bear on its ability to satisfy stated or implied needs. Quality is what the customer says it is.

quality assurance
All those planned and systematic actions necessary to provide adequate confidence that a product or service will satisfy given requirements for quality.

quality audit	An objective assessment of the company's performance by outside consultants or internal specialist staff. Their report should identify the issues affecting quality performance which can form the basis of corrective action, if necessary.
quality circle	A group of employees meeting on a regular basis to solve problems and improve quality in its area. A quality circle is often structured by an overseeing committee which sets projects, reviews progress and rewards the team if it makes a significant contribution.
quality control	The operational techniques and activities that are used to fulfil requirements for quality.
quality management	A broader approach which embraces quality assurance and also the encouragement of innovation and improvement of systems and processes. It involves empowerment of employees and committed leadership.
rack rate	The regular published rates of a hotel. When special rates are quoted they represent a discount from the rack rate.
reach	The percentage of people in a target market exposed to an advertising campaign during a given period.
real jobs supported by tourism	Identifiable positions where individuals' knowledge and skills normally are related to attributes of tourism (Leiper 1999).
recreation	The term is used to embrace the range of activities undertaken during leisure. However, 'leisure' and 'recreation' are sometimes used interchangeably.
Recreation Carrying Capacity Model (RCC)	A park management model based on the definition of the level of recreational use that an area can sustain without an unacceptable degree of deterioration of the resource or of the recreation experience.
Recreation Opportunity Spectrum (ROS)	A park management model that identifies characteristics of different settings and matches them with the recreational opportunities that produces the best results for users and the environment.
recreational vehicle	A motorised self-contained camping vehicle or a truck or van or off-the-road vehicle equipped for travelling.
region	In the domestic context, 'region' refers to an area within a country, usually a tourism destination area; in the international context 'region' refers to a grouping of countries, usually in a common geographic area.
relationship marketing	Activities designed to create a bond between an organisation and its customers. The motivation is the retention of customers.
RPKs	An airline term. Revenue passenger kilometres are the number of passengers who have paid more than 25 per cent of the published fare, multiplied by the distance between the points.
sales promotion	Short-term incentives to encourage sales of a product.
scheduled service	A service operated by a carrier over its approved routes according to published schedules.

seasonality	Change in the level and composition of tourism demand due to the time of the year.
secondary data	Information that already exists, having been collected for another purpose.
sector	(1) One of the industries which is also a component of the overall travel and tourism industry, e.g. airline industry or hospitality industry. (2) A direct flight between two cities.
selective marketing	Targeting visitors who are socially and economically more attractive to the attraction or destination than others.
service	Any activity or benefit that one party can offer to another which is essentially intangible and does not result in the ownership of anything.
situation analysis	An examination of a company or other organisation and where it stands in its environment, its scale of operations, its market share and its relationship to its competitors. The current business definition, mission, marketing strategies and resources are examined critically.
sociocultural	A hybrid term which encompasses change to the social organisation of a group of people as well as reorganisation of a society's culture.
Social impact assessment (SIA)	A process for evaluating the probable effects of a development on the community. It is sometimes made part of the EIA process and at other times undertaken as a separate process.
soft measures (to manage visitors)	Persuasive means, such as marketing, directional signage or incentives for taking some action.
special interest tourism	Prearranged, packaged tourism designed for a group of persons who have a particular interest in a field of study or an activity, such as birdwatching, sports, culture and the arts, scuba-diving, or shopping.
stakeholders (tourism)	Those who have an interest in, or who are affected by tourism. They include travel and tourism companies, governments and host communities.
standard	A published document which sets out technical specifications or other criteria necessary to ensure that a material or method will consistently do the job it is intended to do.
strategic planning	The process of developing and maintaining a strategic fit between the organisation's goals and capabilities and its changing market opportunities. It relies on developing a clear company mission, supporting objectives, a sound business portfolio and coordinated functional strategies.
strategy	(1) A consistent body of policies that will enable an enterprise to get results by organising capabilities, resources and opportunities. (2) The methods and procedures employed to achieve objectives; the plan from which a detailed, budgeted action program is derived.
structural change	A fundamental transformation of some activity or institution. It is permanent; there is no return to the prior level or state.

structure plan	Part of a long-range plan which shows the physical structure of the planned development. For example, it can be presented on a map showing settlements (cities, towns, villages), agricultural lands, greenbelts, industrial land, airports and seaports, access corridors and so on. It guides the location, types and extent of future attractions, facilities, services and infrastructure.
supplier	A business offering products or services sold through travel agencies or, in some cases, directly to the public.
sustainable	Able to be carried out without damaging the long-term health and integrity of natural and cultural environments.
sustainable design	The use of design principles and strategies which help reduce the ecological impact of buildings by limiting the consumption of energy and resources, and by minimising disturbances to existing vegetation.
sustainable development	Achieving growth in a manner that does not deplete the natural and built environment and preserves the culture of the local community.
sustainable tourism	All forms of tourism development, management and operations that maintain the environmental, social and economic integrity and well-being of natural, built and cultural resources.
sustainable transport	Transport which does not harm the environment or use resources that cannot be replaced. It is an ideal rather than a reality.
SWOT analysis	SWOT = strengths, weaknesses, opportunities and threats. The analysis lists the company's internal strengths and weaknesses and its external opportunities and threats.
synthesis (as a step in long-range planning)	The combining and integrating of various components of analysis of survey information about markets and the area. In tourism, synthesis relates the types of tourist attractions to potential markets. Synthesis also integrates the analysis of physical, social and economic factors, including relevant carrying capacities, giving information about the optimum development of tourism.
system	A group of component items that are interdependent and may be identified and treated as an entity.
System of National Accounts (SNA)	A framework designed by the United Nations which provides a systematic summary of national economic activity, and which is adopted by many countries in the production of their national accounts.
taxation	The compulsory transfer of money from individuals, institutions or groups to governments.
temporary change	A temporary alteration in a certain measure or condition from a level or state to which it is likely to return later.
ticket stock	The supply of tickets a travel agency keeps on hand for which the agency has legal responsibility.

timed entry system	A system by which visitors to an attraction are given times at which they may be admitted. Usually this is done when capacity has been reached.
total tourism product	The combination of all the service elements which a tourist consumes from leaving home, to returning.
tour-basing fare	A reduced-rate excursion fare available only to those who buy prepaid tours or packages. Inclusive tour, group inclusive tour, and group round-trip inclusive fares are all tour-basing fares.
tour operator	A business that provides services that include responsibility for the delivery and operation of all facets of a tour, sometimes including an escort. Tour operators may be wholesalers as well as local operators.
tour wholesaler	A business that contracts with hotels, sightseeing and other ground components to be used in combination with air transportation (where appropriate) and whose resultant tour packages are sold through travel agents and other travel sellers.
tourism	The activities of persons travelling to and staying in places outside their usual environment for not more than one consecutive year for leisure, business or other purposes.
tourism-characteristic industries	Industries that would either cease to exist in their present form, producing their present product(s), or be significantly affected if tourism were to cease.
Tourism Compensation Fund (TCF)	A fund to which travel agents must contribute as a condition of licensing. It has been set up under a trust deed to protect the public's money where it has been lost through the default of a travel agent or tour operator.
tourism-connected industries	Industries other than tourism-characteristic ones, for which a tourism-related product is directly identifiable to, and where the products are consumed by, visitors in significant volumes.
tourism consumption	(1) The act of consuming, e.g. a tourist consumes the services of an airline by booking a seat on a flight and travelling on it, and consumes a souvenir boomerang by taking it home and putting it on a mantelpiece. (2) The total expenditure in an economy on tourism goods and services which are used up within a specified time, usually a year.
tourism development policy	A set of statements establishing the basis for developing and managing tourism in a long-term plan.
Tourism Forecasting Council (TFC)	An organisation set up by the Commonwealth Government in 1993 to provide forecasts of future tourism, primarily to help potential investors in tourism plant.
Tourism Futures Simulator	A model for regional development taking into account the environment, both natural and social, and the economy. It was developed by the CSIRO.
tourism market	All the potential customers sharing a particular need or want who might be willing and able to satisfy it by buying a tourism product.

tourism marketing	The management process by which organisations develop destinations, facilities and services as tourism products, identify potential travellers and their needs and wants, price their products, communicate their appeals to target markets and deliver them to their customers' satisfaction and in compliance with organisational goals.
Tourism Ministers Council (TMC)	A body formed by the Commonwealth, state and territory and New Zealand ministers responsible for tourism. The Council meets at least once a year to facilitate inter-governmental cooperation and a coordinated approach to policy development. Representatives of the Australian Tourist Commission, Norfolk Island and Papua New Guinea attend as observers.
tourism multipliers	Mathematical tools which attempt to encapsulate the total effect of tourism on the economy of a destination area. Tourism mulitipliers can refer to the level of tourism expenditure on the level of output, income and employment of the national or regional economy.
tourism optimisation management model (TOMM)	A destination area visitor management model being developed on Kangaroo Island, South Australia. It focuses on optimising the tourism performance of a destination area rather than limiting use.
tourism plant	Facilities, amenities and services specifically built and provided for tourism use in a given area.
tourism policies	Public policies designed to achieve specific objectives relevant to tourism established at the local government, state or territory and Commonwealth level.
tourism product (or total tourism product)	The aggregate of productive activities and services which satisfy the needs of tourists, from the time they leave home, to the time of return. The major portion of the tourism product is consumed at the destination.
Tourism Satellite Account	A set of accounts, using National Accounts concepts, which provide a picture of the place of tourism in the national economy.
Tourism Training Australia	The national industry training advisory body for the travel and tourism industry. It has a network of state- and territory-based branches which consider training issues of local concern. It also advises the Commonwealth Government on the training needs of industry.
tourist	A temporary visitor staying at least one night in collective or private accommodation in the place visited.
tourist destination region (TDR)	A place visited by tourists.
trade cycle	Regular oscillations in the levels of business activities over a period of years, when economic activity changes from a peak (when production, wages and profits are high and unemployment low) to a trough (when unemployment is high and production and profits are low) and back to a peak again.
trade fair (or show)	An organised event to bring people to a location to view a display of products (including services), to exchange information, and/or to buy and sell the

products. Attending important annual trade fairs around the world is part of the marketing routine of many Australian travel and tourism businesses.

transaction	A trade between two parties that involves at least two things of value, agreed-upon conditions, a time of agreement and a place of agreement.
transfers	Transport from an airport, railways station or other terminal to hotel or other accommodation.
transit route region (TRR)	An area tourists must pass through to reach a tourist destination region and return home.
travel account	An indicator of the degree to which a country attracts overseas visitors compared with its ability to persuade residents not to travel abroad. The balance on the travel account is the difference between the expenditures of residents travelling abroad from the expenditures of overseas visitors.
travel advisory	Caution issued by the Commonwealth Government regarding the safety, changing conditions or practices of a travel destination.
travel and tourism industry	The composite of organisations that are involved in the development, production, distribution and marketing of products to serve the needs of travellers. The 'primary trades' are those that directly provide goods or services to tourists.
traveller	A person on a trip between two or more localities.
traveller generating region (TGR)	A place where tourists come from.
trip	A single journey covering the whole period away from home. The National Visitor Survey definition involves a stay of one or more nights but less than three months away from home involving a journey of at least 40 kilometres from home. An international trip to Australia is a journey by any person who resides overseas, enters Australia and stays less than 12 months. The trip can be undertaken for any reason.
usual environment	Can be operationally defined in statistical terms by using various criteria such as some minimum change between localities or administrative territories, minimum duration of absence from usual place of residence, minimum distance travelled and explicit exclusion of routine travel.
verification audit	The process employed by program managers to ensure that tourism businesses continue to operate within documented and approved programs, thereby meeting the standard.
VFR	Classification of travellers whose purpose in travelling is to visit friends and relatives.
visit	An overnight stay at a particular place as part of a trip by a domestic or international visitor.
Visiting Journalists Program	An ongoing program in which the Australian Tourist Commission, with the cooperation of the industry, brings journalists from overseas markets to write or broadcast about Australian tourism assets.

visitor	Any person travelling to a place other than their usual environment for less than twelve months and whose main purpose of trip is other than the exercise of an activity remunerated from within the place visited.
visitor activity management program (VAMP)	A park management model that focuses on marketing rather than the park and the visitor experience.
visitor experience and resource protection model (VERP)	A park management model that incorporates zoning and legislative links with the region's management plan. It uses zoning to prescribe appropriate uses and management strategies for different areas within a park.
visitor impact management model (VIMM)	A park management model that recognises that visitors are not the only cause of impacts. It encourages explicit statements of management objectives, research and monitoring to determine environmental and social conditions, then generates a range of management strategies to deal with the impacts.
visitor management	A planning and operational technique designed to protect valued resources; it is also intended to make visits by tourists more satisfactory. It can be broadly divided into (1) site management and (2) people management.
visitor nights	A statistical measurement which represents the total number of nights spent at a place by all visitors within a specified group.
Warsaw Convention	An international agreement dating from 1929 which limits the liability of airlines.
World Heritage Area	A natural and/or cultural property of 'outstanding universal value' which meets the criteria of the World Heritage Convention, adopted by the General Assembly of the United Nations Educational, Scientific and Cultural Organisation (UNESCO) in Paris in 1972.
World Tourism Organisation (WTO)	The world tourism body, affiliated with the United Nations. Its members include governments of countries and territories and it also has affiliate members from the public and private sectors. Its headquarters are in Madrid.
yield	(1) The net benefit accruing to a country or destination area from visitors. (2) In the accommodation sector the revenue on rooms on one night related to the maximum possible. A 100 per cent yield would require every room to be occupied at the full price or published rack rate. (3) To airlines, earnings per revenue passenger kilometre (RPK). Passenger revenue is obtained by multiplying yield by volume. (4) To a travel agent, retained commission.
zoning	A visitor management technique that delineates where tourism is excluded and where it is an allowed activity.

NOTES

CHAPTER 1

1. Some actual figures from the Australian Bureau of Statistics and the National Visitor Survey were: residents aged 15 years and over took 75.2 million trips within Australia of at least one night's duration in the year ended December 2002 (NVS). ABS figures for calendar year 2002 show arrivals of foreign nationals totalled 4.8 million. Australians took 3,368,000 trips overseas in the year ended 30 June 2002.

2. Jovicic argued that the study of tourism as a complex phenomenon cannot be adequately addressed from within any one existing discipline. He also suggested that the various disciplines that currently house tourism studies, including economics, sociology and geography, failed to grasp the notion of the whole and tried to explain the entity which is tourism by its individual aspects. 'Tourismology' would facilitate the merger of the specialised studies occurring within diverse disciplines and would allow tourism to be examined as a composite phenomenon. Jovicic is cited in Echtner and Jamal (1997), who conclude that while there are some indications that tourism is moving towards becoming a distinct discipline, there are many practical and philosophical reasons that hamper its evolution. In their opinion what is urgently needed is greater collaboration, cross-disciplinary and especially inter-disciplinary research.

3. Leiper sees three contexts in which the word 'tourist' is used to describe or classify an apparent traveller or visitor: 1. popular notions about tourists; 2. technical definitions (such as those of the World Tourism Organisation); and 3. heuristic concepts and definitions (i.e. those intended to help learning). Each context has its definitions. This was an heuristic definition.

4. Measures are necessarily arbitrary. But who is to say a person travelling 39 km is less of a tourist than one travelling 41 km?

5. 'Tourism is now the largest industry in the world by virtually any economic measure, including gross output, value added, employment, capital investment and tax contributions' (Wheatcroft 1994, p. 28). However, other industries sometimes lay claim to being the biggest. The United Nations Environmental Program (Division of Technology, Industry and Economics), says tourism ranks alongside such sectors as construction and petrochemicals as 'one of the world's biggest industries' (UNEP 1999).

6. Australia differs from WTO practice in not excluding as visitors those people from overseas who work when they get here and are paid for it. The variance in aggregates is said to be less than one per cent. Commonwealth, state and territory authorities are working to remove all anomalies in time. It cannot be done overnight.

7. People in transit are not visitors.

8. While most of the definitions are from World Tourism Organisation 1995b, those for 'trips' and 'visits' are from Poole, M (1993).

9. There are two categories of tourism-related industries: (a) tourism-characteristic industries, for which 25 per cent of their output must be consumed by visitors and (b) tourism-connected industries, which have products that are consumed by tourists but are not considered tourism characteristic.

10. Total passengers carried on Australian trunk routes in the year ending June 2001 were 29,625,287. Figures supplied by the Department of Transport and Regional Services.

11. The Automobile Association of Australia has eight members – the eighth being the Royal Automobile Club of Australia, which was founded in 1903 and is in Sydney. It does not offer member services, as do the NRMA and the other organisations.

12. Not all tourism authorities place the return so high, though there is a difference between direct spending and the 'economic impact' of cruise passengers. Tourism Victoria includes the effects of secondary spending. The South Australian Tourism Commission's 'conservative' estimate of average direct spending per ship call is $350,000, which includes port charges and crew spending as well as that by passengers. See also case study pp. 115–16.

13. On the other hand Tourism Queensland's Sunlover Tours is a wholesaler but not a tour operator. It has some 750 Queensland products in its inventory, but usually does not package them.

14. Ratings are on a 1–5 star basis in each category and are based solely on physical features, not service. Consideration has been given to an ASH rating, the acronym meaning Ambience, Service and Hospitality.

15. About 1.3 million in 1998. Old Parliament House, which incorporates the National Portrait Gallery, is also a major attraction. It is managed by the Department of Communication and the Arts.

16. The management arrangements and the creation of the Commonwealth and National Heritage Lists were the result of legislation passed in Commonwealth Parliament in 2003. The Register of the National Estate dates back to 1976 (see pp. 123–4).

17. The Opera House, which has community service obligations, runs at a loss, its revenue from operations making up about 70 per cent of its operating costs. The remainder is made up of 'endowments' from the NSW government, amounting to about $10 million a year.

18. In this sense a distinction has been drawn between 'traveller' and 'visitor'. A traveller at an airport might not be a visitor, but an Australian resident going overseas.

19. Depending on location, service stations could be placed in all but the first category.

20. Some 30 volunteers help staff the Tasmanian Travel & Information Centre in Devonport, which also has a paid staff of three plus one casual. The volunteers have an information role only. The centre is also an accredited travel agency.

CHAPTER 2

1. Tourists from all overseas markets spent $5.16 billion on package tours to and within Australia in 1999 (International Visitor Survey, 1999).

2. As at September 2001. States sometimes change the boundaries and numbers of regions.

3. First research to test the validity of Plog's model by Smith (1990) and others did not support Plog's hypothesis that personality types were linked to destination preferences. However, their methodology

was criticised by Plog (1990) himself responding to Smith in the *Journal of Travel Research*. Later work by Griffith and Albanese (1996) indicates that the Plog model is 'more robust than previously thought'. The study found that Plog's theoretical model provided a firm foundation of psychographic segmentation in travel research and would be 'a fruitful path to travel for both academicians and practitioners'.

4. The report, a landmark event in Australian travel and tourism history, became known as the HKF Report after one of the firms of consultants Harris, Kerr, Forster & Company. The other firm that contributed was Stanton Robbins & Co Inc. The Australian National Travel Association was formed in 1929 to promote Australia overseas. It was an industry body though it had support from governments. It was the predecessor of both the Australian Tourist Commission and Tourism Council Australia, the peak industry body, which went out of existence in 2000 after it failed financially.

5. These are departure figures. Yearly totals quoted in this case study were supplied by the Japan National Tourist Organisation office in Sydney.

6. The actual JNTO figures were 3,909,333 and 11,933,620.

7. The yen was over 90 to the dollar from October 1996 (well up on the 60 of June the previous year) to April 1997, when it was 99. The following month the yen fell to 88 and in the next few years was not to see 90 again. In late 2000 it cost less than 60 yen to buy a dollar's worth of goods and services in Australia.

CHAPTER 3

1. Gross registered tons, applicable in this case, are a measure of volume, not of weight as are tonnes.

2. This reflects what is generally thought about categories – that adventure touring (which includes active adventure with 16 interests) has the most types of interests and cultural tourism is second in that respect. The InfoHub numbers are subject to change, of course. InfoHub does not operate tours itself but provides an Internet guide on which operators can advertise their tours and travel agents and intending tourists can find those that interest them. It claims its guide is the biggest on the Internet, offering in April 2002 10,000 different tours to 170 destinations, including Australia.

3. The National Tourism Strategy said it appeared that the word was coined by Hector Ceballos-Lascurain in 1983 (Commonwealth Department of Tourism 1994, p. 15). Hvenegaard (1994, p. 24) says Ceballos-Lascurain may have been the first to use it in 1987 and Beeton (1998, p. 1) says the term was first used by Ceballos-Lascurain in Mexico in 1988.

4. Australia-wide, about 85 per cent of the estimated 600 ecotourism operators employ fewer than 20 staff, according to a fact sheet placed on the Internet by the Sport and Tourism Division of the Department of Industry, Science and Resources (accessed on 23 May 2000 on www.isr.gov/sport_tourism/publications /factsheets/ecotourism.doc). Ecotourism businesses were estimated to have an annual turnover of about $250 million and to employ total staff of about 6,500, the equivalent of 4,500 full-time staff.

5. They included art galleries, historic sites and museums of many kinds.

6. This was the form of words adopted at a meeting of the Australian Tourist Commission's Aboriginal Advisory Committee in Sydney in 2001.

CHAPTER 4

1. The Organisation for Economic Cooperation and Development (OECD) also compiles international tourism statistics and publishes them annually.

2. According to WTO figures Australia ranked 36th in the world in 1990 in terms of arrivals, 32nd in 1995 and 33rd in 1998.

3. The Australian studies, the International Visitor Survey and the National Visitor Survey, provide data on some other matters. These are the main items.

4. Stynes (n.d.) discusses two Type 2 multipliers which he calls Type II and Type III. The distinction involves a technical difference in how the induced effects are computed. Type II multipliers include households as a sector of the economy, while Type III multipliers do not – the change in household spending is treated as an additional set of final demand changes and is then used to estimate the first round of induced effects.

5. The term 'gross' in GDP indicates that no deduction has been made for consumption of fixed capital (also known as depreciation). Net domestic product, or NDP, is GDP less an allowance for the consumption of fixed capital. See Australian Bureau of Statistics (1994, p. 3).

6. These are not the only possible methods, but those most used in Australia to determine estimates of the economic impact of tourism.

7. On the other hand, Dwyer et al (2000, p. 31) say the claim that CGE modelling is too demanding in its input requirements can easily be countered, particularly when it is appreciated that input–output analysis structure omits key mechanisms for the subject of study.

8. The ORANI model was named after the wife of Professor Peter Dixon, director of the Centre of Policy Studies at Monash University.

9. Opportunity cost is the cost of doing something, measured by the loss of opportunity to do the next best thing with the same amount of time or resources. For example, the opportunity cost of leisure could be measured by the money that could have been earned by working for an equivalent amount of time.

10. This is a small sample of the techniques economists have devised to measure non-market changes in welfare. Gillespie (1999, p. 66) classifies them as market-based techniques, surrogate market techniques and hypothetical market or survey techniques.

11. Leiper quotes a *Sydney Morning Herald* headline in 1997: 'Tourism Now A Million-Job Industry'.

12. Leiper reached this conclusion by estimating from a Bureau of Tourism Research study (O'Dea 1997b) that about 24 per cent of employment directly supported by tourism is in the form of real jobs and the rest is in notional equivalent full-time jobs.

13. The New South Wales Government did introduce a bed tax on accommodation in the Sydney metropolitan area and this was in force from 1997 to 2000 when the GST was introduced. The Northern Territory Government also imposed a bed tax, which was abolished when the GST was introduced. Unlike the New South Wales tax which contributed to general revenue, the Northern Territory tax was used to fund (regional) tourism.

14. Authority to travel to Australia can be processed electronically for short-term visitors from certain countries, including high volume markets such as Japan, the United Kingdom, the United States,

Singapore, South Korea, Hong Kong, Canada and Germany. It is free to travellers entering Australia as visitors, i.e. there is no entry fee for them to come to Australia. However, travellers from other countries have to pay for their visas. Travellers from all countries coming to Australia on temporary business entry visas also pay.

15. The chief executive of the Australian Federation of Travel Agents, Mike Hatton, said in October 2001 that a return ticket from Inverell to Sydney, a typical rural journey, cost $467, but attracted an extra $103.80 in charges. They included $46.70 for GST, $10 Ansett levy, $20 Inverell departure tax and $27.10 insurance levy (imposed to meet increased premiums following the September 11 terrorist attacks in the US). A full business fare between Melbourne and Sydney cost $300, plus $30 GST, extra insurance $7.26, Ansett levy $10 and Sydney noise tax $3.94. A typical around-the-world fare sold in Sydney carried an extra $552 in taxes and levies, not including insurance (*The Australian Financial Review*, 12 October 2001, p. 19).

16. In 1995 average figures the largest amount per day was $401 for visitors who fly to Australia to undertake an 11-day cruise. This compared with $79 per day for all visitors to Australia. The largest injection from foreign exchange came from those tourists who flew to Australia for a 6-day cruise with a 7-day add-on. However, these visitors spent the lowest amount per day, on average, of cruise tourists.

17. P&O operates the only two ocean-going cruise ships with an Australian home port. Captain Cook Cruises, an Australian operator, runs 3- and 4-night cruises from Cairns in Great Barrier Reef waters with the 3000-ton *Reef Endeavour*.

CHAPTER 5

1. There are more than 2800 of these with names like conservation park, environmental park, flora and fauna reserve, nature reserve, state park and wilderness park. There are about 160 conservation reserves in marine areas, with names such as aquatic reserve, fish sanctuary, marine park, marine reserve and marine nature reserve.

2. The code is in nine articles. The points made here were extracted from those that were relevant to social and cultural impacts.

3. This classification was derived from Pearce (1989). It has been modified.

4. Malicious damage is an offence which does not bring material gain to the offender and is not predatory.

5. The difference was that a high level of consensus about these statements was registered for factor 3, while those in factor 1 showed a polarisation of opinion.

CHAPTER 6

1. There is, of course, some expectation that they will fall at some point because of population pressure and environmental disruption.

2. According to UN agency the World Meteorological Organisation, at the end of 2002, 1998 was the hottest year on record with 2002 the second hottest. The 10 warmest years had all occurred since 1987, nine since 1990 (*Herald Sun*, 19 December 2002, p. 33).

3. Dr Terry Done, senior principal scientist at the Australian Institute of Marine Science in Townsville,

noted that some individual colonies survived the trauma which caused coral deaths on some inshore reefs during widespread bleaching on the Great Barrier Reef in 1997–98. This suggested there were genotypes that were ready to take over if the seas did warm. Currents would also tend to transport warm-adapted coral types from the northern Great Barrier Reef region to the warming waters of the south (CRC Reef News, August 1999 newsletter).

4. The mission of the United Nations Environment Program is to 'provide leadership and encourage partnership in caring for the environment by inspiring, informing, and enabling nations and people to improve their quality of life without compromising that of future generations'. The organisation's headquarters are in Nairobi, Kenya (www.unep.org).

5. No emission reduction goals were agreed to for developing countries, which undertook to look at reducing their emissions once developed countries had met their protocol targets. These countries included China, India and Brazil. Australia, along with the United States, Canada and New Zealand, has argued that the protocol should not be ratified without a commitment from developing countries to curb their emissions. Australia, Iceland and Norway were the only countries allowed to increase emissions.

6. *The Australian Financial Review*, 30 March 2001, pp. 1 and 26, and *The Age*, 30 March 2001 (pp. 1 and 6). The White House press secretary, Ari Fleischer, was quoted giving the reasons for the US decision.

7. Australian Greenhouse Office advertisement in *The Age*, 3 March 2001, p. 20. It said this was one of 10 ways Australians could make a difference to the greenhouse effect.

8. Australia's forest conservation policy provides for the protection of:
   - 15 per cent of the distribution of each forest ecosystem that existed before Europeans arrived in Australia
   - 60 per cent or more of the current distribution of forest ecosystems, if rare or depleted
   - 60 per cent or more of the current distribution of old growth
   - all remaining occurrences of forest ecosystems or old growth that are rare or endangered
   - 90 per cent or more of high-quality wilderness.

   State and territory governments have primary responsibility for forest management while the Commonwealth Government coordinates a national approach to environmental and industry development issues. The Commonwealth, state and territory governments are all signatories to the 1992 National Forest Policy Statement (NFPS), which provides the framework for sustainable management of Australia's forests. Australia has 12.6 per cent of its 156 million hectares of native forest in conservation reserves.

9. The most common forest types are eucalypts, which make up 80 per cent of the total. The total area of native forest is about 156 million hectares (or about 20 per cent of the continent). Most of this (116 million hectares) is woodland and mallee.

10. Australian figures are close to the world proportions. In 1995–96 the transport sector consumed 26 per cent of total energy consumed. In the mid-1990s road transport accounted for about 72 per cent of energy use by the transport sector and air transport about 15 per cent (Australian Bureau of Statistics 1997b).

11. Nine million tonnes in 1994, compared with 55 tonnes for road transport (Australian Bureau of Statistics 1997b).

12. *Avionics Magazine* 2001, Vol 25(1), pp. 16–8.

13. The Air Transport Action Group (ATAG) is a Geneva-based coalition of organisations from the air transport industry, formed to press for economically beneficial aviation capacity improvements. Its worldwide membership includes airlines, airports, manufacturers, air traffic control authorities, airline pilot and air traffic controller unions, chambers of commerce, travel and tourism associations, investment organisations, ground transport and communication providers.

14. Adapted from the contribution of the United Nations Environment Program to the United Nations Secretary-General's report on industry and sustainable tourism for the seventh session of the Commission for Sustainable Development, 1999.

15. These conclusions were reached at an Organisation for Economic Cooperation and Development (OECD) Conference on Environmentally Sustainable Transport, Futures, Strategies and Best Practice, in Vienna in 2000.

16. David Lamb, who is also chairman of Axcess Australia Projects Limited, a not-for-profit company that owns the aXcessaustralia cars, said, 'You can safely say that fuel cells are many years away from being affordable in regular cars and that even when the fuel cell itself becomes affordable the problem of distributing the fuel has to be solved'.

CHAPTER 7

1. PATA addressed the issue of managing tourism in a paper called 'Values Based Tourism – Shaping the Future' in 1993. It officially launched 'Values Tourism' at its 1995 annual conference in Auckland. Additions to the list of stakeholders could be (a) universities, TAFE colleges and private providers of tourism courses; (b) future generations.

2. This included three WTO studies, the conclusions of a seminar and presentations at a 'Round Table on Tourism Development and the Role of the State' held at the 10th General Assembly in Bali in 1993. Australia's contribution to the Round Table was made by Ray Spurr, First Assistant Secretary, (Commonwealth) Department of Tourism. He was later associate professor and policy adviser in the World Travel and Tourism Council Centre for Tourism Policy Studies, School of Marketing, University of New South Wales.

3. Superstructure is a term for tourism plant – accommodation, restaurants, attractions, shopping facilities and so on.

4. The TMC operates under a protocol set by the Council of Australian Governments. Among other things this sets down who can be represented, how agendas are formed and liaison with other ministerial councils and local government. Additionally, a 'set of principles' cover where and when TMC should meet, how the field of coverage of the council is determined, a requirement for regular reviews of decisions and their implementation, ways to prevent excessive growth of subcommittees, the role of the New Zealand representative (Federal–State Relations Committee 1998).

5. This has fluctuated from time to time. For about 15 years TMC and ASCOT membership was limited to the Commonwealth and the states/territories. Originally, TMC was a state-only group and at first resisted

extending membership to the Commonwealth. At the same time, the Commonwealth was reluctant to become involved. It was the sensitivities and the possibility of extra funds associated with the establishment of the ATC that provided a catalyst for change.

6. Stroud, a Canberra lobbyist, was the senior tourism bureaucrat in Canberra for more than two decades.

7. A journey is an international journey even though it includes a domestic leg, and different carriers are involved, so long as the airline and the passenger view the domestic leg as part of one international trip.

8. States/territories legislate for all aviation matters except those specifically ceded to the Commonwealth pursuant to the Constitution or by a specific and temporary agreement (Heilbronn 1992, p. 147). In respect to introducing statutory civil wrongs laid down in the Warsaw Convention, the state Acts adopted the Commonwealth Act without amendment for domestic aviation within states.

9. The Trade Practices Act gives the ACCC authority in certain cases to accede to conduct which would otherwise be in breach of the Act so long as it is satisfied that the benefits to the public from the conduct outweigh any detriments.

10. Under the Commonwealth Government accrual accounting requirements all departments and agencies are financed and must report in terms of 'outcomes' and 'outputs'. 'Key result areas' or KRAs are part of this terminology.

11. Following the November 2001 election sport was transferred to another department.

12. The ATC did develop and implement generic domestic tourism campaigns in Australia in the 1970s and 1980s (Richardson 1999).

13. Access was first granted in the 1970s and gave a considerable boost to overseas representation and marketing by the Australian industry. However, access was withdrawn in a later period and still later restored.

14. The Commonwealth's exclusive powers refer to matters like defence, postal services, trade and customs; matters that clearly were considered best provided by a common government. The six colonies which agreed to federation strongly desired to maintain distinct identities and governments in areas where common action was not required. In present-day Australia, the states and territories compete with each other for tourism.

15. Due for completion in 2004, it was being built by a private developer with a substantial loan from the state government. Hobart's convention centre is a commercial operation at Wrest Point Hotel.

16. Formerly the Inbound Tourism Organisation of Australia or ITOA. The name was changed in 1999.

17. 'It is sobering to think that all this effort is miniscule compared to the investment in research in areas like agriculture and mining' (ATR*i* News, March 1998).

CHAPTER 9

1. Cities can have their own infrastructure problems which affect tourists as well as residents. Examples in recent years include water contamination in Sydney and a gas shortage in Melbourne.

2. The proportion of PPP projects is very small compared with those funded by governments and can never be relied upon for the bulk of public infrastructure for roads and water (Athol Yates, senior policy analyst, Institution of Engineers Australia, 2001, pers. comm., 8 December).

3. Twenty organisations made up the Alliance which was disbanded on the completion of the report card. The Tourism Task Force (later TTF Australia) was one of the members.

4. In 1998 319,000 km (about 40 per cent) were sealed with bitumen or concrete.

5. Work carried out in 2000 to improve public vehicular access in the Outback recognised the issue the consultants raised and sought to extend the general network of officially designated 'Public Access Routes'. These are tracks across pastoral land that go to places of interest where some pastoralists want to deny visitor access because of uncertainty about possible public liability claims. The PARs effectively excise the track from the pastoral property and make the Crown responsible – this makes the pastoralists a lot happier to allow visitors to pass across their land (Geddes 2002).

6. This happened on a number of occasions during the tourism building boom of the late 1980s, with unfortunate results for developers and investors.

7. The Versace fit-out per condominium was reported to be from $240,000 to $350,000. Average condominium cost was $1.36 million (MacDermott 2000).

CHAPTER 10

1. Kotler (1991) quotes studies showing a satisfied customer tells three people about a good product experience and a dissatisfied customer complains to 11 people.

2. It is usual to think of education as encouraging analytical thinking and the understanding of conceptual issues in order to contribute to professional and intellectual development. Training is concerned with delivering practical knowledge, skills and techniques, based on competency standards.

3. Its formation came from the merger of four non-profit organisations: Enterprise Australia, the Total Quality Management Institute, the Australian Quality Awards Foundation and the Quality Society of Australasia. The Wider Quality Movement was organised later. It is an informal network of organisations such as AusIndustry, Australian Association of Certifying Bodies, Australian Quality Control Council, Australian Organisation for Quality, Australian Manufacturing Council, Joint Accreditation System of Australia and New Zealand, National Association of Testing Authorities, Australia, National Measurement Laboratory, National Standards Commission, National Supply Group, Quality Society of Australasia, Standards Australia.

4. The main source for this summary is Prokesch (1995), whose article was presented in question and answer form as the result of an interview with Sir Colin Marshall (now Lord Marshall). Changes in the airline industry as the result of the terrorist attacks of September 2001 and the success of no-frills carriers should be taken into consideration. British Airways in the 2000s faces very different challenges from those of the previous decade. However, its culture transformation in the 1990s still holds many lessons for managers concerned with the human factor in their company and its effects on the success of the company.

CHAPTER 11

1. Key stakeholders include residents and visitors, as well as government and the travel and tourism industry. Businesses besides those directly involved with tourism also have a stake in visitor management.

2. This was one of the findings of a survey conducted in 1993 by the University of Venice School of Economics. Views were sought from 422 Venetians on a face-to-face basis.

3. However, eager tourists and surrogate providers can sometimes frustrate access controls. Van Der Borg (1999, p. 132) instances the temporary abolition of ferries to the island of Capri in 1993 to reduce car traffic associated with tourism. Fishermen immediately offered their services and the congestion was more intense than before.

CHAPTER 12

1. Domestic tourism growth was less impressive and harder to measure because of changes of methodology in domestic surveys.

2. Ansett was put into voluntary administration on 12 September 2001 and its planes were grounded on 14 September. A limited service was resumed at the end of the month and ran for four months while the administrators tried to sell the core airline. During that period there was hope that a smaller version of Ansett might return permanently. However, structural change to other parts of the Australian industry (e.g. the retail sector because of the breakup of Traveland) had already begun in September.

3. Telstra has substantial travel and tourism interests through its ownership of Atlas Technologies.

4. Deregulation brought about unprecedented growth in the number of passengers travelling by air within Australia. By the late 1990s average annual traffic on trunk carriers had risen to about twice the annual average of the 1980s. Lower fares for some classes of passengers as a result of periods of competition from two different airlines called Compass, and the introduction of a variety of fare levels because of yield management were the reason. A study by the Bureau of Industry Economics in 1994 concluded that Australia's domestic fares were among the cheapest in the world (Richardson, 1996).

5. It had previously shared the ownership with News Corporation on a 50–50 basis.

6. The (New Zealand) taxpayer-funded rescue came in mid-October 2001 at a cost of NZ$885 million (A$702 million).

7. The American Pritzker family, SPHC's previous owner, retained the Travelodge brand for a new chain of limited-service hotels.

8. The affected markets did not collapse completely. For example, arrivals from Thailand were 81,300 in 1996; 68,600 in 1997; and 49,100 in 1998. The biggest loss was in the Korean market – arrivals dropped from 233,800 in 1997 to 66,600 in 1998.

9. Collier says Australia is unique because restaurants tend to influence what is dished up at home rather than the reverse. Three in four homes now own a wok and rice consumption has more than tripled in the last three decades.

10. On the morning of 11 September 2001, four American airliners were hijacked by terrorists of the al-Qaeda network over the eastern United States. Two were deliberately crashed into the two towers of the World Trade Centre in New York and one hit the Pentagon, headquarters of the US Defence Department, in Washington. The fourth crashed into open land in Pennsylvania apparently after a struggle between hijackers and passengers. The time between the crash of the first aircraft and the fourth was one hour and 20 minutes. The Pentagon was badly damaged and subsequently both World Trade Centre

towers collapsed. All aboard the four airliners, 233 passengers and 33 crew members, were killed. About 1,400 people died on the ground. Most of them had been in the World Trade Centre and included rescue workers – firefighters and police.

11. Media played an important role in encouraging people who had visited the complex to be tested and, where appropriate, undertake early treatment.

INDEX